W9-BJT-580

Comprehensive Legal
and Judicial Development

Proceedings of a Global Conference

Washington, D.C.   June 5–7, 2000

Sponsored by:

The World Bank

in participation with:

African Development Bank

Asian Development Bank

European Bank for Reconstruction and Development

Inter-American Development Bank

International Monetary Fund

United Nations Development Programme

Comprehensive Legal and Judicial Development

Toward an Agenda for a Just and Equitable Society in the 21st Century

Edited by Rudolf V. Van Puymbroeck

The World Bank
Washington, D.C.

The findings, interpretations, and conclusions expressed in this book are entirely those of the authors and should not be attributed in any manner to the World Bank, to its affiliated organizations, or to members of its Board of Executive Directors or the countries they represent. The World Bank does not guarantee the accuracy of the data included in this publication and accepts no responsibility for any consequence of their use. The boundaries, colors, denominations, and other information shown on any map in this volume do not imply on the part of the World Bank Group any judgment on the legal status of any territory or the endorsement or acceptance of such boundaries.

The material in this publication is copyrighted. The World Bank encourages dissemination of its work and will normally grant permission to reproduce portions of the work promptly.

Permission to photocopy items for internal or personal use, for the internal or personal use of specific clients, or for educational classroom use is granted by the World Bank, provided that the appropriate fee is paid directly to the Copyright Clearance Center, Inc., 222 Rosewood Drive, Danvers, MA 01923, USA; telephone 978-750-8400, fax 978-750-4470. Please contact the Copyright Clearance Center before photocopying items.

For permission to reprint individual articles or chapters, please fax a request with complete information to the Republication Department, Copyright Clearance Center, fax 978-750-4470.

All other queries on rights and licenses should be addressed to the Office of the Publisher, World Bank, at the address above or faxed to 202-522-2422.

The article "Law, Relationships, and Private Enforcement: Transactional Strategies of Russian Enterprises" by Kathryn Hendley et al. has since been published in *Europe-Asia Studies* 52, no. 4 (2000): 627–656. For further reference, please visit http://www.tandf.co.uk.

Library of Congress Cataloging-in-Publication Data has been applied for.

Contents

Foreword

"I am glad there is now recognition that a solid foundation for economic and social progress requires the consolidation of democracy as well as respect for the rule of law and human rights: that the enabling environment for economic and social development lies in good governance, respect for the rule of law, the dictates of universal human rights, and the effective pursuit of democratic ideals."

I frequently speak on this topic, but the above statement is not mine: it was delivered by the Hon. S. Amos Wako, Attorney General of Kenya, one of the many presenters at a recent global conference on legal and judicial reform who is personally engaged in a comprehensive law reform effort in his own country.

Recognizing that the rule of law is the cornerstone to sustainable economic development and enduring poverty alleviation, the very first decision I made upon joining the World Bank as General Counsel was to plan for this global conference. The conference was sponsored by the World Bank, in partnership with the African Development Bank, the Asian Development Bank, the European Bank for Reconstruction and Development, the Inter-American Development Bank, the International Monetary Fund, and the United Nations Development Programme. It was held in Washington, D.C., on June 5–7, 2000, and provided a forum to over 600 scholars and practitioners of legal and judicial reform from over 80 countries to exchange views and to learn from each other.

We are pleased to offer a selected, representative list of papers presented at the conference in this book. We wish to support legal and judicial reform efforts everywhere, regardless of whether the World Bank supports them financially, and therefore are glad to share the available lessons of experience as widely as possible.

In organizing the conference, we put the emphasis on *comprehensive* reform. Respect for the rule of law demands incessant action and improvement on many fronts at the same time. Hence, the conference was organized around ten different themes, posed in the form of questions: What are the elements of a successful legal and judicial system? How can governments be held accountable? How to give voice to the poor? What informal mechanisms exist for dispute resolution and contract enforcement? What conditions are necessary for the judiciary to curb corruption? How can the media support the reform process? What are the conditions for an independent, yet accountable judiciary? How can legal training improve participation in the reform process? How does global knowledge sharing foster civil society participation? What are effective reform strategies, and are there models for them?

These are the questions addressed in this book. There are no definitive, universal answers, nor can there be. Reform is a fluid process, shaped by context, individuals, and time. But the experiences recounted here are real. They offer insights into problems that might otherwise have remained unidentified, and opportunities otherwise perhaps left unexplored.

Nor is the search for answers over. In fact, for us in the World Bank, the June 2000 conference marked a new beginning: the start of a real, continuing dialogue with all stakeholders and partners in the reform process. We will continue to publish the ideas, outcomes and lessons learned as we travel together along the road toward a just and equitable society in the 21st century.

Ko-Yung Tung
Vice President and General Counsel

Acknowledgments

The World Bank's Global Conference on Comprehensive Legal and Judicial Development in June 2000 brought together over 600 judges, government officials, academics, managers of economic assistance agencies, and representatives from nongovernmental organizations from all over the world. The event offered the participants (and others connected by Internet and videoconferencing) an unprecedented opportunity to exchange views on reform, to compare results achieved and lessons learned, and to discuss the need for revised agendas and new goals for the future. Participants listened to distinguished members of the legal and judicial community speak about their own experiences and engaged speakers in discussions about broader implications.

While similar conferences have been held before, they tended to have a more limited regional or thematic focus. We believe this was the first time a truly global symposium united practitioners and experts in legal and judicial development in its multiple forms and in the broadest cross-disciplinary sense.

This could only be achieved through the hard work and exemplary volunteerism of many dedicated professionals. Thus it is only fitting that we express our heartfelt thanks to:

- the staff members of the World Bank who assisted me in the organization of the conference, namely Hadi Abushakra, Lubomira Beardsley, Nicolette Dewitt, Maria Gonzalez de Asis, Hans Jurgen Gruss, Linn Hammergren, Natalie Lichtenstein, Waleed Malik, T. Mpoy-Kamulayi, Rick Messick, Friedrich Peloschek, Visu Sinnadurai, and David Varela;
- all speakers, and especially those who could not receive the recognition they deserve by the inclusion of their presentation in this book, namely the Hon. Jan Drognec, Former Justice, Constitutional Court, Slovak Republic; H.E. Hisashi Owada, President, Institute of International Affairs, Japan, and Senior Advisor to the President of the World

Bank; Wang Shengming, Director, Civil Law Office, Legislative Affairs Committee, National People's Congress, People's Republic of China; the Hon. Nan Shuker, Associate Judge, Superior Court of the District of Columbia, Washington, D.C.; the Hon. Gherardo Colombo, Deputy Public Prosecutor, Milan, Italy; Daniel Kaufman, Manager, World Bank Institute, The World Bank; the Hon. Paul Magnuson, Chief Judge, U.S. District Court, District of Minnesota, and Chair, International Judicial Relations Committee of the U.S. Judicial Conference; Luis Moreno Ocampo, Head, Transparency International, Latin America; Sheila Coronel, Executive Director, Philippine Center for Investigative Journalism; Bette Bao Lord, Chairperson, Freedom House, United States; Stephen Denning, former Program Director, Knowledge Management, The World Bank; Dominique Remy-Granger, Director, External Relations Department, Constitutional Court, France; and the Hon. P.N. Bhagwati, former Chief Justice of India, and Chairman, Centre for the Independence of Judges and Lawyers;

- the Hon. Associate Justices of the U.S. Supreme Court Sandra Day O' Connor, Anthony M. Kennedy, and Stephen Breyer, who honored the conference by participating in a special panel discussion;

- the General Counsel and other high-ranking officials of multilateral development agencies who kindly agreed to participate in a special concluding panel discussion on the role of multilateral institutions in legal and judicial development, namely Francois P. Gianviti, General Counsel, International Monetary Fund; Emmanuel Maurice, General Counsel, European Bank for Reconstruction and Development; Francis M. Ssekandi, General Counsel, African Development Bank; G. Shabbir Cheema, Director, Management Development and Governance Division, U.N. Development Programme; Edmundo Jarquin, Chief of the State and Civil Society Division, Sustainable Development Department, Inter-American Development Bank; and Hamid L. Sharif, Senior Counsel, Asian Development Bank; and

- the commentators and moderators for the sessions, as follows:

Session I: Moderator: the Hon. Peter Messitte, Judge, U.S. District Court of Maryland;

Session II: Commentator: Rolf Knieper, Professor, University of Bremen. Moderator: Richard Messick, Senior Public Sector Management Specialist, the World Bank.

Session III: Commentator: George Minet, Senior Specialist, Department of Government and Labor Law and Administration, International Labor Organization. Moderator: Linn Hammergren, Senior Public Sector Management Specialist, the World Bank.

Session IV: Commentator: Tariq Hassan, Advisor to the Minister of Finance, Pakistan. Moderator: Cheryl Gray, Director, Poverty Reduction, the World Bank.

Session V: Moderator: Maria Gonzalez de Asis, Public Sector Specialist, the World Bank.

Session VI: Moderator: T. Mpoy-Kamulayi, Senior Counsel, the World Bank.

Session VII: Moderator: the Hon. Visu Sinnadurai, former Judge, High Court of Malaysia, and Senior Judicial Specialist, the World Bank.

Session VIII: Commentator: L. Michael Hager, former Director General, International Development Law Institute, Italy. Moderator: David F. Varela, Senior Counsel, the World Bank.

Session IX: Commentator: the Hon. Louise Mailhot, Vice President, International Association of Judges, Canada. Moderator: Waleed H. Malik, Senior Public Sector Management Specialist, the World Bank.

Session X: Moderator: Lloyd Cutler, Partner, Wilmer, Cutler and Pickering, Washington, D.C.

Special Session with the Associate Justices of the U.S. Supreme Court: Moderator: Paul Gewirtz, Potter Stewart Professor of Constitutional Law and Director, The China Law Center, Yale Law School

Special Session on the role of multilateral institutions: Moderator: Thomas Carothers, Vice President of Studies, Carnegie Endowment for International Peace.

We also wish to recognize and give special thanks to Prof. Amartya Sen, who inspired the audience at the outset of the symposium with his remarks about the role of legal and judicial reform in the development process.

As is apparent from the foregoing, we owe an enormous debt of gratitude to a great many people for making the conference the stimulating intellectual event that it was. But the person who deserves most credit of all is James D. Wolfensohn, President of the World Bank, whose vision and tireless personal commitment to the cause of justice for all, and especially for the poor and the most vulnerable, has become legendary in his own time. Under his leadership, the World Bank is moving forward with governments from around the world and with all other partners in the development effort to bring greater prosperity, justice, and dignity to all our brothers and sisters on this planet.

Maria Dakolias
Acting Chief Counsel, Legal and
Judicial Reform, The World Bank

Editor's Note

Not all speakers provided papers, and not all papers received could be included in this publication. Nevertheless, there is at least one article for each session, and hence for each topic, and the selection was made so as to provide the reader with the best possible overview of the subject.

Given the wide variety of nationalities, native languages, and writing styles of the contributors, all papers have been edited with a view to ensuring a measure of consistency of style and presentation. However, the editing has purposefully been kept light so as not to obstruct the tone and flavor of the remarks as delivered to the audience.

What Are the Elements for a Successful Legal and Judicial System?

Selected Considerations Anchored in the Universal Declaration of Human Rights

Pierre Truche*

Honorary First Chairman

Court of Cassation

France

All people who consider that their rights have been violated with respect to their persons, property or economic activities should be able to enforce those rights before a tribunal.

All people involved in criminal proceedings, whether as defendants, victims or witnesses, should have the assurance that they will receive an impartial hearing, that their rights will be respected and that, if they must stand trial, they may participate effectively in critical examination of the evidence brought against them by the prosecution.

While such legal disputes, whatever their nature, are always important for those involved in them, they may appear to have only a limited impact on public order, whether we are speaking of personal security or that of commercial transactions. But if disregard for the rule of law is allowed to go unpunished, and especially if it is repeated, a country risks serious disorder that can destroy confidence in its legal system on the part not only of its own citizens but also of those elsewhere who seek to provide it with aid or to invest in it.

The law takes many forms: civil law protects persons and property; commercial law ensures the security of business dealings; social law protects workers; and criminal law punishes the perpetrators of more serious offenses. None of these excludes the others. The goal, by one means or another, is to enforce respect for the rule of law, which will be impossible unless transgressions can be effectively submitted, publicly and in the presence of both parties, before independent and impartial tribunals devoted to upholding human rights.

*Translated into English from the original text in French and edited in English.

This presupposes a specific and demanding role for those who, by whatever right, participate in judicial proceedings, as well as strict rules of procedure to ensure justice and equality for all parties to the case.

Article 10

Article 10 of the Universal Declaration of Human Rights requires the existence of an independent and impartial tribunal.

This means that neither judges nor their courts should have any vested interest in the proceedings. There should be no corruption and no corporatism. To guard against the first of these scourges, judges should not receive direct or indirect remuneration from any source other than the state. However, if their position in society is to be recognized and their dignity respected, their remuneration must be at the highest levels afforded by the public service and be sufficient to maintain a decent standard of living.

In order to reinforce its independence from the executive and legislative branches, it may be proper, at some stage in the history of justice, to allow the judiciary to manage itself in terms of recruitment, appointment, advancement and disciplinary actions. However, such a system need not necessarily be permanent. Corporatism is a risk for any institution when it is associated with the security of tenure essential for the proper functioning of the judicial system. Judges apply the law, and may interpret it, but they are not legislators. The reform currently underway in France consists of amending the role and function of the *Conseil supérieur de la magistrature* [Supreme Council of Justice], which is empowered to nominate and discipline all magistrates. Magistrates will now constitute only a minority of the Council, while unimpeachable personalities drawn from civil society will bring to it an impartial outsider's point of view.

It is clear that public authorities have the obligation to ensure material working conditions that will allow the mission of justice to be properly carried out and, most important, will prevent interference in the course of judicial affairs.

But the impartiality of judges, though affected by the introduction of these structures, also depends on judges themselves. Hence the importance of monitoring recruitment, initial and continuous training, and responsibility.

The system France has chosen combines recruitment through competitions in which candidates must demonstrate their legal knowledge and understanding of changes in society on the economic, social, and cultural fronts, with recruitment based on depth of professional experience. Negotiating this process successfully requires not only a lengthy period of initial preparation, but also the ability to keep up with change, through continuous and varied training in both modern techniques and broader social movements.

All power presupposes responsibility and hence a disciplinary power, which, in France, is exercised by the Supreme Council of Justice. The Council must guard not only against dereliction of duty by a magistrate—for example, failure to perform the tasks assigned—but also, and especially, against failure to respect the ethical principles of dignity, loyalty, honor, and probity.

The Council's duty is to show that this important function occupies a special place. But there can be no impartial tribunal if there are suspicions of bias on the part of those upstream from the judicial decision who provide input to it and those downstream who must execute it. A judicial system cannot be valid unless judges regulate all those who contribute to serving the public, whether they are investigators, officials or experts.

Procedure works to that end.

Article 11

Article 11 of the Universal Declaration of Human Rights requires guarantees of the right to defense and, in criminal cases, the presumption of innocence. The great rule of modern procedure, beyond the classical division into the accusatorial and the inquisitorial, is that the adversarial nature of justice must be respected in all cases.

French criminal procedure has for many years been, and still is, undergoing reform in order to ensure full observance of this principle.

In criminal proceedings, French procedure may be characterized as follows:

- The search for evidence against a person, leading potentially to prosecution, must be conducted before the hearing. It is up to the tribunal to decide whether the evidence produced constitutes sufficient grounds. The case will not be referred to trial if the relevant evidence has not been produced: this occurs in 14 percent of complex cases submitted to trial judges, where a person has been placed under investigation.

- This search for evidence is, without exception, covered by the rule of secrecy, so as not to prejudge guilt. This rule of secrecy applies, however, only to those seeking evidence and not to the persons on behalf of whom proceedings have been initiated. They may therefore appeal to public opinion if they believe that their rights have been compromised.

- To ensure respect for the adversarial nature of justice, French procedure provides for the following:
  - The right of parties to be assisted by counsel, from the beginning of proceedings: the attorney may be of their own choice or one appointed by the court.
  - The right to consult with the attorney while being held in detention, a right that can be extended further.
  - The right to obtain a copy of the record of proceedings at any moment.
  - The right to communicate these proceedings to third parties, in particular an expert, to consider the technical relevance of the evidence produced.
  - The right to demand supplementary investigation and expert testimony.
  - The right of counsel to be informed in advance of any questioning to which his client is submitted, so as to prepare responses with that person in light of his knowledge of the case.
  - The right to demand that proceedings be stayed if rules of procedure are not respected.
  - The right to appeal all important decisions to a higher court.
  - The right, finally, to a public hearing before the court if the case proceeds that far.

Statistically, it has been found that four to five percent of cases that go to a hearing will result in a decision of *nolle prosequi* [refusal to proceed] or acquittal.

- All rights of defense are recognized not only for the person under investigation, but also for the *témoin assisté* [assisted witness], whose rights must be guaranteed for the future in case the evidence found against him is still insufficient. The reform now underway reinforces guarantees for such witnesses.

Victims also may turn to the criminal justice system, have access to the file and be assisted by an attorney, and this extends the adversarial nature of the proceedings to all persons concerned.

- To ensure the integrity of adversarial proceedings, all elements of investigation must be submitted in writing, so as to facilitate consideration and cross-examination. It is only during the hearing that arguments are presented orally.
- Persons responsible for gathering evidence or for providing expert testimony are designated by the judge based on their competence. Experts are selected from lists prepared by the courts, on the basis of their reputation. They are remunerated by the state, and not by the parties to the case, guaranteeing their impartiality.

But what is historically original about the French system is the role of the *ministère public* [public attorney or prosecutor]. To ensure their impartiality, judges cannot decide on their own to hear a case. This task falls to an independent service that represents the interface between society and victims, on the one hand, and judges on the other.

Magistrates, French prosecutors, are recruited in the same way as judges and are subject to the same professional requirements. The Supreme Council of Justice enforces disciplinary measures on them, meaning that the exercise of their function is subject to high ethical standards. They are the first to judge a case, and have the option of not trying the known perpetrator of a violation, but instead submitting the case to mediation, when this solution seems more appropriate. This may take place if the problem has been resolved, the victim has been compensated, or the rehabilitation of the perpetrator seems assured.

Moreover, this role traditionally gives the *ministère public* the freedom to express during the hearing whatever he or she believes to be in the interest of justice. While in the past the Minister of Justice could enjoin the *ministère public* from exercising his discretion, this possibility, already discarded in practice, should also be suppressed in law by the end of the current reform process. It will remain for the government, which is constitutionally responsible for law enforcement, to publish general directives and guidelines based on national crime trends. These directives cannot of course be binding on judges in their consideration of the case before them.

The entire system, however, depends on the monitoring of each player:

- Supervision and control of the judicial police by the prosecutor.
- Control over simple procedures by the court, where charges are referred directly by the prosecutor.
- Control by a judge responsible for investigation in complex procedures—that is, the trial judge—and control of the trial judge by a higher court of appeal. In the current reform there will always be a judge of *détention* [custody/detention] distinct from the trial judge.

Guarantees are no less important in civil and commercial litigation.

To protect their rights, all people may bring a claim before a court, conduct the proceedings themselves, and determine the object of litigation, subject to the arguments of their adversaries. But they also has the duty to prove the facts on which their claim is based and, in order to preserve the adversarial nature of justice, to advise their adversaries, on a reciprocal basis, of the means of evidence that they intend to invoke.

It is important, however, in order to ensure true equality between the parties, that the process be controlled by the judge preparing the investigation phase of the affair, and then by the court hearing the case.

To ensure proper proceedings, judges may set time limits and order such measures as they deem necessary: they may demand explanations of the parties, they may order further investigation, and see to the communication of evidence. They may also attempt to reconcile the parties through mediation entrusted to a third party appointed by the judge, a possibility that is being used more and more frequently.

A further guarantee is the parties' choice of a defense attorney or the possibility of obtaining one appointed by the court if the parties' resources are inadequate. Where would justice be if the poor had no access to it? A recent French law has further strengthened access to justice by creating the *Maisons de la Justice* to which citizens may turn.

Another rule is that trials must be held in public.

Finally, the *ministère public,* by reason of his or her special role in the French judicial system, may express an opinion on points of law raised during proceedings. To this end, he or she must be aware of all procedures concerning the civil status of persons (filiation, guardianship over protected persons) or the difficulties of business enterprises.

Within its inherited traditions, every country must now evolve in a context marked by the globalization of legislation (in particular on human rights) and by exchanges of individuals, goods, services and capital, but also by cross-border criminal activity. Justice is called upon to play an increasing role in this context and therefore demands of those who exercise it a high level of ethics to ensure impartiality within an organization that guarantees its independence, but which does not exclude controls over its functioning. It must at the same time ensure respect for the fundamental liberties of every person.

Rethinking the Processes and Criteria for Success

Bryant G. Garth

Director, American Bar Foundation

United States of America

Discussions on the role and the importance of the rule of law and the judicial system are typically characterized by noble pronouncements—for example, about the independence of the judiciary, the need to improve access to justice, and the like. These are rather abstract terms, however, and they hide the complicated social realities that lie beneath them and give them whatever meaning they have. Nonetheless it is very difficult to gather together lawyers and judges without hearing numerous discussions couched in these terms. They represent formal legal universals that cut across legal systems and contexts, and lawyers are trained to argue in terms of universals. The argument seems almost to be that if enough key people could be made to believe in the independence of the judiciary, the judiciary would be independent. This version of legal idealism, however, has not yet brought much success.[1]

Proponents of better judicial systems and their requirements also are associated with efforts to measure what a successful legal and judicial system would be. The focus again is on specifying what is needed in the internal workings of the judicial system. The effort is to try to avoid generalities and get down to specific indicators of judicial performance. Ideally, this approach takes stock of the more technical aspects of the courts—for example, how efficiently the courts operate, including the cost and duration of proceedings, whether there is corruption, and the quality of judicial training. Those seeking quantitative indicators can also seek to measure—even if only through opinion polls—other factors such as the independence and prestige of the judiciary. The hope riding on such efforts is that they will encourage key local actors to do whatever it takes to improve ratings. This is a form of external

---

1. Most of my observations and the data for this paper are drawn from Dezalay and Garth (forthcoming).

pressure on the actors who have power over the court system. While relatively subtle, it uses external criteria to suggest what must be done in a particular system.

We have had many noble pronouncements about the judiciary and judicial reform from all over the world, and many efforts to improve efficiency, but we have not so far had much to celebrate in moving from judiciaries that are not deemed to be successful toward judiciaries that fit the bill—in other words, moving from lack of respect for the rule of law to respect. The reason for this lack of achievement is not because the major actors in these processes disagree on the legal universals or even the practical fundamentals.[2] The level of agreement is in fact quite striking. It is also not because the development institutions have refused to invest in these programs. So far, however, the conclusion of almost all who have assessed these programs is essentially negative.

Negative conclusions, interestingly, are combined with a pervasive optimism. The reformers seem to be in a cycle that begins with optimism about the wonderful possibilities for a new consensus that will lead to successful legal and judicial reform, and ends with great disappointment and finger-pointing to assess who or what went wrong. This article will try to get beyond the cycle of optimism and disappointment by suggesting areas in which social science research might be more helpful. So far, social science has been used to justify the investment in the rule of law and to measure its achievement in formal legal terms. What might be more useful is a new social science approach that examines the law more critically and situates it in the context of social scientific understandings of the state and the economy—and the processes of import and export of expertise.

This essay will briefly describe the current situation, consider the lessons that we may have learned from the earlier law and development movement, and then move to the topic of the relationship between social structural elements and the rule of law.

---

2. For evidence of the growing global industry promoting the import and export of the "rule of law," see Carothers (1996, 1998, and 1999); McClymont and Golub (2000); Metzger (1997); Pistor and Wellons (1998); Quigley (1997); and Rose (1998). Indeed, a burgeoning group of consultants, think tanks, philanthropic foundations, and national and transnational agencies has come to the conclusion that, whatever the problem, an essential part of the solution is an independent and relatively powerful judicial branch.

The Current Situation: Optimism Amidst Disappointing Results

Thomas Carothers, perhaps the leading commentator on the rule of law, notes in his recent book that "the projects have fallen far short of their goals" (1999: 170).[3] Similarly, the Lawyers Committee for Human Rights is turning out one report after another on the limitations of projects promoting judicial reform (Lawyers Committee for Human Rights 2000). It is difficult to account for these disappointing assessments. The explanations so far proffered by the advocates of reform include the lack of political will within the target countries, the power of entrenched interests, and pervasive corruption (Carothers 1999: 165–77; Hammergren 1998: 270–80). Others suggest the need for more participation by local and global nongovernmental organizations (Lawyers Committee for Human Rights 1996). These criticisms and suggestions appear to be supported by many within the World Bank who have participated in these efforts (World Bank Seminar 1998). There is a search for "best practices" that will avoid the mistakes of the past.

At the same time, there is a burgeoning literature in law and in social science suggesting that the key to success in building democratic states and efficient economies comes from enhancing the rule of law, and that enhancement can proceed through a focus on the courts and the reform of the judiciary. The general optimism is evident in recent writings even on China. For example, the Lawyers Committee highlights the Chinese legal system in its analysis of how U.S. foreign policy should address China:

> One area where it is necessary, feasible and productive for the United States to support internal reform is the legal system. Targeted support is necessary, because Chinese law generally falls well short of international human rights standards. It is feasible, because the Chinese government's interest in legal development dovetails with the US interest in promoting a legal system that is more predictable, transparent and respectful of human rights. And it is likely to be productive, because law is the medium, both intellectually and institutionally, through which Chinese engage in debate and experimentation about human rights and the closely related issues of predictability, transparency and accountability of state action (Lawyers Committee for Human Rights 1998).

---

3. Juan Méndez agrees: "The judiciaries, and those who lead them, have been particularly resistant to change" (Méndez 1999: 223).

Similarly, a recent review by the Ford Foundation of its programs to build "public interest law" highlights the achievements of those who have been the beneficiaries of grants from the foundation (McClymont and Golub 2000). As the Ford Foundation assessments suggest, there remains a kind of general optimism about the ability to export public interest law (Keck and Sikkink 1998; Santos 1995; Sarat and Scheingold 1998). Even if the courts are unsuccessful, perhaps public interest law firms will succeed in mobilizing the law on behalf of the disadvantaged.

In short, whether we consider the courts or other legal institutions, the prevailing opinion today is that we need only to find the right people (and the right consultants), and to ensure that they are "committed," and the noble goals of the rule of law and judicial reform will somehow fall into place. From the perspective of my research, undertaken with Yves Dezalay, the matter is more complex (Dezalay and Garth, forthcoming). The explanations for the failures to date avoid using the tools of social science to explore the structural problems that court reform and efforts to export the rule of law inevitably face. I will explain this definition of the problem in more detail.

Lessons from the First Law and Development Movement

We can learn some lessons by beginning with the "law and development" movement of the 1960s and 1970s, which was a similar effort to export a set of institutions and practices supposed to build the rule of law. The efforts to change the position of law were not very successful at the time. The promised reforms in legal education and legal research—the centerpieces of the efforts—did not take place. Law schools continued to be dominated by part-time professors active in politics, litigation, the judiciary, business, or elsewhere. As a result, the "failure" of the law and development effort was quite quickly conceded (Gardner 1980; Trubek and Galanter 1974). It became an axiom of developmental assistance that an effort to export U.S. models of law had failed.

We can make several points that are often overlooked about this first law and development effort.

First, the effort did not have the kind of backing that we find today. It was a relatively marginal effort to persuade those who were important in development assistance, namely economists, that lawyers had—or could have—some role to play in development rather than simply being obstacles. It will be recalled that the model of development promoted by the economists was state-led development, and the legal establishment was thought to be too closely identified with the old landed elite. They used the "rule of law" to resist new programs. Second, the rhetoric used to kill the program was a bit too dramatic. It was as much a product of a switch in the United States from a focus on legal education to the legal activism of public interest law. Gardner's book, therefore, was as much a product of internal struggles in the Ford Foundation, where he had been a program officer, as it was a critique of "legal imperialism." It is important always to recognize that what is exported as the best technology tends to relate to the politics of the north as much as the needs of the south.

Finally, the conclusion that the first law and development movement *failed* is too simplistic. From the perspective of a generation later, we can see, for example, that Brazilians who gained access to U.S. legal technologies, U.S. credentials, and U.S. contacts through the programs funded as part of the program were able to turn this investment abroad into impressive careers as brokers between their home countries and multinational business investors (Dezalay and Garth, forthcoming). There was a local interest in law and development, and over time it translated into local investment in U.S. laws and institutions—securities, anticorruption, intellectual property. The efforts to reform Brazilian laws according to the expertise that these individuals had acquired did not dramatically change the place of law in Brazil, but it did have an impact both on people and institutions. It also set the stage for the efforts that took place a generation after.

In terms of academic discourse, critics were able to point out a certain naivete in the law and development movement. The proponents had optimistically promoted their own agendas without considering how those would interact with state power in the countries targeted for change. They therefore underestimated the difficulties they faced and could not see the impacts that did take place. The power of these criticisms helped in fact to build the academic movement to study "law in context"—for example, Twining 1997.

Unfortunately, however, the lesson was not learned well. Despite this strong base for skepticism grounded in an awareness of the importance of social context and the structure of the states in which legal institutions operate, the new wave of law and development—including many of the earlier critics—pays very little attention to that context. Even the critics, it seems, are too busy promoting their own projects to reflect more generally on the processes in which they participate. We suggest that we need to revive the project of making sense of the context that leads to law and development and produces particular results.

Structural Complications for the Business of Importing and Exporting the Rule of Law

There are persuasive reasons to expect that the construction of effective judicial systems and stronger societal commitments to the rule of law will be extremely difficult at best. We discuss these reasons in some length in our forthcoming book (Dezalay and Garth, forthcoming). For present purposes, it is perhaps more useful to limit the theory in favor of a set of practical propositions that activists can assess on the basis of their own experience. This list of propositions about the new law and development philosophy is derived from recent research concentrating on Latin America, but it also draws on research in South and East Asia. The research draws on more than four hundred interviews and uses the tools of structural sociology (see also Dezalay and Garth 1996).

First, reforming legal institutions is far more difficult than, for example, reforming central banks. The reason is relatively simple. Law and the institutions connected to it have long histories that associate them closely with the state and state politics. There is typically a close connection, for example, between the faculties of law, the courts, and extended families that make up the political elite. Ambitious people learn to play by certain rules that are set by the patterns of behavior rewarded by those particular institutional structures, and the patterns are therefore extremely difficult to change. Investments of new ideas and new approaches can be absorbed into the old patterns. The law and development movement in Brazil, for example, was unable to dislodge the pattern of part-time professors holding multiple positions in business, government, and politics. There was an impact, as I have noted, but the impact did not change the basic pattern. The same story applies to courts as well as to legal education.

In contrast, central banks could draw on a relatively new expertise, economics, that could be institutionalized in universities according to what had become internationally legitimate requirements. In Brazil, for example, new departments were able to insist on full-time professors and high standards of scholarship. This possibility of setting up new institutions around—or even in opposition to—the more traditional legal ones made it much easier to use investment in internationally legitimate economics to produce major state reforms than comparable investments in legal expertise.

Second, despite many protestations to the contrary, a careful analysis of the processes of import and export shows that the discussions of the rule of law and the role of the judiciary remain dominated by a U.S. image of what those terms mean institutionally. The notion of a strong and relatively independent judicial branch that is able to overrule the other branches of the government in constitutional matters has been picked up in many parts of the world, but the United States is the major proponent of this model of the law and the state.

The more European model—now modified with relatively strong constitutional courts—of a strong state and legislative supremacy is found much more typically in the rest of the world. To be sure, we can say that there is a trend toward a stronger judicial role in the state today, but the trend owes much to the prestige and power of the U.S. model.

Other aspects of the model more closely identified with civil law include the tendency of businesses to avoid the courts except for relatively routine debt collection, and the similar lack of any pattern of translating political issues into legal terms and entrusting them to judges (see, for example, Thome 2000). In terms of the specific patterns of behavior encouraged by the different systems, ambitious individuals in the United States invest in the law and in the ideals of the law and in doing so can be rewarded personally and professionally. They are honored within the profession for their commitments because the legitimacy of the legal profession depends on having lawyers committed not only to business clients, but also to the legal system and to the public interest. This "schizophrenic" aspect of the U.S. legal profession has been essential since the development of the Wall Street firms devoted to the "robber barons" at the turn of the twentieth century.

In contrast, while there are important variations, the politically ambitious and idealistic law graduate in Latin America is more likely to invest not in the autonomy of the law but rather in politics, political parties, and the state. Instead of seeking to speak on behalf of underprivileged groups in courts and analogous institutions as a way of building professional stature (and the legitimacy of the law), these individuals are far more likely to invest in representing underprivileged individuals or particular groups in politics. Part of the reason is that the focus of activity in Latin America is the state and politics, while the U.S. "state" includes a number of institutions located around the state—law firms and think tanks in particular. Because of the centrality of the courts in the United States and the role of the law firms (and also public interest firms), individuals who invest in the law can keep their base of power in legal institutions. In contrast, the investment in the autonomy of the law is much less central to Latin American political settings. The legitimacy of the law depends more on law graduates finding ways to represent different groups in politics than on any commitment to the autonomy of the law—especially as implemented in the courts.

The different patterns mean that it will be difficult to take a U.S. transplant and have it operate the same way in Latin America. The different patterns also suggest caution about insisting that U.S. practices and measures of legitimacy are the only acceptable ones. Another problem is that exporters and importers often tend to idealize the system that is afforded the highest prestige. It may be useful to remind readers that the U.S. system is often subjected to quite vigorous criticisms. Some of the features that are often overlooked about the U.S. legal system should therefore be mentioned.

First, the fidelity to the rule of law is not inconsistent with using the law and its institutions for economic or political ends that have little or nothing to do with what the rule of law might require. The Microsoft antitrust suit, for example, originated out of competition between Silicon Valley companies and Microsoft. There are many examples of business litigation employed as a business strategy—for example, to delay the entry of a competitor into the market. Most of those who followed the battle between Kenneth Starr and Bill Clinton would not see it as evidence of commitment to the rule of law, but rather as examples of individuals seeking to manipulate the law for their political advantage. Within the U.S. context these examples make sense. They are consistent with the rule of law. But similar conduct in other institutional settings may have very different repercussions. In particular, one key to the United States is the importance of the intense scrutiny of academics—situated in numerous law schools competing for attention and recognition—making sure that the strategic conduct of businesses or politicians does not damage the autonomy of the law and the law's legitimacy too much. But this educational system, as I have noted, is unique.

Second, recent examinations of the Supreme Court—for example, Lazarus (1998)—show that the Court is similarly highly politicized, with each side accusing the other of succumbing to political expediency or bad faith. Again, what saves the law in the United States is that the justices feel compelled to keep the public fight according to what can be plausibly justified—again under academic and other scrutiny—as consistent with law. They are constrained to stay in their role through patterns of behavior and scrutiny that have long been in place. These patterns are difficult to reconstruct outside of the particular U.S. legal and institutional setting.

A third point, which we have already mentioned, is that the practices of importing and exporting legal approaches and institutions are themselves embedded in local contexts—on both sides. Those who are involved in promoting reforms of legal institutions in particular countries, drawing on their international connections and credibility, should not therefore be labeled simply as "reformers" or "committed" to reform. They are local actors embedded in local struggles for power and influence. They use the prestige, legitimacy, and resources of outsiders to build their own position at home. At times their interests and positions coincide precisely with the interests and positions of those promoting particular agendas for other countries, but at times they will diverge. A Mexican "reformer," for example, may be committed both to judicial reform and to advancing in the PRI (the Institutional Revolutionary Party—Partido Revolucionario Institucional) hierarchy, and at some point the second priority could easily trump the first. A Brazilian reformer may use the international credibility to move into more traditional roles in multiple positions in and above the law. And an Argentine reformer may use the reform impetus to punish political rivals. These examples are a bit too simple, but the point is that on both sides of the reform dynamic everyone is a double agent promoting reform and his or her own position in a local context.

In a similar example from the north, for example, U.S. proponents of alternative dispute resolution compete for influence in the United States in part by demonstrating their successes abroad. Academics can promote their theories locally by showing influence globally. The same is true for many of the promoters of constitutional reform or court reform. To return to the contrast between law and economics, the relative successes of Chicago economics in Chile were quite important in building its legitimacy in Spain, the United Kingdom, and the United States.

The situation, in other words, is far more contextual and local on both sides than is captured in such terms as "reformer" (or "activist," and so forth). And "successes" in making institutional changes can be traced to structural parallels or homologies that lead actors in the importing and exporting countries to have interests and itineraries that match. This match is far more important than what might be called intent or commitment—which always depends on what the position of the reformer is at a particular moment.

These kinds of structural matches, as mentioned before, are more difficult to find in the law than in some areas that are not so embedded in local histories and power arrangements distilled into social structures. As a result, the approaches identified with neo-liberal economics produced first in Chicago in the United States, for example, have been far more successfully implemented in Latin America than the approaches identified with the U.S. legal system.

Similarly, for reasons that need not be explained in this essay, the corporate law firm in the style—more or less—of the United States and the United Kingdom has also been far more successful in Latin America than has the public interest law firm. Businesses investing in or located in the south are therefore able to use the law and elite lawyers in ways that are unavailable to the poor or to disadvantaged groups more generally. Business law has historically matched better with existing people and institutions than public interest law. Public interest law, interestingly, thrived in the form of the human rights movement in the 1980s, and the successes of that movement help to fuel the optimism that we see today. But today local human rights institutions are no longer very strong. Local activists have tended to follow one of two paths. One is to move into politics and the state, following the longstanding Latin American pattern. The other is to translate the investment in human rights law into the places where it is rewarded more—international institutions typically headquartered in the United States.

This structural analysis is pessimistic as far as it goes. It suggests great difficulty in building and institutionalizing the rule of law and even questions whether the U.S.-based model that is used as a basis for assessment is correct. We might be tempted at this point to conclude that the exercise is too difficult and paradoxical to justify the investment. It does not appear that a collection of best practices or strengthened political commitments or empirical tests will do much to advance the model of the rule of law that is being exported—strong courts occupying a central position in the state, deeply involved in regulating the state and the economy, and with a strong commitment to the autonomy of law.

Rethinking Investment in the Autonomy of the Law

The first problem with this pessimism is that it neglects an obvious social phenomenon. There happen to be numerous individuals and organizations investing substantial resources in reforming legal and judicial systems. Credibility for the economy and the state in international circles—and increasingly also domestic circles—is in fact being measured according to the imported criteria. On the basis of our own research into the importing and exporting countries, we do not expect this activity to stop just because observers suggest caution. It then becomes obvious as well that the accumulation of this investment in the rule of law is going to make a difference.

There are many reasons for this effort. A few can be mentioned to suggest the power of these trends. The international importance of U.S.-inspired law—trade, antitrust, contract, securities, environment, human rights—and U.S. legal practices, in the first place, have helped make an advanced law degree in the United States increasingly important to lawyers from around the world, including Latin America. The students become acquainted with U.S. approaches to the law, including the strong investment of law professors in the United States in the relative autonomy of the law and legal institutions. These students learn to be highly critical of weak reasoning in court decisions and of law that is out of date. They expect supreme courts in their own countries to be important players in shaping political discourse and political agendas. In short, these law graduates develop a stake in legal expertise, and that stake distinguishes them from many of their classmates who did not go abroad.

They invest that expertise to add power and legitimacy to local groups—sometimes only a relatively marginal group of full-time academics or legal philosophers—that have long invested in legal expertise and the autonomy of the law. This investment can change the relative importance of law—for example, in Latin America where the legal world generally is still dominated by gentlemen lawyers connected to extended families descended from an old elite. The investors in the autonomy of the law may even challenge the dominance of the gentlemen lawyers in certain sectors in the name of legal values made more legitimate by their connection to the prestige and credentials that come from the United States.

The places of this enhanced investment in the law and legal expertise vary according to the historical and structural factors unique to each country. We find some of this investment in the courts and in legal education in all places, but owing to historical reasons that we have mentioned, the major places tend to be elsewhere. Business law and commercial arbitration are areas in which there is such investment. Of course, as suggested above, we would naturally expect both areas in Latin America to still have quite strong family components consistent with the longstanding structures of law. In Brazil, according to our research, one key place for investment in the autonomy of the law has been the *procuradors*—public prosecutors. It is no longer possible for a member of the traditional elite simply to parachute to leadership without a requisite investment in the autonomy of law. In Mexico, we can trace these investments into, for example, quasi-state institutions such as the National Commission for Human Rights and the Electoral Commission. They are not autonomous courts, but they have gained some of the features of autonomous courts through this cumulative investment—and they are clearly making a difference in their local settings. Similarly, while there are so far not great successes in reforming the courts in Argentina, despite the World Bank's investment, we can trace international investment into the development of mediation outside the courts and the creation of some entities that—almost uniquely in Latin America—look very much like U.S.-style public interest law firms. All of these changes are significant. The local variations are a function of the strategies of local actors and the spaces that are open to this kind of investment. They both fit longstanding domestic patterns and modify them—without creating what the exporters imagine they will create.

They have not replicated the conditions that are so essential to the U.S. approach as it has been institutionalized in the United States. In none of these settings, therefore, have the traditional law schools connected to the political elites been transformed. Educational reform has been quite limited and found mainly in private schools acting parallel to and competing with the traditional law schools. The courts, as we suggested, are not even close to the model according to which they are increasingly being measured. But what is interesting is that the investment in the people connected to judicial reform contributes to the momentum for the rule of law that is translated into more indigenous patterns of reform.

As suggested before, we cannot ascertain the impact of "legal reform projects" without taking into account all the (perhaps) unintended and even paradoxical impacts of the investment. In this respect, therefore, the conclusion of the Lawyers Committee for Human Rights, repeated in several studies, is misleading:

> Government commitment should be assessed before the Bank agrees to finance a judicial reform proposal. This assessment should be one of the most important issues in the Bank's initial appraisal of the climate for reform in a given state. Judicial independence is the most important measure of commitment—the willingness of the government to take concrete steps to reduce political influence in judicial appointments and court operations.... (Lawyers Committee for Human Rights 1996, 2000)

Certainly it is important to do all that can be done to protect the independence of the judiciary from political influence, but the conclusion of the Lawyers Committee that the effort in Peru was a waste of time and money does not necessarily follow. Before we can make such a determination, we need to know much more about those who were involved in the project, what they are doing, and whether there are any institutional outlets promoting the relative autonomy of the law that have been strengthened as a result.

Indeed, if we consider the local context carefully, it is clear that we cannot expect the legislative and executive branches of the government to grant complete autonomy to the courts just because it is a good idea to have an independent judiciary. The problem is the same one that comes from thinking that what is widely accepted in the United States is universally valid. We know what "judges" are in the United States—where they come from, what values they hold, and what institutional incentives they face because of the role of law in the United States. But someone labeled a "judge" in another country may be a very different kind of person. The label is not enough to separate those called judges from local politics, families, political feuds, or clientelism. And if there were such a separation, we might still question whether a government would really want to create a new ruling group in the guise of a completely independent judiciary unless it had gradually granted that autonomy and observed the concomitant development of institutional constraints—faculties of law, for example, and patterns of behavior that come to define the operating rules of the courts.

Practical Conclusions

My conclusions, therefore, point in two seemingly opposite directions. One is that we need to be more modest in defining our prescriptions and assuming that we know what is best for any given country. We make mistakes both in the diagnosis and in the cure, even when we think that we have completely taken into account the perspectives of local actors. The local actors are embedded in the same hierarchies that lead us to think our "universals" are indeed universal. The second point, however, is that assessments of the results of legal investment need to be broadened. Local impacts that are typically neglected by those who can only imagine success as "independent" courts involved in major policy arenas must be considered. The general conclusion—which takes into account both these points—is simply that we need a much better understanding of the local contexts that produce importers and exporters of the rule of law on the one hand, and the processes themselves on the other. Rather than elaborate further on the more general point, however, I will conclude with some practical observations.

First, even though reformers resist this characterization, there remains a strong tendency in the analyses of problems and the diagnosis of remedies to use the United States as the template. This problem is evident in general approaches and in particular calls for precise features of U.S. law such as case management and alternative dispute resolution (defined precisely to correspond to U.S. taxonomies). At the very least, reformers should be sensitive about which "universals" they promote.

The second problem, which is related, is that there are other potential models for legal legitimacy, including those that contemplate a stronger state with accountability through the legislative processes. Alternative models, whether they come from civil law or elsewhere, are on the defensive, but it is not clear why they cannot also be consistent with the rule of law and democracy. The prestige of U.S. legal institutions, the attractiveness of advanced degrees in the United States, and the power of U.S. actors on the world scene may be leading reformers to overlook virtues associated with other approaches.

Third, it is also important to see that there can be spaces outside of the courts and the traditional legal academies where local actors can invest in and build commitments to the autonomy of law and the importance of legal expertise as a language of governance. Those concerned with the rule of law should expand their gaze to consider other places where there can be major social impacts. They may not fit the U.S. or even the European ideal, but not even the U.S. always fits its ideal of, for example, independence from politics. Those who study the rule of law should be alert to transformations that do not seem to fit the U.S. rule—or are outside the realm of traditional courts and legal academic circles.

Fourth, despite my argument that we need to consider other potential models, we still need to recognize that there are powerful pressures to converge around a U.S. model, and they will undoubtedly continue. I therefore would like more sensitivity to the limits of that approach and other possibilities, while at the same time taking into account these very strong pressures. It does not make sense for me to argue that the U.S. legal model (or U.S. junk food or U.S. blue jeans) should be rejected.

Fifth, given this pressure to converge around a particular model, we have to be concerned with some problems that have tended to be neglected to date. In particular, a key ingredient of the U.S. model—often not well understood in the United States—is the role of legal education and especially academic scholarship produced by full-time law professors. There is a huge production of legal scholarship in the United States that takes virtually any issue or group or expertise, translates it into legal terminology, and thus makes it available to keep the law in tune with academic, social, and political trends. At the same time, this academic production also keeps judges accountable to the basic canons of formal legal scholarship. Both sides—formalizing inside and importing from outside—are necessary to maintain the position of law in the United States. This kind of scholarly investment is rare outside of the United States. In Latin America, in particular, most professors remain part-time.

Without this investment, there is no one except the media to police the politics of the courts and to hold the courts accountable, but the media are limited and cannot by themselves adjust the law locally to keep it up to date. They can help avoid corruption, but that kind of policing is not enough. As noted before, in contrast to economics, which was relatively new, it has been very difficult to transform legal education—hence the failure of the first law and development movement.

Sixth, and finally, the various trends that put increasing pressure on the countries of the south to build the rule of law according to U.S. standards raise questions of legitimacy that should be considered. The incompleteness of the U.S. model as imported means that it is not "indigenized" or made local. The ideas and approaches from abroad can be criticized by opponents of globalization, for example, as unsuited for local situations. The problem obviously relates to the difficulty of changing legal education or the courts, which then seem not to match the ideas that are coming in from the north.

Furthermore, the relative success of business law firms as opposed to public interest law firms means that the institutions of legal representation in the south are far more asymmetrical than they are in the United States. To the extent that the legitimacy of the business law firms depends on having counterparts with un- or underrepresented clients, the legitimacy of law is bound to be further undermined. The situation is of course quite complex. Structural reasons make it more difficult to build public interest law than business law. It may be easier to build the legitimacy of imported law through such public interest institutions, however, than by concentrating too much energy on the courts and the legal academy—the two institutions most resistant to change.

BIBLIOGRAPHY

Carothers, Thomas. 1991. *In the Name of Democracy: U.S. Policy Toward Latin America in the Reagan Years.* Berkeley: University of California Press.
——. 1996. *Assessing Democracy Assistance: The Case of Romania.* Washington, D.C.: Carnegie Endowment for International Peace.
——. 1998. "The Rule of Law Revival." *Foreign Affairs* 77(2): 95–106.
——. 1999. *Aiding Democracy Abroad: The Learning Curve.* Washington, D.C.: Carnegie Endowment for International Peace.
Dezalay, Yves, and Bryant G. Garth. 1996. *Dealing in Virtue: International Commercial Arbitration and the Construction of a Transnational Legal Order.* Chicago: University of Chicago Press.
Dezalay, Yves, and Bryant G. Garth. Forthcoming. *The Internationalization of Palace Wars: Lawyers, Economists, and the International Reconstruction of National States.*

Gardner, James. 1980. *Legal Imperialism: American Lawyers and Foreign Aid in Latin America*. Madison. Wis.: University of Wisconsin Press.

Hammergren, Linn. 1998. *The Politics of Justice and Justice Reform in Latin America: The Peruvian Case in Comparative Perspective*. Boulder, Colo.: Westview Press.

Keck, Margaret, and Kathryn Sikkink. 1998. *Activists Beyond Borders: Advocacy Networks in International Politics*. Ithaca, New York: Cornell University Press.

Lawyers Committee for Human Rights/Venezuela Program for Human Rights Education and Action. 1996. *Halfway to Reform: The World Bank and the Venezuelan Justice System*. New York: Lawyers Committee for Human Rights.

Lawyers Committee for Human Rights. 1998. *Beyond Linkage and Engagement: A New Approach to US–China Policy*. New York: Lawyers Committee for Human Rights.

——. 2000. *Building on Quicksand: The Collapse of the World Bank's Judicial Reform Project in Peru*. New York: Lawyers Committee for Human Rights.

Lazarus, Edward. 1998. *Closed Chambers: The Rise, Fall, and Future of the Modern Supreme Court*. New York: Times Books.

McClymont, Mary, and Stephen Golub, eds. 2000. *Many Roads to Justice: The Law Related Work of Ford Foundation Grantees Around the World*. New York: Ford Foundation.

Méndez, Juan. 1999. "Institutional Reform, Including Access to Justice." In Juan E. Méndez, Guillermo O'Donnell, and Paulo Sérgio Pinheiro, eds. *The (Un)Rule of Law and the Underprivileged in Latin America*. Notre Dame, Ind.: University of Notre Dame Press.

Metzger, Barry. 1997. "Law and Development. An Essential Dimension of Governance." Proceedings of a Seminar in Fukuoka, Japan on *Governance: Promoting Sound Development Management*. May 1997. http://www.asiadevbank.org/law/proceedings/1997/governance/governance.htm

Pistor, Katharina, and Philip A. Wellons. 1998. Revised. *The Role of Law and Legal Institutions in Asian Economic Development 1960–1995. Final Comparative Report*. Prepared for the Asian Development Bank, March 1998.

Quigley, Kevin. 1997. *For Democracy's Sake: Foundations and Democracy Assistance in Central Europe*. Washington, D.C.: Woodrow Wilson Center Press.

Rose, Carol V. 1998. "The 'New' Law and Development Movement in the Post-Cold War Era: A Vietnam Case Study." *Law and Society Review* 32: 93–140.

Santos, Boaventura de Sousa. 1995. *Toward a New Common Sense: Law, Science and Politics in the Paradigmatic Transition*. New York: Routledge.

Sarat, Austin, and Stuart Scheingold, eds. 1998. *Cause Lawyering: Political Commitments and Professional Responsibilities*. New York: Oxford University Press.

Thome, Joseph. 2000. "Heading South But Looking North: Globalization and Law Reform in Latin America." Paper for LASA Meeting, March 15–19, Miami.

Trubek, David, and Marc Galanter. 1974. "Scholars in Self-Estrangement: Some Reflections on the Crisis in Law and Development Studies in the United States." *Wisconsin Law Review* 1974: 1062–1102.

Twining, William. 1997. *Law in Context: Enlarging a Discipline.* Oxford: Oxford University Press.

World Bank Seminar. 1998. Seminar on judicial reform: "Lessons of Experience." May 12.

What Alternatives Exist for Holding Governments Accountable?

Principal Institutions and Mechanisms of Accountability

Denis Galligan

Professor of Socio-Legal Studies and

Director of the Centre for Socio-Legal Studies

University of Oxford,

Visiting Professor

Central European University

Budapest

Introduction

In making government and administration accountable, various institutions and mechanisms are available and commonly deployed in modern constitutional systems. These include the processes of courts and ombudsman bodies, inspectorates and auditors, special appeal tribunals that are external as well as complaints procedures that are internal, and others. What we mean by accountability is that one official or organization is required to explain and justify its actions to another body or authority, according to specified criteria, where the body or authority, to which account is given, normally has power to take remedial action when the criteria are not met. The main point of accountability is to ensure that the primary institutions of government perform their functions properly according to legal and other relevant standards. The object of this paper is to give a brief overview of the different institutions and processes of accountability of government and administration.

The Objectives of Accountability

Although accountability may take many forms, I shall restrict the present analysis to those that have an express legal role and duty in that regard. Before examining the particular forms of accountability, it may be helpful to outline the objectives to be achieved through accountability.

The first objective is to improve the quality of administration. Accountability may advance this objective in several ways. First, the very fact that accountability mechanisms exist may influence the behavior of officials toward better decision-making. Second, when an act or decision is brought under scrutiny by a court or ombudsman or other institution, it may be changed for the better. Third, scrutiny in a specific case may have consequences beyond that case. A court's decision, for instance, may contain a more general ruling about how some aspect of administration should be conducted; or an ombudsman's investigation in a particular case may lead to recommendations about a more general practice.

The second objective of accountability is to protect the rights of citizens who are affected by the administration. A feature of government and administration that is easily overlooked is that their actions often have direct and serious consequences for the rights and interests of citizens. Citizens encounter government and administration in many different contexts in which benefits are conferred or withheld, or in which burdens are imposed. Sometimes the interests at stake are fairly minor, but often vital matters are left to the power and discretion of administrative bodies. The main consideration in such encounters between citizen and state is that the laws governing the matter should be fairly and accurately applied, and that discretion should be exercised in a fair and reasonable manner. Accountability mechanisms are directed to ensuring that these standards are observed, and in particular that specific actions are taken legally, fairly, and reasonably. It may be suggested that the right of a citizen to seek recourse from an administrative decision, by way of appeal, review, or investigation, is an important constitutional right.

The third objective of accountability is to increase the general legitimacy of government and administration. Legitimacy is a complex notion that we need not examine here beyond noting that it is variable depending on various factors. In relation to government and administration, the legitimacy of an institution is partly dependent on the two matters noted above, the quality of decisions and the treatment of citizens. But legitimacy also depends on other factors, such as openness and transparency, on notions of fairness in matters of procedure and substance, and on being subject to outside scrutiny. Accordingly, accountability mechanisms may contribute to legitimacy in two general ways: one by examining such matters as openness and transparency to ensure that they are respected; the other by the very process of requiring the primary body to make account. In other words, the extent to which government and administration are subject to accountability mechanisms is itself an indicator of legitimacy. Of special importance here is the way that accountability can help to generate intermediate standards which in turn contribute to the general objectives. Such standards include openness and transparency, participatory procedures, independence and impartiality, and reasoned and reasonable decisions.

A Common Model of Administrative Accountability

While every country has its own history and traditions, among many a common and broadly agreed concept of administrative accountability is emerging. The common concept has developed to some extent in each country, although there appears to be a consensus that certain kinds of accountability are necessary features of a sound system of government and administration. The common concept draws on several sources:

1. The law and practice of the countries of Western Europe, a law and practice that has close parallels in countries such as Australia, Canada, New Zealand, and the United States;
2. The law and practice of the European Union, in particular the jurisprudence of the European Court of Justice and the practices of the Commission and the Council;
3. The influence of the European Convention on Human Rights and its interpretation by the Commission, the Court, and the Council of Europe; and
4. The writings and commentaries of jurists.

The main features of the common concept are that accountability mechanisms should include a combination of the following: appeals to courts on issues of legality; appeals to internal and external bodies on the substantive merits of decisions; complaints to investigative bodies such as the ombudsman's office concerning poor quality administration; general supervision by a range of audit bodies and inspectorates, including the very specific supervision of public finances; and an extensive system of parliamentary committees. Most Western European countries have made good progress toward a system of accountability based on these features, while the newer European democracies are working toward that end. Some of these institutions are more important than others; courts, ombudsman bodies, and audit commissions, for instance, are often embedded in constitutions, while others, such as internal appeals, are included in codes of administrative procedure. Other institutions, such as special inspectorates or appeal tribunals are left for creation by law.

Principal Institutions and Mechanisms of Accountability

I turn now to a brief analysis of the main institutions and mechanisms of accountability of government and administration.

Judicial Supervision

Judicial supervision of the administration is an essential feature of a system of government and administration based on the rule of law. By judicial supervision we mean the process by which an independent court examines an administrative action to determine whether it complies with the principle of legality. And by the principle of legality we mean the legal rules deriving from the constitution, statutory legislation, international treaties, and judicial decisions that apply to the administration. Judicial scrutiny is normally initiated by a person, organization, or interest group whose interests are affected in some tangible way by the administrative action. Most legal systems also make provision for a special public authority, such as the prosecutor, commissaire du government, or attorney general to bring the action before the courts.

The procedures for bringing judicial review vary considerably, with the adversarial approach of Anglo-American courts at one end of the spectrum and the investigative approach of the French Conseil d'Etat at the other end. However, the essential character of judicial supervision is the same, namely, to determine whether an action of an administrative or executive body is in accordance with law. The court systems across Europe also vary greatly, with some countries such as France and Poland having separate administrative courts, while others, such as Hungary and Romania, have administrative review conducted by the ordinary courts. However they are organized, the main requirement is that the courts should be independent of the administration and executive in the performance of their functions. Independence does not depend on whether the court is classified as part of the administrative arm of government, as in the French system, or is entirely separate from it, as in Britain.

The principles on which judicial scrutiny is based are that public administration should be conducted within a framework of laws and that the courts are responsible in the final resort for deciding whether particular actions are within those laws. The principle of legality, or the framework of laws, consists of different kinds of legal standards: laws defining the powers of administrative bodies and their limits; laws imposing standards on the manner in which decisions are made; and laws prescribing the procedures to be followed. The assumption behind the first set of legal standards is that the authority has only the powers conferred by law, and that actions not authorized by law are by definition outside the law and of no legal effect. The second group of legal standards is aimed at the decision process itself, imposing principles such as good faith, rationality, proportionality, reasonableness, fairness, and equality. The third category of standards is procedural in nature, and includes notions of procedural due process. It can be seen that the principle of legality has an open and dynamic character, and can be the vehicle for conveying a range of values to government and administration.

Although accountability of the administration through judicial supervision is essential in a society based on the rule of law, it should be recognized that this is a limited form of accountability. It is limited in several ways: (i) judicial supervision is confined to the legality of specific administrative acts and decisions; (ii) it depends normally on a person or group affected by the action taking the initiative to challenge it and so is likely to be sporadic; (iii) it is a costly process, often for the party bringing it, and always for the public purse; (iv) the judicial process is often very slow in reaching a conclusion; and (v) there are functional limits on the courts' capacity to review administrative actions. The strength of judicial scrutiny is that it protects rights in specific situations. Its limitation is that it is likely to have only marginal impact on the general practices of the administration. A successful action in the courts will mean that the particular act or decision is remedied, but the wider implications for the administration may be negligible. Some notable judicial rulings in the course of an action for judicial review may become general principles of law providing guidance for the future, but that is rare.

Internal Mechanisms: Appeals and Complaints

In the countries of Central and Eastern Europe, during the communist period, the usual form of accountability of administrative bodies was to a superior authority within government and administration. There was little scope for external scrutiny, so that complaints and grievances were dealt with within the administrative system. We know little about how these accountability systems worked in practice. They remain the principal form of recourse within those countries, although now an unsuccessful internal appeal may be followed by some form of external scrutiny by a court or ombudsman.

While it is understandable that internal systems of accountability are somewhat discredited in Eastern Europe, they are in fact an important form of accountability and have considerable potential as an instrument for improving the quality of administrative decision-making. The recent trend in Western countries is to pay more attention to internal forms of supervision and accountability, partly because of that potential and partly because of the limited efficacy of external mechanisms. A standard approach is for a department or agency to create an internal appeal structure from the primary decision to a superior or other body within the organization. Appeals are often supplemented by complaints procedures of a more comprehensive kind; in the United Kingdom, the Citizens' Charter, introduced in the 1990s, required all public bodies providing services to the public to specify the standards of service accompanied by suitable mechanisms for complaining when the service obligations were not met.

The advantages of internal accountability mechanisms are several: (i) they are informal, easy to initiate, usually fast, and fairly cheap; (ii) they have the advantage of the appeal or complaint being dealt with by an official who is experienced in the field of administration; and (iii) they can be wide in their scope and they need not be confined to matters of law. Internal procedures also have disadvantages: (i) it is difficult to keep separate the primary decision-maker and the appeal body or investigator; (ii) secrecy and a lack of transparency often characterize internal procedures; and (iii) the quality of the internal procedures is often low owing to lack of training or proper organization.

External Appeals

By external appeals we mean a process by which a person dissatisfied with an administrative action may appeal to a body that is independent of the administration. Such appeals may raise questions of law, but their main attraction is that they can consider the facts and substance of the action. This appeal function is sometimes performed by lower or specially created courts; alternatively, special appeal bodies may be set up—these are not courts, but they do make an independent adjudication in respect of the matter. However the appeal body may be comprised, the essential idea is to examine the evidence, the facts, and the primary judgment about these to determine whether the appeals body is the best or most supportable in the circumstances.

Appeals on the merits to external bodies are familiar in some Western systems of administration, although they have no place in the traditions of Central and Eastern Europe. The French *Tribunaux Administratives,* which are the first-instance administrative courts, have the power to examine the merits as well as legality in certain contexts. A more extensive system of external appeals can be seen in the tribunal system of the United Kingdom. This is an extensive system that covers most, but not all, areas of administration. The usual pattern is to have a chairperson who is a lawyer accompanied by two lay members who are experienced in the field of administration. However, the most highly developed system of external appeals is to be found in the Australian Administrative Appeals Tribunal (AAT), which consists of one main set of tribunals similar to but with more extensive powers than the British system. The AAT not only has the power to examine the primary decision to see whether it was wrong in some way, it has the additional duty of considering the matter afresh and substituting the decision it thinks best, even if no error can be found in the original decision. Where discretion has been conferred on the original authority, the AAT is obligated to reconsider and re-exercise the discretion.

External appeals are normally allowed only after internal appeal mechanisms have been exhausted (when there are such mechanisms). The main difference between the two is that the latter are conducted within the administration by administrative officials, while the former are heard by an independent semi-judicial body. The scope of appeal is similar in both cases, usually allowing a full re-examination of the merits of the case. Internal mechanisms are likely to be very informal, although emphasis on informality is also an important feature of external appeals. The two go well together. Most errors or sources of grievance can be remedied at the internal stage, and can be done so with speed and efficiency. This in itself is a good reason for having internal mechanisms and requiring that they be invoked as the first instance. Where grievances persist after the internal process, they can be dealt with still reasonably quickly and informally by an external appeal body. The added value here, however, is the appeal body's independence and its capacity to provide a level of scrutiny that may not be possible within the department or agency itself. In addition to their role in dealing with individual cases, through their decisions in such cases, internal and external processes can also have a role in setting general standards of good administration. Just how effective they are in that role is a matter that needs further research.

The relationship between these two forms of substantive appeals and judicial supervision should be noted. Judicial supervision is concerned with the legality of administrative actions and is a necessary feature of a rule-of-law system. It does not examine the substantive merits of an action but has the function of ensuring that the administrative body has legal authority for what it does and that in exercising its authority it has complied with other relevant legal principles. Appeals, whether internal or external, are primarily concerned with the facts and the substantive decision made on the facts. Issues of legality may arise, and where they do they will be dealt with; but the main point of these processes is to re-examine the merits.

Ombudsman

The idea of the ombudsman as a mechanism of accountability is rapidly gaining ground in Europe and elsewhere. Although a relatively new form of accountability, except in Sweden from which the modern form is derived, the ombudsman appears to meet a need that otherwise would not be adequately met. It is particularly popular in the new democracies of Eastern Europe, although there may be some confusion there as to both its essential functions and its limits.

The essential idea of the ombudsman is an independent statutory body whose task is to investigate complaints made by individuals or groups about the actions of administrative bodies. The ombudsman may have a general, wide-ranging power to investigate all aspects of administration, or it may be given supervision over specific areas, such as the police, prisons, and the health service. An ombudsman is usually created under a statute or law that specifies its powers and makes it accountable to parliament. Since its main function is to investigate, scrutinize, and possibly criticize government and administration, it is essential that it be independent of both.

An ombudsman's role is often marked by several characteristics. First, it investigates complaints in order to determine whether there are faults in the procedure or substance of the administrative action. Second, an ombudsman usually has extensive powers to question officials and to require them to produce documents. Third, when an investigation does disclose fault or impropriety on the part of the administrative body, the ombudsman recommends a solution or some form of remedy, rather than impose a sanction. It is then for the agency or department to remedy the defect in accordance with the ombudsman's recommendations, encouraged undoubtedly by the desire to avoid adverse publicity and an unfavorable report to parliament. The usual recommendations are reconsideration, reversal, or the payment of compensation.

The question arises as to what kinds of defects an ombudsman investigates. The answer is that there are several, and indeed ombudsman bodies may be quite different in their purpose and function according to the nature of the defect. Broadly three main categories can be identified. The *illegality* model: according to the classic Swedish model, an ombudsman investigates complaints alleging illegality on the part of the administration. Illegality means that the administration has breached a statute, regulation, court-made rule, the constitution, or a principle of international law. The idea that an ombudsman should concentrate on complaints concerning the actions of the administration has been influential in the new European democracies. The Polish ombudsman, created in 1987, was considered a great success because it investigated with an independence of mind violations of the law and principles of community life and social justice.

The *constitutional and human rights* model has been especially prevalent in the new European democracies where complaints concerning the abuse of rights are of particular concern. This has resulted in the creation of various kinds of ombudsman institutions to deal with the abuse of rights. The rights model may be seen as a variation on the *illegality* model; instead of embracing all forms of administrative illegality, an ombudsman of this kind focuses on illegality relating to the violation of constitutional and human rights.

The *maladministration* model is based on the idea that good administration requires more than staying within the law, and that there are many defects that may broadly be considered maladministration. This term is not easily defined, but it includes improprieties on the part of the administration that go beyond illegality, although of course illegality is itself an instance of maladministration. Carelessness, undue delay, lack of cooperation, unfairness, and procedural irregularity are all covered. This model of ombudsman has been adopted in many places including the European Union, France, Britain, Australia, and New Zealand.

While the three models overlap to a considerable degree, the emphasis and function of each is different. A country considering the adoption of an ombudsman should consider which model best meets its needs at the time and which best fits in with other forms of accountability. In countries where the court system is weak or discredited, there may be an argument for incorporating the legality model, at least as a temporary measure; in the other countries the pressing need may be to protect human rights. The maladministration model is something of a luxury and generally should be considered only after a strong court system has been established and human rights issues are under control.

One of the dangers to guard against is the idea that an ombudsman can perform many functions, some of which are traditionally left to other institutions, and that an ombudsman may even remove the need for other institutions. Unawareness of this danger is sometimes apparent in the new European democracies where the proliferation of ombudsman institutions is most noticeable—often without careful consideration of their functions and their relations to other institutions, however. One danger that should especially be avoided is to imagine that an ombudsman is a suitable substitute for courts. On the contrary, ombudsman bodies serve a different function—investigating complaints—and should complement courts, whose task is to uphold legality. The ideal should be to develop both a strong system of courts and an efficient ombudsman mechanism.

This is not to deny of course a certain overlap between the two, especially in cases in which the illegality model of the ombudsman is adopted. However, the general lines separating the two should be kept clear. Courts are judicial bodies with the final responsibility for deciding questions of law; they can impose remedies such as declarations of nullity or liability, but they can inquire into and rule upon only specific cases that come before them. An ombudsman for its part is a nonjudicial body with responsibility for investigating complaints against the administration; it may recommend that certain action be taken, which may go beyond the specific complaint. An ombudsman is usually more easily accessible than the courts and the procedures are quite different.

Other Accountability Mechanisms

Other accountability mechanisms that I shall mention rather than analyze in detail include inspectorates, standard-setting bodies, parliamentary processes, and especially the committees of parliament. Inspectorates are of many kinds and usually consist of specially created bodies with powers to monitor, scrutinize, and report on the actions of a primary administrative body. While their activities now range widely, probably the most important is the audit authority, which supervises the financial management of agencies and departments. Standard-setting bodies are perhaps less common, but the general idea is to create a supervisory body, one of whose main tasks is formulating standards of behavior and service with respect to the area of administration that is subject to it. Such standards then become one of the grounds for holding the administrative body accountable. The parliamentary process is the ultimate form of accountability, and is now normally conducted through a committee system, which is becoming a standard feature of modern democracies.

Evaluation and Reflections

It can be seen from this brief account that a considerable range and variety of accountability mechanisms for the supervision of government and administration are available. Well-developed, modern democracies are likely to have elements of all or most of them in some form or another, although just precisely what form they take and how they fit together as a whole is bound to vary greatly. The general idea is that different mechanisms serve different functions in securing accountability, and the aim should be to devise over time a pattern of mechanisms that are adequate in their cover of government and administration, and which are reasonably compatible with each other but without too much overlap or duplication. The more comprehensive and coherent the pattern is, the more effective it is likely to be in making government and administration accountable. The corollary is that there is no one single mechanism that will serve all purposes; a realistic view is that each adds in its own small but distinctive way to achieving satisfactory levels of accountability.

While a network of accountability mechanisms is a worthwhile ideal for all modern democracies, it cannot be achieved overnight, nor can it be achieved without committing substantial resources to it. As to the first point, it is generally wise for newer democracies to develop accountability mechanisms step by step, with an order of priority clearly stated, and in line with the available resources. For example, a first priority should be the creation of an independent and effective court system, which may but need not necessarily be accompanied by an ombudsman system. An ombudsman is important, but courts should come first. Parliamentary committees have great potential for accountability, but they take time to establish themselves and to define their areas of expertise, and so on. It is vital, moreover, that each institution or mechanism be adequately funded so that it is effective. Nothing is more likely to bring discredit and a sense of illegitimacy than the creation of an institution that quickly proves to be ineffective because of a lack of funding. The ombudsman system in Eastern Europe provides a good example; one does not have to look far to find ombudsman bodies that are swamped with complaints that they cannot possibly even read, let alone investigate. Similarly, while elaborate laws and regulations regarding parliamentary committees can be seen all over Eastern Europe, most of them are largely dormant.

Now while these points are easily made, the newer democracies face a dilemma. On the one hand, they are under great pressure from many quarters—western governments, international organizations, nongovernmental bodies, and the financial and business sectors—to develop accountability mechanisms quickly and comprehensively. On the other hand they do not have the expertise or the resources to make those mechanisms effective. This often results in the creation of dysfunctional institutions and low levels of accountability.

There is of course no easy solution to this dilemma. The sensible approach, however, is for each country, with the benefit of outside help, to formulate its own plan of development, based on its own needs as understood against its social and historical conditions, and according to its economic capacity. Such a plan should identify needs and priorities, taking care to ensure that any proposed accountability mechanism adds distinct value to the existing arrangements. It should also include techniques for monitoring the effectiveness and quality of the institution and its processes. This is only a beginning, but I suggest that it is a necessary beginning in the creation of sound and lasting forms of accountability.

The Role of the Ombudsman

Bience Gawanas

Ombudswoman

Republic of Namibia

I am very pleased to be with you today and to share my time with such distinguished panel members. I wish to commend the World Bank for the invitation, as I am representing an occupation, the ombudsman, that is so crucial in accountability discourse, yet is always overlooked at conferences of this nature. This forum will no doubt, afford us with the opportunity for an in-depth discussion on accountability. I will therefore address the topic by looking at the ombudsman institution as an alternative for holding government accountable. However, before doing so, I wish to make some preliminary points.

Discourse on Accountability

I attended a conference last year in Toronto and, among the many useful observations and statements made, the issue of the use of private sector language to describe accountability in public sector institutions came under scrutiny. This discourse on accountability obviously begs the question as to the language that we all use so easily to define accountability. As such it is not only a question of a definition, but also the need to find a common language and a common lens through which we all can look at issues of accountability as a principle of good governance.

At the conference, we were reminded to reclaim the language of government, which includes the following:

- Public good;
- Common good;
- Serving the public;
- Fairness, dignity; and
- Respect, honesty.

Traditional Means of Ensuring Accountability

The constitution is always taken as the starting point for accountability, as it is the fundamental law that establishes structures and instruments for good governance. This is followed by an emphasis on the rule of law based on the principle that public affairs must be conducted on the basis of legality. It requires among other things the adherence to principles of good administration, as set out by the Commonwealth Secretariat, which are as follows:

- Be just, fair, and equitable;
- Be transparent and honest, and not corrupt;
- Conduct oneself in the interest of the public at large and do not serve the private interest of public servants;
- Carry out duties in accordance with the rules of financial good practice;
- Be responsive to the needs of the public;
- Conduct operations in an efficient manner, that is, without undue delay and inconvenience to the citizens; and
- Remain open to public scrutiny.

Coupled with the above is the need to create an environment of transparency through legislation such as freedom of information acts, whistleblowers protection acts, and codes of conduct.

There are also various governance structures that work to promote accountability and, among others, these are:

- Parliament;
- Auditors general;
- Judiciary;
- Anticorruption agencies;
- Human rights commissions;
- Election commissions;
- Public service commission;
- Civil society organizations including the media; and
- Ombudsman offices.

It is the ombudsman offices, in particular those in the developing world, that will be primarily addressed here as alternative mechanisms.

In the 1990s many countries transformed themselves from autocratic states to constitutionally created democratic states. Although many of them have introduced multiparty democracies with an entrenched bill of rights, they have yet to consolidate a framework for democratic governance. Therefore, unlike in established democracies where a culture for the respect of the rule of law has been firmly established, in developing countries, checks and balances expected to exist among the various arms of government are either nonexistent or do not function effectively. Human rights abuses occur and the search for good governance is an ongoing struggle. Coupled with this, corruption has become a major issue. It permeates every sector of society and has become accepted as a way of life. In the absence of a viable alternative, the economic and social rights of citizens are insufficiently guaranteed or met.

This is also a time when demands are being made for good governance—namely, political pluralism, an end to corruption, more respect for human rights accountability, transparency, and effective and efficient administration. Multiparty democracy refers not only to elections but also to the relationship between the state and the citizen. When people vote their leaders into power, they have expectations that the leaders will serve the public, be fair and act reasonably and according to law, provide effective and efficient services, be accessible and follow the rules of natural justice, and provide visionary and accountable leadership. As such, governments must first and foremost be held accountable by the people themselves in a given country.

People will have confidence in public institutions only if they can be assured of honesty and being served in a transparent and open manner and if there are mechanisms through which they can hold government accountable. However, effectiveness of control of the two most important check and balance mechanisms—parliament and the courts—are hampered, first, by the fact that although separation of powers is an important feature of a democratic dispensation, absolute separation between parliament and the other branches of government is not possible, and second, by the expense and slowness of litigation which inhibit effective access to courts.

The importance of independent monitoring bodies including the role of civil society can therefore not be overstated. The ombudsman can be said to fill the gap by playing a complementary role to parliament and the courts. It is not, however, a substitute for proper values or an internal complaints mechanism, as the best solutions and controls are usually found within an institution itself.

The Role of the Ombudsman

It is within the context outlined above that the role of the ombudsman assumes a wider dimension in that he or she is expected to be the defender of human rights, including the right to good governance. The concept of the ombudsman is understood in various ways; the following are provided as examples:

- The ombudsman is a concept entrenched within a democratic system as a safeguard against governmental abuses of individual liberties.
- It also serves to enforce executive accountability for the good of ordinary citizens.
- It is a mechanism necessary for the enforcement of the rule of law.
- It offers informal methods for resolving disputes free of charge to the complainant and relatively quickly and inexpensively for government compared to litigation. It does not replace the courts but is a compliment to the courts in dispensing quick and just remedies.

As an important role-player in the democratization process, the ombudsman fulfills a much broader mandate than do traditional ombudsman institutions. Therefore, I believe that our role in emerging democracies should be geared toward the following:

1. *Search for justice by promoting respect and protecting the rights of the individual.* I assume that when countries choose the democratic path, they also pledge to move away from oppression and injustice and toward improving citizens' quality of life, toward an environment in which human rights and fundamental freedoms are observed and enjoyed. Yet, whether knowingly or systemically, violations do occasionally take place within these government administrations—indicating a gap between theory and reality. Individuals who have been subject to the impact of maladministration or corruption or have suffered violations of their human rights should be aware that they have a right to complain

to an independent and impartial ombudsman and know how to make such a complaint. Officials must also be made aware that their decisions and actions are subject to scrutiny to determine whether these adversely affect citizens.

2. *Promote the rule of law.* In a democracy, all government institutions, be they at the central, regional or local level, are required to act within and uphold the rule of law. This means that the actions of government must be reasonable, fair, and just. Public officials must at all times act in a manner that is not arbitrary or contrary to public interest. Their decisions must be in accordance with previously defined rules and procedures.

   The ombudsman is there to ensure that the rule of law is implemented in terms of protecting the rights of the people as set out in the constitution and according to the mandate of the Ombudsman Act and other laws and regulations. When officials do not adhere to these principles, their decisions adversely affect the rights of the ordinary citizen and lead to maladministration. Authorities and their officials can cause maladministration as a result of abuse of power, arbitrariness, mistake, and neglect.

   Therefore, in promoting good governance and effective administration, it is incumbent upon the ombudsman not only to seek a remedy for the grievances of individual citizens, but also to pursue a policy of prevention—which means pointing out deficiencies within the public service that need improvement and which were revealed while investigating a complaint. These broader systemic issues may require corrective action, which may include the adoption of rules and procedures that will promote and create a public service culture that is responsive and adheres to standards.

3. *Eliminate corrupt practices and promote ethical standards in public life.* I believe that the basic tenet of democracy is that public institutions must carry out their work in a transparent manner; if they are not willing to subject themselves to public scrutiny, these institutions will fail to gain the public's trust. The expectation of the public is that officials will

perform their duties to the highest possible standard. Therefore, there is a need to define good ethical administrative practice in a code of conduct. Where administrative behavior falls short of this code, officials must be held accountable and their decisions must be challenged whether it is through the courts or by filing a complaint with the office of the ombudsman. The office of the ombudsman views the abuse of power, corruption or unfair, discourteous or other improper conduct on the part of an official not only as affecting the rights of a citizen but also as an indication of the deterioration of ethical standards.

Ethical issues are becoming more and more the standard against which people measure elected officials. Increasing corruption and declining integrity are perceived as major causes for poor service delivery. They also undermine the processes of institutional development, good governance, and overall socioeconomic development. Therefore there is a clear link between the quality of service delivery and integrity. Service delivery has to take place in a culture of honesty and integrity. Communities expect their leaders to lead with integrity and deliver quality service.

4. *Promote and advance democracy and good governance.* It is essential that we recognize that the concept of governance includes the active participation of people in the processes of government, such as the exercise of power and the making of decisions that affect people's lives. Therefore I believe that democracy should not only be about setting up institutions or structures, and elections should not be regarded as the end-all of democracy. The framework must involve a process of establishing values that form the basis of any democratic society. These values, when exercised within a multiparty democracy, must of necessity include tolerance of differences and opposing viewpoints, inclusiveness, and respect for human rights. In this way, people's participation within political processes will be promoted.

For example, it is no use talking about women's participation in public life if we continue to erect barriers in front of them using tradition, religion, and stereotyped notions of their proper role and place.

From my perspective as the ombudswoman of Namibia, I want to see within this debate on accountability the issue of viewing human rights as basic tenets of good governance. As such, measurements of accountability as a principle of good government cannot solely be in terms of dollars, but have much more to do with human values of dignity. What is the point of holding governments accountable only insofar as it concerns their efficiency in terms of deficits if this forces them to cut social spending? What is the essence of holding governments accountable externally, if indeed the public is excluded from such accountability frameworks?

In my view, accountability is achieved when the citizens of a country, based on equal participation in the processes that affect them, can call governments to account regarding the effective and efficient provision of the services they need and which should be based on the core values of serving the common good. People who are aware of their rights will not be willing to suffer in silence or merely be called upon to vote at elections. They will increasingly make demands for more transparency and accountability in their dealings with the administration, and also from their elected representatives.

The slogan "bringing government closer to the people" can only become a reality if concerted efforts are made by the political leadership to reach out to the people through public education and awareness campaigns. One may need to ask the extent to which a country can be regarded as democratic, including an accountable government, if people generally continue to be excluded from decisions affecting their lives. Is it enough to have formal declarations of democracy and good governance, if in fact people continue to be denied their right to question their leaders and demand accountability from them? Is it enough to ask for votes every four or five years without also asking what people's views, experience, needs and concerns are and to take these into account when formulating policies and plans? I would therefore submit that government should be held accountable by those it serves—as they include the illiterate, the downtrodden, the marginalized whose voices are rarely heard. They and they alone can tell when a government fails to live up to their expectations. They and they alone know when they are treated as second-class citizens in their countries. They know when they are hungry, thirsty, homeless, and destitute even though they may not be able to define what accountability is.

The role of the ombudsman has been and will continue to be to promote participation and assist the people in understanding and holding public office bearers accountable through public education and outreach efforts, which include visits, distribution of leaflets, radio and television and public speaking engagements at schools and conferences, and so on.

Can Laws and Institutions Give Voice to the Poor?

Barricades or Obstacles

The Challenges of Access to Justice

Martín Abregú

Executive Director

Center for Legal and Social Studies (CELS)

Argentina

Introduction

When I first asked some colleagues the question that is the topic of this session, I heard some very different answers, so I have chosen a few that I would like to share with you:

- "It is obvious that laws and institutions can give voice to the poor, but do they want to?"
- "If laws and institutions cannot give voice to the poor, what are they for?"
- "Laws and institutions are not able to give voice to the poor, but at least they should consider how to assure people a free translator."

Others preferred to raise previous questions, such as:

- "What do we mean when we say 'give voice'?"
- "What do we mean when we say 'the poor'?"

Confronted by all these questions and answers, I decided to try to articulate all of them, to try to approach this issue in a way that allows us to consider the extent, but also the limits, of the subject we have to deal with.

There is no doubt that to "give voice to the poor"—understood as protecting the weakest ones, within a rule of law framework—is in the very nature of the establishment of any law and institution. Beginning with Hobbes' justification of the state in his *Leviathan*, but also considering other liberal explanations—not to mention any of the other much more interventionist modern theories—the notion of a "legal" state has always included the principle that there has to be a fair way to solve disputes regardless of the qualities of those involved in the confrontation.

We could conclude, then, that the very notion of the modern state necessarily includes a component on how to manage people's conflicts with some rational trend. Therefore, this rationale has to consider (a) how to make sure that everybody will be able to have access to these "legal" solutions; and (b) how to deal with the actual differences between the parties in order not to favor the privileged ones but to secure equity among them, which might include some unequal rules to protect those disadvantaged.

The administration of justice, therefore, must have a teleological aim that goes far beyond the mere resolution of conflicts. As has been said, it is not by chance that the ministry of justice is the only ministry that is named after a virtue.[1]

Within this context, the question that we have to answer in this session should not be understood as questioning the postulates of the modern states, as questioning what is due under the rule of law—since such an understanding would mean an outdated proposal for the new century. The question should not be understood as questioning the possibility to reach those objectives either, such as whether the principle to give voice to the poor must be left aside as another modern utopia.

On the contrary, this session must be viewed as an inquiry into the conditions to ensure that laws and institutions would give voice to the poor, into the actual challenges that the rule of law has to face to aim this objective. It is in this sense—but only in this sense—that we have to celebrate that we are discussing this question, as a necessary step to tackle the current deficiencies of our legal systems. Until recently, the World Bank "only very indirectly addressed the more sensitive issues of judicial independence, access to justice and related constitutional and legislative reforms"[2] and, therefore, our discussion is an important move forward.

---

1. Bielsa, Rafael. 1986. *El concepto de la reforma orgánica del servicio de justicia* en Cuadernos de FUNDEJUS. Buenos Aires.

2. Lawyers Committee for Human Rights. 2000. *Advancing Judicial Reform. An Environmental Case Study in Bolivia.* March (see p. 3).

Since we are considering this issue at a conference entitled "Comprehensive Legal and Judicial Development: Toward an Agenda for a Just and Equitable Society in the 21st Century," the question on the voice of the poor is a question on the access to justice in a broad sense. Assuming that the poor do not have actual access to the courts, we have to consider which are the obstacles that people find in order to get justice done, how we are supposed to avoid them, and which kind of response we think the courts have to give them.

Access to Justice: The Role of the Center for Legal and Social Studies

Now that we have identified the problems that we have to face, let me explain my background. I work for a domestic human rights law-oriented nongovernmental organization, the Center for Legal and Social Studies (CELS). We have a rights-based approach to human rights issues. We are not experts on the administration of justice, but we have the expertise of those who use the system every day to "get justice done," in a strict sense. Our experience, therefore, is exclusively related to Argentina—even though we might easily consider it just an example of Latin American judiciaries.

Actually, CELS was created, in 1979, to confront the denial of justice to those victims of the dictatorship that ruled Argentina from 1976 to 1983. During those years political dissidents disappeared under the "dirty war" and CELS' founders—four very well-known lawyers—decided that it was necessary to have a legal strategy and began to file habeas corpus petitions about the fate of their loved ones. These were systematically rejected, and that was the beginning of our work to build some new roads to the courts.

Since then, we have been dealing with many serious obstacles that stand in the way of justice for those who have been victims of human rights violations. Probably the most outrageous example of denial of justice is the one related to cases of police brutality. As it has been extensively denounced and demonstrated, victims of police brutality are systematically confronted with a lack of response—or even complicity with the suspected policemen—from judges and prosecutors.[3]

During the last few years, however, we had to begin considering the access to justice question in a much broader sense. After the transition to

---

3. CELS—Human Rights Watch. 1998. *La inseguridad policial: violencia de las fuerzas de seguridad en la Argentina*. Eudeba, Buenos Aires.

democracy, we started receiving many different complaints and demands from low-income people. Either we went to distant neighborhoods or they came to our downtown office, but it was always the same story: poor people, not necessarily victims of gross human rights violations, but unable in one way or another "to get justice done." People came asking for legal counseling and representation on matters as diverse as labor laws, health care, immigrants' rights, and family issues.

At the beginning we tried to develop some tools to help them, but there was an underlying question that we had to face: Why were they coming to us instead of going to some state-sponsored office? The answer was also obvious: the state was rejecting them, the state was ignoring them. Therefore, their only way to claim their rights was through a nongovernmental human rights organization.

As a human rights organization, the issue of access to justice for us became an instrumental one.[4] Our experience revealed clearly enough that there was no possibility for the actual enjoyment of basic rights if there was not a fairly established way to secure access to justice. In other words, the routine denial of basic rights was what brought us to the access to justice problem, whose solution would pave the way to a rational system of solving conflicts among people.

We decided then to carry out various projects to approach this issue. Probably the most important one is the research that we are carrying out currently with the Defensoría del Pueblo de la Ciudad de Buenos Aires (The Ombudsman—actually, the Ombudswoman—Office of the City of Buenos Aires). We are interviewing all the legal aid offices in the city, including the bar association and the law school clinics, but we are also interviewing the clients of these services.

What we would like to determine is:

- Who are the users of these services?
- Are the users finding the response that they are seeking?
- Which are the cases that never reach the courts (the most important ones for us)?

---

4. I am aware different concepts of access to justice exist. However, I prefer not to discuss those points of view; I will instead just explain our practical approach to the issue. To read about alternative concepts, see Bielsa (1986: 12), cited above in note 1.

This research illustrates our concern: how (in)accessible are the courts for those who cannot pay for a lawyer, or, in much more realistic terms, if you do not have money to pay for a lawyer, do you have any possibility of bringing your conflict to be resolved before an impartial judge?[5]

Obstacles

Let's go back then to our original question: Can laws and institutions secure access to justice for the most vulnerable groups? Even at the risk of sounding like an economist, my first answer is that it depends. As I will try to demonstrate, it depends on many operational matters but, much more important, on some other deeply rooted problems that we will have to cope with if we really aim to secure justice for all. I will try then to identify those obstacles that prevent the most disadvantaged sectors of society from accessing justice, and I will suggest some very general but key principles that should guide any serious effort to revert the situation, to move from our skepticism toward a more positive answer to our dilemma.

Operational Obstacles

As has been already suggested, we should differentiate between operational obstacles and structural ones. If we accept this classification, we should consider "operational problems" to be those related to the efficiency and effectiveness of the administration of the justice system, and "structural problems" to be the ones that are in the very nature of our judiciaries as they are currently organized. There might be some difficulties in differentiating one kind of obstacle from another—and, of course, there is some discretion on this classification. But what we should keep in mind is that a clear line could be drawn between obstacles that could be reverted from inside the judiciary and those that are far beyond any endogenous solution.

---

5. The relevance of this question is fundamental: "Since the legitimacy of rule of law is based on the effective implementation of the principle of equality before the law, inequalities to access to justice compromise the legitimacy that a democratic State must preserve and increase permanently." However, it must be assumed that the right to effective judicial protection is a myth. Access to justice is always available, but only in theory. As has been said, it is like the Sheraton Hotel, "everybody can come in; the only thing that you need is money" (Garro, Alejandro. 1999. *El acceso a la justicia y el "derecho de interés público."* In *Justicia y Sociedad. Hacia un mejor servicio público de justicia,* April No. 2, pp. 37–39)

We will mention just a few of these operational obstacles:[6]

- There is no comprehensive plan that facilitates the coordination of efforts, avoiding overlaps.
- There is a growing unprotected social sector, since legal aid services have not evolved with the increasing population and its needs.
- These services do not have a general approach but a specific one—to protect only certain rights.
- The quality of legal assistance has been traditionally related to the payment of lawyers' fees.
- Public defense has been oriented to criminal cases and as a consequence is notoriously inefficient in dealing with other issues.
- The path to a civil process that avoids the payment of litigation costs goes through a preliminary judicial process.
- There are no serious data on the clients of these legal services.
- Legal aid services normally have their offices in downtown areas and are not easily accessible to those living in suburban areas—who are, in most of the cases, the ones who need these services the most.
- The process cost is proportionally more expensive for small-amount disputes.
- An adequate or appropriate pretrial counseling system is not in place.
- There is a dearth of appropriate advice to avoid unnecessary processes.

Those of you who are experts on the administration of justice and have been working and criticizing the reform process that has been carried out during the last decade have a clear knowledge of these difficulties and have some answers on how to deal with them. Most of the bibliography emphasizes these barriers, and there is a lot of material and interesting research about them, but this is not the information that we have been working with, so I will not analyze but just mention it. Actually, I hope that some others on this panel might help me find some tools to mitigate this problem.

---

6. Garrido, Carlos M. "Informe sobre Argentina." In *Situación y políticas judicales en América Latina,* Special Publications Series No. 2, Escuela de Derecho, Universidad Diego Portales, Chile, pp. 81–82.

Structural Obstacles

I would rather consider the structural obstacles, those that are not just judicial problems but, on the contrary, are problems that have to do with the very basic forms of societal organization. These issues are prior to the judicial response to any specific case brought before a tribunal, but are inherently linked to the administration of justice.

At least three of those major obstacles need to be mentioned:

1. The very organization of the judiciary "turning its back" on the people;
2. The situation of vulnerability of those we have considered here as "the poor"; and
3. The lack of awareness of those vulnerable groups of their right to claim their rights.

As has been said before, these obstacles go far beyond the judiciary. However, they have to do with the very reason of the establishment of a judiciary—as we have seen at the beginning of this presentation—that is, to secure a rational and legal way of conflict resolution. It has to do with considering not how the courts deal with people, but how we manage to have more people dealing with the courts.

A footnote might be needed at this point: this is not a call for a uniform bureaucratic judicial response to any conflict that might arise. This does not have to do with judicial versus other informal ways of conflict resolution. This has to do with the fact that, in order to live in a fair and equitable society, everybody must have the possibility of bringing his or her conflicts before a tribunal—whether that is a court, a justice of the peace, or any other other rational system.

If we do want to give voice to the poor, if we do want to secure access to justice for the vulnerable, we shall certainly have to find a way "to get justice done" for everyone and not only for those who reach—or try to reach—the courts. If we do want to give voice to the poor, these are the first obstacles that we will have to face and, even though they are not just judicial questions, the judiciary has a lot to offer in solving them.

It is necessary, therefore, to consider in more detail each one of these obstacles.

1. The judiciary was established following its own necessities, developing its own logical thinking, and thus creating "barricades" for those from the outside who want to trespass the "judicial land." A few examples of those barriers include:

   - The location of the tribunals. Courts are always at specific downtown locations. People not only face long trips to get there, but the courts are also conceived as an autonomous part of the city, where everybody has to go to file their complaints. The very idea of a "judicial city" is the best example of the judiciary's thinking of itself as a differentiated property.
   - The design of judicial buildings and tribunals. Once you get there—the judicial land—it is not easy to find your way to the particular court. Huge and labyrinthine buildings, full of symbols that remind you that you are not at home but at some virtuous palace, send a threatening message to those who try to get to the courts without due guidance. By the same token, if you happen to reach a court, with or without a lawyer, you will not be able to pass through the entrance desk (*mesa de entrada*), which separates those who impart justice from those who wait for it.
   - The development of its own "legal" language. Lawyers, judges and prosecutors speak their own dialect. Even at oral trials, most of us have witnessed how it is virtually impossible for the accused to understand the reading of their sentence. It is commonplace at the judiciary's meetings to blame the media for not having journalists who are "experts" on justice issues. On the contrary, what is annoying—at least for me—is that one has to be an expert to understand when "justice is done."
   - The reification of the clients of the judicial service. Users of the judicial system, once they get involved in a case, are no longer persons with a conflict that has to be solved but plaintiffs or defendants, accused or victims. Their whole life will be suddenly reduced to their primordial role: the one that they have to play during the process. This reductionism and standardization transforms the complaints into something that has nothing to do with real life.

It is not necessary to point out that these problems do not affect only the poor. But it is also obvious that you might easily reduce these inconveniences if you do have the possibility of hiring your own "city" guide and translator, and if you have enough money or prestige not to be considered just a plaintiff or an accused.

2. The second obstacle that was mentioned before was the vulnerability of the weakest members of society. In this case, the difficulty is intrinsically related to the fact of poverty. People with no jobs and no social security rights are too vulnerable to stake a claim for their rights. Since they are "beneficiaries" of social programs and they have no right to demand social assistance, they are permanently afraid of upsetting their official "donors."

   A couple of examples might illustrate this vulnerability. A few years ago, we studied the lack of public defenders for noncriminal cases in the Province of Buenos Aires, the biggest and, in some areas, the poorest Argentine province, and we focused on some very poor, high-population suburban neighborhoods. Among them, there was a very disturbing one, La Matanza, where the numbers speak for themselves: there were only two public defenders for noncriminal cases for a total population of 1,173,190, of whom 347,917 had unsatisfied basic needs. But the two public defender offices were not yet working. We were looking for a client of those defenders for years, but we could not find a single person who wanted to file a complaint against the local government. They were all afraid that there might be some kind of retaliation, such as cutting off their social benefits.

   During 1999, some beneficiaries of a well-known social program came to CELS inquiring about a possible action to restore the funding that had been cut off. There was no ground for a judicial request so we decided to file a complaint before the World Bank Inspection Panel, since the program was founded by a loan for a structural adjustment program and, we claimed, the Argentine government was not appropriately using these funds. Again, one of the problems we had to face to file the complaint was that none of the beneficiaries wanted to sign it. It was necessary to assure them that the denunciation would be anonymous and that the government would only learn about CELS' representation, but not the names of those represented. Only under these conditions did we manage to collect more than a hundred signatures.

Eventually, we did file the complaint before the inspection panel, and the government then decided to restore the original budget for the program. When the panel had to decide the issue, it had already become moot, but, among other rulings, the panel recognized the right of the beneficiaries to denounce it anonymously. Anonymity, then, was the key element that allowed the beneficiaries to succeed in their demands.

What those two examples clearly show is that those who depend on a social program do not want to confront the state because they are afraid they might lose their benefits. Since they do not have a right to that social assistance which is essential for their very subsistence, they prefer not to press for their rights at all.

This vulnerability is old news. It is the very same vulnerability that provoked the consolidation of the social state during the first decades of the twentieth century. After the consolidation of liberal democracies in western countries, a trend of social constitutionalism sprang up in those countries. With the irruption of the welfare state, governments aimed to organize not only civil and political rights but also economic, social, and cultural ones depending on the role that each person has in the labor market.[7]

However, it is important to keep in mind that those social rights, as they have been postulated even in international treaties, were inherently related to the requisite of being an employee. Therefore, with the welfare state crisis and the increasing unemployment rates, those who depend on social programs are no longer people with rights, but with benefits. On the road from a liberal and social state to the newest

7. As Cappelletti has explained, "the access to justice movement constitutes a central part of the modern social State or welfare State." Using the "waves" theory, he points out that at a first stage, the aim was to elude the obstacles related to poverty, and, second, this movement was focused on more complex and articulated difficulties, such as those related to the vulnerable groups in industrial societies. (*Cappelletti*, Mauro. 1999. "Acceso a la justicia." In *Revista del Colegio Público de Abogados*. La Plata. See pp. 248–49.)

"assistential" state, the poor became more vulnerable if they chose to pursue their traditional rights. To some extent, they are in the very same situation they were before the recognition of those rights, since they do not feel free to lay claim to them.

3. Last but not least, the third structural obstacle to access to justice that was mentioned above was the lack of awareness of the right to demand basic rights. This is not the session to analyze the educational issues related to this topic. But what might be important to consider in this session is that, quite frequently, the most vulnerable groups do not even know that they have a right to lay claim to their rights. Even though they are probably aware of their rights to freedom of speech or association, to health and education, they may not have any clue about how to exercise them.[8]

Another footnote might be needed at this point: there are plenty of problems regarding the lack of awareness of basic rights. Of course there are some people who are not even aware of their very basic civil and political rights. There are also some other people who—a bigger number than the previous one—consider social rights, generally speaking, as unjustifiable political gifts. However, I do not think we should consider these educational gaps at this session.

What I do want to analyze is that, even though many people may be aware of their rights, in most cases they do not think about their everyday conflicts from a rights-based point of view. Therefore, they do not even consider the possibility of filing a complaint before a tribunal.[9]

The right to access to justice could be described, in this sense, as the most ignored right, since, for a full understanding of this right, a

8. In Roberto Berizonce's words, "the lack of rights protection is frequently related to the ignorance of legal tools and the distrust of the judicial systems and its agents, provoked by formalism and bureaucratization of the proceedings... The common faith of being aliens before the system erodes the confidence on judicial matters and manners, particularly for the disadvantaged sectors." (Berizonce, Roberto. 1993. *Administración de Justicia en Iberoamérica*, J. Ovalle Favela coord., U.N.A.M. Mexico. See pp. 41–65.)

9. Luis Moreno Ocampo, former prosecutor and speaker at this Conference, used to have a very interesting TV program, in which he was an arbitrator between two parties who presented their cases in front of the camera. The educational achievement of that program was that ordinary people learned about solving their differences through an impartial process.

person has to (a) be aware of his or her rights, (b) be aware that there is also a right to exercise those rights, and (c) be used to reading some of his or her social conflicts as legal questions.

Guidelines and Proposals

As has been already explained, these issues go far beyond judicial matters and could be ignored if we take an endogenous approach to the problem of the access to justice. However, an actual response to the question about securing voice for the most vulnerable segments of society calls for a comprehensive view that should confront these problems or, at least, incorporate them.[10]

At this stage it is important to point out that there are some interesting responses that the judiciary could offer to diminish the aforementioned barriers to access to justice, including taking organizational measures regarding those classified as operational obstacles. In this sense, there are some very basic principles and guidelines that must be followed in order to reverse this diagnosis. A few examples might help for a better understanding of these ideas.

1. There is a crucial necessity to bring the tribunals closer to the people. Some of these measures could be considered as operational ones, following the classification that we proposed before. However, what is supposed to be behind these proposals is the basic idea put forth by John Jay, first chief justice of the United States Supreme Court, about bringing justice to the threshold of the house of each citizen.

   This idea encompasses the following:

   - Courts should be decentralized. It is a key element of any program striving to increase access that the tribunals should be moved from cities (downtown) to the neighborhoods. To be sure, there will be some centralization of activities, but it is important to try to keep it as minimal as possible.
   - Since access is not just a matter of location, it is also crucial that court buildings look like an open public place. If courts are

10. See also Bielsa (1986: 4). See note 1 for full reference.

decentralized, they do not need to be huge buildings. Actually, ordinary houses might be perfect.

A good example in Argentina is the new Prosecutor District Office in a Buenos Aires suburban area, Saavedra. Even though there has been some very strong opposition to this proposal, the office is doing a great job, forging strong links between the people and, at least, one area of the judicial system.

- It is also necessary that we start moving in the opposite direction regarding the use and abuse of a legal dialect. Some safeguards might be very useful to deter this tendency.
- A jury system should be established. If ordinary people would play this fundamental role, lawyers would have to adapt legal terms to plain words. Arguments against the jury system invariably support some kind of elite justice, which always goes in the opposite direction of our original intent—that is, ensuring justice.
- It may be also extremely useful to establish some kind of media office within the judiciary. Judges and other judicial agents frequently do poorly when communicating through the media. Therefore, if some specific office would "translate" judicial decisions for the media, that might help people understand the decisions and would keep judges "safe" from journalists.
- Another important requisite for making the courts more accessible is to turn the relation between courts and clients into a much more informal one. In order to do so, a key element for the organization of the administration of justice is that it must be shaped by the requirements of its eventual clients, thus not demanding that the clients adapt themselves to the courts' bureaucratic logic.
- The "Justices of the Peace" (Jueces de Paz) in some rural areas in Peru could be a good example of an informal and flexible system, responding to local needs. On the other extreme, the Argentine establishment of compulsory mediation is a good example of how we could transform good principles into bad rules.
- When we are carrying out a reform process of the administration of justice, it is necessary to include every actor in the process. As has

been explained, "the experience and perspective of the users of the judicial system, often represented by nongovernmental organizations and public interest lawyers, can make a valuable contribution to the identification of reform needs and priorities. If judicial reform is to contribute to improving the basic relation between state and citizens in a country, the reform process should, fairly early on, provide citizens with a greater sense of ownership and control over the judicial system."[11]

The Lawyers Committee for Human Rights has certainly applauded a World Bank experience in this trend:

> A small but noteworthy Ministry of Justice sub-component of the (Bolivian) project focused on analyzing the traditional judicial system used by several of Bolivia's indigenous communities. Regional NGOs with experience with indigenous communities were contracted to carry out the studies. The studies were undertaken in recognition of the fact that large sectors of Bolivian society—in particular, indigenous groups—lack access to the national justice system. In addition to the lack of access to "formal" justice, indigenous law persists, because the populations often prefer to use traditional forms of justice to solve conflicts within communities or between neighboring communities of the same ethnic background. The national legal system lacks legitimacy for these groups.... This component of the project, if carried forward, offers a groundbreaking opportunity to integrate different legal traditions in a way that should strengthen the overall legitimacy of the justice system. It could also potentially improve access to justice in a significant way at the community level for groups that have long been left outside the bounds of any effective formal means of conflict management.[12]

2. The question of the vulnerability of those depending on social programs is, no doubt, the most difficult one to solve from a judicial

---

11. Lawyers Committee for Human Rights (2000). See note 2 for full reference. This reflects one of the lessons learned of the World Bank experience, namely "that these projects should be conducted through a participatory approach. Participation is needed in order to gain ownership and commitment from the government and stakeholders," including different branches of government, bar associations, law schools, NGOs, and citizens. (World Bank. 1999. *Initiatives in Legal and Judicial Reform, Legal and Judicial Reform Unit.* Legal Department. Washington, D.C.)

12. Lawyers Committee for Human Rights (2000: 13). See note 2 for full reference.

perspective. To eradicate or at least diminish this social problem, it is necessary to recreate the rights that have been abolished since the crisis of the welfare state and, therefore, the judicial response will be a very mild one.

- However, it is important that, assuming this vulnerability, the courts grant broad criteria for standing—that is, for organizations to represent individuals. To secure actual, effective protection—not merely nominal—of those rights and interests, not only on an individual but also on a collective level, it is necessary to allow and even promote and facilitate the access of the representatives (public and private) of unorganized groups with nondefined—and probably not definable—boundaries.[13]
- We should recognize that class actions, *acciones de tutela* or *amparos colectivos,* are necessary tools to overcome this obstacle. It is also extremely important to grant autonomous standing to NGOs, so that they can represent those interests that no one individual can represent.
- Nevertheless, to allow the NGOs the necessary procedural tools to enable them to freely access the courts is only the first step. It is also necessary to give the judges the training and administrative infrastructure to handle these collective claims.

3. Finally, if we want to secure the right to access to justice, we should also promote a rights-based understanding of social conflicts. This has nothing to do with education but with building links between the people and the courts. Individuals might not need to learn themselves about their rights and how to exercise them but they do have to have a familiar counterpart to advise them.

- Some experiences show that lay lawyers or paralegal officers could be key actors in this role. In some countries where lawyers are scarce, these agents have revealed themselves as encouraging entities for people to bring their cases before the courts.

---

13. Cappelletti (1999: 249). See note 7 for full reference.

- But, again, it is important not to limit us to these alternatives. In some cities of Argentina, for example, where there are thousands of lawyers with few cases and low income, it would be much more practical not to train lay lawyers but to promote the involvement of actual lawyers in minor cases.
- It is important to point out that even though the state should fulfill its responsibility to secure justice for all, in Latin America, owing to budget constraints, the biggest expectations for success rest on lawyers and other legal professionals working with NGOs and other civil associations, since "these legal services might acquire a preventive or consultative form, not necessarily limiting themselves to active representation of legal defense."[14]

At CELS, for example, we are carrying out a joint project with a suburban university (the Universidad Nacional de General Sarmiento) in one of the poorest neighborhoods of the Province of Buenos Aires, to assist the local bar association in establishing a legal aid program. In order to do so, we are not "exporting" any other model but we are trying to, first, determine needs and resources, and second, organize an indigenous system. What might be very important for the success of this project is that the whole community has been involved in the discussions that we are promoting.

It is worth mentioning that if we happen to be successful in this goal, there is going to be an "explosion" of cases presented before the courts. However, this should not deter us from moving ahead. Even though it is crucial to prevent these side effects and, therefore, to secure the institutional operational requirement to face this demand, it should not be forgotten that only such an explosion might be the welcome consequence of a push for justice for all.

Final Remarks

These are just a few suggestions on how to promote equitable access to justice. The ultimate question, however, is what response the vulnerable will receive from the judiciary. It is not worth repeating that access to tribunals is meaningless if justice is not to be served. However, this is another issue that is

---

14. Garro, Alejandro (1999: 50). See note 5 for full reference.

different from the instrumental character of the right to access to justice that I preferred to point out in this presentation.

It is clear by now that we are not talking about just some minor or esthetic reforms of the judiciary, but about a second reform of the state—one that focuses on the rebuilding of its basic duties to secure the rule of law. It is imperative, therefore, to push for these changes as the only fruitful path to sustainable development.

Paraphrasing Ferrajoli, we might conclude then that "access to justice" has nothing to do with mere legalism, formalism, or procedural issues. On the contrary, it consists of the protection of fundamental rights which represent the values and the interests that institute and justify the existence of those artifices that are the law and the state, of which enjoyment for all constitutes the substantial basis of democracy.[15]

15. Ferrajoli, Luigi. 1995. *Derecho y Razón.* Madrid. See pp. 28–29.

Engaging and Empowering Communities

Grizelda Mayo-Anda

Assistant Executive Director

Environmental Legal Assistance Center, Inc. (ELAC)

Philippines

Years of developmental legal advocacy work with indigenous peoples, fisher-folk, farmer communities, and the rural and urban poor in the Philippines have provided alternative or public interest lawyers like myself with a different perspective in viewing and using the law. Law generally reflects the perspectives of the elite and powerful in society. Law, in both content and process, by articulating only a dominant perspective also reflects the current balance of political and social conflict.[1] Not all laws are just, equitable and socially relevant. A disparity exists between policy rhetoric and actual practice. Given these realities, laws are dynamic and open to interventions by people.

The so-called myth of the law and the reality of the poor are continuing dilemmas that we face. The poor and powerless usually find it difficult to deal with the law. More often than not, laws and institutions are unable to comprehend and address the realities faced by the poor—their culture, intricate problems, interests, and aspirations. There have been attempts to address these inadequacies, such as the passage of new legislation, creation or reformation of institutions, and strengthening of regulatory mechanisms. However, these efforts are at times fragmented, unsustained, and still inadequate to respond to the mounting economic and social problems faced by the poor.

The Need and Opportunities for Engagement

Notwithstanding the aforementioned difficulties, it is important for the poor to make use of the law, participate in legal processes, and work with existing institutions.

1. Leonen, Marvic. 1994. "Engaging the Rhetoric: Law and Its Interface with Community Action." Issue Paper 94–02, , p. 2. Legal Rights and Natural Resources Center—Kasama sa Kalikasan, Manila.

First of all, the existing legal framework provides opportunities for the participation of marginalized and underprivileged communities in the formulation and implementation of policies.

In the area of resource management and environmental protection, for instance, the constitution of the Philippines provides the following:

1. Democratization of access to resources: Direct users of natural resources, such as farmers, forest dwellers, and marginal fisherfolk, are guaranteed the right to continue using such resources for their daily sustenance and survival in accordance with existing laws.[2] Hence, the constitution introduced the concept of small-scale utilization of natural resources as a mode of natural resource utilization.[3]

2. Social justice: There is a bias for the underprivileged as regards the development and management of natural resources such that land and other natural resources shall be made accessible to them. Municipal waters, for example, are reserved for the preferential use of subsistence fisherfolk.[4]

3. The right of the people to a balanced and healthful ecology: The constitution protects the right of the people to a "balanced and healthful ecology in accord with the rhythm and harmony of nature."[5] The state is mandated to protect, advance, and promote the people's right to ecological security and health. In the case of Oposa vs. Factoran,[6] the Supreme Court had occasion to rule on the interpretation of the constitutional policy on the environment. In this case, the Supreme Court declared the "right to a balanced and healthful ecology" as a self-executory right and recognized the primacy and centrality of ecological security and health among the many rights ensured by the constitution.

2. See 1987 Philippine Constitution, Article 13, Sections 4, 6 and 7.
3. See 1987 Philippine Constitution, Article 12, Section 2, paragraph 3.
4. See 1987 Philippine Constitution, Article 12, Section 3.
5. See the Constitution, Article 2, Section 16.
6. 224 SCRA 792.

4. Due process clause: The constitution guarantees the right of the people to life, liberty, and property to be free from undue intervention and usurpation without due process of law. Thus, surface owners or occupants whose rights are based on a Torrens title or valid tenurial instrument issued by the government and whose rights may be impaired by development and exploration activities can assert their right to due process.

5. Fundamental liberties: Besides the right to due process, important provisions include the right to information and the right to people participation, where the state recognizes and promotes the right of youth, women, labor, indigenous communities, nongovernmental organizations (NGOs), and community-based or sectoral or people's organizations (PO). There is a provision for a people's initiative and referendum on proposing, amending, rejecting, or enacting laws. These policies serve as a basis for community groups to participate in establishing, conserving, managing, and formulating policies and resource management plans.

Environmental statutes also provide for the preferential treatment of the underprivileged and for community participation. For example, the Philippine Fisheries Code of 1998[7] provides for the following:

- Protecting the rights of fisherfolk, particularly of municipal fisherfolk communities, in the preferential use of municipal waters;
- Providing primary support to municipal fisherfolk through appropriate technology and research, adequate financial and marketing assistance, and other services;
- Managing fishery and aquatic resources in a manner consistent with the concept of integrated coastal area management in specific natural fishery management areas; and
- Establishing Fisheries and Aquatic Resources Management Councils (FARMCs) at the municipal and barangay[8] level to assist local government units in formulating and enforcing policies.

7. Republic Act (RA) 8550.
8. A barangay is considered the smallest political unit of government.

The Local Government Code[9] provides for participatory policymaking as follows:

- Representatives for NGOs and POs have seats in almost all councils, leagues, and boards;
- Resource use or management plans can be enacted into ordinances through the local people's initiative;[10]
- Resource use plans formulated by fisherfolk in several barangays or municipalities may be implemented through the league of barangays and municipalities.[11]

In the case of Pala'wan, its unprecedented and landmark legislation known as the Strategic Environmental Plan (SEP) for Pala'wan[12] provides for the use of participatory approaches in the realization of its goals and programs.

Second, poor communities cannot rely solely on government to convert such policy rhetoric into reality.

Government's failure to enforce laws has always been a pervasive problem and has caused poverty and violations of human rights. Hence, poor communities such as marginal fisherfolk and farmers, indigenous peoples, and other segments of the rural and urban poor must be empowered to effectively engage with laws and institutions.

Third, community participation in legal processes, complex as it may seem, can help shape or refine policy and enrich pro-poor legislation, programs, and institutions.

Poor communities have shown that, when organized and capacitated, they are able to develop approaches that utilize existing laws and institutions to effectively respond to their needs. Here, interventions of nongovernmental groups and to a certain extent, government, play a crucial role.

At this juncture, allow me to share with you some experiences of NGOs in our country, particularly my own NGO, the Environmental Legal Assistance Center, Inc. (ELAC), in assisting poor communities of fisherfolk, farmers, and indigenous peoples to effectively engage with laws and institutions.

9. RA 7160.
10. RA 7160, Section 120.
11. RA 7160, Sections 491 to 507.
12. RA 7611.

Raising Law from Rhetoric to Reality: Empowering
Communities through Various Approaches

Developmental Legal Aid

Developmental legal assistance or DLA philosophy, as alternative law groups (ALGs) or public interest law groups call it, involves the use of law, legal education, or service as a means to empower local communities confronted with problems.[13] This is distinguished from traditional legal aid, which views legal service as an end in itself and works strictly within the existing framework of the legal system. According to DLA philosophy, citizens cannot solely rely on the legal system to address or resolve their problems. Their own creative forms of community action are necessary to effectively enable them to assert their rights and interests.

In implementing the DLA perspective, ALGs have departed from the traditional legal aid in that they seek to empower client communities to enable them to develop their own legal and political strategies. In his article, "Participatory Justice in the Philippines," Stephen Golub aptly sums up the nature and impact of the work of ALGs in the Philippines as follows:

> Their activities embrace both conventional and unorthodox legal work. They may litigate; appear before quasi-judicial proceedings, such as labor and agrarian reform tribunals; negotiate with corporate leaders regarding environmental and labor issues; and provide legal assistance and guidance regarding strikes and protest activities. They may also secure government services for partners; organize communities; train paralegals; pursue efforts to affect jurisprudence; conduct research; produce scholarly articles and publications; advise advocacy groups; and work on legal and regulatory reform.

> ALGs' activities, then, can be seen as an effort to make client populations more legally and economically independent. They aim to inject fairness, accountability, and predictability into a legal system that is often abused or ignored by elite interests. More broadly, ALGs seek to democratize access to state-allocated resources and policymaking processes.[14]

---

13. See Golub, Stephen. 2000. "Participatory Justice in the Philippines." In Mary Mc-Clymont and Stephen Golub, eds., *Many Roads to Justice, The Law Related Work of Ford Foundation,* p. 219. Golub identifies the contribution of alternative law groups to policy implementation as "helping their partners raise Philippine law from rhetoric to reality."

14. Golub (2000: 200, 202). See note 13 for full reference.

The Muro-Ami Story: Saving Poor Children and Adult Fishworkers and the Degraded Marine Environment from Distress

Muro-ami[15] is a type of commercial fishing that has long been banned by law owing to its use of child labor and its adverse impact on the coral reefs. Despite the ban, this destructive fishing practice has continued in the Philippines to this day. The commercial fishing operations continue under the guise of *pa-aling*[16] which has been allowed by government. These are operated by powerful businessmen from the province of Cebu, Central Visayas in southern Philippines. Operations are focused mainly on the waters of Pala'wan where coral reefs and marine resources still abound. Almost ever year, children and adult fishworkers escape from the *muro-ami* fishing vessels and seek refuge in various areas in Pala'wan. Some of them narrate their stories of abuse, oppression, and maltreatment at the hands of the "maestro" or foreman of the fishing operations. Government enforcement agents apprehended a few of these vessels in the past, but no cases have been filed.

In November 1999, the F/B Prince Arnold, a commercial fishing vessel owned by the ASB Fishing and Development Corporation, was apprehended by elements of the Philippine Navy in southern Pala'wan. The fishing vessel, with about 400 men on board, was towed to the port of Puerto Princesa City. While anchored in the port, more than 30 people escaped. The navy turned over the vessel and pertinent documents to the fishery personnel in charge in the hope that a case would be filed. To the navy's dismay, the vessel was released. The case was exposed by the media when some of the minor and adult fishworkers who escaped were interviewed.

The navy, media, and an NGO sought the assistance of ELAC in instituting the appropriate legal action against the owner-operator of the fishing vessel and also against the inept government personnel. ELAC filed three cases—one for child abuse, another for *muro-ami* fishing, and still another for violations of the labor code.

continued

15. Muro-ami is defined by law as a fishing method that uses diving and long hoses with stones and metals tied at the end, to pound the coral reefs and other habitat to entrap and catch fish.

16. Pa-aling is a modified form of muro-ami in that instead of using stones and metals, bubbles are used to scare the fish in order to entrap them.

The Muro-Ami Story (continued)

ELAC's interview with the minor and adult fishworkers-escapees produced disturbing revelations. All of the fishworkers had been recruited from poor fishing and farming communities in Negros Oriental. They were promised good pay, but they ended up dismayed by the hardship and suffering they were subjected to. All the interviewees disclosed that they were ordered to use stones to pound on the corals. Armed only with a long hose linked to a compressor, they had to dive some 20 to 30 meters to scare the fish.

The majority of the fishworkers could barely read and write (mostly with elementary level of education, specifically from grades 1 to 4). They were led to believe that the fishing activity they would engage in would be safe and pay well. Some of them, especially those between the ages of 18 and 24, left without the knowledge of their parents. Because they were poor, the fishworker—escapees initially thought that they were in no position to complain about their plight. They never realized that their plight could generate attention and support.

The operating company was ordered to temporarily stop its fishing operations as a result of the complaints lodged against it. ELAC also initiated a campaign to ban *pa-aling* as a type of commercial fishing, since the government is currently reviewing the existing fishery regulation governing such type of fishing activity. As a result of these initiatives, government attention was generated. Labor and social welfare offices provided financial assistance. NGOs convened a meeting in order to solicit financial and material assistance to the fishworker-escapees. The case also caught the attention of the national media.

In the area of policy reform, ALGs have helped prepare critical national legislation that would advance the cause of the poor, such as the Urban Development and Housing Act, the Indigenous Peoples' Rights Act, the Philippine Fisheries Act, and the Clean Air Act. While these laws may not be perfect, having been muddled by lawmakers during the legislative process, they have been able to articulate certain policies and programs in favor of poor and marginalized communities. ALGs have also helped develop administrative regulations or executive agency policies to implement new and relatively progressive statutes.

Opposition to the Pala'wan Cement Project: A Study on Public Advocacy

The public debate on the Pala'wan Cement Project provides a good example on how ALGs helped achieve a solid environmental lobby together with NGOs and people's organizations in opposing a dubious development project that even had strong political endorsements.[17] The lobby of NGOs was coordinated by the Pala'wan NGO Network, Inc. (PNNI), backed by good information and research, and complemented by media advocacy and network building. PNNI launched a "cyberspace advocacy" campaign primarily to gain international support for the struggle of the Pala'wan indigenous community and to counter the disinformation being spread by the project proponents.

A Canadian company called Fenway Resources, working with a local partner, was proposing to build a U.S. $470 million cement plant in the municipality of Sofronio Espanola, south of the province. With a projected annual output of 2 million metric tons of cement, Fenway was claiming that it was going to be the biggest cement plant in the country.

The project was contentious from the start owing to the refusal of the Pala'wan indigenous community to accept the project. It also became a controversial issue when the project proponents secured an endorsement/approval from the Pala'wan Council for Sustainable Development[18] (PCSD) in 1996 without even a public hearing or consultation called for that purpose.

With the help of ALG lawyers, the NGOs and POs were able to raise the following issues:

   a. Serious adverse environmental impacts of the project, particularly on the forestal, coastal, and tribal ancestral land areas;

continued

---

17. Excerpt from Mayo-Anda. 1999. *Case Studies on Mining and Environmental Impact Assessment..*

18. The PCSD is mandated under the Strategic Environmental Plan for Pala'wan to provide policy direction and govern the implementation of the SEP.

Opposition to the Pala'wan Cement Project (continued)

b. Absence of technical and financial capability of the project proponent, Fenway Resources, and its speculative trading practices in the Vancouver Stock Exchange where it was publicly listed;

c. Unresolved legal issues: (i) quarrying would cover old-growth forest that was considered a core zone and protected area under existing policies; (ii) quarrying site would have an impact on the ancestral domain of the Pala'wan tribal community; (iii) wharf site would entail the destruction of some four hectares of mangrove forest and coral reefs that were classified as core zones; (iv) plant site was located on agricultural lands covered by Certificate of Land Ownership Awards (CLOAs) which could not be transferred within a 10–year period, thereby precluding its reclassification into an industrial zone.

Owing to the strong environmental lobby spearheaded by the Pala'wan tribes and the NGOs, the PCSD decided to refer the project to the Department of Environment and Natural Resources (DENR) without endorsing it. This was a change from its original position of endorsement-approval. The DENR, for its part, has not acted on the Environmental Compliance Certificate (ECC) application, as it had no PCSD endorsement. Some Pala'wan politicians, however, are still lobbying the DENR to issue an ECC to the project.

At the Vancouver Stock Exchange (VSE), the share prices of Fenway began to plunge when reports on the real status of the project and its prospects began to find its way onto the Internet. In early 1998, the VSE delisted Fenway shares from its trading board, on findings that included insider trading and nondisclosure of critical information.

This, however, has not completely led to the demise of the project, as its proponents are currently working to get the same project listed in other areas. The NGOs and indigenous communities have remained vigilant because there is still the possibility that sheer political influence alone can allow the company to get an ECC from the DENR.

As regards law implementation, ALGs have actively engaged in education work, organizing paralegals, information and media advocacy, and building linkages or coalitions to achieve greater community participation in implementing progressive laws and in advocating for stronger government accountability. Ultimately therefore, law is brought to the grassroots level.

In asserting their rights, poor communities are often harassed with lawsuits. While these suits usually get dismissed, the presence of a criminal complaint or warrant of arrest still shakes and stresses concerned community residents, PO leaders, and barangay officials. Community or PO members know that ALG lawyers will be there to assist them, but their strong distrust of the justice system causes them to worry. To address this community concern, lawyers together with NGO partners hold community consultations and assemblies to discuss the nature and effects of the lawsuits. In these meetings, the community members agree upon an action plan or strategy with the support of NGOs. A cohesive community or PO usually decides to continue with its ongoing initiatives despite harassment suits.

In one case, barangay officials and fisherfolk who vigorously opposed the encroachment of commercial fishing into the bay area were swamped with a string of cases—libel, illegal assembly, abuse of authority, and threat. In another case, barangay officials and farmer residents who opposed illegal quarrying activities undertaken by a former mining company were sued for illegal assembly and trespassing. These harassment suits were dismissed after almost two years. During the period of time that these cases were pending, the village officials and community residents affected proceeded with their advocacy initiatives. The continuing partnership between the affected PO members, village officials, and NGOs strengthened the community's resolve.

Paralegal Trainings: Tool for Community Empowerment

Paralegal trainings consist of two- or three-day workshops, lectures, and group dynamics on the law, national policies on resource use and environment; on specific environmental laws, legal and metalegal[19] remedies; skills training on investigation, arrest, and search; and preparing complaints and

---

19. In ALG parlance, metalegal refers to community actions undertaken to assert or dramatize community issues in order to generate government action.

affidavits. Local communities—ranging from marginalized fisherfolk, farmers, and indigenous communities to youth, NGOs, and barangay officials—participating in these became cognizant of their rights and available remedies through their acquired knowledge of significant environmental laws, the legal system, and procedures and paralegal skills.

Since 1996, local communities in Pala'wan undertook concrete actions to address community-specific environmental problems, such as the use of citizen's arrest or seizure and confiscation of illegally gathered forest or fishery products, quarry resources, and paraphernalia used in the commission of environmental crimes; conduct of community patrols; monitoring and reporting of these violations to concerned authorities and NGOs such as ELAC; and filing of criminal and administrative complaints against violators and derelict or corrupt government officials.

Besides increased awareness and knowledge, members of local communities who used to violate environmental laws were mobilized to actively join the community's environmental protection efforts. A good example is the agreement forged between fishpond owners, barangay officials, and ELAC on the protection of the remaining mangroves in Barangay Babuyan, Puerto Princesa City. Besides being forward-looking, the agreement serves as a compelling factor to ensure the commitment of existing fishpond developers and barangay officials to protect the remaining mangroves in the barangay.

In 1999, paralegal development efforts got the support of the city mayor. The series of paralegal trainings in the city of Puerto Princesa culminated in the deputization of selected paralegals from five barangays by the city mayor as volunteer community paralegals (VCPs). The deputization of VCPs, embodied in an executive order issued by the mayor, is a first in the history of the city and province. At this point the VCPs have undertaken initial action plans that include, among others, conduct of community patrols and monitoring, establishment of marine sanctuaries, and organizational development activities.

Community-Based Resource Management

The Environmental Legal Assistance Center (ELAC) was organized as an alternative law group that seeks to empower communities as resource managers through the use of law and capacity-building strategies. This is expressed in our vision, thus:

ELAC envisions communities that are empowered and self-determining stewards of natural resources. These communities are vigilant and assertive of their environmental and human rights.

Its DLA philosophy inspired ELAC to evolve its legal assistance work into community-based resource management which entailed, among others, community organizing and participatory research activities and involvement in local policy advocacy.

ELAC focused its efforts on strengthening existing POs. Besides conducting trainings and seminars, ELAC organized exchange visits by community organizers (COs), key community leaders, and barangay officials to other fishing communities with similar situations. Their meetings with fellow fisherfolk as well as their visits to community-initiated projects such as sanctuaries provided participating PO leaders, barangay officials, and COs with fresh insights and a broader perspective on resource management and community development.

Advocacy capacities of community leaders and members were strengthened as they became members of Fisheries and Aquatic Resource Management Councils (FARMCs) and barangay committees. While FARMCs were recommendatory bodies insofar as fishery resource planning and policymaking were concerned, the active participation of PO leaders had an impact on law enforcement and drew support from the local government. In one instance, local government and the DENR were compelled to address community issues such as fishpond development and quarrying. In another instance, apathetic barangay officials were encouraged to support the stoppage of commercial fishing activities in their barangay.

Also in the area of local policy advocacy, fisherfolk in partnership with ELAC played a key role in the formulation of the citywide fisheries ordinance in early 1997. Fisherfolk leaders, together with NGOs, participated in various workshops facilitated by such institutions as the local government, DENR, and PCSDs to discuss coastal/marine guidelines and tourism guidelines for Pala'wan. Residents in two barangays recently undertook the prerequisite steps to establish a marine sanctuary in their areas.

Communities have learned gradually that innovative approaches are important in advocacy work. For instance, they know that it would be valuable to identify key players in policy formulation and implementation and establish links with these policymakers, even on an individual basis. Through dialogue and other forms of communication with policymakers and government implementers, communities are able to change the attitude of government and eventually engender their trust in the capability of communities for resource management.

They also have learned the value of building coalitions and networks—especially through cases in which traditional politics intervene. In advocating for the expeditious identification and delineation of ancestral domain claims in the province of Pala'wan, NGOs and POs working with indigenous communities formed themselves into a working group. The working group prepared a short-term plan, met with key government officials, submitted an alternative guideline which was later approved by PCSD, and pushed for a budget to carry out the delineation process.

Moreover, communities have realized the value of media advocacy. On their own, some community leaders have gone to radio stations and written newspapers to air their concerns and expose the ineptness of government agencies.

As regards research work, community members have participated in resource profiling and assessment. One approach that has effectively been used is called Environmental Investigative Missions (EIMs). An EIM is designed to be a participatory, multipartite effort to determine the possible impacts of a development project on the community. Community participation is an integral component of the EIM.

Environmental Investigative Missions were conducted to determine the environmental impact of trawl and purse seine fishing activities in Honda Bay and the proposed shipyard and shipbuilding development project in Coron. The research has been used both as an advocacy and planning tool. The community's appreciation of the research results is one immediate consequence of the EIM activity.

Community members have also been trained to undertake monitoring and evaluation activities as part of the resource management planning process and environmental defense efforts. In Coron, for instance, the completion of a participatory rapid appraisal of the natural resources in the area of a proposed ship repair facility in one barangay strengthened the community's position on the project.

*Tenurial Security for Poor Communities: Addressing the Need for
Resource and Land Access*

Without some form of legal instrument allowing poor communities to occupy foreshore or forestal areas, these communities do not have equitable access to our natural resources and consequently they are discouraged from participating in any management or protection scheme. In the past, some of the poor fisherfolk, farmers, and indigenous communities were actually employed by illegal fishers, loggers, and wildlife smugglers to engage in destructive methods of resource use.

In the coastal zone, tenurial instruments, which are also in the nature of management schemes, help deter the "tragedy of open access." For indigenous communities, the instrument is called the Certificate of Ancestral Domain Claim (CADC) or the Certificate of Ancestral Domain Title (CADT) under the new Indigenous People's Rights Act.[20] For fisherfolk and farmers, there

How the Tagbanuas of Coron, Pala'wan Secured their Ancestral Territory

In July of 1998 the Tagbanua indigenous community of Coron, northern Pala'wan had bestowed upon it the first-ever ancestral waters claim in the Philippines. Consisting of 22,000 hectares of land and seas, the ancestral territory was covered by a Certificate of Ancestral Domain Claim (CADC). The CADC gives the tribe the right to manage their ancestral land and seas. The indigenous community has already prepared its ancestral domain management plan, which will serve as the basis for the management of its resources and zoning of its territory.

It had taken the Tagbanua community five years to secure its CADC. Now the people are glad that they will be able to have primary control over the management of their ancestral territory and regulate the entry of tourists and migrants. The Tagbanua's victory shows the way for other indigenous tribes.[21]

20. IPRA law or RA 8371.
21. Rimban, Luz. 1998. "Paradise Regained." *The Investigative Reporting Magazine* (Manila) 4(3): 19.

is the Community Based Forest Management Agreement or Certificate of Stewardship Contract.

A critical element to complement land tenure and sustain any resource management initiative is the provision of alternative livelihood or appropriate enterprise activities. Farmers who have lived on slash-and-burn farming and fisherfolk who are wont to use cyanide or dynamite need livelihood assistance to enable them to live decently. In the experience of the fisherfolk of Sitio Honda Bay, a group of fisherfolk attempted to address the problem concerning dwindling fish catch. They generated the support of NGOs and the city government in their plan to set up a tourism-related enterprise to supplement their current fishing activity.

The Story of HOBBAI (Honda Bay Boatmen Association): Developing a Community-Based Tourism Enterprise

Over the past three years or so, Honda Bay, Puerto Princesa City, Pala'wan, has been one of most popular tourist destinations in Puerto Princesa along with the world-famous Underground River. In 1997 alone, out of the 100,000 tourist arrivals in Puerto Princesa, approximately half visited Honda Bay.

Ferrying of tourists around Honda Bay used to be controlled and monopolized by only five families who had enough capital and established connections with the hotels and inns in the city proper. The rest of the community members would get a rare chance of earning from the visitors if and only when the so-called cartel was unable to accommodate all the guests on their boats. It was only in such situations that they would "pass" the excess tourists on to other boatmen. Even then, the boatmen would not get the full amount for the service they rendered, since cartel members would as a "norm" get the lion's share of the gross income.

The system began to change when some 30 fisherfolk sought ELAC's assistance in organizing themselves into a boatmen association in the latter part of 1996. They called themselves the Honda Bay Boatmen

continued

The Story of HOBBAI (continued)

Association, Inc. or HOBBAI. What these small boat operators wanted was some opportunity, if not an equal opportunity, to earn from the growing tourism industry (the City Tourism Office called it "a phenomenal growth"). It took almost a year for the boatmen association to finally start operation since the new boatmen did not want to start without their registration papers in hand.

Despite initial resistance from the original group of five families, HOBBAI members proceeded to get the support of the City Tourism Council. After a series of dialogues and representations with the city officials, the city mayor issued an executive order giving exclusive right to HOBBAI to operate tourist servicing in Honda Bay.

Another interesting insight in the organization of HOBBAI is the vital role of women in the management of the community enterprise. As its name reflects, the community involved did not have an explicitly gender-oriented approach to forming the HOBBAI. Rather, women's concern, skills, and leadership grew organically through the project's use of participatory planning and research methodology. By using technologies of participation, HOBBAI made significant progress toward equitable and community-wide sharing of both responsibilities and profits. A secondary result has been the sustained involvement of village women in local tourism politics and legal defense of their marine and coastal resources. The HOBBAI experience demonstrates the importance of (1) having NGO support for community organizing with visible women leaders and trainers; (2) allowing women to participate in the design of planning and research methods; (3) recognizing existing gender roles and strategically evaluating how to maintain or subvert them; and (4) building gender analysis into participatory monitoring and evaluation of the community-based tourism project as a step toward more explicit gender-focused programming in the future.[22]

22. Mayo-Anda, Grizelda, John Galit, and Abigail Reyes. 1998. *The Women's Hand in a Boatment's Cooperative: Organizing the Honda Bay Tour Boat Operators in Puerto Princesa, Pala'wan.* UNED–UK Report for the United Nations Commission on Sustainable Development.

Community-Based Law Enforcement

NOTHING IS REAL UNLESS IT IS LOCAL. This is a common perspective shared by local communities. Laws and government programs will have no meaning for them unless the people experience the benefits, witness their favorable impacts or participate in their implementation.

One important area that has started to draw the interest of communities is in enforcing the law. In the area of environmental protection, local communities always hear of rampant violations committed by powerful people and that government agents appear helpless in curbing environmental crimes. This compelling situation encourages community members to pursue a community-based law enforcement program. Armed with increased knowledge of the law and legal processes and motivated by the desire to protect their remaining resources, some community paralegals have joined community law enforcement initiatives either with or without government agencies.

In pursuing community law enforcement initiatives, some communities have found it useful to build linkages and partnerships with enforcement agencies because the latter usually have police powers and ammunition to support their efforts. In doing so, local communities seek the help of NGOs in identifying reliable players in law enforcement to ensure that their efforts will not be imperiled by corrupt public servants. In several instances, fisherfolk and FARMC members of Honda Bay have coordinated with individual policemen and DENR personnel in the seizure of forestry products, and in stopping illegal fishpond development and quarrying activities.

Among indigenous peoples, their existing customs and traditions on conflict resolution and decision-making have provided us with interesting insights on alternative enforcement mechanisms. Unfortunately, some local government officials and government agencies, instead of appreciating the complementary value of indigenous systems, are threatened by such initiatives.

Seizure and Confiscation: An Alternative Enforcement Mechanism

In Pala'wan, it usually takes an average of two to three years for an environmental case to start trial. It then takes the same amount of time for the trial to reach a conclusion. Given the slow process in adjudicating cases, communities have sought an alternative enforcement mechanism by which they

Asserting Their Tribal Justice System Is a Continuing Struggle for the Tagbanuas of Coron

Quite often, the Tagbanuas of Coron hear about the lackadaisical attitude of law enforcement agencies toward illegal activities. Since illegal fishing activities continue to beleaguer their communities, they decided to initiate their own community action to address the problem.

On September 28, 1999, members of Bantay Dagat/Kalikasan, a special task force of the Tagbanua Foundation of Baragay Malawig, Coron, Pala'wan—apprehended a group of fishermen engaged in blast fishing within the ancestral domain (waters claims) of the Tagbanua. The illegal fishermen were on board a motorized banca owned by a resident of the same barangay. The members of the Bantay Dagat confiscated the fishing boat and all the fishing paraphernalia. The items were taken into custody by members of the Tagbanua Foundation.

After the apprehension, the Tagbanua community met to discuss its options. One option considered was to take all the seized items to town and turn them over to the police for their custody while preparing all the legal documents for the subsequent filing of a case or cases against the illegal fishers. Another option was to try the case under the tribal justice system and impose traditional sanctions. This is perfectly legal under Sec. 15 of the Indigenous Peoples Rights Act (RA 8371) (IPRA). The tribal council agreed to meet and settle the case on October 2, 1999.

In the afternoon of October 1, 1999, two municipal officials, aided by members of the local police, visited the Tagbanua community and ordered the release of the seized motor banca and fishing paraphernalia. The barangay captain, a Tagbanua himself, invoked the rights of the Tagbanuas under their customary laws. To diffuse the tension and avert any possible violence, the barangay captain reluctantly agreed to turn over the custody of the confiscated banca and other items to another barangay official.

This was not the first time that the municipal government officials interfered to suppress the initiatives of the Tagbanua in guarding their ancestral territory. On July 30, 1999, Tagbanua villagers of Tara, Coron, who apprehended fishermen using cyanide, were also ordered by a municipal official to release the banca and all the confiscated paraphernalia.

can impose sanctions and deter violators from committing environmental crimes.

Taking off from the tribal justice concept of indigenous communities, ELAC, in partnership with some indigenous communities and barangay officials, is in the process of advocating for an ordinance or tribal law that would ensure swift justice for the communities beset with environmental problems. It is being studied and proposed that in cases in which apprehending and suing violators would not be feasible, the local government officials and indigenous communities will seize, confiscate, and appropriate for the benefit of the community the seized products and paraphernalia used for committing the environmental crime. Paraphernalia consist of chainsaws, boats, equipment, fishing gear, and other items. This proposal would definitely entail some legal research and advocacy, but experience has shown that violators would find it deleterious to have their paraphernalia confiscated instead of being sued.

Lessons and Insights

The approaches mentioned above are just some of the various initiatives undertaken by NGOs to enable poor communities to engage with laws and institutions. Various interventions have showed us some of the crucial considerations in ensuring that laws and institutions would articulate the voice of poor communities, thus achieving the following:

- Cohesion or organization of communities, as this expresses power, leadership, and credibility in dealing with various institutions;
- Continuing empowerment activities (initially in partnership NGOs, but later by the PO or community group on its own) to ensure that communities can achieve some level of flexibility or adaptability to new, emerging legal trends;
- Developing and sustaining partnerships between local communities, NGOs, and government institutions, in whatever form, which would help sustain efforts that address community concerns;
- Effective use of tribal and community-based systems of decision-making and law enforcement;
- Monitoring and evaluation mechanisms (usually informal) so that community members would learn to reflect on lessons and in the

process gain a better understanding of how to move toward greater self-reliance;

- Effective combination of NGO interventions with government efforts and the legal/policy framework in order to produce a lasting impact; and
- Continuing decentralization of laws and institutions so that they become localized and accessible at the grassroots level.

Other noteworthy insights that community empowerment initiatives have shown us include the following:

1. Tribal and community-based systems exist whether the national or local law provide for these. Preexisting community traditions and customs relating to decision-making and dispute resolution must be enhanced. Likewise, such indigenous systems must be developed as enforcement mechanisms in light of the problems that plague the justice system.
2. The question of property rights is always a core concern in any community empowerment initiative. Tenurial security and equitable access to resources must be addressed in order to sustain community-based initiatives.
3. Interaction among poor communities must be facilitated so that the people can learn from their experiences and constitute a movement that could effectively voice the concerns of the poor.
4. Interventions of NGOs and government, if effectively combined with a supportive legal framework, play an important role in converting policy rhetoric into reality.
5. Monitoring and evaluation mechanisms must be built into the community empowerment program. This is an important element of the community or PO's organizational development as well as the NGO's institutional development.
6. Education must be a continuing or never-ending process. We must continue to be creative in seeking new ways to sustain education.

Undoubtedly, replete with insights, our work is a continuing and challenging one. Looking for appropriate mechanisms to interface existing laws and institutions with local community initiatives must therefore continue to remain high on our agenda.

Access to Justice

A Truncated View from Bangladesh

Shahdeen Malik

Madaripur Legal Aid Society

People's Republic of Bangladesh

Bangladesh, with a land area of less than 150,000 square kilometers, is a country with more than 120 million people now, cramming more than 1,000 individuals per square kilometer, if one excludes the uninhabitable water bodies and hilly areas. The country is divided into 64 court districts, yielding an average of, in round figures, 2 million people per court district. If one excludes the two districts with the main cities, Dhaka and Chittagong, with around 20 million people, the average is more in the region of 1.5 million persons per court district or less. In terms of territorial jurisdiction, the court districts are not large. The distance to the district court building in any district would hardly be more than 50 kilometers. But these 50 kilometers are often a very long distance to travel. Money (for litigation expenses) and time required (for the case to meander through the snail-paced system) discourage most travelers from undertaking the journey. One simply has to be reasonably well-off and tenacious.

By the latest count, close to a million cases are pending in the court system. Even the mandatory appeals against death sentences pronounced by trial courts take at least three years before being taken up by the High Court Division. Complicated land disputes are often passed on to sons and grandsons to complete the legal process to resolve the disputes.

Such an unflattering account of the formal legal system is compounded by the prevailing poverty and increasing corruption. The delay and perception of corruption, at least at the lower tiers of the judicial system, are increasingly making the legal system marginal. However, at the same time, there is an unmistakable process of centralizing the legal system in national discourse and perception.

Grinding poverty and the failure of development efforts have propelled a new interest in the legal and judicial systems over the last few years. These interests have manifested in the establishment of a number of nongovernmental organizations (NGOs) focusing on law- and human rights-related issues. Moreover, some of the large developmental NGOs such as BRAC (the former Bangladesh Rural Advancement Committee) and Grameen Bank have begun to take up law-related programs and actions. A number of official institutions such as the Judicial Administrative Training Institute and the Law Commission of Bangladesh have been set up. The Office of the Ombudsman and a National Human Rights Commission are under active consideration by the government and there is a growing interest in legal and judicial reform. Newspapers have begun to report what they deem to be important court cases on the front page, and discussions and workshops on law and judicial reform are also regularly reported by the media.

At another level, two recent judgments by the Supreme Court have directed the government to finalize the formal process of separating the judiciary from the executive, by constitutional amendment if necessary.

Now, where do all these leave the poor in terms of access to justice? Mostly, exactly where they were, as if the formal system did not exist. Even the not-so-poor, the investors and the businesses, increasingly those who can afford it, are taking recourse to arbitration clauses in their contracts to avoid the judicial system.

The recent spate of stern laws in the context of the country's deteriorating crime situation and increasing criminalization of acts are resulting in excessive police power, not only by the police themselves but also by an increasing number of other governmental agencies—further compounding the problems. For example, without proof of criminal motive or intent to defraud, one could go to jail for failing to repay bank loans; often attempts to commit crime is equated with crimes committed in terms of punishment, and so on. Similarly, in matters such as environmental degradation and pollution, only the relevant governmental agency is authorized to file cases. The environmental courts are excluded from entertaining complaints regarding violations of the Environment Preservation Act by anyone but the duly authorized government official.

I mention these, as it were, eclectic examples, in the hope of providing you with glimpses of the system, instead of attempting an overview in five minutes.

Access for the Poor

I assume that access to justice has now been recognized as an essential precondition for economic development. Issues such as the rule of law, independence of judiciary, due process or process of law, equality and non-discrimination have transcended the confines of lawyers and courts and are becoming central concerns of development discourse.

In this newly fashioned realm of concerns, the issue of access to justice in Bangladesh is in danger of bypassing the formal avenues and institutions. Increasingly, in addition to the arbitration clauses mentioned earlier, the NGOs are undertaking mediation in far corners of the country to settle disputes through negotiation and compromise. Increasingly, responses from poor and marginalized people to these efforts are creating alternative sites of dispute resolution, further undermining the formal system. What we, in the NGO sector, term "traditional mediation" by the local elite, though sometimes biased in favor of the rich and the powerful, is also being increasingly utilized by various disputants. Occasionally, even murders and rapes are compromised locally by the traditional mediation process (for instance, when relatives or heirs of the murdered person are financially compensated by the murderer or the murderer's family). This is done not because that is the prevailing notion of justice in such matters, but because the formal system is perceived as costly, time consuming, and lacking muscle in terms of really punishing the criminal, whose identity is locally known. Hence, financial compensation is preferred as being better than no punishment through the process of formal criminal trial.

The lack of confidence in and access to the formal justice system we have summarized up to this point leads to alternative sites for dispute resolution. In the short run, even at the risk of further marginalizing the formal legal and judicial systems, I predict an increase in resorting to mediation as a means of limited justice. Increasing intervention by the NGOs leads to a formalization of the mediation process as well as enhanced awareness about laws and rights. These developments, in the long run, may generate enough pressure for reform of the formal system to make it fair and accessible.

In addition, probably influenced by the activism of the Indian Supreme Court, our Supreme Court has become more proactive, in the process liberally issuing rulings against the government. However, political disputes fashioned as matters of fundamental rights now often end up in court, raising concerns about the politicization of courts. Nevertheless, this phenomenon of public interest litigation is at least enhancing the formal due process perception and creating pressure for the accountability of governmental action. These, in the long run, will translate into better access to justice.

Overcoming Barriers

As indicated, formal interventions by governmental circles to enhance access to justice are still negligible. Recently there have been some efforts to induct mediation into the trial process, and retired judges have suddenly become enthusiastic about these negotiated processes. The government has been toying with the idea of village courts for quite a while now. This is, however, tinkering at the margins only.

The issues of impunity, not only referring to the actions of law enforcement agencies and governmental bodies, but increasingly of the elite of political parties; perception of corruption (that judgements can be bought, at least at the trial level); criminalization of acts; stringent laws opening further avenues of abuse; and virtual absence of reform movements or campaigns—and not poverty *per se*—are the main barriers to access to justice facing litigants.

Also, the absence of accountability of the legal profession and rudimentary systems of professional monitoring provide ample scope to unscrupulous lawyers to exploit uninitiated litigants, further undermining the confidence in the formal legal system.

These, however, are not too difficult issues to resolve; neither are they barriers that are impossible to overcome.

It needs to be remembered that we have had a central system of appointment of judges since at least the eighteenth century. High courts with power to issue writs have been functioning for more than a century and until recently, most of the prominent political leaders came from the legal profession. A quarter of a century ago, almost half of all the elected members of parliament used to be lawyers, though the present representation of lawyers is less than one sixth. It is this formal legal tradition, the centrality of legal concerns and lawyers in the public domain along with the homogenous nature, perception, and culture of the population that can constitute a bedrock on which meaningful reform can be built. Despite grinding poverty, a long-functioning system of local elected bodies, though with limited official powers, is another institutional force of well-entrenched due process practices, which can be prodded to take up the issue of access to justice.

In other words, there are a plethora of sites, institutions, and players that can push for legal reform and enhanced access to justice. Also, there are more than 25,000 enrolled lawyers, a good number of whom have been trained in western, and particularly North American countries with a high level of professional competence. The law departments of Bangladeshi public universities attract the best candidates, and the competition for entrance is fierce. Given these positive elements, the stumbling block is the absence of initiatives at the national policy level. In competition for scarce resources, law and judicial systems have failed to be a central concern. However, the government's revenue from the legal and judicial system is three and a half times more than the budget allocation for this sector. Such a financial scenario also indicates the possibility of easy intervention.

These interventions may take the path of creating institutions of checks and balances, particularly the Office of the Ombudsman and National Human Rights Commission; ensuring the independence of the judiciary with its own financial autonomy; and establishing systems of accountability and monitoring of the judiciary and the legal profession. These are the policy level issues that can be addressed and implemented. Without them, the issue of access to justice, in our conditions, can only be tinkered with at the margins, with stopgap measures such as mediations and alternative dispute resolution exercises or even reform of procedural laws. With these institutions in place and policy commitments made, there are ample resources—human and others—to deliver justice to the poor.

To conclude, let me reiterate that in our context, the increasing marginalization of formal legal and judicial systems is at the root of the problem of accessibility. Only when these institutions are refashioned in a manner that will infuse confidence in the fairness of the process will the poor generate pressure for access. This, in turn, will result in the opening of doors of justice to the poor. Even most of us, who are trained as lawyers and started our interventions for the poor to enhance their access to the justice system are gradually opting for ways of dispute resolution, wherever possible, outside the court. That itself tells the story of accessibility.

In the short run the initiative to changes in institutions, policies, and priorities lies with the state. Should the state fail to respond, other avenues would emerge to ensure justice for the poor.

Women and Access to Justice

The Case of Ecuador

Rocío Salgado Carpio*

Director, Corporación Mujer a Mujer

Ecuador

Prior to the 1967 Constitution, the legal capacity of married women in Ecuador was abridged specifically by virtue of their marital status: a wife could not perform any legally binding act without her husband's consent. A set of laws in force up until that time gave a husband legal authority over his wife and her property. Article 160 of the Civil Code, for one, expressly barred married women from appearing in court as plaintiff or defendant in their own right or represented by an attorney. Excepted from the rule were women in professional practice and mothers acting on behalf of legitimate children in a suit against their father.

The 1967 Constitution affirmed the fundamental equality of husband and wife, whereupon sections of the nation's secondary laws had to be rewritten. Ecuadorian women were formally accorded the right of access to the justice system. The word "formally" is significant: in practice, the doors of the system have only opened part way. This holds true both in substantive law and in a pervasive set of criteria and biases that are brought to bear when laws are interpreted and applied. There still are statutes on the books that restrict the remedies available to a woman who wants to file a complaint against her spouse. Specifically, Article 28 of our Code of Criminal Procedure prohibits a married woman from lodging a complaint against her husband.

The official justice system and its formalities thus have operated as an apparatus of exclusion, betraying the system's lack of understanding of the sum total of the society it is supposed to serve. Sizable sectors of the population have lost faith in a system that they feel has failed them. Concurrently,

---

*Translated into English from the original text in Spanish and edited in English.

however, civil society organizations have been fighting for a stronger voice and alternative avenues to justice for women. In recent years Ecuadorian women have brought fresh ideas to legislation and to the interpretation and application of laws, two milestones being the creation of women's bureaus and the enactment and implementation of the law prohibiting violence against women and the family. The process that led up to that statute pointed up not only just how difficult it is to administer and enforce such legislation in a patriarchal legal system, but also how the behavior of the citizenry and the institutional culture are evolving as far as attitudes toward the administration of justice are concerned.

Women in Ecuador are gaining more and more say in the design, monitoring and evaluation of justice being meted out, notably in such spheres as domestic violence, family and children's rights, and political participation, with the backing of civil society organizations and through joint state-civil society initiatives such as the network of women's bureaus.

The notion of entitlement to justice has evolved over time. At one point, as Loli and Rodríguez recall,[1] it had to do with access to the protection of the courts, that is, the formal right to bring action or defend oneself against an accusation. Today, effective access to justice is viewed as a primordial entitlement among the new suite of individual and societal rights, since having a right counts for nothing if there is no machinery in place for an individual to exercise it.

Two important questions when we look at access to justice are how civic participation has affected justice and how the official justice system is configured, what groups it protects or is designed to protect. Bringing a gender perspective to the analysis, women are questioning the status quo and shedding new light on these issues. When we talk of "justice" we mean more than just the court system: judges' determinations in contentious or voluntary jurisdiction are only part of the picture. These are cross-cutting social concerns as well, so there need to be avenues for citizens' participation, to "produce justice" in the sense of picking up initiatives and proposals for participatory mechanisms being advocated or set in place in various quarters.

Among these approaches are legal aid bureaus and other legal advisory services, and information campaigns to make citizens aware of their rights. In

---

1. From a paper by Silvia Loli Espinoza, *La administración de justicia y los derechos humanos de las mujeres,* presented on August 28, 1999. Quito.

Ecuador, human rights organizations have led this charge. Though their efforts may not have had a large-scale, nationwide impact, they have been crafting strategies to secure access to justice for the poor and the disadvantaged. These services are revealing why the system has remained out of reach for the poor: an absence of mechanisms whereby society can scrutinize and have a say in the workings of the system *per se*; the preponderance of the written word in lawsuits; features of the larger justice-administration apparatus that make it difficult for people to find out directly how their case is progressing; little if any knowledge about rights and procedures; high attorneys' fees; protracted proceedings; and so on.

While it is true that much of the population has to contend with these same obstacles, they nevertheless affect women disproportionately because of the discrimination women encounter in society generally. To the state, justice is premised upon an abstract concept in which all human beings are equal and the laws are gender-neutral; it takes no heed of social, historical, cultural, economic, or gender contexts. This abstract notion is perhaps one of the most critical roadblocks for groups seeking access to justice: until the law recognizes that society is heterogeneous and moves to narrow the gap between the included and the excluded, justice for the latter will continue to be a pipe dream.

What does access to justice entail for women, the poorest of the poor? Rodríguez and Loli have explored a number of elements that I shall outline here.

Exercise of the Right of Effective Recourse to the Competent Authorities so That Complaints Will Be Heard and Ruled On

We would equate such "effective recourse" to the "simple and prompt recourse" mandated in Article 25(1) of the Inter-American Convention on Human Rights, and we thus would presume that all competent authorities having legal jurisdiction should be receiving complaints and petitions.

On this point I might refer specifically to Ecuador's law prohibiting violence against women and the family. According to the pertinent article, some 1,170 officials and forums are to hear domestic violence cases and act on them according to that law—national commissioners, chiefs of police, political leaders of *parroquias* (small rural territorial subdivisions), criminal law judges and the criminal courts. But, in practice, only 21 women's bureaus are actually handling such matters. According to research done last year by the National Council on Women (CONAMU) to review how Law 103 has been administered and enforced in the five years it has been on the books, it is clear that the law is being applied patchily at best. The courts and criminal law judges tend to regard domestic violence as a private matter requiring professional help; political heads of small *parroquias* are simply uninformed.

But issues of access to justice also can be analyzed from a gender perspective, since the socially ascribed roles of men and women create different kinds of conflicts that can end up in the courts, and the two sexes thus make different use of the law. The majority of complaints filed by women have to do with violence in the home and with maternal obligations—maintenance allowances, custody, visitation, and so on. Centers set up to help low-income women see all too many complaints of these kinds, which are directly associated with a woman's financial subordination to her partner or father of her children. According to a World Bank report, 38 percent of poor urban women are not part of the work force because they simply do not have the skills or knowledge that employers are demanding. A number of studies have illustrated the particular toll that poverty takes on women. Those who do manage to enter the labor force are at a disadvantage because of the few avenues of justice open to them and their lack of judicial protection.

When women do decide to go to court, they run into daunting obstacles. One is the cost of the proceedings, in which lawyers' fees often far exceed the support for which the woman is petitioning. The quality of representation a woman can count on has much to do with the fees she can afford: as a rule, more money buys superior professional counsel. The duration of family court proceedings is a second impediment. In Cuenca, for instance, it can take up to three months just for a judge to review the complaint or petition. Women are unaware of their rights and of alternative remedies and are uninformed about procedural formalities. They may be mistreated by judicial officials and be fearful of stepping into the public arena.

Though a number of groups in Ecuadorian society run into these same difficulties, the situation is worse for women because of entrenched gender discrimination.

In 1998 the cities of Quito, Guayaquil, and Cuenca launched a project to help low-income women secure access to justice. In the space of two years about 5,000 women have used the project's services. Some 68 percent of these clients needed help with support petitions and 55 percent with divorce suits; 70 percent of them reported abuse and 15 percent sought other kinds of aid.[2] Funded by Projusticia, these advocacy and counseling centers have given women new tools to obtain justice on better terms. Meanwhile, the National Council on Women has been setting up women's bureaus in several provinces to channel gender-based complaints. These resources are unquestionably bringing justice to large sectors of the population.

Observance of Due Process Rights Before and During the Handling of a Dispute

Due process refers to the core set of elements that must be present in all legal proceedings in order for justice to be validly meted out in any given case. Though basic guidelines of due process are amply developed in criminal law, due process is by no means restricted to that sphere: it is a consideration in any dispute submitted for settlement. Women are pointedly calling into question the due process guarantees in our laws. For one thing, with a single nod to victims' rights, due process requirements are geared to protecting the rights of the accused. Women who are victims of domestic violence or sexual assault are particularly defenseless, and a high percentage of the perpetrators go unpunished. This cannot help but undermine their confidence in the institutions governing our society.

The object of due process standards should be to afford genuine assurances to the victim and the accused alike that justice will prevail, and to make the court system credible to the larger public. According to research done in 1997 in the criminal court system in Quito, Guayaquil, and Cuenca,[3] barely 220 of 1,904 assault complaints filed had made their way through the system, and in only half of those cases had a sentence been handed down. These telling indicators of the weakness of Ecuador's justice system explain why so few women look to the courts for redress. Instead, they are taking their problems to the women's bureaus, which are geared to their needs and offer simpler procedures.

2. Database of the Legal Services for Low-Income Women project funded by Projusticia for CEPAM–Quito, CEPAM–Guayaquil, and Corporación Mujer a Mujer–Cuenca. 1999.

3. Corporación Mujer a Mujer. 1999. *La justicia presa*. Cuenca.

The Right to Have Basic Human Rights Standards Observed in Dispute Settlements

The clearest sign that the justice system is meant for a privileged few is its disregard for fundamental rights. Until the system is truly universal, justice will remain the province of a minority. Guarantees of freedom from gender-based discrimination, which date to the Universal Declaration of Human Rights, lie at the heart of notions of human rights. So long as a single form of discrimination persists in a society, its human rights are not being respected. Each of Ecuador's constitutions has recognized this right, which is closely tied in to the principle of equality. But statements of principle are only the starting point: the next move is to devise concrete mechanisms to turn principles into practice. Ecuador's new constitution accords supra-legal status to the human rights conventions and accords the nation has ratified. Among these is the Convention on the Elimination of All Forms of Discrimination against Women, which women consider a key instrument in the campaign to end discrimination.

In recent years, nongovernmental women's advocacy organizations have sponsored information and awareness campaigns about the use of these laws, targeted at judicial officials and attorneys in private practice. The impact of their efforts is already evident in a number of cases in which judges have invoked, in their decisions, international standards for protecting women from discrimination, but these instances are still the exception. Ecuador has yet to develop a judicial culture in which respect for and protection of human rights is the norm. To truly open the justice system to women and ensure the observance of basic human rights standards, these principles need to be part of university and professional studies and training, law school curricula, and training for judges and other justice system officials. Without such a shift in the culture, the recognition of the aforementioned rights will continue to be a formality, not an effective guarantee on which women can rely.

That every human being has human rights is indisputable. Thus, human rights principles and guarantees are not negotiable in out-of-court settlements or decisions of conciliation boards or hearings. In many domestic violence or sexual assault cases there are nudges toward financial settlements whereby the perpetrator can sidestep punishment. This practice should be stopped. If a community's judicial machinery cannot promise its residents swift and effective remedies, they are likely to resort to nonjudicial options of that kind, on terms that often violate fundamental principles. There is of course a place for reparations to victims, but not in exchange for impunity for their aggressors.

The Right to Have Final Rulings on Disputes Enforced, Including Reparation Orders, and to See Offenders Punished

If final decisions on their complaints or petitions are never enforced, women are left with the feeling that justice has not been done. In the legal system we see all too many instances of unenforced judgments, in which court-ordered reparations never materialize.

Women's organizations that assist low-income women play an important role since they actively pursue the enforcement of judgments. A statistical study showing the correlation between the support provided by ethical professionals who are advocates for women in need and the percentage of cases in which judgments are enforced would be most illuminating. The issue of financial reparations for victims is one of these organizations' core focuses. Unless women's complaints can be carried through to that final stage, their rights may be affirmed but will never be truly protected.

Conclusions

By way of conclusion, I would like to leave you with some thoughts that come out of our experience in working with low-income women.

1. Ecuador has made impressive strides in developing alternative legal services to help settle the kinds of disputes that arise in a society in crisis, as ours is. The approach chosen by women's advocacy NGOs is a constructive one that marries the law and real-life considerations. To see the difference, we have only to look at the outcomes. For instance, support petitions handled by women lawyers working with Corporación Mujer a Mujer in Cuenca, taking an approach that explains the problems women face, are bringing significantly higher figures than those obtained by other practitioners.

   As for efforts to eradicate gender discrimination, the courts' pervasive sexist bias has been tempered. One particularly welcome development is the trend away from evidence that purportedly seeks to establish a woman's "honor" but in fact perpetuates a double standard in which women's sexual conduct is judged by the standards of a patriarchal society. That tradition is giving way to psychological testing, which reveals victims' emotional scars, thereby painting a more complete picture of the problem. Anthropology and the sociology of law also are contributing their knowledge of key elements of interpersonal relationships, helping to apprehend the power that some persons wield over others. Traditionally, the crux of sexual assault cases has been physical force; today, other considerations can be factored into the analysis.

2. When we look at the high percentage of poor women who are seeking legal assistance and the recurring abuse in most of their lives, it becomes clear that national policies are needed to tackle poverty and domestic violence as fundamental barriers to justice. Poverty takes a terrible toll wherever it lodges, but the situation of poor women who turn to the courts for relief is particularly acute. Even women from higher income brackets run up against harsh financial realities if they are separated from their husbands or want to file for divorce, because with few exceptions it is men who hold the purse strings.

3. A first step toward a universally accessible justice system will be a rethinking of the very notions of law and justice. This will mean curriculum changes in university law faculties and more legal research to be able to gauge how the administration of justice affects male and female members of society. The ultimate aim will be to find ways to open the door to the huge ranks of the hitherto excluded, assuring that the justice system takes due account of the heterogeneous society it serves.

4. One constructive move is to instill practices that, in conformity with the constitution, enable aggrieved parties to seek justice through alternative dispute resolution arrangements. This will mean regulating nonjudicial forums in which controversies can be settled and fundamental rights will be strictly observed. Women's organizations that have been working in this direction are getting results for their clients, who need their cases handled quickly and inexpensively.

5. Information campaigns to make people aware of their rights and how to exercise them need to be stepped up, and citizens must become more involved so that they can identify with the system on which they rely and not remain on the outside looking in.

6. It is urgent that the state move resolutely to make orality a central feature of the judicial system, as a way of lowering costs and speeding decisions.

What Informal Mechanisms Exist for Dispute Resolution and Contract Enforcement?

Law, Relationships, and Private Enforcement

Transactional Strategies of Russian Enterprises

Kathryn Hendley*

Associate Professor of Law and
Political Science and
Director of the Center for Russia,
East Europe, and Central Asia,
University of Wisconsin-Madison

Peter Murrell

Professor of Economics and
Chair of the Academic Council
of the IRIS Center,
University of Maryland

Randi Ryterman

Economist, The World Bank

*Thanks are due to Alla V. Mozgovaya of the Institute of Sociology of the Russian Academy of Sciences, who coordinated the survey throughout Russia, to James H. Anderson, Berta Heybey, Todd Koback, and Michael Morgalla for research assistance, and to Rachel Kranton and Young Lee for helpful comments. We gratefully acknowledge the support of the National Council for Eurasian and East European Research, the World Bank, and of the U.S. Agency for International Development under Cooperative Agreement No. DHR–0015–A–00–0031–00 to the Center on Institutional Reform and the Informal Sector (IRIS). The findings, interpretations, and conclusions expressed in this paper are entirely those of the authors. They do not necessarily represent the views of the World Bank, its Executive Directors, or the countries they represent.

Published in *Europe-Asia Studies*, 52, no. 4, (2000): pp. 627–656. For further reference, please visit http://www.tandf.co.uk.

Introduction

How do Russian industrial enterprises do business with one another? The "Wild East" image of Russia suggests that extra-legal tactics are used on a day-to-day basis, and that law is largely irrelevant. The reality is quite different. In this article, we provide an overview of the mechanisms that enterprises use to enforce agreements and to solve problems that arise in their relations with other enterprises. Using both quantitative and qualitative information, we analyze the significance of relational contracting, self-enforcement mechanisms, social networks, and legal institutions. We also consider the extent to which the legacies of the planned economy continue to affect inter-enterprise relations. Our objective is to fill the empirical lacuna on the transactional behavior of Russian enterprises by systematically presenting information on the strategies employed by enterprises and by making judgments on which of those strategies seem most important.

The Soviet legacy presents special challenges for Russia. Under the old system, legal institutions were highly permeable. Laws bent to the political winds, as did the courts (Hendley, 1996). In view of this history and the difficulty of quickly legitimizing carryover legal institutions, many commentators have argued that law is not terribly relevant in the emerging Russian market and that the shortcomings of the legal system are a key factor stymying development. (E.g., McFaul, 1995, pp. 95–96; Aslund, 1995, pp. 5–7, 138; Eckstein et al, 1998, p. 146; Ernst et al, 1996, p. 292.) Some take this argument much farther and contend that enterprises are turning to private security firms for assistance, and that these firms are performing state functions (Volkov, 1999; Hay and Shleifer, 1998; Hay, Shleifer, and Vishny, 1996; Leitzel, Gaddy, and Alekseev, 1995; Shelley, 1995, p. 830). Thus, we examine whether these security firms—the mafia of popular lore—are important in inter-enterprise relations.

As a general matter, the efficiency and predictability that firms desire in their business relations have many different sources. A traditional perspective embodied in the classical view of contracting and implicitly in neo-classical economics saw a world of arm's length trading supported by powerful state legal institutions.[1] Similarly, an evolving state capacity to enforce contracts is

---

1.Williamson (1985, p. 20) refers to this as the legal centralist point of view in which "Most studies of exchange assume that efficacious rules of law regarding contract are in place and are applied by the courts in an informed, sophisticated, and low-cost way." Legal scholars tend to refer to it as the classical or neoclassical theory of contracts. (E.g., Macaulay, 1977, pp. 508–10; Feinman, 1990, pp. 1285–87)

an essential element of North's (1990) description of the rise of the west and the process of economic development.[2]

An alternative view was stimulated most notably by Macaulay (1963) and spurred by developments in transactions-cost analysis (Williamson, 1985) and game theory (e.g. Telser, 1980 and Kreps et al., 1982). The alternative view maintains that the importance of law in contractual relations has been vastly overstated and that economic agents construct productive relationships largely without reference to the legal system.[3] To support economic relationships, agents use a variety of purely private mechanisms such as personal trust, calculative trust, reputation, and constructed mutual dependence.[4] Stated provocatively, the fundamental difference between the traditional and alternative views subsists in the relative roles of trust and law in promoting cooperation (Deakin, Lane, and Wilkinson, 1997).

In more sociological analyses, a common theme is that personal interaction and impersonal state institutions tell only part of the story (Greif, 1996). Relationships are embedded in a broader social structure (Evans, 1995; Granovetter, 1985). Social, or network, relations affect the interaction between trading parties and provide powerful enforcement mechanisms (Galanter, 1974). Relationships are supported by community reputation and by the costs and benefits of information exchange. This group- or network-oriented approach has been increasingly popular in the last decade,[5] spurred

2. Weber's (1967) historical-theoretical analysis of the rise of capitalism in Western Europe focuses on the importance of private property as an impetus for merchants to rely on law. As Macaulay (1977, pp. 509–10) argues, Weber assumes that law and litigation are integral to contract enforcement.

3. One could cite a host of studies, some of which have as their central thesis that the legal system is irrelevant and others which take this thesis as an assumption while showing the alternative mechanisms that transactors use to support their relationships. For an example of each of the genres, see Macneil (1985) and Klein and Leffler (1981).

4. This is not the place for an extended discussion of "the elusive notion of trust" (Gambetta, 1988, p. ix). In the following, we will maintain Williamson's (1993) distinction between calculative and personal trust. Calculative trust occurs when each of two parties calculates that is in the other party's own interest to cooperate, basing that calculation on a systematic exploration of both party's goals and possibilities. In contrast, personal trust is closer to a human passion, in which the two parties have an implicit agreement not to calculate, not to monitor closely, since either of these would destroy the presumption that each party assumes that the other party has good intentions. As is made clear in later sections, personal trust and calculative trust correspond to two different transactional strategies. Our discussions of trust do not refer to citizens' attitudes toward the government. See generally Mishler and Rose (1997).

5. Landa (1994, p. 101) calls the "ethnically homogenous middleman group" an "institutional alternative to contract law."

by the recognition of the importance of networks of traders in such varied settings as East Asia[6] and New York (Bernstein 1992, Uzzi 1996), and by the historical-theoretical analysis of Greif (1989, 1994; see also Greif, Milgrom, and Weingast, 1994) and North (1990; see also, Milgrom, North, and Weingast, 1990).

The relative importance of each of these mechanisms of governing relationships is still an open question, as is the variation in their importance across situations and societies. Indeed, there is so little consensus that Williamson (1994, p.174) identifies an "...exaggerated emphasis on court ordering (by the institutions of the state) over private ordering (by the immediate parties and affiliates to a transaction)..." while Deakin, Lane, and Wilkinson (1997, p. 105) observe "...a wide consensus to the effect that the institutions of contract law are largely marginal to the processes of business contracting." Similarly, in the economics literature one frequently encounters the assumption that contracts are not enforceable by the government or any other third party (Klein and Leffler, 1981, Klein, 1996) while legal scholars tend to assume a more central role for law and legal institutions in contractual matters.[7]

Our data indicate that, much like their Western counterparts, Russian enterprises use a wide variety of mechanisms to govern their exchange relations. Russian enterprises exhibit a strong preference for using direct enterprise-to-enterprise negotiations to solve potential contractual problems. Similarly, there is a reliance on long-term partners, suggesting that personal trust plays an important role. This is hardly surprising given the chaotic nature of the Russian marketplace, and the difficulty of assessing the credibility of potential trading partners.

Contrary to common wisdom, Russian enterprises do not reject the use of law and legal institutions when disputes arise.[8] Many enterprises use the courts.[9] This is not to say that a legalistic strategy is preferred, but merely that

---

6. Jones (1994, p. 216) refers to the "the role of guanxi networks as an alternative to the legal regulations of exchange" in China. See also Winn, 1994.

7. An evaluation of competing theories of contract law is beyond the scope of this article. Feinman (1990) and Hillman (1997) provide comprehensive critical assessments.

8. A detailed discussion of the relevance of law and legal institutions to the process of negotiating the terms of business deals is beyond the scope of this article, but we do provide some examples in presenting our empirical information.

9. Johnson, McMillan and Woodruff (1999) come to similar conclusions.

such a strategy is considered feasible. Consistently, we found little evidence of enterprises resorting to private law enforcement. These findings suggest that the supposed connection between the ineffectiveness of law and the rise of the mafia is overstated. Finally, the legacies of the old administrative enforcement mechanisms seem few, although enterprise networks built up during the Soviet days are rather resilient.

In the following section of the paper, we briefly examine the available transactional strategies, setting up the framework for our presentation of the data. We go on to describe the source of the information we use, the primary element of which is a survey of 328 Russian enterprises. Then, we catalog the prevalence and the effectiveness of the various transactional strategies.[10] We analyze complementarities between the use of the different strategies, an analysis that provides important clues about the sources of institutional change in Russia. A conclusion summarizes the lessons emanating from the paper.

The Available Transactional Strategies

What alternative strategies could Russian enterprises pursue in search of efficiency and predictability in their business relations with other enterprises? In this section, we describe a set of seven strategies, which we consider to cover the broad range available. For expositional convenience, we place these strategies on a spectrum, with reliance on relationships at one end and reliance on law at the other.[11] The ordering of points on the spectrum roughly correlates with variations in some of the properties of the strategies, such as reliance on reputational effects or the involvement of official third parties. Nonetheless, we cannot emphasize too strongly that we do not view enterprises as moving up or down the spectrum in a linear fashion, as they change their approach to ordering relationships. Certain elements of the spectrum might be unavailable to some enterprises; some enterprises might find that abandoning a strategy at one end of the spectrum will force them to move to the other end. Moreover, any given enterprise will likely use a combination of strategies.

---

10. For analysis of regional variations in the use of strategies, see Hendley, Murrell and Ryterman (1999b).

11. Macaulay et al. (1995, p. 235) conceptualize contracts as existing "on a spectrum from discrete transactions to long-term continuing relations." See also Galanter (1974).

Table 1 sets forth the seven basic strategies, along with examples drawn from present-day Russia and plausible values for the properties of strategies. The Table serves as a framework for the presentation of our empirical information, focusing on what enterprises do to prevent or to solve problems in existing relationships. This is, of course, only one part of making relationships work. There are also the formative steps, for example, the setting of contractual terms or the choice of customers and suppliers. We do provide information on some formative issues below, but this is not the heart of our empirical information. Our focus is on the enterprise's approach to problem-solving, as one lens through which we can understand the more general phenomenon of how enterprises make their relationships work.

At one end of the spectrum is *relational contracting*.[12] When two enterprises trade with one another over an extended period, their officials might develop bonds of personal trust that override any fears of contractual non-performance. Then, the relationship no longer depends upon a detailed calculus of the other party's motives. In such cases, the written contract is largely superfluous (Macaulay, 1963). Any specific element of agreement between the two parties can only be understood in the context of the whole relationship. If problems arise, they are resolved through negotiations, without involving outsiders. Adjustments occur without recontracting. Resorting to the courts or even bringing in lawyers can be corrosive, since such actions signal a defraying of personal trust.

In *self-enforcement*, the relationship is based on the calculus of mutual interest, each party deciding that the other has a self interest in fulfilling the agreement.[13] This is a relationship of calculative, rather then personal, trust. However, a succession of self-enforcing agreements might lead to the development of personal trust. Hence, in practice, the borderline between relational and self-enforcing agreements is fuzzy.[14]

---

12. See Macneil (1985). Schwartz (1992) suggests that relational contracting refers to the same phenomenon as the notion of incomplete contracts in economics.

13. See Telser (1980) for example.

14. Indeed, being worthy of personal trust might be operationally indistinguishable from having a reputation for fair dealing and being receptive to complaints. In one description of the process of building a relationship, the parties interact and then social and psychological factors lead to personal trust. In another description, the parties have an incentive to build a reputation as a good partner and they do so in a calculating manner. The only factor distinguishing the two types of processes could be the pattern of thought that leads to behavior.

Table 1: Seven strategies that enterprises use in pursuing efficiency and predictability in business relations

	Strategy	Russian examples	Enforcement methods	Reliance on outsiders	Personal trust in counterpart	Reliance on reputation	Use of law
1	Relational contracting	Meetings, especially between lower level officials	Personal pressure; fear of erosion of personal trust	Low	High	Medium -- personal trust dominates	None
2	Self-enforcement	Threats to stop trading; pre-payment, barter	Calculative trust based on future interactions; fear of erosion of reputation	Low	Low	High -- enterprises aim to accumulate reputational capital	Low
3	Third-party enforcement	Telling others, e.g. other enterprises	Shame; lost economic opportunities from group	High - not state	Varying - depending on nature of group	High -- especially third-party reputation	Low
4	Private enforcement	Private arbitration; "mafia" or security service	Judgment of impartial actor; threats and/or violence	High - not state	Low	Varies: low for reputation of transacting party; high for reputation of enforcer	Varies: extra-legal means might be used to enforce legal rules
5	Administrative levers of state	Asking a governmental organ for help	State munificence or harm	Significant - state	Medium	Medium	Medium
6	Shadow of law	Penalties; Pretenzia;[2] Collateral	Threats to go to court; negotiated settlement	Significant - state	Medium	Medium	High
7	Legalistic	Arbitrazh court[3]	Court order	High - state	Low	Low	High

Notes:

1. *Pretenzia* are letters requesting payment sent by the wronged party to their contractual partners before filing a complaint in the court. Prior to 1995, *pretenzia* were mandatory.

2. *Arbitrazh* courts hear business disputes between legal entities.

In self-enforcing arrangements, the contract determines outcomes. Since parties are expected to be calculating, lawyers may play a more significant role than under relational contracting and going to court need not necessarily signal the end of all future interactions. Nevertheless, self-enforcing agreements most often arise in situations where use of the official legal system is not envisaged. The threat of stopping trade is the basic enforcement mechanism. The parties also build in conditions that encourage performance.[15] (Later in the paper, we discuss how Russian enterprises use barter and prepayment to this end.)

When the relationship between two parties is embedded in a wider network of relations, *third-party enforcement occurs.*[16] The network can provide benefits to the two parties, for example, through an elevation in social status or by sharing information about trading partners. It can also impose costs such as the shame of being branded as untrustworthy or the lost profits from foreclosed trading opportunities with network members. These benefits and costs provide the carrot and stick that can induce contract fulfillment between two network members. This mechanism represents a step away from self-reliance, but does not yet presume state involvement or extra-legal remedies of self-help.

Private enforcement occurs when the parties to a contract use the services of a private entity that does not have any pre-existing relations with them. The standard example in developed economies is the inclusion of arbitration clauses in commercial contracts. In transition economies, private enforcement also brings to mind uglier mechanisms, such as calling upon the mafia or a private security firm to secure performance by a trading partner. Such enforcement assumes a lack of confidence both in the trading partner and in the capacity of the legal system to provide acceptable relief, although private enforcers may simply implement judgments of the courts. This strategy is typically one that is multi-layered, often beginning with implicit threats, and sometimes culminating in the use of violence. While violence is not an essential element, intimidation is.[17]

---

15. See for example Williamson's discussion of hostage models (1985, Chapters 7 and 8.)

16. The term is taken from Greif (1996, pp. 246–47). He also uses the term "collectivism," but given the history of Russia use of this term would create much confusion here.

17. If the intimidation and violence is undertaken by the private armies of the contracting parties, then this would be classified as self-enforcement.

Enforcement could be provided by any entity that can impose costs or bestow benefits on the contracting parties. Given the history of state involvement in Russia's economy, an obvious suspect for that role would be the *state administration*.[18] Enterprises that are still close to the state would naturally ask government officials to pressure a trading partner who is not performing. Governments have many levers of influence over enterprises and might be willing to use them. Presumably, the non-performing enterprise will change its behavior rather than risk the state's ire.[19]

As we approach the other end of the spectrum, law plays a central role. Often, the role can be as mere backdrop: the possibility of a credible threat to use the courts will be enough to establish an important role for legal rules in determining the character of outcomes. The threat induces the parties to bargain to agreement within the *shadow of the law* (Mnookin and Kornhauser, 1979; Jacob, 1992; Cooter et al., 1982). When relations between trading partners are characterized by a low level of trust, their contracts often include confiscatory remedies designed to protect the parties. Examples of these are collateral arrangements or penalty clauses. In case of default, correspondence between enterprises would include threats to initiate lawsuits and to enforce these confiscatory contractual terms. Settlement comes because it is cheaper than litigation, not out of any desire to protect a reputation or to maintain a long-term relation.

At the opposite end of the spectrum from relational contracting is *litigation*. Submitting a dispute to the courts implies an acceptance of the legitimacy of the institution, and a willingness to abide by its decision (Shapiro, 1981). Filing a lawsuit typically indicates a breakdown in the relationship between the trading partners. They would not appeal to court, given litigation costs, if settlement could be reached through negotiation. In a stable economy, litigation is also expensive in relationship terms. Harsh words are exchanged, and the trading relationship is often irretrievably severed.

The Survey and the Data

Between May and August of 1997, we surveyed 328 Russian industrial enterprises. The sample included enterprises from six cities (Moscow, Barnaul,

---

18. State bodies also provide such services in market economies, the prototypical case being a local official mediating between a developer and a construction company.

19. Sometimes the punishment comes from a private entity responding to pressure from the state rather than from the state directly. For example, the state (in some capacity) might convince the enterprise's bank to call its loans.

Novosibirsk, Ekaterinburg, Voronezh, Saratov), with each city represented roughly equally. The enterprises were concentrated among ten industrial sectors.[20] Enterprise size ranged from 30 to 17,000 employees, with a median of 300 and a mean of 980. Most of the enterprises were established during the Soviet era, and about three-fourths (77%) are privatized. In virtually all of those privatized, some stock was in the hands of insiders, and nearly a third were entirely owned by insiders. Outsiders (non-employees of the enterprise) held some stock in 60% of the enterprises.

In each enterprise, Russian surveyors administered different survey instruments to four top managers: the general director, and the heads of the sales, purchasing (supply), and legal departments. In this paper, we focus primarily on the data reported by the heads of the sales and the purchasing departments.[21] Our discussion centers on the answers to two composite questions, one addressed to each of these two enterprise officials, focusing on how the enterprises deal with problems, potential or actual, in transactions.[22] In Boxes 1 and 2, we reproduce English versions of the questions as they were addressed to enterprise officials.[23]

The structure of the questions was partially determined by the desire to maximize the amount of information collected in the face of constraints on respondents' time. We wanted to examine both the strategies that were used to prevent the occurrence of problems and the strategies used to deal with partners that did not perform. We also wanted to explore both sales and purchasing transactions. With infinite respondent patience, which we did not have, this would have dictated four composite questions. Instead, we settled for two: the purchasing question dealing with the prevention of problems and the sales question dealing with non-performance. This match was natural in the present Russian transactional climate, with non-payment rife.[24]

20. The industrial sectors are (number of enterprises in parentheses): food processing (67); textiles, clothing and leather (60); fabricated metal (34); machinery and transport equipment (23); electronics (34); chemicals and petroleum (33); construction (18); wood products (8); paper and printing (5); and other (46).

21. When the enterprise did not have a formal department, the person who carried out the relevant duties answered the survey.

22. We use responses to other survey questions to expand on the information from these two composite questions.

23. There is a small change in format from the Russian versions, in order not to confuse the reader with the instructions given to the surveyors.

24. The national-level statistics on *arbitrazh* court caseload provide one indicator of the growth of non-payments as a problem. In 1992, such cases made up 19% of the total cases decided. By 1995, they had grown to constitute the majority (51%) of cases decided. (Sudebno-arbitrazhnaya statistika, 1997)

Table 1:The question posed to the purchasing department

During the past two years, how important were the following methods in helping your enterprise to prevent and/or resolve problems arising in relationships with suppliers? First, please tell us whether you used the method. If the method was used, then please evaluate its effectiveness on a scale from 0 to 10. A '0' means either that the method was not used at all or that it was not effective and a '10' means that the method was very effective.

Method	1 = Yes, it was used during the past two years. 2 = No, it was not used during the past two years	On a scale from 0 to 10, how effective was the method during the past two years?
Formal business meetings between lower level officials of the trading partners.		
Formal business meetings between the general directors of the trading partners.		
Informal meetings between counterparts in the two enterprises, for example, in a restaurant, banya, recreational facility, or civic organization.		
Intervention by other enterprises.		
Intervention by officials of a business association or a financial-industrial group.		
Use of private enforcement firms (security firms, collection agencies, mafia, etc.)		
Intervention by banks.		
Intervention by representatives of political parties or movements.		
Intervention by officials of the local government.		
Intervention by officials of the federal government.		
Use of *arbitrazh* courts.		
Use of *treteiskie* courts.		

Note: Treteiskie courts are private tribunals that arbitrate business disputes at the request of the parties.

Table 2: The Question Posed to the Sales Department.

Listed below are some possible methods of dealing with customers that did not honor their agreements with your enterprise. First, please tell us whether your enterprise has used or threatened to use this method during the past two years. Then, please tell us how effective either the threat of using these methods or their actual use has been in getting them to honor their agreements. Convey your views by choosing a point on a scale from 0 to 10. A '0' means either that the method was not used at all or that it was not effective and a '10' means that the method was very effective.

Method	Has your enterprise used or threatened to use this method during the past two years? 1 = Yes 2 = No	On a scale from 0 to 10, how effective is this method for getting other firms to honor their agreements with you?
Telling other enterprises about the behavior of an enterprise that did not honor its agreement.		
Forcing the enterprise to pay a financial penalty.		
Stopping trade with the enterprise.		
Filing a complaint against the enterprise with an antimonopoly committee.		
Sending *pretenzia* or other notices suggesting a possible court action.		
Filing a claim in arbitrazh court.		
Reporting the enterprise to a local government organ.		
Reporting the enterprise to a federal government organ.		
Reporting the enterprise to a business association or a financial-industrial group.		
Reporting the enterprise to social, religious, or civic organizations.		

In constructing the question posed to the purchasing department (Box 1), we assumed that a potential for disputes always exists and that the means of addressing that potential are indicative of the transactional strategy undertaken. Thus, we listed twelve methods of presenting and resolving problems, and asked enterprises whether they used the method and how they rated the effectiveness of the method on a scale of 0 to 10.

Table 2 summarizes the responses to the question reproduced in Box 1. In column (1), we associate each method of addressing potential disputes with one of the strategies on the spectrum summarized in Table 1. Column (2) lists the percentages of enterprises that use each method. Column (3) summarizes the evaluation of the effectiveness of each method by presenting the mean scores of the 0 to 10 scale, including only the responses of the enterprises that used the method. The final column combines the information on extent of use and effectiveness. Assuming that the effectiveness of a method is 0 for those enterprises that did not use it, one can calculate a mean effectiveness score across all enterprises. These mean scores appear in the fourth column.

The question posed to the sales department (Box 2) focused on the actions taken when customers did not honor their agreements. The responses are presented in Table 3, whose construction is identical to that of Table 2. Given that non-performance is a presumption of the question, it lists methods that are more ominous than those addressed on the purchasing side (e.g., "stopping trade," "reporting...," "filing..."). But these stronger methods might be very effective as threats alone and therefore the question includes the possibility that the threat of use, rather than actual use, is the method of dealing with non-performing customers. In turn, this led to the necessity of posing a different set of methods in the customer question than in the purchasing question. (The threat of a meeting sounds hardly credible!) For these reasons, the questions posed in Boxes 1 and 2 are not identical.

How do we view the quality of the data contained in these Tables? Given the constraints of survey procedures and the non-quantitative nature of the phenomenon with which we are dealing, the numbers presented should be regarded as crude indicators. But this imprecision has to be taken in the context of the limited amount of information that exists on the mix of transactional strategies that enterprises undertake. This statement is as true for developed market economies as it is for Russia. Thus, we view Tables 2 and 3 as shedding a glimmer of light on territory where the rays of the accountant, the industrial census, and the quantitative surveyor do not normally shine. We welcome more refined procedures, but for now, the numbers in Tables 2 and 3 provide much more detailed information than exists elsewhere, certainly on Russia and probably on most countries.

In the next Section, we examine the results of Tables 2 and 3 in context. The Russian transactional environment is in flux, somewhere en route from hierarchical central planning to the market. There are echoes of this path's starting point in the current decisions of firms. Moreover, the present transactional environment contains many features that are specific to the transition and to Russia. Thus we provide pertinent information both past and present. We also introduce additional details from our data set, from in-depth enterprise case studies, and from related research on the *arbitrazh* courts, in order to explain and to amplify the picture provided by the Tables.[25]

The Russian Picture

During the Soviet period, the principal dynamic was vertical. Fulfillment of the national economic plan was the overriding goal for enterprises. Ministries provided enterprises with contracts consistent with plan goals. These contracts bore only a superficial resemblance to those in a market-driven system, given that enterprises had almost no control over the identity of trading partners or the terms of trade. Breaches could be appealed to an administrative agency, known as state *arbitrazh* (or *gosarbitrazh*), but the arbiters' central concern was with plan fulfillment, rather than with legal niceties (Pomorski, 1977). When appealing to *gosarbitrazh*, enterprises were usually more interested in signaling the cause of production problems than in obtaining damages or other relief (Kroll, 1987).

Given the shortages prevailing in Soviet times, enterprises often had difficulty obtaining key planned inputs. Appeals to ministerial superiors were helpful in resolving these problems. Ministry decisions about which enterprises to help were inevitably colored by the importance of the output and the relationship with the enterprise. Thus, it was critical for enterprise

---

25. Related case studies and analyses of the courts appear in Hendley (1999 & 1998a,b,c).

Table 2: How the Purchasing Department Deals with Problems with Suppliers

(1) Methods of preventing and/or resolving problems in relationships with suppliers. (The number in the left hand column identifies the strategy in Table 1 with which this method is associated)	(2) Percentage of enterprises using method	(3) Average scale score for those using method	(4) Average scale score across all enterprises (assuming score = 0 if don't use)
1 Informal meetings between counterparts in the two enterprises, for example, in a restaurant, banya, recreational facility, or civic organization.	23.01	7.39	1.70
1,2 Formal business meetings between lower level officials of the trading partners.	76.38	7.51	5.73
1,2 Formal business meetings between the general directors of the trading partners.	56.44	8.52	4.81
3 Intervention by other enterprises.	15.34	5.34	0.82
3 Intervention by banks.	5.21	4.71	0.25
3 Intervention by representatives of political parties or movements.	0.31	3.00	0.01
3 Intervention by officials of a business association or a financial-industrial group.	3.99	4.85	0.19
4 Use of private enforcement firms (security firms, collection agencies, mafia, etc.)	2.76	6.22	0.17
4 Use of treteiskie courts.	1.84	4.33	0.08
5 Intervention by officials of the local government.	10.43	4.41	0.46
5 Intervention by officials of the federal government.	3.37	4.45	0.15
7 Use of Arbitrazh courts.	25.46	5.40	1.37

management to maintain a good relationship with ministries, both the industrial ministry and the procurement ministry. (See generally Berliner, 1957.) Relationships with Communist Party officials were also important because these officials could pressure the contractual partner (or sometimes the ministry). Helping enterprises was often in the officials' self-interest (Granick, 1961, pp. 165–77), since evaluation and remuneration were inextricably linked to economic performance. Thus, in the Soviet era, governmental and third-party relationships were especially important.

Table 3: How the Sales Department Deals with Customers that Did not Honor Agreements

(1) Methods used or threatened in dealing with customers that did not honor their agreements. (The number in the left hand column identifies the strategy in Table 1 with which this method is associated)		(2) Percentage of enterprises using or threatening method	(3) Average scale score for those using or threatening method	(4) Average scale score across all enterprises (assuming score = 0 if not used)
1,2	Stopping trade with the enterprise.	65.85	5.76	3.76
3	Reporting the enterprise to social, religious, or civic organizations.	0.91	2.33	0.02
3	Reporting the enterprise to a business association or a financial-industrial group.	2.74	3.00	0.08
3	Telling other enterprises about the behavior of an enterprise that did not honor its agreement.	47.56	4.41	2.08
5	Reporting the enterprise to a local government organ.	14.02	2.39	0.32
5	Filing a complaint against the enterprise with an antimonopoly committee.	7.32	2.91	0.20
5	Reporting the enterprise to a federal government organ.	7.93	3.46	0.27
6	Sending pretenzia or other notices suggesting a possible court action.	58.23	5.16	3.00
6	Forcing the enterprise to pay a financial penalty.	57.32	4.65	2.65
7	Filing a claim in arbitrazh court.	60.98	5.69	3.45

Although the formal structure of the Soviet system emphasized vertical links, the pressure to fulfill the plan routinely forced enterprise management to seek inputs through informal horizontal channels. Behind the scenes, enterprises worked with so-called "pushers" (*tolkachi*) who specialized in offering incentives to contractual partners for contract fulfillment and in finding deficit goods from other sources (Berliner, 1988, pp. 34–36, 76–78). These transactions were illegal under Soviet law, but meeting the plan justified skirting the law. Few enterprises could have survived without some participation in the second economy. (See Grossman, 1977.) Thus, Russian enterprises were familiar with horizontal relational transacting before the 1990s.

In the late 1980s and early 1990s, the old system declined in fits and starts. The legalization of trading in goods for profit—the Soviet crime of "speculation"—saw the tolkachi and the second economy emerge from the shadows. Reforms hastened the decline of the administrative command system, while bureaucratic resistance slowed the process. With profit replacing plan as the key motivating force for enterprises, the ministries gradually lost their raison d'être. By 1992, the flagship Soviet ministries in charge of planning, prices, and supplies had been eliminated, and the industrial ministries had been largely decimated.[26] But the overall size of the Russian state bureaucracy has not declined and the Soviet era imparts a powerful legacy, suggesting that it is important to look for vestiges of the old system of administrative contract enforcement. At the same time, old relationships might persist in a different setting. For example, our survey reveals that 88% of sales directors believe that contacts with former officials of the old Soviet supply organizations have facilitated customer relations.

The reforms and the vast structural economic changes mean that enterprises have faced a massive shift in the transactional problems. During Soviet times, suppliers were more likely to default. Ubiquitous shortages left customers constantly fearful of late deliveries, though the tight ministerial control over the substance of contracts severely limited the ability of parties to protect themselves through careful drafting. Now goods are abundant, but a large proportion of enterprises lack liquidity and it is extremely difficult for suppliers to know which customers can pay. Thus, the increased contractual freedom, so desired by the old Soviet enterprises, has led to a variety of new challenges, which could have hardly been anticipated. In the following, we examine the popularity and effectiveness of the various strategies that enterprises are adopting in the face of these problems.

Relational Contracting

Relationships have always been important to the smooth functioning of the Russian economy. This basic truth is not unique to Russia. Almost

---

26. In some industrial sectors, ministries continued to exert power through their control over licensing and regulatory functions. (E.g., Hendley, 1998c, pp. 99–100) Some other ministries reconstituted themselves as *kontserny* and served as middlemen. (Kroll, 1991) Their ability to perform this function lasted only so long as their information about, and connections with, potential suppliers was superior to that of the enterprises themselves.

everywhere, personal trust inevitably affects how partners deal with one another in routine transactions and what they do when problems arise. Tables 2 and 3 provide data consistent with that picture. The most frequently used methods of solving problems, and the most effective ones, are those that rely solely on enterprise-to-enterprise interactions. Foremost are formal meetings between lower level officials. Such meetings allow trading partners to resolve potential problems in a non-confrontational and relatively cheap manner.

More than three-fourths (77%) of the surveyed enterprises have held formal business meetings between lower level officials in an effort to prevent or resolve problems with suppliers. Older enterprises are more likely to employ this tactic. Among enterprises formed after 1990, use drops to 71%. Larger enterprises use such meetings more frequently than smaller enterprises.

There remains the question of the source of the personal trust that is implicit in relational contracting. One potential source is a history of working together. However, relationships in Soviet times often began with shotgun marriages arranged and enforced by ministries. These arranged marriages are most likely to survive into an era of transactional freedom when the parties have developed a relationship of personal trust, though mutual dependence may also play a role. Even though enterprises can now freely decide to whom to sell output and from whom to buy inputs, many have chosen to maintain old ties. Among the surveyed firms, about half (48%) of customers and suppliers dated from the Soviet period.

Formal links between the enterprises can also serve to cement trust.[27] In 11% of enterprises, suppliers are shareholders. In 16%, customers are shareholders. Similarly, there are representatives of suppliers on the boards of directors of 8% of enterprises, and representatives of customers on 12%. When there are such links, enterprises are more likely to use formal business meetings between lower level officials to resolve problems. For example, of the enterprises that have suppliers on their boards, 95% utilize such meetings.

Trust may arise more quickly when the relations between the officials of the two firms have a personal character. Personal trust has become a valued

27. When we use the word trust without the adjectives personal or calculative, both types are implied.

commodity in post-Soviet Russia, where default on contractual payments is commonplace. Many managers believe that the limited resources of their trading partners tend to go toward paying debts to companies to whom a personal obligation is felt. Our survey indicates that there is a personal dimension to the relationships with contractual counterparts in 50% of transactions.[28] But the data do not suggest that such personal contacts lead to extensive use of informal meetings. Table 2 shows that formal contacts are much more important than informal ones taking place in a non-business setting.[29]

Self-Enforcement

The autonomy that came to Russian enterprises after the fall of the administrative-command system gave rise to an increased need for self-enforcing agreements. Absent personal trust, enterprises sought mechanisms that would induce their counterparts to perform without outside enforcement.

When markets have imperfections and when information about alternative trading partners is limited, the desire to keep trading with a partner can provide incentive for performance. When problems loom, the threat of stopping trade reminds the partner of the costs of default. If the problems are not solved, carrying out the threat is the ultimate remedy. This is the tactic most commonly used for dealing with buyers who renege (Table 3), and it is regarded as the most effective. In the chaotic Russian environment, where non-payment has become almost routine, the threat of stopping trade could even be consistent with maintaining relational contracting. For example, 77% of enterprises that have customers on their boards of directors use this strategy, in contrast to 66% of all enterprises. But, we can fairly assume that severing trade reflects a complete erosion of the trust that undergirds a relationship.

To construct self-enforcing agreements, enterprises can also adopt contractual terms that make contract fulfillment more likely, or use other

---

28. In the survey, we also collected data on specific transactions undertaken by the enterprises.

29. This suggests that the informal meetings referred to in Table 2 might be laden with symbolism to a greater degree than the use of the word "informal" implies. This point is supported by the observation later in the paper that the strategy of using informal meetings is associated with the strategy of using contacts with third-party enterprises.

mechanisms. For example, echoing Williamson's (1985) hostage model, enterprises maintain possession of the customer's property in 8.6% of sales transactions; in 7.5% of procurement transactions, supplier's property is held. However, these percentages pale in comparison with those for prepayment and barter, two mechanisms whose use is consistent with a self-enforcing transactional strategy.

With most enterprises operating at far below capacity, goods are easily available, but many enterprises lack the liquid resources to pay for them. A significant proportion of enterprises are seriously in debt to tax authorities and suppliers. (Over 75% of surveyed enterprises are in arrears to the tax authorities. Over 90% of enterprises have customers in arrears.) Many enterprises are technically insolvent, but most muddle through without resort to bankruptcy protection (Hendley, 1999). Creditors seek payment from debtors' bank accounts. When the funds are insufficient, petitions are registered with the bank, and any money that comes into the account is automatically transferred to creditors, in the order mandated by legislation.[30] This institutional framework has prompted debtor enterprises to avoid using liquid resources and to hide them.[31] The most common schemes are to have customers pay suppliers directly or to create affiliated companies and funnel money through their bank accounts. This system, combined with the general absence of credit rating agencies, makes it extraordinarily difficult for suppliers to assess whether potential customers are able to pay.[32] In contrast, ability to supply goods is usually easy to check—finished goods inventories and spare production capacity are easily monitored.

---

30. There are separate registers (or *kartoteki*) for private and governmental debt. The priority for payment is established by article 855 of the Russian Civil Code, as modified by a December 1997 decision of the Russian Constitutional Court. (*Vestnik Konstitutsionnogo Suda Rossiiskoi Federatsii*, no. 1, pp. 23–31, 1998) In most instances, a court judgment is a prerequisite for placing a debt on the kartoteka.

31. Payments are further complicated by the perpetuation of the dual money system created during the Soviet period. Most payments are made using "noncash" (*beznalichnye*) money, i.e. through bank accounts. Interviews reveal that some enterprises have resorted to paying their bills in person with "cash" (*nalichnye*) money. But doing so raises obvious personal safety and logistical issues.

32. Enterprises used a credit rating agency to investigate the ability of customers to pay in only 4% of transactions. Fafchamps (1996a, pp. 427–28) stresses the absence of a "mechanism by which information about bad payers is widely shared among firms" as a cause of problems in contract enforcement in Ghana.

Prepayment is one solution to this fundamental informational asymmetry, in which the customer's ability to pay is much more difficult to ascertain than the supplier's ability to produce. Demands for prepayment are certainly widespread. In a sample of transactions collected in the survey, 75% of enterprises included a clause in their sales contract requiring some sort of prepayment. Forty-one percent of enterprises demanded full (100%) prepayment. The average prepayment commitment of customers was 54% and the amount actually paid was 48%. Seventy-four percent of contracts for material supplies required some prepayment, with 45% of such contracts requiring full prepayment. For procurement, the average contractual commitment was 58%, with actual payments amounting to 50% of the total price.

Interviews conducted during case studies suggest that the level of personal trust is inversely correlated with the amount of prepayment. Enterprise managers consistently stressed that they are less likely to insist on prepayment from long-term partners who have a track record of paying on time. Thus, first-time customers paid 60% of the purchase price in advance, whereas other customers paid 44% of the total price.[33] Other mechanisms of self-enforcement serve as substitutes for prepayment. Advance payments average 36% when the supplier holds some of the customer's property, but 49% otherwise. Market power is also a substitute: an enterprise is less likely to breach when it has few alternatives and knows that it will have to return to the same contractual partner at a future time (Kranton, 1996). Thus, customers pay 44% in advance to dominant suppliers, while non-dominant suppliers are pre-paid 53%.[34]

Of course, self-enforcement of transactions in goods is not the only reason for prepayment. Lack of available credit has left some enterprises unable to finance the costs of production. This is particularly a problem for those enterprises with a long production cycle or those that manufacture big-ticket

---

33. Review of sales department records in several enterprises in early 1998 shows that first-time customers are often asked to provide various sorts of certificates of good standing from bank, tax authorities, and corporate registry offices. These documents, while helpful, did not entirely calm the fears of sales managers, who still preferred prepayment. Their ability to demand and obtain prepayment was also affected by the market power of the potential customer.

34. Dominance is defined as more than 65% of the market, as in the Russian anti-monopoly law (Art. 4, "O vnesnenii," 1995).

custom-made equipment. Of the surveyed enterprises, 68% received advance payment sufficient to cover the cost of the material inputs needed for production.

Barter is another mechanism that has elements of self-enforcement, but which has many other causes (Aukutsionek, 1998). Barter can help self-enforcement in several ways. Barter removes some of the difficulties of checking on the partner's financial circumstances: the ability to pay depends more on production capacity and inventories, which can be easily monitored. When two enterprises supply each other's production needs, the mutual ability to hold-up the other enterprise can create an incentive to perform. Perhaps most important in the Russian environment, a seller might more reliably collect a barter payment, since indebted enterprises are always likely to have their monetary resources taken by creditors, including the tax authorities.

The desire for self-enforcing agreements is only part of the explanation for the current prevalence of barter, and its dramatic increase over the past six years.[35] Barter transactions can take many different forms depending on the circumstances. Sometimes they are bilateral; in other cases they involve an entire chain (*tsepochka*) of enterprises. In this latter case, barter transactions might fall into the category of third party enforcement: there are many examples of barter chains where intermediaries (including former Soviet officials) have constructed chains of mutual dependence among enterprises.[36]

Third-Party Enforcement

Other enterprises are the critical third party players for Russian transactions. Table 3 shows that almost half of all enterprises use the possibility of damaging a customer's reputation with other enterprises as a way of reacting to non-performance. More generally, 90% of sales directors surveyed reported that their contacts with non-customer enterprises have been helpful in customer relations. When researching the ability of their customers to pay, 22%

---

35. In 1992, an average of 10% of the sales of surveyed enterprises took place via barter, whereas by 1996, this figure had risen to 39%. Likewise, the average percentage of material supplies that were obtained by barter in 1992 was 10.5, compared to 42% in 1996. For a breakdown of barter rates regionally, see Hendley, Murrell, and Ryterman, 1999b.

36. Since high debt levels often limit enterprises' access to their bank accounts, making it impossible for them to pay for goods directly, they can only obtain inputs with the help of third-party intermediaries.

of enterprises sought information from other enterprises, more than for any other source. Those enterprises that sought such information were more likely to use the enforcement strategy of telling other enterprises about non-performance.

Table 2 indicates that 15% of procurement directors have sought the assistance of other enterprises when problems arise with their suppliers. The relative standing of the "other enterprises" option is the same in both tables—this is the most used option apart from direct enterprise-to-enterprise contacts and litigation (or its shadow.) The differences between the frequency of use of the other enterprise option between the sales (48%) and procurement (15%) sides is not surprising. Defaults are more common in sales than in procurement transactions.

The use of informal enterprise networks for enforcement has only a weak formal counterpart. The data in Tables 2 and 3 show the peripheral role of business associations and financial industrial groups (FIG). Despite the fact that 28% of the surveyed enterprises belong to some sort of business association or FIG, only a small proportion of enterprises call upon these associations for help in solving transactional problems.[37] In addition, only 3.5% of enterprises used associations or FIGs to check up on the ability to pay of prospective customers.[38]

Table 2 confirms the unimportance of political parties or movements in post-Soviet inter-enterprise relations despite the heritage of Communist Party officials as the universal fixers of the Soviet economy (Granick, 1961). Only one of our 328 surveyed enterprises had sought help from a political party to prevent or solve its problems with suppliers, reflecting the disintegration of the old Communist Party structure and the changed role of the new political parties.

Private Enforcement. Two basic strategies for private enforcement exist in Russia, as in most countries. The first, dispute resolution through private arbitration, is benign. The second, enforcement by private agents often through intimidation, is more ominous, both for the parties and for society

37. Germany and Great Britain, in which industry and trade associations have been institutionalized, provide interesting contrasts to Russia. See Lane and Bachmann, 1997, pp. 234–43.

38. Our data suggest that the importance attributed to FIGs by some commentators is overstated. E.g., Eckstein et al., 1998, pp. 87–92.

more generally. Our data indicate that neither is important for Russian enterprises.

Private arbitration tribunals, known as *treteiskie* courts, have always existed in Russia (Vinogradova, 1997; Pistor, 1996; Halverson, 1996). During the Soviet period, their use was restricted mostly to transactions involving foreign companies. Even this use was limited, since foreigners preferred Stockholm to Moscow. Disputes between Soviet enterprises that could not be resolved through negotiation were generally submitted to *gosarbitrazh*.

During the past few years, new *treteiskie* courts have begun to sprout up across Russia.[39] Russian law places no restriction on their use. (See Hendrix, 1997; O'Donnell and Ratnikov, 1997.) Any enterprises can agree that disputes will be decided by a particular *treteiskii* court and in the presence of such an agreement the *arbitrazh* courts will usually decline to hear the case, respecting the bargain of the parties to cede jurisdiction to the *treteiskii* court.[40] (Arts. 23, 85–3,107, 1995 APK) Notwithstanding the elimination of the institutional barriers to the use of *treteiskii* courts and the increased ease of access, the data in Table 2 indicate that few enterprises are using them.[41] Those enterprises that have used the *treteiskie* courts have found them effective, thus suggesting that their judgments have been respected.[42] A full analysis of the reasons why Russian enterprises shy away from the *treteiskie* courts is beyond the scope of this paper, but interviews with enterprise lawyers suggest that the cost and

39. The creation of such courts is often funded by Western sources, based on the assumptions that the arbitrazh courts are hopeless and that instituting alternative dispute resolution mechanisms is the best response to this problem.

40. Absent such a clause, the *arbitrazh* courts exercise jurisdiction. Of course, if all the parties agree, any dispute can be submitted to a *treteiskie* court or to international commercial arbitration.

41. Halverson (1996, p. 92) notes that "in spite of the many domestic arbitration tribunals that have been established in Russia during recent years, these tribunals are seldom utilized by Russian businessmen." According to Hendrix (1997, p. 1080), about 500 cases are filed each year with the International Commercial Arbitration Court in Moscow, the busiest of the *treteiskie* study. The caseload has remained at this level since 1992. By contrast, the *arbitrazh* courts decided more than 340,000 cases in 1997, more than 11% of which were heard in Moscow. (See Sudebno-arbitrazhnaya statistika, 1998) The total number of cases heard in 1998 exceeded 398,000, an increase of more than 16% (Sudebno-arbitrazhnaya statistika, 1999).

42. As with other private tribunals, enterprises must pay to use these *treteiskie* courts. The amount is substantially greater than the filing fees required by the *arbitrazh* courts. (See Hendrix, 1997, p. 1081) Enterprises are unlikely to go forward with a case in these *treteiskie* courts unless sure that the other side will comply. *Treteiskii* court judgements can be enforced by *arbitrazh* courts, but this is not a desirable outcome.

the unfamiliarity of procedural rules more than outweigh the speed and confidentiality that come with private arbitration.

When the issue of private enforcement in Russia is raised, few think first of *treteiskie* courts. The more common image is of the nefarious Russian mafia, i.e., non-state agents using coercion.[43] A common wisdom has emerged in the media and even among scholars, that Russian enterprises routinely rely on private enforcement and, absent such services, would not be able to stay in business. For example, Leitzel et al. (1995, pp. 28–29) argued that, "...perhaps [the mafia's] main benefit is contract enforcement....Unsavory as the mafia's enforcement tactics are, they give Russian business people the confidence to enter into contracts that would otherwise be too risky." (See also Shelley, 1995, p. 830; DiPaola, 1996, pp. 158–64; Hay, Shleifer, and Vishny, 1996; Varese, 1997, p. 580; Syfert, 1999) This is grounded in the assumption that the *arbitrazh* courts are unworkable (Volkov, 1999, p. 742; Shlapentokh, 1997, p. 875; Black and Kraakman, 1996, p. 1926). However, our data indicate that the assumed futility of appealing to the courts is much overstated. When we asked general directors to compare the courts and private enforcement along key criteria, the directors rated private enforcement superior only on one criterion, speed. They considered the courts better on competence, cost, certainty of enforcement, and confidentiality. This evidence hardly suggests that enterprises are turning to the mafia out of frustration with the *arbitrazh* courts.[44]

Table 2 shows only a very limited use of private enforcers to encourage contractual compliance, less than 3% of enterprises having used private firms to prevent or resolve problems with suppliers.[45] Further buttressing this interpretation is the fact that only 2.5% of enterprises use private security firms to

---

43. We offer no definition of the term mafia. We use the term in the manner it is commonly used, a colloquial, hopelessly imprecise reference to all manner of semi-legal and illegal groups.

44. In the study reporting on the pilot for this survey (Hendley et al., 1997), some enterprises reported that sometimes the mafia simply implemented the judgments of the *arbitrazh* courts.

45. On the assumption that the mafia specializes in debt collection, it is tempting to conclude that this result reflects our inclusion of this question in Table 2, which focuses on supplier problems, rather than in Table 3, which focuses on customer problems. But even if the assumption is correct, the conclusion is not. More than half of the contracts studied involve prepayment, so that supplier non-performance is the most likely cause of a breach.

investigate customer's ability to pay. If contract enforcement were really the domain of such firms, then it would be unlikely that they would have such a small a role in providing information on the probability of contract fulfillment.

To be sure, there are powerful criminal groups in Russia and enterprises are concerned with security. Half of the surveyed firms either have an internal security service that assists in collecting debts and delivering output or have hired an outside security firm to perform these services.[46] These results suggest that security services have the more prosaic mandate of protecting money or property, rather than the task of enforcing contracts through intimidation of trading partners.

Administrative Levers of the State

Contract enforcement during the Soviet period was intimately tied to the planning and supply systems. Enterprises could expect help from ministries and other state agencies in obtaining the resources necessary to meet the plan. Soft budgets guaranteed continued existence. This institutional heritage was common to the vast majority of the surveyed enterprises, since 88% were state-owned at some point. These enterprises are now generally privatized and the state's ownership stake has been eliminated in most.[47] The mutually re-enforcing system of plan dictates and soft budgets has vanished.

The tendency to turn to the state had become deeply ingrained over the decades of Soviet power. Enterprises remain in fairly close contact with the state: in 66% of enterprises, senior managers meet with local or oblast government officials at least once a month and in 27% of enterprises meetings occur this frequently with federal officials. Regular meetings do not necessarily indicate a continuation of the old patterns, however. The Russian government, like governments in all market economies, exerts considerable regulatory power. The key issue in this paper is whether these meetings deal with enforcement of agreements.

---

46. More specifically, 24% of enterprises use internal security services (11% on a daily basis), and 38% use outside security firms (8% on a daily basis). Some, of course, use both.

47. Seventy-seven percent of enterprises surveyed have been privatized. Local and oblast-level governments own shares in 10% of the enterprises; the federal government owns shares in 13%.

The results of Tables 2 and 3 indicate that few enterprises look to the state for help in solving problems with customers and suppliers. Not surprisingly, petitions to the local or oblast government are more frequent than to the federal government. Such contacts are easier to organize and more likely to be grounded in a personal relationship. What is particularly revealing is that enterprises rate this strategy's effectiveness (column 3) very low compared to all the other options included in the Tables. Similarly, while general directors of 16% of the surveyed enterprises reported that the local or oblast government had attempted to solve problems with suppliers or customers, on balance, they viewed such mediation as detrimental.

The simplest explanation of these results is that some actors continue old patterns of behavior in new circumstances where the behavior is much less effective. Thus, older enterprises are more likely to adopt a strategy of seeking state intervention in solving problems with trading partners.[48] Enterprises' use of this strategy is strongly correlated with their receipt of direct subsidies from the state, but only 8.5% of enterprises receive such subsidies.[49] The strategy of seeking the state's help with transactional problems is unrelated to the level of present state ownership, but strongly correlated with prior state ownership. Of the enterprises that were previously state owned, 11% used this strategy, whereas only 5% of enterprises that were never owned by the state did so. These results suggest that the state's tightening fiscal constraints are more important than privatization in changing the long-established patterns of behavior.

The transition to the market has witnessed the introduction of a significant number of new institutions, including bankruptcy commissions, the securities commission, and anti-monopoly committees (AMC). The AMCs are potentially important at the level of enterprise transactions, because, in theory, their task is to stamp out any anti-competitive behavior, for example, by punishing a dominant enterprise that uses its market power to force a trading partner to accept a contractual breach. (See Sahlas and Reshetnikova, 1997.) If an enterprise is subject to such behavior on the part of a trading partner, it can appeal to the local AMC for relief. Although this structure has been in

---

48. Of firms formed in 1990 or before, 11% have used this strategy, but only 6% of firms founded after 1990 have used it.

49. Of enterprises receiving direct state subsidies, 21% use this strategy. Only 9% of those not receiving subsidies use it.

place since 1991, it remains peripheral in transactional issues. Only about 10% of the surveyed enterprises had turned to the AMCs for assistance on any matter during the two years preceding our survey.[50] And as Table 3 reveals, enterprises view the AMC's as ineffective in matters connected to transactions. These data and interviews with enterprise officials suggest that enterprises are not actively mobilizing the new market-oriented state institutions on their behalf.

Shadow of the Law

There are strategies that raise the specter of litigation, often through the threat of filing suit or of pursuing punitive remedies. In Russia, as elsewhere, such warnings often spur greater interest in negotiated settlements. Prior to 1995, enterprises had to send letters (*pretenzia*) demanding performance from defaulting trading partners before filing a lawsuit.[51] *Pretenzia* remain in widespread use, despite the fact that they are no longer a pre-condition to a lawsuit. Table 2 indicates that well over half of the enterprises use *pretenzia* as a method of dealing with problem customers, and that this tactic is seen as relatively effective. Surveyed enterprises report on average that they send a warning letter to 38% of delinquent customers. Enterprises with legal departments are much more likely to send *pretenzia*. While 71% of such enterprises resorted to *pretenzia* at one time or another, only 50% of those without a legal department ever sent them. Thus, even though *pretenzia* are not formal legal documents, many firms view their preparation as primarily within the purview of lawyers.

The continued use of *pretenzia* might be the result of routinized behavior that persists even though no longer mandatory. But sending these letters was never an empty gesture: it was part of the effort to pressure a recalcitrant counterpart. *Pretenzia*, which typically include a threat of litigation, ratchet up the pressure from merely reminding the counterpart of missed deadlines. In the sample of transactions collected in the survey, 24% of enterprises reported receiving an informal or verbal complaint about their performance. *Pretenzia* were received by 8% of enterprises. Penalties were assessed against

---

50. An additional 10% of enterprises had been the target of an AMC investigation during the past two years.
51. Failure to send a *pretenzia* was automatic grounds for dismissal of the claim. (Arts. 79, 80, and 86, 1992 APK)

5%, and paid by 3%. Litigation commenced with respect to 1%. This implies that the vast majority of problems are resolved through informal reminders, without even having to send *pretenzia*, and that most of the remaining disputes are resolved prior to initiating lawsuits.[52]

As the forgoing indicates, penalties are an element of bargaining within the shadow of the law, rather than a mechanism of self-enforcement or of relational contracting. Enterprises that routinely include penalty clauses in their sales contracts emerge as more likely to send *pretenzia*.[53] In contrast, when general directors believe that demands for penalties will damage the relationship with the customer, *pretenzia* are used less frequently.

Penalties for contractual non-performance are traditionally permitted in civil law countries, and Russia is no exception.[54] During the Soviet period, penalties were assessed mostly for late delivery or sub-standard quality. The amounts were minimal, providing a signal to ministries rather than punishment to enterprises. As inter-enterprise arrears mounted in the early 1990s, penalties for late payment became routine.[55] The surveyed enterprises report that 53% of their sales contracts include a clause penalizing late payment. But inclusion of penalties in a contract does not imply that late payment immediately triggers demands for penalties. Although more than half of enterprises have threatened delinquent customers with a demand for penalties in the two years prior to the survey (see Table 3), sales directors report that penalties are actually collected in only 8% of cases where payment is overdue. These data, buttressed by interviews, imply that penalty clauses are used mostly to provide negotiating room.

---

52. These data suggest that for every 100 transactions, 24 experience potential disputes. Of these, 16 are resolved through informal complaints, 7 are resolved through threats of litigation and/or penalties, and 1 will be litigated.

53. Of the enterprises whose use of penalties in sales contracts is above the median level, 68% use *pretenzia*, whereas usage drops to 49% among enterprises below the median level.

54. U.S. law allows parties to predetermine the damages that would result from a breach, but such liquidated damages must be reasonably related to actual losses. Penalties are not enforceable. See Restatement (Second) Contracts, Section 356(1); Section 2–718(1) of the Uniform Commercial Code; and Clarkson, Miller and Muris (1978).

55. A 1992 presidential decree authorized industrial enterprises to charge penalties of up to 0.5% of the amount owed per day for their sales and procurement contracts (Postanovlenie, 1992). Article 395 of the Civil Code also allows for penalties calculated on the basis of the Central Bank's annual discount rate. A 1997 plenum of the Higher *Arbitrazh* Court attempted to clarify what sorts of penalties can be awarded by the courts. See Postanovlenie, 1996.

While collateral arrangements are commonly used in market economies as a means of enforcing contractual obligations without resorting to litigation, this practice has not yet emerged among Russian industrial enterprises. Only 4% of enterprise sales and procurement contracts incorporate a formal collateral arrangement. Interviews suggest that the cost of the mandatory notarization (1.5% of the value of the transaction) discourages many enterprises from using collateral as security. The use of informal collateral, the possession of the other party's property discussed above, is more common.

Litigation

Going to court is rarely the preferred method of resolving disputes. Russia is no exception. As elsewhere, only a small fraction of disputes between trading partners ever end up in court.

Russia has a dual court system. The *arbitrazh* courts, which came into existence in 1991 as an institutional successor to *gosarbitrazh*, exercise jurisdiction over business disputes involving legal entities. (Art. 22, 1995 APK, Iakovlev and Iukov, 1996, pp. 43–63) Courts of general jurisdiction hear all other legal matters. As market reforms have progressed, the disputes submitted to the *arbitrazh* court have grown more and more complicated. Not surprisingly, cases now take longer to process. The increased use of penalties means that the amounts being demanded are no longer symbolic. The *arbitrazh* courts have struggled to come up with mechanisms for ensuring compliance by the losers. (See Hendley,1998b) It is hardly surprising, therefore, that the surveyed enterprise lawyers expressed nostalgia for the halcyon days of *gosarbitrazh*. They believe that *gosarbitrazh* was quicker and cheaper to use, and that decisions were better implemented. But this is surely a consequence of the greater complexity of dispute settlement in a market economy.

An odd consensus has emerged among commentators that the *arbitrazh* courts are not up to the task before them and irrelevant to the needs of the economy. These courts, according to this consensus, are compromised by the judges' lack of competence in market economics, the persistence of outside influence (the "telephone law" familiar from the Soviet period), and the difficulty of enforcing judgments. As a result, enterprises are shunning the courts in favor of private enforcement. (See, for example, Halverson, 1996, pp. 100–103; O'Donnell and Ratnikov, 1996, pp. 838–41; Black and Kraakman, 1996; Hay and Shleifer, 1998; Hay, Shleifer, and Vishny, 1996 pp. 560–62;

Syfert, 1999, p. 381.) Our data refute key elements of this common wisdom. Enterprises were asked to rate the importance of eight potential obstacles (enforcement, cost, competence, etc.) to submitting their disputes to the *arbitrazh* courts. The lack of enforcement was rated as the most important problem, whereas the judges' lack of knowledge was rated as relatively unimportant. Moreover, as we have made clear above, enterprises rate the courts as superior to private security firms on most criteria.

Enterprises clearly regard the courts as a viable option when negotiated settlements prove elusive.[56] For example, during 1996, 40% of the surveyed enterprises had initiated 6 or more lawsuits; and 28% had been sued 6 or more times by other enterprises.[57] Tables 2 and 3 show that 61% of enterprises have filed claims, or threatened to file claims, against delinquent customers at some time in the two years prior to the survey, and 25% of enterprises have done so against suppliers. Moreover, as those Tables demonstrate, enterprises give the courts a relatively high ranking in terms of effectiveness. It is clear that, apart from direct enterprise-to-enterprise contacts, threatened or actual use of the courts is the most important method of contract enforcement in Russia.

In the view of Russian lawyers, the inability to enforce judgments is the single biggest shortcoming of the *arbitrazh* courts. The chairman of the Higher *Arbitrazh* Court, which stands at the apex of the *arbitrazh* court system, has acknowledged that implementation is the Achilles' heel of the system (Vasil'eva, 1996; see also Hendrix, 1997, pp. 1098–1100; Hendley, 1998a). Yet when asked whether improving the enforceability of *arbitrazh* court decisions would help in developing transactions with new suppliers, general directors felt this would have little impact. Thus, despite the perennial complaints about enforcement, enterprises do not believe that reforms in this area would make much difference.

Enterprises with legal departments go to court more frequently: 77% of enterprises with legal departments have gone to *arbitrazh* court, in contrast to

56. In a 1997 survey of 269 Russian enterprises, Johnson, McMillan and Woodruff (1999) found that a majority (54.4%) of enterprises that had disputes with other enterprises had initiated a claim in *arbitrazh* court.

57. Significant numbers of enterprises had not used the *arbitrazh* courts at all during 1996. Twenty-eight percent had no cases as a plaintiff, and 42% had no cases as defendant. For a more detailed breakdown of litigation patterns, see Hendley, Murrell, and Ryterman, 1999a.

51% of the enterprises without legal departments. As with *pretenzia*, this indicates that firms regard litigation as the responsibility of lawyers. These results may seem natural to Western observers, but are intriguing in the Russian context, since legal representation is neither required nor routinely observed in *arbitrazh* cases. (See Hendley, Murrell, and Ryterman, 1999a.)

Complementarities Between Strategies

An interesting question arising from Tables 2 and 3 is whether the propensities to use different strategies are related. Examining this question gives insights into the nature of transactional strategies and the development of Russian institutions. For example, is relational contracting inconsistent with law-related approaches (Macaulay, 1963, Williamson, 1985)? Do vestiges of the old Soviet system appear in market enforcement mechanisms? Is there a separation between those enterprises that use networks and those that use legal institutions (Kali, 1998)? Does government enforcement activity bolster market institutions? What are the differences between the roles of the federal and local governments?

Of course, most strategies will be substitutes; if an enterprise has the help of other enterprises in enforcing its contracts, for example, then the enterprise will have less need to go to court or to enlist private enforcement firms, other things equal. Thus, we will not focus on patterns of substitutes. Rather, the more interesting question is which strategies are complements: are increases in the use of strategy X associated with greater use of strategy Y, *ceteris paribus*?

We look for complementarities using simple correlations, employing a transformation of the data summarized in Tables 2 and 3. Let N be the number of methods of dealing with problems in relationships that are listed in Tables 2 and 3.[58] Denote by S_{ij} the effectiveness score given by enterprise i to method j. (These are the scores in the last columns of Tables 2 and 3.) Searching for complementarities using the S_{ij} would give misleading results: it would be natural for S_{ij} to be positively correlated with S_{ik} simply because enterprises with many problems will use many methods of addressing these

---

58. N equals 15 in this analysis. In Tables 2 and 3, there are 17 conceptually distinct methods listed. (Some methods are repeated in the two tables.) We exclude from the analysis the two methods (political parties and social, religious etc. organizations) that are used by fewer than 1% of the enterprises.

problems. Thus, use of the S_{ij} does not reflect an adjustment for the basic *ceteris paribus* condition in the notion of complementarity; i.e., one should compare patterns of strategy use adjusting for overall use of problem-solving strategies. This suggests that the data will reveal complementarities more incisively if we examine the relative use of strategies. Thus, we focus on:

$$S_{ij} = S_{ij} / \sum_{k=1}^{N} S_{ik}$$

We judge strategy j to be complementary to strategy k if s_{ij} is significantly positively correlated with s_{ik} across enterprises, i.[59] Diagram 1 summarizes the results of this search for complementarities. Any two strategies that are complementary to each other appear together in an enclosed oval. If two strategies are not contained in the same oval, then they are not complements.[60]

Of course, given a sufficiently tangled web of geometric shapes, it would be possible to represent any set of complementarities in such a way. Thus, the diagram's message lies in its simple structure. For example, although there are many complementarities between the various third party and governmental enforcement mechanisms, the mechanisms can be arrayed so that these complementarities appear only as links between neighbors. The legal system complements only adjacent elements of this linear arrangement of third-parties.

What insights does the diagram offer?

1. The relational contracting strategies largely stand on their own, supporting the conclusion that these strategies do not naturally combine with others that look outside the bilateral relationship.

---

59. We use 5% levels of significance in one-sided tests.

60. The Diagram very closely represents the patterns of statistically significant correlation coefficients, with some slight modifications to simplify its structure. There are 19 correlation coefficients that are significantly greater than zero at a 5% level of significance. The Diagram shows 22 pairs of complements: 19 that correspond to the statistically significant correlation coefficients, plus three more. The three additional pairs are: informal meetings of enterprise personnel and informing other enterprises (positive and significant at the 10% level), informing other enterprises and reporting to a business association (positive and significant at the 10% level), and the intervention of banks and the use of pretenzia (indistinguishable from zero). In imposing a slightly more simplified structure on the diagram than that derived from a purely mechanical exercise, we view that diagram as a theory suggested by the data. None of the conclusions that we draw is dependent upon these simplifications.

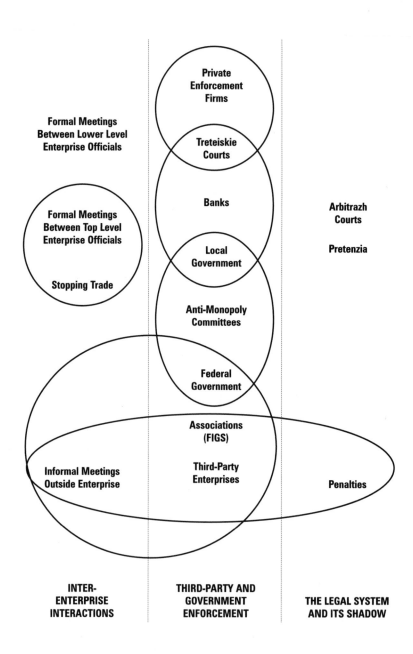

DIAGRAM 1: THE COMPLEMENTARITIES BETWEEN TRANSACTIONAL STRATEGIES

2. The joint complementarity of five mechanisms appearing in the lower part of the diagram is notable. Older enterprises are more likely to rely on contacts with third-party enterprises; enterprise associations are often attempts to recreate defunct Soviet structures; the federal government is the institutional successor of the only powerful element of the Soviet government; penalties are a traditional remedy for contractual non-performance dating back to Soviet days (though the amount and impetus for seeking them has changed); and lastly informal contacts outside the enterprise suggest long-standing ties. Hence, all the strategies that involve remnants of the old system seem to be complements. The fact that the federal government is associated with this group of strategies suggests that its role in encouraging the use of the new market-related institutions has been ambiguous, at best.

3. One set of complementary strategies combines the use of institutions that have effectively been reinvented in the post-Soviet era. Banks, courts, and local government, which are together in the diagram, represent institutions whose status and independence has risen dramatically in the 1990s.[61] Enterprises using these strategies base their transactions on decentralized institutions breaking with the past in their transactional behavior. It is notable that local governments, rather than the federal government, are an element in this approach.

4. Some enterprises prefer to rely on the state, with the role of anti-monopoly committees reflecting their position as an arm of government, rather than their mandate as a facilitator of competition.

5. Finally, private enforcement firms and the *treteiskie* courts seem to be complements, but so few enterprises use these alternatives that we would attribute little significance to this observation.

---

61. Independence and status are, of course, relative concepts. While the courts have undergone substantial reform over the past decade, few would regard them as truly independent or high status institutions. Yet progress in this direction has been made. See generally Solomon (1998).

Perhaps the most fascinating insight in the diagram is the light that it sheds on the impetus behind institutional development.[62] The federal government is associated with an approach to transactional strategies that emphasizes the vestiges of the Soviet system. Appeals to the local government are complementary with the use of institutions that are central to a market economy. The development of institutions designed to facilitate market transactions may have been adversely affected by the ongoing struggle between center and periphery. Legal reforms centered on the federal government might have fallen afoul of the connections between it and the legacies of the Soviet system. The federal government's failure to embrace the forces for change at the local level may have lessened the effectiveness of institutions that are important in aiding the efficiency and predictability of business relations.

Conclusions

This article represents a first attempt to fill in the gaps in our knowledge about how Russian enterprises do business. We have focused on the strategies pursued in efforts to prevent or solve problems with trading partners. Our analysis shows a tendency to work out problems without resorting to outsiders (whether private or governmental). In the chaotic world of the transition, strategies that use trust—both personal and calculative—emerge as critical. Interviews with managers confirm the importance of personal relationships or at least having an opportunity for face-to-face meetings to judge integrity. Equally important is an assessment of the material interests of potential (or long term) partners. Whether the relatively important role of trust-based strategies will wane as the Russian market develops remains to be seen. Certainly, the costs of evaluating the trustworthiness of potential counterparts should decrease over time, since many of these costs are associated with transitional phenomena, such as the presence of large numbers of indebted enterprises.

At first glance, our finding that many Russian enterprises have filed claims in the *arbitrazh* courts may seem to conflict with the propensity to work out problems through direct contacts. Yet, on-site interviews reveal

---

62. In making these comments, we assume that our six cities are representative of Russia as a whole.

that enterprises regard these two strategies as parts of a larger whole. Rarely do they respond to non-performance by immediately filing a lawsuit. Instead, they try to work out problems, resorting to the *arbitrazh* courts only when negotiations break down. The decision on when to abandon negotiations is affected by myriad considerations, including the length and depth of the underlying relationship and the relative market power of the two parties. (See generally Felstiner et al., 1980–81)

The idea of litigation as a last-ditch alternative—but an acceptable one— may seem obvious to many readers. But to those who are familiar with the literature on Russian legal developments, this idea is somewhat surprising. Almost without exception, this literature contends that the *arbitrazh* courts are not being actively used, and that their pervasive flaws have doomed them to peripheral status.[63] As our data show, this impression is simply wrong. Why commentators have been so willing to write off the *arbitrazh* courts is something of a mystery. Perhaps the usual carping of litigants about delays and perceived injustices were taken too literally, or perhaps Western observers have held the Russian courts to an unrealistically high standard. While we are not arguing that the *arbitrazh* courts are anywhere near perfection, our data clearly document that they play a significant role.[64]

Our analysis also sheds light on the role of the mafia in Russia. A common view of the mafia's rise is that it is a functional response to the weakness of official contract enforcement mechanisms (Shleifer, 1994, p. 103; Leitzel et al, 1995; DiPaola, 1996). An alternative view is that there is little redeeming social value to the mafia; it is strong because the state is weak in controlling crime and because the institutional environment engenders criminal activity through corruption (Handelman, 1995). Our data strongly suggest that the

---

63. Not all commentators have completely dismissed the *arbitrazh* courts, e.g., Hendrix (1997), Pistor (1996), Halverson (1996).

64. In a previous study (Hendley et al, 1997), based on the pilot interviews for the survey whose data are reported here, we reached conclusions that might be interpreted as assigning a smaller role to law and legal institutions than we do in this paper. In that study, we focused, much more than in the present paper, on active strategies for restructuring relationships and less on the role of the shadow of the law and the use of courts in resolving disputes in existing agreements. We nevertheless noted the relative esteem in which the courts were held, at least compared to other institutions, and the frequency with which enterprises were using courts.

first view is greatly over-stated and that the rise of the mafia has little to do with the demand for contract enforcement.

We began this paper by pointing to the paucity of detailed empirical information on the relative importance of the various strategies that businesses use to govern their transactions. This gap in empirical knowledge is as true for developed economies as it is for transition countries. Thus, the results appearing above have a significance that is wider than simply understanding present-day Russia. Of course, Russia has many special characteristics, making generalization to other countries hazardous. Indeed, it is now commonly assumed that the mix of transactional strategies depends critically on deep underlying characteristics of the country in question (Greif, 1996; Uzzi, 1996). This is of course a theory based on anecdotal observation, a theory that has not been tested systematically.[65] At the very least, we have provided a methodology that could be replicated for other countries and the results for Russia, which could form the basis for testing this theory.

BIBLIOGRAPHY

Arbitrazhnyi protsesual'nyi kodeks Rossiiskoi Federatsii [1992 APK]. *Vestnik Vysshego Arbitrazhnogo Suda Rossiiskoi Federatsii*, no. 5, pp. 5–47, 1992.

Arbitrazhnyi protsesual'nyi kodeks Rossiiskoi Federatsii [1995 APK]. *Vestnik Vysshego Arbitrazhnogo Suda Rossiiskoi Federatsii*, no. 6, pp. 25–79, 1995.

Aslund, Anders. *How Russia Became a Market Economy.* Washington, D.C.: The Brookings Institution, 1995.

Aukutsionek, Sergei. "Industrial Barter in Russia." *Communist Economies & Economic Transformation*, 10:2, pp. 179–88, 1998.

Berliner, Joseph S. *Factory and Manager in the USSR.* Cambridge: Harvard University Press, 1957.

Berliner, Joseph S. *Soviet Industry from Stalin to Gorbachev: Essays on Management and Innovation.* Ithaca: Cornell University Press, 1988.

Bernstein, Lisa. "Opting Out of the Legal System: Extralegal Contractual Relations in the Diamond Industry." *Journal of Legal Studies*, 21:1, pp. 115–157, 1992.

Black, Bernard, and Reinier Kraakman. "A Self-Enforcing Model of Corporate Law." *Harvard Law Review*, 109:8, pp. 1911–82, 1996.

---

65. One exception is Sako's (1992) study, examining the relative roles of relationships and the law in the UK and Japan.

Clarkson, Kenneth W., Roger LeRoy Miller, and Timothy J. Muris. "Liquidated Damages v. Penalties: Sense or Nonsense?" *Wisconsin Law Review,* 1978:2, pp. 351–390, 1978.

Cooter, Robert, Stephen Marks and Robert Mnookin, "Bargaining in the Shadow of the Law: A Testable Model of Strategic Behavior" *Journal of Legal Studies,* XI(2), pp. 225–251, 1982

Deakin, Simon, Christel Lane, and Frank Wilkinson. "Contract Law, Trust Relations, and Incentives for Cooperation: A Comparative Study" in Simon Deakin and Jonathan Michie, eds., *Contracts, Cooperation, and Competition.* Oxford, 1997.

de Soto, Hernando. *The Other Path: The Invisible Revolution in the Third World.* New York: Harper & Row, 1989.

DiPaola, Peter Daniel. "The Criminal Time Bomb: An Examination of the Effect of the Russian *Mafiya* on the Newly Independent States of the Former Soviet Union." *Indiana Journal of Global Legal Studies,* 4:1, pp. 145–81, 1996.

Eckstein, Harry, Frederic J. Fleron, Jr., Erik P. Hoffmann, and William M. Reisinger. *Can Democracy Take Root in Post-Soviet Russia? Explorations in State-Society Relations.* Lanham, Maryland: Rowman & Littlefield, 1998.

Ellickson, Robert C. *Order without Law: How Neighbors Settle Disputes.* Cambridge: Harvard University Press, 1991.

Ernst, Maurice, Michael Alexeev, and Paul Marer. *Transforming the Core: Restructuring Industrial Enterprises in Russia and Central Europe.* Boulder: Westview Press, 1996.

Esser, John P. "Institutionalizing Industry: The Changing Forms of Contract." *Law & Social Inquiry,* 21:3, pp. 593–629, 1996.

Evans, Peter. *Embedded Autonomy: States & Industrial Transformation.* Princeton: Princeton University Press, 1995.

Fafchamps, Marcel. "The Enforcement of Commercial Contracts in Ghana." *World Development,* 24:3, pp. 427–48, 1996a.

Fafchamps, Marcel. "Trade Credit in Zimbabwean Manufacturing." Stanford University, September 1996b.

Fafchamps, Marcel and Bart Minten. "Relationships and Traders in Madagascar." Stanford University, June 1998.

Feinman, Jay M. "The Significance of Contract Theory." *University of Cincinnati Law Review,* 58:4, pp. 1283–1318, 1990.

Felstiner, William L.F., Richard L. Abel, and Austin Sarat. "The Emergence and Transformation of Disputes: Naming, Blaming, Claiming ..." *Law & Society Review,* 15:3–4, pp. 631–54, 1980–81.

Galanter, Marc. "Why the 'Haves' Come Out Ahead: Speculations on the Limits of Legal Change." *Law and Society Review,* 9:1, pp. 95–160, 1974.

Gambetta, Diego. *Trust: Making and Breaking Cooperative Relations*. Oxford: Basil Blackwell, 1988.

Granick, David. *The Red Executive: A Study of the Organization Man in Russian Industry*. Garden City, N.Y.: Doubleday, 1960.

Granovetter, Mark. "Economic Action and Social Structure: The Problem of Embeddedness." *American Journal of Sociology*, 91:3, pp. 481–510, 1985.

Grazhdanskii kodeks RF (chast' pervaya) [GK]. *Sobranie zakonodatel'stva Rossiiskoi Federatsii*, no. 32, item 3301 (1994).

Greif, Avner. "Cultural Beliefs and the Organization of Society: A Historical and Theoretical Reflection on Collectivist and Individualist Societies." *Journal of Political Economy*, 102:5, pp. 912–50, 1994.

Greif, Avner. "Contracting, Enforcement, and Efficiency: Economics beyond the Law" in Michael Bruno and Boris Pleskovic, eds., *Proceedings of the World Bank Annual Conference on Development Economics 1996*. Washington, D.C.: The World Bank, 1996.

Greif, Avner. "Reputation and Coalitions in Medieval Trade: Evidence on the Maghribi Traders." *Journal of Economic History*, 49:4, pp. 857–82, 1989.

Greif, Avner, Paul Milgrom, and Barry R. Weingast. "Coordination, Commitment, and Enforcement: The Case of the Merchant Guild." *Journal of Political Economy*, 102:4, pp. 745–76, 1994.

Grossman, Gregory. "The 'Second Economy' of the USSR." *Problems of Communism*, 26:5, pp. 25–40, 1977.

Halverson, Karen. "Resolving Economic Disputes in Russia's Market Economy." *Michigan Journal of International Law*, 18:1, pp. 59–113, 1996.

Handelman, Stephen. *Comrade Criminal: Russia's New Mafiya*. New Haven: Yale University Press, 1995.

Hay, Jonathon R., and Andrei Shleifer. "Private Enforcement of Public Laws: A Theory of Legal Reform," *American Economic Review*, 88:2, pp. 398–402, 1998.

Hay, Jonathan R., Andrei Shleifer, and Robert W. Vishny. "Toward a theory of legal reform." *European Economic Review*, 40:3–5, pp. 559–67, 1996.

Hendley, Kathryn. "How Russian Enterprises Cope With Payments Problems." *Post-Soviet Affairs*, vol. 15, no. 3, pp. 201–34, 1999.

Hendley, Kathryn. "Growing Pains: Balancing Justice & Efficiency in the Russian Economic Courts," *Temple International and Comparative Law Journal*, vol. 12, no. 2, pp. 302–32, 1998a.

Hendley, Kathryn. "Remaking an Institution: The Transition in Russia from State Arbitrazh to Arbitrazh Courts." *American Journal of Comparative Law*, 46:1, pp. 93–127, 1998b.

Hendley, Kathryn. "Struggling to Survive: A Case Study of Adjustment at a Russian Enterprise." *Europe–Asia Studies*, 50:1, pp. 91–119, 1998c.

Hendley, Kathryn. *Trying to Make Law Matter: Legal Reform and Labor Law in the Soviet Union.* Ann Arbor: University of Michigan Press, 1996.

Hendley, Kathryn, Barry W. Ickes, Peter Murrell, and Randi Ryterman. "Observations on the Use of Law by Russian Enterprises." *Post-Soviet Affairs,* 13:1, pp. 19–41, 1997.

Hendley, Kathryn, Peter Murrell, and Randi Ryterman. "Do 'Repeat Players' Behave Differently in Russia? An Evaluation of Contractual and Litigation Behavior of Russian Enterprises." *Law & Society Review,* forthcoming, 1999a.

Hendley, Kathryn, Peter Murrell, and Randi Ryterman. "A Regional Analysis of Transactional Strategies of Russian Enterprises." *McGill Law Journal,* 44:2, pp. 433–72, 1999b.

Hendrix, Glenn P. "Business Litigation and Arbitration in Russia." *The International Lawyer,* 31:4, pp. 1075–1103, 1997.

Hillman, Robert A. *The Richness of Contract Law: An Analysis and Critique of Contemporary Theories of Contract Law.* Dordrecht, The Netherlands: Kluwer Academic Publishers, 1997.

Iakovlev, V.F., and M.K. Iukov, eds. *Kommentarii k Arbitrazhnomu protsessual'nomu kodeksu Rossiiskoi Federatsii.* Moscow: Kontrakt, 1996.

Jacob, Herbert. "The Elusive Shadow of the Law." *Law & Society Review,* 26:3, pp. 565–90, 1992.

Johnson, Simon, John McMillan, and Christopher Woodruff. "Contract Enforcement in Transition." Mimeo, January 1999.

Jones, Carol A.G. "Capitalism, Globalization and Rule of Law: An Alternative Trajectory of Legal Change in China." *Social and Legal Studies,* 3:2, pp. 195–221, 1994.

Kali, Raja. "Endogenous Business Networks." ITAM, Mexico, 1998.

Klein, Benjamin, and Keith B. Leffler. "The Role of Market Forces in Assuring Contractual Performance." *Journal of Political Economy,* 89:4, pp. 615–41, 1981.

Klein, Benjamin. "Why Hold-Ups Occur: The Self-Enforcing Range of Contractual Relationships." *Economic Inquiry,* 34:3, pp. 444–63, 1996.

Kranton, Rachel E. "Reciprocal Exchange: A Self-Sustaining System." *American Economic Review,* 86:4, pp. 830–51, 1996.

Kreps, David M., Paul Milgrom, John Roberts, and Robert Wilson. "Rational Cooperation in the Finitely Repeated Prisoners' Dilemma." *Journal of Economic Theory,* 27:2, pp. 245–52, 1982.

Kroll, Heidi. "Breach of Contract in the Soviet Economy." *Journal of Legal Studies,* 16:1, pp. 119–48, 1987.

Kroll, Heidi. "Monopoly and Transition to the Market," *Soviet Economy,* 7:2, pp. 143–74, 1991.

Landa, Janet Tai. *Trust, ethnicity, and identity: Beyond the new institutional economics of ethnic trading networks, contract law, and gift-exchange.* Economics, Cognition, and Society series. Ann Arbor: University of Michigan Press, 1994.

Lane, Christel, and Reinhard Bachmann. "Co-operation in inter-firm relations in Britain and Germany: the role of social institutions." *British Journal of Sociology,* 48:2, pp. 226–54, 1997.

Leitzel, Jim, Clifford Gaddy, and Michael Alekseev. "Mafiosi and Matrioshki: Organized Crime and Russian Reform." *The Brookings Review,* 13:1, pp. 26–29, 1995.

Macaulay, Stewart. "Non-Contractual Relations in Business: A Preliminary Study." *American Sociological Review,* 28:1, pp. 55–67, 1963.

Macaulay, Stewart. "Elegant Models, Empirical Pictures, and the Complexities of Contract." *Law & Society Review,* 11:3, pp. 507–28, 1977.

Macaulay, Stewart, John Kidwell, William Whitford, and Marc Galanter. *Contracts: Law in Action,* vol. 1. Charlottesville, Virginia: The Michie Company, 1995.

Macneil, Ian R. "Relational Contract: What We Do and Do Not Know." *Wisconsin Law Review,* 1985:3, pp. 483–525, 1985.

Masten, Scott E., ed. *Case studies in contracting and organization.* New York and Oxford: Oxford University Press, pp. xii, 344, 1996.

McFaul, Michael. "Why Russia's Politics Matter." *Foreign Affairs,* 74:1, pp. 87–99, 1995.

McMillan, John and Christopher Woodruff. "Networks, Trust, and Search in Vietnam's Emerging Private Sector." University of California, San Diego, March 1998.

Milgrom, Paul R., Douglass C. North, and Barry R. Weingast. "The Role of Institutions in the Revival of Trade: The Law Merchant, Private Judges, and the Champagne Fairs." *Economics & Politics,* 2:1, pp. 1–23, 1990.

Mishler, William, and Richard Rose. "Trust, Distrust and Skepticism: Popular Evaluations of Civil and Political Institutions in Post-Communist Societies." *Journal of Politics,* 59:2, pp. 418–51, 1997.

Mnookin, Robert H., and Lewis Kornhauser. "Bargaining in the Shadow of the Law: The Case of Divorce." *Yale Law Journal,* 88:5, pp. 950–97, 1979.

North, Douglass C. *Institutions, Institutional Change and Economic Performance.* Cambridge: Cambridge University Press, 1990.

O'Donnell, Neil F., and Kirill Y. Ratnikov. "Dispute Resolution in the Commercial Law Tribunals of the Russian Federation: Law and Practice." *North Carolina Journal of International Law and Commercial Regulation,* 22:3, pp. 795–873, 1996.

"O vnesenii izmenenii i dopolnenii v Zakon RSFSR 'O konkurentsii i ogranichenii monopolisticheskoi deyatel'nosti na tovarnykh rynakh,'" no. 22, item 1977, *Sobranie zakonodatel'stva Rossiiskoi Federatsii,* 1995.

Pistor, Katharina. "Supply and Demand for Contract Enforcement in Russia: Courts, Arbitration, and Private Enforcement." *Review of Central and East European Law,* 22:1, pp. 55–87, 1996.

Pomorski, Stanislaw. "State Arbitrazh in the U.S.S.R.: Development, Functions, Organization." *Rutgers–Camden Law Journal,* 9:1, pp. 61–115, 1977.

Postanovlenie Prezidiuma Verkhovnogo Soveta Rossiiskoi Federatsii i Pravitel'stva RF "O neotlozhnykh merakh po uluchsheniiu raschetov v narodnom khozyaistve i povyshenii otvetstvennosti predpriyatii za ikh finansovoe sostoyanie." *Vedomosti S"ezda narodnykh deputatov i Verkhovnogo Soveta RSFSR,* no. 23, May 25, 1992.

Postanovlenie Plenuma Verkhovnogo Suda RF i Vysshego Arbitrazhnogo Suda RF "O nekotorykh voprosakh, svyazannykh s primeneniem chasti pervoi Grazhdanskogo kodeksa RF," no. 6/8, *Rossiiskaya gazeta,* no. 151, August 10, 1996.

Sahlas, Peter J., and Elena Reshetnikova. "Competition Law in the Russian Federation." *Review of Central and East European Law,* 23:1, pp. 49–71, 1997.

Sako, Mari. *Prices, quality, and trust: inter-firm relations in Britain and Japan.* New York: Cambridge University Press, 1992.

Schwartz, Alan. "Relational Contracts in the Courts: An Analysis of Incomplete Agreements and Judicial Strategies." *Journal of legal studies,* 21:2, pp. 271–318, 1992.

Shapiro, Martin. *Courts: A Comparative and Political Analysis.* Chicago: University of Chicago Press, 1981.

Shelley, Louise. "Post-Soviet Organized Crime and the Rule of Law." *John Marshall Law Review,* 28:4, pp. 827–45, 1995.

Shlapentokh, Vladimir. "Bonjour, Stagnation: Russia's Next Years." *Europe–Asia Studies,* 49:5, pp. 865–81, 1997.

Shleifer, Andrei. "Establishing Property Rights" in Michael Bruno and Boris Pleskovic, eds., *Proceedings of the World Bank Annual Conference on Development Economics 1994.* Washington, D.C.: The World Bank, 1995.

Solomon, Jr., Peter H. "The Persistence of Judicial Reform in Contemporary Russia." *East European Constitutional Review,* 6:4, pp. 50–56, 1997.

"Sudebno-arbitrazhnaya statistika: O rabote arbitrazhnykh sudov Rossiiskoi Federatsii v 1995–96 godakh." *Vestnik Vysshego Arbitrazhnogo Suda,* no. 4, pp. 131–33, 1997.

"Sudebno-arbitrazhnaya statistika: Osnovnye pokazateli raboty arbitrazhnykh sudov Rossiiskoi Federatsii v 1996–97 godakh." *Vestnik Vysshego Arbitrazhnogo Suda,* no. 4, pp. 21–23, 1998.

"Sudebno-arbitrazhnaya statistika." *Vestnik Vysshego Arbitrazhnogo Suda,* no. 3, pp. 8–14, 1999.

Syfert, Scott D. "Capitalism or Corruption? Corporate Structure, Western Investment and Commercial Crime in the Russian Federation." *New York*

Law School Journal of International & Comparative Law, 18:2, pp. 357–406, 1999.

Telser, L.G. "A Theory of Self-enforcing Agreements." *Journal of Business,* 53:1, pp. 27–44, 1980.

Uzzi, Brian. "The Sources and Consequences of Embeddedness for the Economic Performance of Organizations: The Network Effect." *American Sociological Review,* 61:4, pp. 674–98, 1996.

Varese, Federico. "The Transition to the Market and Corruption in Post-socialist Russia." *Political Studies,* 45:3, pp. 579–96, 1997.

Vasil'eva, M. "Nel'zya zhit' po zakonam dzhunglei." *Chelovek i zakon,* no. 7, pp. 54–59, 1996.

Vinogradova, E.A., ed. *Treteiskii sud.* Moscow: INFRA, 1997.

Volkov, Vadim. "Violent Entrepreneurship in Post-Communist Russia." *Europe–Asia Studies,* 51:5, pp. 741–54, 1999.

Weber, Max. *Max Weber on Law in Economy and Society.* Edited by Max Rheinstein. Cambridge: Harvard University Press, 1967.

Williamson, Oliver E. "Calculativeness, Trust, and Economic Organization." *Journal of Law and Economics,* 36:1, Part 2, pp. 453–86, 1993.

Williamson, Oliver E. *The Economic Institutions of Capitalism: Firms, Markets, Relational Contracting.* New York: Free Press, 1985.

Williamson, Oliver E. "The Institutions and Governance of Economic Development and Reform" in Michael Bruno and Boris Pleskovic, eds., *Proceedings of the World Bank Annual Conference on Development Economics 1994.* Washington, D.C.: The World Bank, 1995.

Winn, Jane Kaufman. "Relational Practices and the Marginalization of Law: Informal Financial Practices of Small Businesses in Taiwan." *Law & Society Review,* 28:2, pp. 193–232, 1994.

What Conditions Are Necessary for the Judiciary to Curb Corruption?

Role of the Rule of Law and Judiciary Independence in Combating Corruption and Protecting Development Programs

Maher Abdel Wahed*

Attorney General

Arab Republic of Egypt

In the Name of Allah, the Compassionate and the Merciful

Judiciary independence and its role in combating administrative corruption were among the topics of the Thirteenth International Conference held by the International Society for Social Defense in Lecce, Italy, in 1996 in cooperation with the UN Committee for Crime Control and Criminal Justice and the UN Office in Vienna, Austria under the auspices of the Italian Ministry of Justice. I participated in the Conference in my capacity as a member of the Board of Directors of the above Society representing Arab and African countries. The Conference discussed constitutional and general legal measures for protecting the civil service and the judiciary from corruption. We also touched on judiciary independence and its role in combating the corruption phenomenon, in addition to applied experiments in some countries, constitutional and legal measures used for combating corruption, and criminal law procedures for dealing with new forms of corruption.

Egypt has a vital interest in legal and judiciary reform as a means of supporting the rule of law and judiciary independence to create the environment necessary for fostering development and attracting investments. To adequately emphasize this interest and the importance of the subject of corruption in particular, it is essential to frame the Egyptian experience from perspectives defined by its constitutional, legal, and applied aspects. This will stress the fact that an independent and robust judiciary under the rule of law

*Translated into English from the original text in Arabic and edited in English.

is the first and most important institution for combating corruption. Moreover, judges must be covered by judicial guarantees—which will be addressed in an introductory section dealing with legislative and judiciary reform in Egypt. This will be followed by two sections; the first deals with the rule of law and its guarantees under the criminal justice system, while the second deals with the role of legislation and the judiciary in combating and curbing corruption.

Legislative and Judiciary Reform in Egypt

I am fully convinced that the role played by the judiciary is a key factor in achieving any progress. Justice is the basis of government. It is the rudiment underpinning society in establishing rights and duties as well as striking a balance between competing interests and differing directions.

Justice can only be served by providing the legislative base that meets societal needs, accommodates new local and international developments, and ensures streamlined litigation procedures. Equally important is the presence of an effective and consummate judiciary system. It safeguards rights, transactions, and persons in order to achieve social, economic, and financial stability.

Egypt has chosen the political and economic system that is conducive to achieving its national aspirations and expectations. This system is based on the fundamentals of democracy and constitutional legality. As well, it is based on full economic freedom in ownership and production in the context of a new global system whose major issues are the communications revolution, trade liberalization, and movements of capital and investments by giant corporations in all countries and continents.

In formulating plans in the areas of justice, legislation, and courts, the Egyptian Ministry of Justice has adopted an approach to reach the following goals:

1. Upgrading judiciary services to increase their ability and adequacy, and to expedite and streamline litigation procedures for all citizens.
2. Taking stock of all legislation efforts, consolidating them, and improving them in order to meet societal needs.
3. Ensuring adequate numbers of judiciary staff and their technical and specialization levels through a comprehensive master plan.

4. Disseminating the relevant modern technology and computerizing litigation procedures.
5. Developing and upgrading court buildings to make them bastions of justice in appearance and in essence.

In formulating its policy to achieve the above objectives, the Ministry of Justice has taken the following facts into account:

- The rule of law is being strengthened and deepened as the basis for government and all forms of daily activities in Egypt through the proper legislative base as well as a competent and definitive judicial system. This will streamline litigation and render it safe and secure for all citizens and any person with a legitimate interest in Egypt.
- Any facilitation leading to helping owners of rights obtain their rights in a speedy and conclusive manner will conserve their efforts and free up their energies for use in development.
- Strengthening litigation in a manner conducive to speedy settlement of disputes and establishment of justice is in essence, and in the temporal dimension, a precondition in an environment that aspires to increase investments and nurture the growth of the national economy. This can only be achieved through a legislative base that makes the path smooth and free from obstacles, and through a judicial system that is effective and competent in safeguarding rights and protecting transactions.

The policy of streamlining litigation procedures is based on two foundations: legislative reform and improved judiciary performance.

Egyptian Legislative Reform Policy

A crucial priority is the examination of legislation related to litigation procedures with a view to introducing further streamlining and simplification that is conducive to shortening procedures and time needed. Slow litigation procedures are blatant injustice.

Accordingly, Egypt has paid due attention to addressing legislative problems in its drive to streamline litigation procedures, by consolidating, revising, coordinating, simplifying and condensing laws, and eliminating any ambiguities or contradictions therein. This has ensured harmony and agreement with the provisions of the constitution, as well as keeping abreast with the needs of today's Egyptian society, the requirements of social and economic reform, and the need to eliminate restrictions that hamper market activities, investments, and development.

In the context of efforts exerted to achieve the above objective, a review was conducted leading to improvements of the Code of Civil and Commercial Procedures, the Penal Code, the new Code of Commerce, the Personal Status Law, the Maritime Trade Law, the Law Concerning Control of Narcotics and Narcotics Trafficking as well as the Arbitration Law to accommodate modern international trends related to local and international commercial arbitration.

Amendments have been made to provisions of the Criminal Procedures Law aimed at addressing the problem of backlog of criminal cases leading to delays in hearing such cases as well as related civil cases. This was achieved by the following actions:

1. Introducing the conciliation system in respect of contraventions and many misdemeanor crimes and making it a cause for abatement of criminal lawsuits.
2. Introducing controls to prevent misuse of the right to institute legal proceedings.
3. Holding urgent evening sessions, without adherence to scheduled attendance, to try defendants put under precautionary incarceration for misdemeanors specified in decrees issued by the Minister of Justice and in cases in which the defendant was caught red-handed.
4. Expanding the system of criminal writs by increasing the ceiling of fines in cases in which a criminal writ may be issued by a judge of summary jurisdiction and the district attorney concerned.
5. Regulating the procedures for placing the property of a defendant under precautionary custody in a manner consistent with the provisions of the constitution to facilitate execution of a ruling establishing a fine, reimbursement, or compensation. Such measures include managing or prohibiting from disposal those assets that have been involved in crimes of embezzlement, encroachment on public property—as well as in crimes affecting properties owned by the state or its agencies, enterprises, and units. Such measures may include taking over the property belonging to a defendant's spouse or minor children if there is

adequate evidence that such property is derived from the crime being investigated. The respective custody writ must be issued by a ruling of the competent criminal court pursuant to a request by the office of the Attorney General. A writ may be issued by the Attorney General when necessary in urgent cases provided that the writ is submitted to the competent criminal court for review within a period of seven days as of the date on which it was issued. Otherwise, such a writ will be null and void.

Improving the Performance of the Judiciary

The judicial reform policy is designed to strengthen judiciary independence and streamline the litigation system and its procedures. An improved system will achieve speedy and facile establishment of justice by ensuring the following: numerical, scholarly and technical adequacy of judges and public prosecutors in the Department of the Attorney General; adoption of a specialization system; upgrading of court buildings; dissemination of the use of advanced computerized systems in automating litigation procedures; and paying attention to judicial workers and ensuring that they perform their duties satisfactorily.

Egypt's population growth and increased awareness of individual rights and increased transactions as economic activities grow—thereby increasing the number of disputes and creating the problem of lengthened litigation periods—have resulted in a shortfall in the number of judges dealing with an ever-increasing number of disputes. To manage this problem, the retirement age for judges has been increased to 64 and the number of those appointed at the lowest rungs of the judiciary hierarchy has been increased. Moreover, a plethora of legislative measures simplifying and mainstreaming litigation procedures have been enacted. These measures have helped, and will continue to help, in solving the problem of backlogs and slow procedures.

Strengthening the Scholarly Competence of Judges and Members of the Department of the Attorney General

It is necessary and important to technically prepare judges; develop their capacities; strengthen their abilities; deepen their sense of invulnerability, independence, and neutrality; and imprint the sanctity and sublimity of their mission on their conscience.

Top-notch training and good preparation of judges and public prosecutors in the Department of the Attorney General has become a requirement for good and timely performance as well as speedy decisions on legal cases, in addition to serving the cause of justice.

The essence of educational training is not confined to familiarity with and mastery of jurisprudence; it must include knowledge of various humanities disciplines that complement jurisprudence and enhance understanding of the law and the ability to enforce it.

Moreover, judges' capacity to be methodical in addressing issues, and in reaching their core, without stopping at appearances, must be developed.

Training and education must not be confined to those at the very beginning of their judiciary careers. The effort must extend in scope to include each new career stage that judges go through. Such training and education can be provided through organizing remedial and specialized seminars that are consistent with their status. Swift developments are taking place all over the world today as borders open and large international trading blocks emerge. Technology is also developing and the communication revolution is making great leaps in conveying ideas with lightning speed across the globe. Such developments are opening new fields and areas never known before, creating for judges and public prosecuters at the Department of the Attorney General great responsibilities requiring strenuous efforts in serving the mission of justice.

The Egyptian Ministry of Justice, armed with a strong belief in the importance of educating and training judges to equip them with the scholarly know-how needed for their judiciary work, established the National Center for Judiciary Studies in 1981. Through an overall training plan, the Center contributes to the creation of an atmosphere of confidence and reassurance that stimulates development and investments. It also diversifies its programs in terms of specialization and duration, training attendees in the use of modern technological means. This will also enable the tracking of global developments and amazing achievements in scholarly, technological, and economic fields—and in turn serve the state's objectives of developing the Egyptian economy and enhancing the prospects for investments. Moreover, the center will serve as an organization that initiates seminars and conferences addressing various legal subjects related to the work of judges.

A study is being conducted to develop the center into an institute that would train public prosecutors. Such training would be made compulsory for persons willing to pursue judicial careers. Trainees would be required to successfully pass programs as well as educational, practicum, and psychological tests. Such tests will measure the trainee's aptitude and qualification for judicial work as well as his or her ability to serve the mission of the judiciary. The Supreme Judiciary Council will select candidates from law school graduates through competitions for enrollment in the Center. Candidates selected must spend no less than two years before being appointed for judiciary positions. Upon successfully passing examinations and tests at the end of this period, graduates would be appointed at entry levels in the Department of the Attorney General. The Center provides various other training and education programs as well.

In the context of its plan for judicial reforms, the Egyptian Ministry of Justice looks forward to the future, having drafted ambitious plans based on the belief in the importance of training and educating judges as well as public prosecutors from the Attorney General's Department and their auxiliaries as a foundation for strengthening and increasing their scholarly and technical competence. The plan includes the establishment of a modern judicial academy that includes three institutes: (1) an institute for judges, public prosecutors, and all members of judicial bodies; (2) an institute for staff supporting judges such as court secretaries, clerks, summons servers, and chiefs of civil and criminal sections; and (3) an institute for experts of all specialties. Measures are being taken to start implementation of this judicial project.

We believe in the need for judges who match the pace of our age and the challenges it poses, face the new developments it involves, interact with their society and its issues, and participate in formulating its future in a manner conducive to prosperity and growth as well as security and safety for each individual living on our national territory.

Specialization of Judges

Specialization of judges is a component of judiciary reform. It is a way of achieving excellence and thoroughness. Judicial specialization in a specific type of conflict has become necessary to improve performance and reach just rulings in an environment marked by increasing conflict proliferation and

diversification. Therefore, specialized training courses and seminars are organized to handle civil, trade, summary, and criminal justice cases as well as
family and labor disputes.

The Rule of Law and Guarantees under the Criminal
Justice System

In its preamble, the 1971 Egyptian Constitution provides that the rule of law
is not only a guarantee required for freedom of individuals but also the sole
basis for the legitimacy of authorities.

The Constitution has devoted a chapter to the rule of law. It provides that
"... the rule of law is the basis of government in the State" (Article 64).

The Supreme Court, in its ruling of January 23, 1992 (in respect of case
No. 22 of Legal Year 8) concludes that "the Legal State is the one that
complies, in all its activities—regardless of the nature of its powers—with
legal rules that are superior to the State and form the controls over its
various business and actions. The exercise of power is no longer an individual
privilege; it is exercised on behalf and for the benefit of the community."

Egyptian legislators were careful to establish the sublime meanings of this
principle in the following constitutional provisions: "The State shall be subject to law. The independence and immunity of the judiciary are two basic
guarantees to safeguard rights and liberties." (Article 65)

"Penalty shall be personal.

There shall be no crime or penalty except by virtue of the law. No penalty
shall be inflictd except by a judicial sentence. Penalty shall be inflicted only
for acts committed subsequent to the promulgation of the law prescribing
them." (Article 66)

"Any defendant is innocent until he is proved guilty before a legal court,
in which he is granted the right to defend himself.

Every person accused of a crime must be provided with counsel for his de-
fence." (Article 67)

"The right to litigation is inalienable for all, and every citizen has the
right to refer to his competent judge.

The State shall guarantee the accessibility of the judicature organs to litigants, and the rapidity of statuting on cases.

Any provision in the law stipulating the immunity of any act or administrative decision from the control of the judicature is prohibited." (Article 68)

"The right of defense in person or by mandate is guaranteed. The law shall grant the financially incapable citizens the means to resort to justice and defend their rights." (Article 69)

"No penal lawsuit shall be sued except by an order from a judicature organ and in cases defined by the law." (Article 70)

"Any person arrested or detained should be informed, forthwith with the reasons for his arrest or detention. He has the right to communicate, inform, and ask the help of anyone as prescribed in the law. He must be faced, as soon as possible, with the charges directed against him

Any person may lodge a complaint to the courts against any measure taken to restrict his individual freedom. The law regulates the right of complaint in a manner ensuring a ruling regarding it within a definite period, or else release is imperative." (Article 71)[1]

The chapter related to the rule of law concludes with the following provision:

"Sentences shall be passed and executed in the name of the people. Likewise, refraining to execute sentences or obstructing them on the part of the concerned civil servants is considered a crime punishable by law. In this case, those whom the sentence is in favour of, have the right to sue a direct penal lawsuit before the competant court." (Article 72)[2] Such a provision is in agreement with the International Covenant on Civil and Political Rights as already ratified.

The Egyptian Constitution established the principle of the rule of law in both its related prongs: submission by the state to the law and independence and immunity of the judiciary. Accordingly, court rulings must emphasize this principle and be an expression of it. Based on this vision, the constitution has accorded court rulings all protection and means of execution. Moreover, civil and public servants who refuse to execute, or hinder the execution of, court rulings shall be punished.

The constitution has been careful to provide guarantees to grant effectiveness to the principle of the rule of law as evident in the following provisions:

---

1. Heller, Peter B. 1991. "Egypt" in *Constitutions of the Countries of the World*. Eds. Albert P. Blaustein and Gisbert H. Flanz. Debbs Ferry, New York: Oceana Publications, Inc.
2. See note 1 for full reference.

1. Revision of constitutionality of laws (Article 189). In a supreme court ruling issued on January 23, 1992 in Case No. 22 of Constitutional Judiciary Year 8, the following is stated: "Submission by the State to the law shall mean non-violation by State legislation [and laws] of the rights deemed in democratic States to be a basic and preliminary basis of law-abiding states and a basic guarantee of human rights, dignity and wholesome personality. This shall include a plethora of rights considered to be closely related to personal freedoms guaranteed by the Constitution."

2. Judiciary independence and immunity:

"The Judiciary Authority shall be independent. It shall be exercised by courts of justice of different sorts and classes, which shall use their judgements in accordance with the law." (Article 165)

"Judges shall be independent, subject to no other authority by the law.

No authority may intervene in the cases or in justice affairs." (Article 166)

"The status of judges shall be irrevocable. The law shall regulate the disciplinary actions with regard to them." (Article 168)[3]

The above principles are enshrined in the United Nations Declaration on Independence of the Judiciary issued in 1965.

In implementation of these principles, penal laws enacted in Egypt since 1883 provide penalties for civil servants if they intervene with judges or courts of law on behalf of a litigant or if they attempt to prejudice any litigant before the court, whether by order, request, plea or recommendation.

If, as a result of any such intervention, the judge fails to issue a proper ruling, the criminal code provides severe sanctions. Any such conduct is classified as a felony punishable by imprisonment, fine, and dismissal. Failure by a judge to issue rulings in other situations is punishable by fine and dismissal (Criminal Law, Articles 121 and 122).

Another such principle is the provision enshrined in the current Judiciary Branch Law No. 46 of 1972 as amended by Laws No. 17 of 1976 and 25 of 1984 "... judges shall not be transferred, seconded

---

3. See note 1 for full reference.

or loaned save as in cases and in the manner specified in this Law" (Article 52).

Article 67 of the above law provides that judges and public prosecutors in the Department of the Attorney General—except assistant attorneys general who are at the lowest rung of the career ladder—shall be unremovable.

It should be noted that the Department of the Attorney General in Egypt stands alone by deciding that its members, headed by the Attorney General, be immune and unremovable since the Department is an integral part of the judiciary branch. According to Egyptian laws, the Department of the Attorney General combines the power to investigate with the power to prosecute in public cases. Consequently, the public prosecutors of the Department of the Attorney General have traditionally been accorded the immunity that applies to judges. They also enjoy the same guarantees accorded to judges in respect of appointment, transfer, and retirement in terms of the need to secure approval by the Supreme Judiciary Council. This attitude by Egyptian legislators is in agreement with the Declaration of Judiciary Independence as adopted by the UN's Seventh Convention held in Milan during August 26–September 6, 1985. The declaration states that the independence of prosecutors is as indispensable as the independence of judges. It is a guarantee that is necessary for establishing justice, as it requires that members of the Department of the Attorney General be treated equally with their colleagues, the judges, in terms of immunities.

A guarantee of judiciary independence that the Judiciary Independence Law provides is that assemblies formed at each court comprising all its members shall exclusively have the competence to distribute and arrange court business, and determine the number of circuits and sessions and second members to work at criminal courts (Article 30).

The Supreme Judiciary Council is the body that is deemed legally competent to examine all matters related to judges and public prosecutors of the Department of the Attorney General such as appointment, promotion, transfer, secondment, loaning, and all other affairs as specified in the Law.

The Supreme Judiciary Council shall comprise the following: The Chief Justice of the Cassation Court (Chairman), the Attorney General, two most senior Cassation Court Counselors, and three most senior Court of Appeals Counselors (members). (Article 77 bis (1) and Article 77 bis (2)).

Decisions on applications submitted by judges and public prosecutors in respect of revocation of final administrative decisions related to judges and members of the Office of the Attorney General shall be exclusively entrusted to the civil circuits of the Cassation Court. These departments shall also decide on compensation applications and disputes related to salaries, pensions, and allowances (Article 83).

The disciplining of judges and public prosecutors shall be entrusted to a council to be composed of the Chief Justice of the Cassation Court (Chairman), three most senior chief judges of courts of appeal, and three most senior Court of Cassation Counselors (members). Sessions of this council shall be confidential.

In cases other than those involving individuals caught red-handed, a judge or a public prosecutor shall not be arrested and put in custody except after securing a writ from a competent judicial committee. In cases of an individual being caught red-handed, the case shall be referred to the said committee within 24 hours. This committee shall exclusively have the right to decide on continued imprisonment or order the release of the person concerned. No investigation procedures in respect of criminal actions by such a person shall be initiated before securing a permission from the said committee. Penalties taking away freedoms of judges and public prosecutors shall be executed in special places (Article 96).

3. Ensuring the right of individuals to sue, be they Egyptian nationals or foreigners on Egyptian soil, is a measure to protect their rights under the law, taking into consideration the basic guarantees required for administering justice in an effective manner similar to that in developed states (Article 67 / 1 of the Constitution, and the ruling by the Constitutional Court rendered on January 23, 1992).

4. Right of access to self-defense of individuals is emphasized as a condition for establishing the legality of a trial as the accused is innocent until proven guilty in a due process that guarantees the right of the accused to defend himself or herself.

The Constitutional Court of Egypt emphasized the fact that the right to defense is a mainstay of a just trial as required by Article 97 of the constitution (Supreme Constitutional Court, May 16, 1992, Case No. 6 of Constitutional Judicial year 13).

The constitutional value of the defense right covers the following elements:

1. The right to have thorough knowledge of the charge concerned and all evidence thereof.
2. The right of the accused to express himself or herself freely.
3. The right to enlist a defender—the right to have access to defense in person or by proxy.
4. Striking a balance between the rights of defense team members and prosecution team members.
5. The right to have an equitable and just trial.

An equitable and just trial would have the following characteristics:

- Trial procedures should be public except when the court concerned decides the trial is to be conducted behind closed doors for the sake of public order or morals. In all cases, verdicts should be rendered in open sessions.
- The state should ensure speedy judgment of cases (Article 68 (a) of the Egyptian Constitution). This is in agreement with Article 14.3(c) of the International Covenant on Civil and Political Rights. This Covenant provides that an individual should have the right, when accused of a crime, to have a trial without unreasonable delay.
- No penalty or punishment may be imposed without a court ruling (Article 66 of the Constitution).Verdicts should be justified and supported by reasons.
- A defendant should not be tried for the same deed more than once.

The Role of Legislation and the Judiciary in Combating and Controlling Corruption

Discussing criminal justice and its role in achieving stability in society by providing the people with peace and security leads to the supremacy of the authority of law in community interaction—and in turn presents us with the problem of corruption, and by extension the role of legislation and the judiciary in combating and controlling it. Corruption is one of the factors that destroys a community, so the problem receives great attention at both domestic and international levels.

The importance of this problem becomes clear with respect to developing countries where the issue of development constitutes a vital basis for their advancement and progress and where government corruption is an axe of destruction that cuts down all hopes ascribed to plans for development. Since governments of most developing countries strive to keep up with the world economic order, these countries have become more vulnerable than before to the risks brought on by various forms of corruption, starting with tax and customs evasion, bribery, drug trafficking, money laundering, and organized crime that damages social and political systems and hampers development plans.

We need to define what is meant by government corruption in light of the distinction between government and governmental administration. The government draws up the policies and the administration executes or implements such policies.

Corruption takes numerous forms, including trading in public posts, abuse of public funds—such as the crimes of embezzlement, misappropriation of public money, and tax and customs evasion—as well as crimes of graft involving those officials in the areas of government procurement and those in charge of implementing economic and service projects.

Among the reasons for corruption are the following:

1. The emergence of new economic blocs and the orientation of countries toward open markets under international agreements, participation of certain investors with huge amounts of capital in multinational companies, free movement of capital between countries leading to organized economic crimes that transcend national borders, with the end result that the negative impact of corruption on any country is no longer restricted within that state.

2. Weakness of control over functional work, poor administrative organization and amorphous responsibility, lack of specification of

competence, low wages and pensions, imbalance in the social structure, and the existence of negative social values, lack of awareness,
and weak commitment.

3. Laxity in applying laws and regulations and non-adherence to their
   provisions, lack of control and monitoring of employees by officials,
   and for the most part, the turning of a blind eye to the mistakes of public officials and not taking the legal measures that should be taken
   when offenses are committed.

4. The large number of government regulations and instructions involving a multiplicity of complicated procedures causing ambiguity so that
   it is difficult for the layperson to know his or her rights; this forces one
   to pay to get those rights. The briber finds graft a quick way to have his
   or her interests taken care of, and the bribed finds an easy way to make
   a profit.

5. Weakness of moral and religious deterrents in respect of certain
   employees.

Importance of Political Will in Combating Corruption

It is necessary to emphasize the political will of the government to take measures to provide the appropriate environment for achieving the highest rates
of social and economic development. As part of this process the government
is determined to combat manifestations of corruption that waste the country's economic resources which are vital to various development operations.

Becoming aware of this, the political leadership in Egypt devised systems
that provide the appropriate environment for combating corruption and fur-
thering development processes without the hindrances that have a negative
impact on their implementation. Specific measures include the following:

1. The political leadership adopted the principle of openness and transparency to make citizens aware of the economic difficulties and
   the forms of dysfunction that confront society. This creates the appropriate environment for implementing economic reform programs and
   addressing negative ramifications in order to curb corruption in society.

2. An appropriate environment was created in support of the democratic process, introducing opportunities for a variety of opinions and trends to be expressed through constitutional institutions, the press, and various mass media, resulting in numerous cases of corruption coming to the attention of control and judiciary agencies entrusted with dealing with such cases.

3. The leadership kept abreast of global and local economic changes through enactment of laws and legislation governing various activities and transactions resulting from such changes and giving full support to implementation procedures without exception, with a view to filling the gaps through which those who corrupt the system sneak in, and to dealing with those who are tempted to embezzle public funds and interfere with the interests of the state and citizens.

4. The tendency of the state to relax its control on economic activities and adopt policies and measures that reduce the government's role in managing public projects, subsidizing goods and services, and controlling the currency market creates incentives for misusing public resources, hampering economic growth, and provides an environment conducive to the growth of corruption. The state is taking into consideration the social dimension in adopting such policies.

5. More room, increasing year after year, is being granted for the private sector to play a greater role in implementing economic development operations in Egypt, and rules are in place that govern and monitor the actions of the private sector in order to avert practices that do not take into consideration public interest and thus have a negative impact on development plans.

6. Censorship and security agencies constitute the legal framework for combating all forms of corruption in Egypt, and have been given an enhanced role, and are in charge of dealing with all forms of financial and administrative corruption. These agencies are the following:

a. The Central Accounting Agency: an autonomous body responsible to the President and entrusted with the control of the funds of the state and other public bodies; it assists the People's Assembly in performing its functions in such control as specified by law.

b. The Central Agency for Organization and Administration: entrusted with formulating the policies that simplify the procedures for rendering services to citizens, and combating bureaucracy in government agencies in order to address manifestations of corruption.

c. The Administrative Censorship Agency: exercises its function by addressing infraction and corruption in government bodies, public institutions and private sector corporations that undertake public works, as well as all the bodies in which the state participates in any way, and in most cases the government initiates instructions to the agency to search and investigate administrative and financial violations that it discovers, and to uncover and control criminal acts.

d. The Public Department for Combating Public Fund Violations: one of the departments within the police specializing in combating crimes of bribery and infringement of public funds, including crimes of embezzlement, misappropriation of public money, counterfeiting, forgery, and smuggling.

This is in addition to the role of the internal departments of the administrative agencies of the state in tightening control over government spending and implementing the financial laws, regulations and instructions, such as the departments of planning and follow-up, finance, security, and personnel. Administrative regulations and decrees regulate the powers and competence of each department.

The Legislative Framework for Penal Safeguards to Combat Corruption in Egypt

The legislative framework for penal safeguards to combat corruption in Egypt is embodied in the provisions of the penal code that incriminate and punish perpetrators of corrupt practices including crimes of bribery and related offenses.

A crime of bribery can be committed by any public official or employee of a government department or other departments under its supervision, or any member of public or local prosecution commissions, whether elected or appointed, as well as arbitrators, experts, agents of debtors, liquidators, official receivers, or any person entrusted with public service, members of boards of directors, and managers and staff of institutions, corporations, societies, organizations, and establishments, if the state or one of its public agencies contributes to their funds whatever the share involved.

In bribery cases, the punitive penalties provided for in the articles referred to shall be instituted, and in all events, the amount paid by the briber or mediators by way of bribery shall be confiscated.

The provisions of the penal code specify crimes of misappropriation of public funds such as the following: embezzlement, larceny, misappropriation of funds of stock companies, treachery, profiteering, encroachment on real estate benefits, violation of the system of distribution of goods, intentional malice of public funds, unintentional malice of public funds, negligence in the maintenance or use of public funds, intentional breach in the execution of certain contractual obligations, unpaid labor, and sabotage of public funds.

In all cases, the felon would be charged with restitution of the funds subjected to embezzlement or larceny, and be ordered to repay the value of the funds misappropriated, destroyed, or burned, as well as the compensation required.

In view of the close linkage between crimes of corruption and crimes of money laundering, legislation should be enacted targeting specific money laundering operations. This is a matter under study especially since Egypt joined the United Nations Vienna Convention of 1988. Certain provisions, however, already contribute to combating money laundering—such as the Illegal Gains Law, the Protection of Values Law, the Penal Code, and the Law Against Narcotics.

This is in addition to crimes and felonies defined as harmful to public interest and addressed by the penal code as well as crimes of forgery, tax and customs evasion, and other legal provisions that punish public officials for illegal gains.

The Judiciary's Role in Combating Corruption

An autonomous and neutral judiciary with safeguards and immunity for its custodians would be capable of confronting and combating corruption at the national level by taking decisive judicial measures, applying legal provisions, and reinforcing them with deterrents in the form of strict judgements and serious and unrelenting follow-up of execution measures.

The Prosecution Unit at the Department of the Attorney General is the competent authority to investigate and deal with crimes of corruption. It is capable of carrying out investigations and promptly implementing corrective action.

The Prosecution Unit has established specialized prosecutor's offices for investigating certain crimes that constitute forms of corruption—such as the Supreme Prosecutor's Office for State Security, the Supreme Prosecutor's Office for Public Funds, the Prosecutor's Office for Financial Affairs, and the Prosecutor's Office for Tax Evasion Control—in order to expedite the completion of investigations into cases submitted. This office prepares cases for action and refers them to the competent courts in urgent session. Examples of cases within the jurisdiction of the Supreme Prosecutor's Office for State Security would be investigating crimes of bribery. The Office exercises its competence throughout the republic. This would not prevent other ordinary prosecutor's offices nationwide from investigating cases of bribery submitted to them. Such prosecutor's offices should submit their completed investigations, ready to be acted upon, to the Supreme Prosecutor's Office for State Security to be dealt with. This is an organizational rule whose infringement would not result in invalidation. Referring action in such cases to a specialized prosecutor is preferred because the specialized office has the particular expertise of those handling such cases, and also because of the ease that comes with having one measure for dealing with them.

It is to be noted that public prosecutors investigating this type of case are interrogation judges, and therefore have all the authority vested in interrogation judges in accordance with the law.

The Supreme Prosecutor's Office for Public Funds specializes in investigating and dealing with crimes stipulated in chapter 4, volume 2 of the penal code, and related crimes, including crimes of larceny of public monies and both deliberate and unintentional misappropriation of public funds and profiteering in all parts of the Republic. It investigates crimes impinging on public funds, in the districts of Cairo and Giza, and may investigate such crimes in other districts.

Other judiciary bodies under the Ministry of Justice include agencies for examination and investigation in the area of illegal gains. These are formed of counselors and judges upon approval of the Supreme Judiciary Board. Their competence is examination of the declarations of financial assets by employees of the state and those dealing with the state, in order to evaluate the elements of their financial assets and to determine their sources and any increase in their wealth, and discover whether there is any suspicion of illegal gain. The law obligates state employees to submit declarations of their financial assets periodically every five years. The inspection and investigation agencies verify the declarations or any complaints concerning them, in order to prove or disprove the existence of unlawful gain. If they find that the documents include evidence of illegal gain, they conduct their investigation and prepare it for action, referring it to the competent criminal court.

Judiciary agencies that specialize in considering corruption cases and dealing with them include the Administrative Prosecution Agency, which is an autonomous judiciary agency specializing in financial and administrative violations committed by civil servants of the state, and employees of public agencies, societies, and private agencies that are specified by a law or a presidential decree. The Administrative Prosecution Agency interrogates these individuals and conducts investigations by referring them either to disciplinary tribunals or to the Department of the Attorney General to be dealt with in accordance with the penal code.

Combating Corruption of Officials in the Judiciary Bodies

I had explained earlier that the judiciary is the most important body entrusted with fighting corruption in view of the legal and judiciary powers and the safeguards that enable judges to execute such tasks. If corruption encroaches onto the judiciary and its bodies, that means the collapse of the plans and programs that are devised to protect society from the negative impact of the various forms of corruption. This will affect the resources of the state, and bring down the rate of development and economic programs.

We should distinguish between corruption of employees of the judiciary and corruption of the judges themselves. Employees of judiciary bodies are considered public officials of the state, governed by control and disciplinary laws that govern other state employees. However, in view of the serious tasks vested in them, and their linkage with the operations of the judiciary, the handling of cases and the execution of rulings, special laws have been enacted concerning them. These laws govern these employees' appointment and performance, organize their work and transfers, determine their responsibilities and discipline in order to set firm control over them, prevent their infraction and expose corruption among them, and take deterrent measures against them in the event that laws and regulations are violated. Their accountability is measured against stricter criteria since they, as "managers" of justice, act as a protective shield for society.

Monitoring agencies have been established within the judiciary bodies that undertake inspection, review of work, and submission of periodic reports for evaluating judicial employees' performance and their accountability— and imposing penalties on them is the prerogative of judges who are assigned to supervise administrative work in judiciary bodies.

How the Judiciary Can Combat Corruption

The Egyptian judiciary system is one of the oldest in the world. It is well known for its neutrality and objectivity. The constitution and the laws grant it autonomy and immunity, and its members cannot be dismissed. The laws governing the judiciary bodies single out a special system for judges with respect to appointment, transfer, and secondment. The Supreme Judiciary Board handles these affairs. A special panel deals with their discipline, accountability, and trials, under special rules as a safeguard for their independence and judicial immunity. Over the years, judges have developed judiciary values and traditions and moral principles that are considered their shield against any infraction, to the point that it can be said that society has put them at a rank closer to prophets, and there is truly a belief that a judge cannot be imagined to commit any form of corruption.

The legislative body has set legal rules that prevent encroachment of corruption onto the judiciary, and guarantee its purity. Thanks be to God, the judiciary bodies are pure, as a result of the system provided by law that holds them severely to task in the event of the commission of any form of infraction, by the judiciary body that deals with their affairs—that is, the Supreme Judiciary Board. Among these rules are the following:

1. Only the best elements are selected to be judges from among the graduates of the colleges of law. The Supreme Judiciary Board selects them from a pool of candidates after the security and control bodies have conducted tests and investigations into their families, and their

cultural, moral, and social status. Upon appointment, they go through basic training sessions that cement the values and traditions of the judiciary that they should acquire and believe in throughout their working life as judges.

2. Judges and public prosecutors are, throughout their working life and until they are promoted to the grade of counselor, subject to inspection cycles in order to be evaluated technically; their promotions are proposed by the judiciary body composed of a group of counselors, judges, and public prosecutors. Candidates are selected from among the most prominent qualified judges and public prosecutors. They are also entrusted with the investigation of complaints in order to prevent the encroachment of corruption to them.

3. There are laws that stipulate rules for questioning judges and public prosecutors, whether by disciplinary or penal measures, in the event of the commission of any misconduct or any form of corruption. If a judge or a prosecutor has failed to perform his or her duty, a verbal or written warning is served after hearing his or her testimony. A judge or a prosecutor may raise objections to the written warning in front of an ad hoc judiciary committee. Should the violation be repeated or continue after a final warning, disciplinary action will be taken against him or her.

   Judges and prosecutors of all grades are disciplined by a disciplinary board composed of seven ex-officio members, based on their seniority at the top of the judiciary body, under the chairmanship of the head of the Court of Cassation. If it is established that an infraction has taken place, the disciplinary board may order the suspension of the judge or prosecutor from performing his or her duties, or may decide to grant him or her mandatory leave pending the end of the trial—the sessions of which are videotaped—and disciplinary action may result in a reprimand or dismissal. The Minister of Justice implements the actions issued by the disciplinary board and a presidential decree is issued for effecting punitive dismissal.

   If a judge or a prosecutor commits a crime or a misdemeanor, the law requires that permission be obtained from the ad hoc judiciary committee chaired by the head of the Court of Cassation before arresting him, or placing him in custody, or taking any measure of investigation or penal action against him, with the exception of the case of being caught in flagrante delicto. In the event of arrest or placement in custody, the Attorney General must refer the matter to the said committee within the time specified for making a decision in that respect.

The ad hoc judiciary committee is appointed based on a request from the Attorney General by the panel that has the authority to decide the punitive action, even if the crime is not related to the post of the accused.

A judge or a prosecutor who is penalized by restriction of his freedom is imprisoned in a location separate from those specified for keeping other prisoners.

A judge or a prosecutor may lose his authority at any time for any reason of loss of competence other than health. The disciplinary board is empowered to consider the request of the Minister of Justice in this regard. After hearing the prosecution and the defense of the judge, the board will issue its ruling: in the event of conviction it will refer the judge to pension or transfer him to another nonjudiciary post; if the judge or prosecutor is found not guilty, the board will dismiss the prosecution's case.

4. The Egyptian judiciary system is based on a multiplicity of levels of courts. There are lower courts, courts of first instance whose rulings are appealed in appellate courts, and whose rulings in turn may be contested in front of a court of cassation. Likewise, decisions of the Prosecutor-General's Office can be appealed to a senior body up to the Attorney General. In such a system it is difficult for corruption to encroach in absolute terms, since it is possible to catch it if it happens at a higher level.

The International Conference for Combating Corruption and Ensuring Impartiality of Staff in Security and Legal Bodies was held in Washington, D.C. from February 24 to 26, 1999 under the chairmanship of then-U.S. Vice President Al Gore. Egypt participated in this conference with a high-level delegation from the Administrative Control Agency, the Ministry of Justice, and the National Security Agency. Among the proposals discussed during the sessions of the International Conference for Combating Corruption were the following:

- Courts or competent judiciary agencies are granted the power and the right to issue instructions to banks allowing either review of or reticence on banking, financial or trade records, in a way that safeguards non-hindrance of the law of confidentiality of accounts or restriction or reticence on such records.
- Promoting among government officials religious values that urge them to be impartial and combat corruption, is important.

The conference issued a final communiqué that urged government representatives in the conference to cooperate through local or global bodies and to focus their efforts on adopting effective principles against corruption and finding ways to assist each other through mutual evaluation.

Analyzing the proceedings of the said conference shows increased international attention to combating corruption among government officials in view of its clear negative impact on the stability of economic reform and development plans. The United States proposed the establishment of an international agreement to combat corruption under the auspices of the United Nations that would be binding to signatory states, to take effective measures to combat and prevent corruption.

The Tenth United Nations Congress on the Prevention of Crime and Treatment of Offenders held in Vienna from April 10 to 17, 2000 dealt with crime, justice, and confrontation of the challenges of the twenty-first century. Among the topics covered were strengthening the supremacy of law, enhancing the criminal justice system, and promoting international cooperation for combating transnational crime. The conference issued the Vienna Declaration, which states the following in paragraph 16:

> We further commit ourselves to taking enhanced international action against corruption, building upon the United Nations Declaration Against Corruption and Bribery in International Commercial Transactions, the International Code of Conduct for Public Officials, relevant regional conventions and regional and global forums. We stress the urgent need to develop an effective international legal instrument against corruption, independent

of the United Nations Convention Against Transnational Organized Crime....

Conclusion

We conclude from the above that combating and addressing corruption requires the following actions:

1. Establishing a special international network to address crimes of corruption.
2. Finding a new formula for technical, legal, and judiciary cooperation among public prosecutors' offices in various countries of the world under the auspices of the United Nations in the areas of arresting and trying suspects in cases of corruption.
3, Stressing the role of civil society in raising awareness of combating corruption.
4. Making punishment severe for crimes of corruption and confiscating proceeds arising from them.
5. Paying attention to the role of international and national organizations as partners in combating corruption.
6. Paying attention to clear, applicable, ethical charters.
7. Encouraging competence by allocating material and moral awards.
8. Emphasizing addressing problems of corruption, achieving justice, and endeavoring to restitute the funds and assets obtained from crimes of corruption, irrespective of the time they were committed or the designation of the violator, within the framework of fair criminal justice.
9. Stressing the importance of disseminating the culture of respect for the law.
10. Expediting action in cases of corruption through simplifying their procedures and removing any restriction imposed by law on the competence of the prosecution in instituting criminal cases against those who commit such crimes.
11. Spreading awareness that although fighting corruption has a high financial cost, failing to spend on combating programs would cost more in view of the clear ramifications of the spread of corruption and its impact on development programs.

12. Taking into consideration the necessity of preparing an international agreement to combat corruption that draws its effectiveness from the political will of the countries.
13. Establishing an independent judiciary with a strong structure endowed by the law with a system that protects it from corruption or any other form of deviation of the judiciary authority in charge of the judicial system.

Addressing the phenomenon of corruption requires continued development of the legislative and judiciary structure and those bodies combating crime in various countries. This requires similar development of regional and global international cooperation to mobilize all capacities in order to combat this phenomenon. This is the role hoped for and targeted by the United Nations through the Commission for the Prevention of Crime.

Egypt, in its statement to the Tenth United Nations Congress for the Prevention of Crime and Treatment of Offenders held in Vienna in April 2000, called for international efforts to formulate a global strategy to combat corruption at various levels, and stressed the necessity of devoting special attention to external causes and elements of various manifestations of corruption that may be linked to certain practices of multinational corporations or certain major trade monopolies that may sometimes be linked to certain aspects of performance in external support programs. In our opinion, the impact of such external factors is as serious as the impact of internal elements or causes of corruption that we address, and should be addressed with as much vigor by all countries.

How Do the Media Support the Reform Process?

Freedom of Expression, Freedom of Information, and the Requirements of Justice

Hon. Geoffrey Robertson

Queen's Counsel

United Kingdom

The assumption behind this conference is that justice matters. It matters to rich and poor and to high and low alike; all and sundry must be guaranteed access to a court system for settlement of disputes quickly and fairly. In a functional, work-a-day sense, the law is the mechanism for reducing the level of grievance in any society. Unless there is confidence in the system itself, both in its rules and in the officials who apply them, then anxiety and bitterness will breed discontent and resort to bullying and intimidation—a situation in which the weak have no protection against the powerful. Justice, in any society, must arm the weak with the *possibility* of winning against the strong, even against the state itself.

Although justice is for most of the time a work-a-day matter of finding the appropriate rules for settling disputes and resolving grievances and trying accused persons with basic fairness, no justice system can be worthy of that name unless it provides for judges who are independent of the state that appoints them, operating without any pressure to decide cases in favor of government. Such "David and Goliath" contests underline the importance of judicial independence—bearing in mind the need for openness, the need for accountability in the exercise of power and expenditure of public money, and the need for informed public confidence in judicial officers.

The fundamental principles that must guide legal and judicial reforms in every country are to be found in the Universal Declaration of Human Rights, 1948, notably Article 7 (protection against discrimination), Article 8 (the right to an effective legal remedy), Article 9 (the rule against arbitrariness), Article 10 (the right to a fair and public hearing by an independent tribunal), and Article 11 (the presumption of innocence, expanded in terms of defense rights by Article 14 of the United Nations (UN) Covenant on Civil and Political Rights). These principles have become, in the view of most scholars, binding rules (or norms) of international law, with what is termed a *jus cogens* force—that is, "a rule accepted and recognized by the international community of states as a whole from which no derogation is permitted" (see Article 53 of the Vienna Convention on the Law of Treaties).

The task for all states is to erect and maintain justice systems according to these principles—not an easy matter even for the wealthiest and most advanced democracies, as recent decisions of the European Court of Human Rights against Britain, France, Denmark, and so on attest. For developing countries, or those lacking (or transiting to) democracy, legal systems often fall abjectly short of these fundamental requirements. Progress depends in part on resources and in part on government resolve, but the role of the media is important too, both in spotlighting defects in the system and in raising critical consciousness of the need for reform. To this end, the media's role is supported in international law by Article 19 of the Universal Declaration (supplemented by Article 19 of the Covenant, and equivalent articles in regional human rights treaties and in many national constitutions):

> Everyone has the right to freedom of opinion and expression; this right includes freedom to hold opinions without interference and to seek, receive and impart information and ideas through any media and regardless of frontiers.

This right is not absolute, as (absent of malice) is the free speech right in the first amendment to the U.S. Constitution. However, it may be said that international law provides a presumption in favor of free speech, which may be overridden only on clear proof that it is outweighed by a countervailing public interest—for example, in national security or protecting individual reputation from unjust attack or in maintaining the authority of the judiciary. But the media in many democratic countries, especially those with common law traditions, is unnecessarily constrained by these exceptions, owing to the failure of national courts to honor and apply this presumption in favor of freedom of expression. Exceptions to it should be narrowly construed, and not given *equal* weight.

This is because the right to freedom of expression is fundamental to democratic society. It is an essential human right which must be guaranteed to every citizen, and even to noncitizens, in respect of opinions however shocking or unattractive. That is why it must be protected by laws that are up to date, workable, and comprehensive, and that contain only such exceptions as are necessary to protect other values in a free and fair society. That there must be some exceptions admits of no doubt: there can be no freedom (as a great American judge once pointed out) falsely to shout "Fire!" in a crowded theatre: people may be killed in the panic to escape. Since the free speech principle is grounded in the public interest, it must give way on occasions when the public interest points the other way—to secure a fair trial, to protect citizens against damaging falsehoods or unwarranted invasion of their privacy, and to prevent incitement to racial violence or breaches of vital national security. The exceptions should be embodied in laws that are narrowly and carefully defined.

So far as the government and the judiciary are concerned, the media's job is faithfully to report their decisions, and to analyze and criticize them for any perceived mistakes. Law should hold the balance and enable both the media (the "fourth estate") and the other estates (executive, legislative, judiciary) to do their jobs, permitting "creative tension" between them, which is an incident of every healthy democracy. The law should provide the media with machinery to access official information and encourage it to expose malfeasance and corruption, while at the same time providing the authorities with power to stop media behavior that imperils national security or undermines the democratic fabric or propagates "news" that is false or inaccurate. Media organizations and the journalists in their employ sometimes forget that they themselves exercise a form of power when they use their right to free speech to criticize others, in print or on television, so they too cannot be immune from criticism, for instance for dishonesty or bias on unethical behavior. The law in a progressive society should therefore conduce to healthy, informed, and responsible criticisms of journalists and editors, especially since the right to free speech permits them, necessarily, a certain amount of unhealthy, ill-informed, and irresponsible criticism of politicians and judges and other wielders of power.

It must be accepted that defects in a justice system are often not as apparent, and certainly not as emotionally moving, as the results of genocide and torture and other familiar human rights violations. While there are blatant examples, such as secret or "kangaroo" courts, matters such as judicial corruption or susceptibility to political pressure require sophisticated behind-the-scenes investigation. This calls for reporters who are knowledgeable about the law itself as well as its systems and personnel, and for editors and proprietors who will not buckle under government threats to put the reporters in jeopardy before the very judges they have criticized. It also requires a degree of transparency in the justice system, including a willingness by its professional denizens to open their rituals and practices to public scrutiny and complaint. It also calls for media practitioners who are skilled not merely in reporting the courts, but in presenting legal cases in comprehensible and interesting ways.

It has to be acknowledged that this range of media expertise is lacking, to a greater or lesser extent, in every country except perhaps the United States. There, the commitment to democratic transparency at every level of the justice system and the reporting freedom provided by the first amendment has produced a reasonable level of media interest in and exposure of systemic defects and the need for reforms. Whether seen in examples of widespread public discussion of court cases and judicial appointments, or in legal magazines and the Court TV channel, the media is able to provide the public with the evidence it needs to assess the workings of the legal system. This does not of course mean that the legal system is above reproach—far from it, as the state of many U.S. prisons and the barbaric implementation of the death penalty attest. But this results from popular choices made by those elected to public office—the media is able to inform that choice, and does so in a reasonably insightful and accurate, if sometimes overly sensationalized, way. The problem in other countries is to equip the local media (and the international media, in some respects) both with the expertise to report on the legal system and with the right to publish reports on it that are adverse.

Training journalists to a familiarity with law and legal procedures is not undertaken by many media groups, and although media law is a module in many communications courses it generally covers only the laws that have an impact on professional writing. In some countries the more serious media employ legal commentators and carry contributions from practicing lawyers arguing for specific reforms, but it is rare to find articles or television programs that investigate the legal system or expose judicial corruption. Those that do run a very high risk of litigation, since lawyers are prone to sue to protect their reputation and judges in many countries have power to punish their critics for contempt of court. One notable example was an article in an international legal journal a few years ago that alleged improper behavior in a number of commercial cases decided by a group of judges in Malaysia. The publishers received a flurry of writs both from the lawyers the article named and the lawyers' clients, while the concerned individuals who were quoted in the article were also sued for libel. Heavy damages were awarded against one (the secretary of the Malaysian Bar Association) while another (Param Cumeraswamy, the UN Rapporteur on the judiciary) had to have the libel action against him removed to the International Court of Justice to establish his immunity from suit. This case provides a good example of the difficulty even for international publishers of conducting a thorough investigation of allegations of corruption within a national legal system. The result is that corruption within legal systems flourishes to a much greater extent than is recognized.

It might be expected that support for such investigations would come from professional associations and especially from the International Bar Association (IBA). Regrettably but predictably, these self-interest groups tend to be supportive of lawyers; the IBA is quick to protest when the human rights of any of its members are threatened, but has done nothing to encourage critical examination of members who operate in ways that are contrary to the public interest. It has not supported examinations, for example, of the judicial corruption that in some countries has become institutionalized partly as a result of low judicial salaries. Given that the legal profession in any given country will have a vested interest in maintaining the status quo, this is further proof of the need for an active and informed media that can operate without unnecessary constraints in its coverage of the legal system.

If the media is to play its proper role as a watchdog over the justice system, it is vital that national laws should give it protection from reprisals. Although some constraints are necessary to secure the fairness of trials, and to safeguard individuals from invasions of their privacy or reckless attacks on their reputations, these should always be proportionate and must not have a chilling effect on public interest journalism. Regrettably, many if not most countries have in place laws and punishments that do exert such a chilling effect. Examples include the following:

1. Laws that provide for the jailing of journalists

   Progressive societies no longer send people to prison for what they write or publish. But many legal systems still threaten—and sometimes impose—imprisonment for crimes of sedition, insulting officials, contempt of court, criminal defamation, inciting disobedience, and spreading false news. Such punishments are usually unnecessary and disproportionate, except in cases (the broadcasting by Radio Mille Collines in Rwanda, for example) in which incitements to serious crime or race hatred are concerned. Penal laws against the press are otherwise unnecessary.

2. Laws or courts that impose massive fines or damages on the media

   There is a tendency for libel damages in many systems to be "at large"—that is, at the discretion of the judge or the jury. The result can be bankruptcy for the journalist or liquidation for a publishing company, as the result of a single error. Media operations are such that some errors are inevitable; there are means of correcting them and compensating for them that do not have a chilling effect on future investigations. The European Court of Human Rights has ruled (in *Tolstoy v. UK*) that damages (in that case, of over US$2 million) should be moderate in media cases, but this has no influence in some countries, where politicians and their business cronies can expect to collect millions of dollars against newspapers that criticize them.

3. Licensing or restricting publication

   This is the most common form of censorship. Although licensing can be justified in some circumstances—for example, for radio and television stations—it should always be conducted according to fair and rational rules, and never be used as a means of silencing critics of official conduct. There can be no justification for limiting licenses to government channels, or to publications that support the government. Lee Kuan Yew's government, for example, acted objectionably on this score in punishing international newspapers for criticizing Singapore courts or politicians, by limiting their circulation to a very small number of copies.

4. Prior restraints

   Common law systems offer many opportunities for gagging the media ahead of time, by "interim injunctions" and similar orders. While these may in rare cases be justified, many courts grant them routinely and without reference to the public interest.

5. Forum shopping

   An unattractive consequence of wide variations in press laws across the globe is that wealthy and powerful public figures seek out the forum with the most plaintiff-friendly law for their actions against newspapers, books, and magazines that are distributed for worldwide sale, as well as against satellite television and the Internet. (The favorite forum at present is the United Kingdom, which places a heavy burden on the media to prove the truth of the stories and permits libel actions if only a few copies of the offending publication are circulated within the country.) Forum-shopping is often encouraged by national courts that are overly impressed by their own abilities—see the case of Boris Berezovsky v. Forbes Magazine, last month, in which Britain's House of Lords decided to entertain a libel action between two foreigners. This ability to forum-shop for the jurisdiction that is least tolerant to free speech should be curtailed: in a global village it makes no sense for an entire new breed of "international" public figures to enjoy different reputations in different parts of town.

*   *   *   *   *   *

Article 19 of the Universal Declaration bestows a right to "seek" information as well as to receive and impart it. This must imply more than a right to ask questions, and may be used to support three implications of the Article 19 right:

1. To impose duties on governments to divulge information;
2. To protect whistleblowers who breach secrecy laws and employment contracts in order to speak out, in conscience, from within a government agency or court administration or lawyer's office; and

3. To permit journalists to refuse to divulge their confidential sources for stories, no matter how much the identity may be of interest to police or security services, or to government or courts or big business.

In this last respect, in 1996 the European Court held in *Goodwin v. UK* that the right to freedom of information carries the implication that journalists must be permitted to protect their sources, otherwise there would be no information to be free with—sources of news would "dry up." The Court has yet to consider the case of the whistleblower (who might enjoy additional support from the "freedom of conscience" guarantee in Article 18). Freedom of information legislation is common enough in advanced political systems, where it is seen as a part of the definition of democratic culture, bolstered by reference to the "democracy rights" in Article 21 of the Universal Declaration of Human Rights, including the right to participate in government and to have "equal access" to public service. But most countries have no interest in moving toward such openness—quite the contrary.

Many states are at present trying to restrict access to the Internet, either by criminal laws that prohibit it entirely (in Libya, Iraq, Democratic People's Republic of Korea, Myanmar, and the Syrian Arab Republic) or by controlling a sole service provider (in Saudi Arabia, all traffic goes through a ministry, which disallows access to sites offering "information contrary to Islamic values"). A similar "firewall" has been erected by China, not only to stop information coming in other than through the official gateway, but to stop "official secrets" (in other words, criticisms of the regime) being e-mailed abroad. (China's surf wars are fascinating to watch, given popular expertise with the technology; the Falun Gong cult, for instance, was banned more for its ability to organize demonstrations by e-mail than for its meditation techniques).

The utility of the Internet as a free speech tool is being undermined in countries like Australia and Britain where courts have permitted local plaintiffs to sue the owners of foreign Internet sites on which they are mentioned, even though the site has no connection with local jurisdiction and any access to it from the locality is by deliberate choice of the accessor, not of the Internet publisher. This assumption that net libels are "published" (and hence actionable) whereever they can be downloaded means that authors and publishers and website proprietors can be sued anywhere—or everywhere—in the world.

To enable the media to give greater support to the process of law reform it will be necessary to remove or mitigate some of the legal deterrents to investigative journalism. This will mean reforming laws that jail journalists or hit them with heavy damages or ban papers through a licensing system. In countries (there are 50 or so) that base themselves on English common law, it will mean reforming the law of libel so that the burden of proof is placed on the plaintiff and unfair presumptions—that a plaintiff is of good character, that every defamation causes damage—are removed. The advent of a Bill of Rights in Britain, with a free speech guarantee, has already produced (by judicial creativity) a new public interest defense of "qualified privilege," and this modernizing process must continue.

Where coverage of the courts is concerned, local laws must rigorously uphold the "open justice" principle, which is based on the notion that justice is not done unless it is seen to be done (as Jeremy Bentham put it, public access to courts "keeps the judge, while trying, under trial"). This transparency must extend to the court file—all pleadings and evidence submitted should be open to public scrutiny. There should be obligations upon chief judges to present annual reports of court performance, and greater opportunities for radio and television coverage, at least of appeals and of civil matters.

The time has come also to give attention to the scope of the power of courts to punish their own critics. The English common law offense of "scandalizing the courts" remains a crime in many Commonwealth countries (in Scotland it is known as "murmuring judges") and it permits the punishment of journalists who allege corrupt behavior by judicial officers. It has been invoked recently in Kenya, Ghana, Mauritius, and Singapore; in Malaysia it was used last year to jail a *Far East Economic Review* reporter, Murray Hiebert, and against several of the barristers defending Anwar Ibrahim. It permits judges, in effect, to act in their own cause, and therefore is a breach of the fair trial principle as well as of the free speech guarantee.

The performance of the media in supporting judicial and legal reform varies from country to country: the only generalization that can be made is that it is uneven and underwhelming. The challenge of law reform is twofold: to the media itself, in equipping its practitioners with the skills to understand and explain to the public the importance of having an advanced justice system, and to governments and legislatures and courts in appreciating the importance of giving the media more freedom to investigate and expose, however uncomfortable (and, sometimes, erroneous) the conclusions of its investigations may be. Legal systems must themselves be more transparent, and more welcoming of media scrutiny on the principle that justice must be seen in order to be done.

What Conditions Are Necessary for an Independent yet Accountable Judiciary?

Independence and Accountability

A Holistic View

Hon. Omar Azziman*

Minister of Justice

Kingdom of Morocco

Ladies and Gentlemen,

I would like to begin by commending the World Bank for its initiative and by congratulating the organizers. I am among those who, for a long time, have been advocating recognition of the role played by law and justice in development, and I am delighted with what I heard here yesterday, during the opening remarks, on the subject of comprehensive development, interdependence, and the link between social, economic, political, legal, and judicial factors.

I was asked to address the conditions necessary for an independent and credible justice system and I must begin by saying that I do not have any magic formulas and that I do not believe in universal legal and judicial models or in the notion of a manual for the perfect judge. However, I do believe fervently in the value of dialogue, the exchange of ideas, the sharing of experiences, the usefulness of comparative analyses, and the interaction of cultures as a source of progress. For this reason, I will merely offer, for your critical assessment, a number of burgeoning ideas and provide you with food for thought on the subject of independence and justice.

I would like to begin by attempting to provide clarification regarding the independence of judges and the political role played by justice.

I would then like to demonstrate, that while institutional guarantees are necessary for independence, they are insufficient, since much more is needed in order to meet the requirement for independence.

* Translated into English from the original text in French and edited in English.

Finally, I would like to illustrate that independence is a necessary, but not a sufficient condition for a reliable and credible justice system.

The Independence of Judges and the Political Function of the Justice System

An independent justice system, construed in a categorical, absolute, and unqualified manner is, at best, an illusion or utopia, and at worst, deception or hypocrisy.

Since the removal of justice from the private realm, it has become, just about everywhere, one of the essential functions of the state and one of the most conspicuous state powers. Consequently, justice is eminently political, provided that its etymological meaning, according to which it cannot be reduced to the politics practiced by politicians or partisan politics, is assigned to it.

The judge is a figure of authority charged by the state with the task of settling disputes. This organizational and regulatory mission of restoring peaceful social relations and appeasement is, by nature, political. The intervention of a judge is sought when rules, defined beforehand by the authorities in place, are not observed. The aim of the judge's intervention is the restoration of order. Is it possible to imagine a function more political in nature than maintaining law and order?

Furthermore, the mission of the judge is not only to provide a reading of the law; he or she also contributes, through his or her work, to the development of law and thus participates, in his or her own way and to the extent possible, in the drafting of rules by fulfilling a regulatory role. The expansiveness of this role may vary, but it is always by nature in the political realm.

Does this mean that the notion of independent justice is devoid of meaning and substance? Absolutely not. The judge ensures respect for law and order but does not follow orders. The judge is the servant of the law, his role is to serve the law and to disregard desires that are contrary to the law, regardless of what they might be.

This independence is therefore not an isolated abstraction; instead, it is an affirmation and recognition of the specificity and autonomy needed to perform judicial functions in relation to the other functions of the state. The independence of the justice system lies, quintessentially, in this unflagging vigilance and this resistance to all forms of pressure, and justice derives its substance, meaning, and greatness from this capacity to serve as a counterbalance and to act in the interest of the law.

Independence Presupposes the Existence of Legal Instruments and Institutional Guarantees

An independent justice system calls for constitutional and institutional guarantees. The principle of an independent justice system, in the case of both the legislature and executive, must in some way be solemnly enshrined in the constitution. This constitutional guarantee is even more indispensable in the case of societies that have a tradition of subordinating judges to the authority of the executive branch and of interpenetration or confrontation between the executive and the judiciary.

Institutional measures and legal instruments are also necessary to shield judges from any interference by the executive branch and to allow them to escape all pressure, particularly in the area of their appointment, advancement, assignment, nomination to positions of responsibility, their control, and respect for professional discipline. The methods used vary from one country to another (supreme council of justice, judiciary, absence of a ministry of justice, and so on), but are all aimed at protecting judges from any interference or influence by government.

Important safeguards must also be put in place to monitor and evaluate the work of judges, their efficiency, performance, quality of their decisions, and their respect for the code of ethics.

In this case also, methods vary widely from one country to another and there is some combination of appeal procedures and inspection duties, which are assigned to the most senior and experienced judges or to an organ of the judiciary. In essence, while monitoring is necessary, it must take place in a context of respect for the independence of judges.

In short, let us bear in mind that the independence of the justice system is meaningful only if it is recognized, established, and guaranteed by the law through a legal mechanism, violation of which is duly sanctioned. However, legal instruments and guarantees are not enough. Many countries meet all these conditions, and their justice system is not always independent.

Independence is therefore not limited to legal instruments for the following reasons:

Independence Transcends Legal Instruments

First Reason

At the moment, justice is central to the development of our societies since it influences and determines whether democracy will take root in societies, the strengthening of the rule of law, legal security, and economic growth and development.

Consequently, the issue is no longer simply one of protecting the justice system from the government and parliament by defining strict boundaries between their respective authorities but of shielding the judge from any form of pressure and source of influence. This involves the following:

- Protecting the judge from the influence of economic power, which is becoming increasingly invasive and impersonal;
- Protecting the judge from the influence and seduction of the media;
- Protecting the judge from the whims and vicissitudes of public opinion, which can be fairly emotional;
- Protecting the judge from the influence of all forms of corporatism, including judicial corporatism;
- Protecting the elected judge from the pressure of those who elected him;
- Protecting the judge from himself and from the intoxication and conceit inherent in the exercise of ever-increasing power and from becoming enamored of honors and distinctions.

Thus, an independent justice system is appearing more and more as a requirement and an aspiration that far exceed legal instruments aimed at protecting the justice system from encroachment by the legislature or the excesses of the executive.

This independence is therefore taking on a new dimension that is prompting a thorough reexamination of the independence of the justice system.

Second Reason

An independent justice system is not the product of improvisation, and it is not decided upon by decree. It is the result of historical developments that were often turbulent and always fraught with conflict, which gradually shaped a social conscience and a collective memory. It is the result of a long process of democratization that has triumphed over absolutism, authoritarianism, and the nonseparation of powers. It is the condition and consequence of the equality of everyone before the law and one of the most powerful guarantees of impartial justice.

In order to take root and thrive, an independent justice system must therefore chart its own course, its own historical trajectory, in terms of ideas and experiences, and must be ever-mindful that historically and culturally, it rests on a foundation of democracy, equality, respect for freedoms and liberties, and the primacy of the law.

An independent judge is not someone whose independence is solemnly proclaimed in the constitution. An independent judge is an individual who is conscious of the importance of the universal accomplishment that an independent justice system represents, who adheres to its underlying democratic values, who practices independence, viewing it as human progress, and considers it his or her duty to preserve and improve upon this accomplishment.

More than the institutional aspects, the value of which I am not underestimating, this cultural facet of an independent justice system seems to me to be decisive, since it is what determines, in the final analysis, whether a judge will instinctively resist any interference or any form of influence, regardless of its source, nature, or objective.

Third Reason

The concept of independent justice was not forged in order to confer prestige on judges or to ensure their comfort. It was not designed to be a title of nobility or a badge of distinction conferred on the persons charged with the task of judging or as a way of paying homage to judges. An independent justice system is not even an end in itself or a moral value (as is justice or equity).

Independent justice was thought to be indispensable to the smooth functioning of judicial institutions, the condition for and guarantee of sound justice; that is, a condition for and guarantee of freedom of judgement, protection of freedoms, and preservation of the rights of each person.

Viewed in this manner, independent justice ceases to appear as the privilege of an office or as a right or attribute of the judge and assumes the form of a claim or right, of the person to whom the law applies, to independent justice—and an obligation or duty on the part of the judge to be independent. Consequently we have moved well beyond the mere demarcation of boundaries between the judiciary and the other powers in place.

This shift in perspective reveals to the judge the true importance of his or her independence and prompts him or her to demonstrate heightened vigilance so as not to replace one form of dependence with another.

This shift in perspective sheds new light on the issue of responsibility since independence must not in any way lead to immunity and even less so to impunity, and freedom of judgement must not be distorted to assume the form of arbitrariness. This leads directly to the issue of the responsibility of judges; not their incontestable and indisputable responsibility as citizens, but their professional responsibility arising from the discharge of their duties, something that is necessary, but that must be regulated in such a way that it does not hinder the independence of judges.

Further Conditions for True Independence

An independent justice system is essential if justice is to be soundly dispensed but is not enough to ensure a reliable and credible justice system that enjoys the confidence and respect of persons to whom the law applies.

Other conditions are necessary that pertain both to the judge and to the context in which he or she works. Given the time constraints, I will simply list and outline them.

Conditions Pertaining to the Judge

Moral and intellectual integrity. The work of a judge can be properly performed only by a judge who is honest and whose integrity, from a moral and intellectual standpoint, is beyond reproach; hence the need to institute a system for monitoring professional ethics that is both rigorous and respects the independence of the judge. Stiff sanctions must therefore be imposed in instances of ethical lapses and judges must be properly remunerated to ensure that they do not yield to temptation.

The rapid development and growing complexity of law makes the issue of the competence of judges a most pressing one; hence the need to put in place training structures that are flexible and rigorous and to make provisions for continuing education. This leads to the delicate issue of the specialization of judges.

Conditions Pertaining to the Work Context of the Judge

Judicial organization, procedures, and the modus operandi of courts also have an impact on reliable and credible justice. For this reason, issues related to access to justice, respect for the right to defense, the merits of proceedings in which the parties are heard, rules related to a fair trial, and the existence of appeal procedures are important.

Decisions emanating from the justice system are made by the judge but also by a number of players who exert a positive or negative influence on the quality of justice; namely lawyers, legal counsels, and experts. The same rigorous and strict standards must be applied to all persons who provide legal support.

Independence and Accountability

Issues of Power and Control

Rogelio Pérez-Perdomo*

Academic Director

Stanford Program for International Legal Studies

Stanford, California

Professor, Instituto de Estudios Superiores de Administración

Caracas

As I was putting together notes for this paper in early May 2000, the newspapers brought home pictures more disturbing than the scholarly books: Iranian judges had ruled for a shutdown of reformist newspapers and the arrest of their editors, allies of President Khatami. During the first round of parliamentary elections weeks earlier, reformist groups had won a resounding victory; the court's move was read as a delayed reaction on the part of conservatives. Meanwhile, a world away in Chile, judges were clearing away procedural obstacles to a trial of senator-for-life and former president Augusto Pinochet. It was hard not to think of the situation some years back, when Chile's justices upheld the coup, treated Pinochet as a champion of judicial independence, and declined to act on the widespread human rights violations his government had countenanced.[1]

Both these moves are controversial, but their political significance is unmistakable. On what authority does a court take such a course? Are judges answerable for their acts and omissions? Should they be? And to whom would they be accountable?

Asking judges to be both independent and accountable would appear to be a contradiction in terms. Judicial independence refers, *grosso modo*, to a state in which other powers are prohibited from interfering in a case

* Translated from the Spanish original. The author thanks J. Thome and J. J. Toharia for their comments and the correction of the English version.

1. Correa Sutil (1993); Frühling (1984).

brought before the courts; accountability refers to the consequences that judges' decisions—or failures to decide—may have for them. Common sense would dictate that the more mechanisms there are in place to ensure an independent judiciary, the more difficult it will be to hold judges accountable, and the more one insists that judges be held to account for their acts, the less independent they can be. But, as the name of this session suggests, under certain conditions independence and accountability are not antithetical. What we propose to do here is examine those conditions and to look at definitions of these terms and at societal contexts in which the values of independence and accountability can coexist.

Legal historians have recounted how judges' accountability to parties to an action evaporated in the Napoleonic order, leaving only disciplinary liability in cases such as willful misconduct or fraud (Giuliani and Picardi 1978: 37). The chief law officer—namely, in this case, the justice minister—is the disciplinary authority.

This approach mirrored the absolutist model in which judges were seen primarily as public servants, depositaries of the prince's authority. By the same token, if judges are viewed as mere mouthpieces of the law, independence presumably will not be a requirement for their work, and one can hardly hold them accountable for decisions if they are simply following the dictates of the law. Latin America showed one of the limits of the ideology that to be blindly faithful to the law, judges needed to be independent of the executive. For many judges, the law and formalities of administration of justice were mere trappings, masking the personal agendas of those holding political power. The virtue of *legalism* thus was brandished against the vice of personalism (Muñoz Tebar 1891).[2] Note that the legalist notion of justice does not concern itself with accountability, and requires at most a modicum of independence.

The perception of a judiciary with no power was borne out in practice until the mid-twentieth century, but it was not exclusive to the civil law tradition. A work on comparative constitutional law of the era that looks at the relationship between law and politics (García Pelayo 1961)[3] takes in England, the United States, France, Switzerland, and the Soviet Union, but its

---

2. For an analysis of the historical role of the judiciary and the law in Latin America see Pásara (1982); Zaffaroni (1994); and Pérez Perdomo (1978, 1990).

3. The work was first published in 1950.

analysis of judicial power is confined to the United States. Though English judges may have enjoyed elevated social status, the principle of parliamentary supremacy made them politically irrelevant.[4] We thus should not approach this as an issue of differences between common law and civil law. It is more to the point to note that, in our era, certain distinctive features of the interaction between the judicial and political systems in the United States have spread (Friedman 1985, 1994; Shapiro 1993). A historical analysis reveals that the shift began in continental Europe and Latin America before it was felt in the United Kingdom (Pérez Perdomo 2000).

In fact, the powerlessness of the judiciary was hardly absolute. In France, where the notion of the "judge as mouthpiece" was perhaps most deeply entrenched, the primacy of judge-made law and the political weight of the judiciary is evident in the evolution of administrative law—that crucial corpus for dealings between the state and the citizenry—which came out of judicial practice (Labaudère, Venezia, and Gaudemet 1999).[5] Hence, a more accurate way to frame the argument would be to say that judges have had a great deal of power in configuring the law, even during eras in which they were considered to be entirely subservient to the laws (Dawson 1968). It is a hallmark of our times that more and more major issues, some of them in the political terrain, are being placed before the courts, and that we no longer think of judges as being subservient to the law or to tradition (Cappelletti 1989: 3ff).

If we accept that judges do have real power and their decisions are more than mere mouthings of the law, then questions about their independence and accountability must come to the fore as intertwined concerns. Power and accountability must go hand in hand (Astuti 1978). Judges do exercise a political power; when we inquire about independence and accountability we are asking about the legitimacy and bounds of that power. This paper will refer to a handful of the issues examined in works I have cited as references, focusing on several of the knottier concerns.

---

4. Forbath (1991) compares the roles of judges in England and the United States and explains the important implications this has had for political life in the two nations. See also Van Caenegem (1987); Griffith (1991); and Jowell (1999).

5. France has a dual judicial system and the Conseil d'État and the administrative judges were not thought of as a judicial body until recently.

The Power and Independence of the Judiciary

If we grant that the judiciary wields real public power, our first question must be whence its legitimacy—in other words, why should we obey judges, and why should the political authorities obey them? The notion of judicial independence brings the issue into sharp focus: if judges are independent of the political authority, what then is the source of their power?

In the past half-century the winds of democracy have swept through political systems. Taking root in the process is the idea that those in power should not interfere in judicial matters. Note that it is democratic states that grapple with questions about an independent judiciary: this is not something that absolutist or authoritarian states hold dear (Giuliani and Picardi 1978; Becker 1970). "Judicial independence" has meant independence from the executive branch, the principal seat of political power and the most centralized of the branches of government. To judge from recent trends, we would need to lengthen the list of sources of power to include political parties and the media.

Today, we expect judges to remain outside the political fray and to act accordingly in their courtrooms. Judicial independence means that we believe, normatively, that judges should not be parties to the political process—that is, they should evince no sympathy for the governing authorities or political parties, and should not be guided by them or by opinion polls or the media. We look to judges to rule *according to law,* that is, by reference to a corpus of knowledge that society prizes, and we expect them, as individuals, to be impervious to the lure of political or financial rewards. Independence is a value that is instrumental for judges' impartiality and their fidelity to the law and legal principles.

Judges are human beings and, like their fellow citizens, they are unlikely to be politically neutral. It would seem desirable that they share in the broad political trends at work in their society (Toharia 1999; Zaffaroni 1994). But to discharge their office they must put respect for the law and legal values above any partisan loyalty.

We would maintain that the legitimacy of the judiciary's power is rooted not in democracy but in legal ethics.[6] This calls for a brief clarification: ac-

---

6. Elsewhere we have termed this legitimacy *aristocratic,* as Aristotle used the word (Pérez Perdomo 1993). It is rooted in the assumption that judges have, or ought to have,

cording to some in-depth analyses (Dahl 1989), one sine qua non of modern democracy is the protection of individuals and minorities, so that they can take part in the political system. This is, at heart, the political meaning of the law in modern nations. Thus, the language of the law is above all a language about rights. Protecting rights and the rule of law is not at odds with the workings of a democracy: it is both part and parcel of democracy and its counterweight.

This answers the question about the purpose of an independent judiciary. What we are dealing with is an instrumental value—this is an independence for something, not for judges to use as they think best. An independent judiciary is one that will be able to rule according to law, will safeguard individuals' fundamental rights, and thus will be genuinely impartial within the general guideline of the law.

With that in mind, let us go back to the events I mentioned at the start. The Chilean justices who condoned massive human rights violations failed in their mission, forfeiting their ethical-legal legitimacy. Ethically, they were not free to protect or fail to protect human rights, regardless of what percentage of the Chilean population may have backed the government's policy at the time. I find the Iranian judges' moves to stifle freedom of the press to be alarming for the same reason, though I am too far removed from that particular set of circumstances to be able to offer fitting comments.

Independence resides in each judge (Becker 1970). This is tied to the normative image of the judge, and we think it would be reasonably safe to say that there exists a basic consensus regarding that normative image (Toharia

---

more intellectual training in the law and must be held to a higher ethical standard than the rest of the citizenry. They would be more *virtuous* than the man on the street, using "virtue" as it was understood in classical Greece. I fear that the word *aristocracy* may be misunderstood, since the modern European meaning of the term is the one now in currency. Positions on this issue range widely, from those who maintain that we should consider the power of the judiciary to be democratic because its purpose is democratic (Zaffaroni 1994) to those who see the judicialization of politics as a threat to the democratization process (Linz 1978). Santos (2000) maintains in the same article that "in continental Europe [the rising protagonism of courts] is above all the symptom of the failure of the state, as democratic state" (p. 402), and that "the rule of law and the judicial system are a central component of democracy I" (the liberal democracy). In democracy II (the more socialist one proposed by Santos) they are as important as in democracy I, but "less central because they must be conceived as part of a much broader set of participatory institutions and social movements" (Santos 2000: 425). We believe that the present analysis can cast light on this divergence.

1999). On the contrary, the institutional configurations to make certain a judiciary will be independent and cultural elements at work alongside them, may differ considerably from one society to another. This is an important consideration in an era of transplantation efforts. We should take care not to confuse judicial independence with those institutional setups, as many are wont to do.[7] For the most part their object is twofold: independence, and control or accountability. Their modus operandi will depend very much on the social and political backdrop.

In short, if the judiciary's power is to be legitimate, the judiciary cannot appear to be one more arm of the political authority, however democratic the government. Judicial power also is necessary to rule out political controls and answerability demands. This calls for a delicate balance, a demarcation of the spheres of independence and accountability or control. We will look at these areas along with the institutional setups that countries have devised to make for an independent and accountable judiciary.

Control and Accountability

Control and accountability are distinct but interrelated notions. Control refers to an institutional apparatus charged with making certain that judges do not deviate from the commonly accepted values of the collective. Questions of control generally are examined in the context of judicial appointments and promotions. Accountability speaks to the consequences of judges' wrongful acts or omissions. In practice, these areas are intricately intertwined, and demands for accountability can be one form of control.

A prime focus of the literature on accountability is the array of liabilities that can attach to judicial activity (Cappelletti 1989). So-called disciplinary liability refers to judges' answerability to a judicial-system oversight authority, which may be judicial agencies proper or involve political institutions. The latter variant is sometimes referred to as "political accountability," though that usage seems infelicitous to me. The criminal liability of judges goes to their unlawful acts; civil liability has to do with reparations that judges may have to make to parties who have suffered injury as a result of judicial mis-

---

7. For a discussion of methodological considerations in constructing justice—system performance indicators, and the easy move from deciding what is a desirable behavior to indicating the structural feature most likely to produce it, see Hammergren, undated.

conduct. Such liability is personal, existing in each judge, though nowadays civil liability also can attach to the state because the judge acts on the state's behalf. We will not explore these forms of answerability here, but will look in a moment at one other type that we consider to be true political accountability—a collective, diffuse form of answerability.

Questions of independence and control first come into play when judicial posts must be filled. We are accustomed to thinking that in democratic societies all power comes, or should come, from the people. Even so, we generally maintain—with very good reason—that judges should not be popularly elected, as that would make them heavily dependent on the political process and beholden to campaign funders or political organizations that backed their candidacy. Thus, in those jurisdictions that do elect judges, the tendency is to do away with election campaigns or the more democratic features of the electoral process (Merryman 1999: 122ff). In most selection exercises there are safeguards to make certain that a candidate is an ethical person and knowledgeable about the law.

In the English tradition, some elements of which were passed on to the United States, professional politics plays a clear role in the choice of judges. As a rule justices are recruited from among experienced, distinguished lawyers, and both professional and political circles have a say in the selection (Griffith 1991; Merryman 1999; Jacob 1972). Giving judges life tenure is a way of insulating them from political pressure in the concrete cases that will subsequently come before them. Very commonly the institutional mechanisms in place will color judges' general political orientation (Griffith 1991). The system does not forestall serious conflicts between the judiciary and the political authority.

Most nations steeped in the civil law tradition have depoliticized the process of appointing judges to the bench: competitions and judicial training institutions are designed to keep politics out of the selection process. Judges enter the profession not long after finishing their judicial studies, largely on the strength of academic merit (Merryman 1985). This opens a career path to young judges. The problem then becomes one of who controls that career path and what factors decide who will be promoted, since managing judges' promotion expectations can mean effectively controlling them. Hence the tendency to shift that function from the executive branch to judicial councils or comparable specially created bodies (Fix-Zamudio and Fix-Fierro 1996).

This takes us to the question of who should sit on such councils, and how one evaluates a judge.[8]

To decide on the domain of independence it is useful to look at the various facets of judicial activity. A judge's inherently judicial responsibility is jurisdictional—the hearing of cases and rendering of judgments. This is the independent realm of action of each judge, as an individual. Obviously, for judicial systems to operate properly there need to be checks on other activities in which any given judge may engage. First, there is the meaning of the activity itself: a judge is not free to rule on this or that case, and failure to rule constitutes a denial of justice. Undue delays are another potential form of denying justice. In most nations, denial of justice is a crime—one of the few criminal acts that only judges can commit. The system should be alert to situations of justice denied, which tend to far outnumber cases in which the courts actually impose penalties for this crime.

Second, judges can commit wrongful acts and omissions associated with the discharge of their office. Extortion and complicity in bribery are two examples, which most legal codes class as grave offenses. Breaches of internal rules are another potential area of misconduct. Delays, nonfeasance, and patently below-norm performance records create, or ought to create, disciplinary and civil liability. Other transgressions may involve violations of codes of ethics, such as inappropriate relations with the parties to an action, or with attorneys. Soliciting loans is a sanctionable act in some countries. Clearly, some liability attaches to such wrongful acts.

Finally, disciplinary liability can attach in some instances unrelated to judicial office because judges, by virtue of the source of their legitimacy, are expected to be exemplary citizens. Alcohol or drug abusers, perpetrators of violence, and those who do not fulfill family obligations should not sit on the bench.

Can the existence of these kinds of liability or accountability affect a judge's independence? Theoretically the answer would be no, since such behaviors are entirely extraneous to judges' jurisdictional mandate— or they are the manifest failure to perform that mandate. In practice, however, any accountability system can be misused to punish independence,

---

8. For the subtle mechanism (and its transformation) in the French high judiciary, see Bancaud (1993).

particularly if there is a double standard at work, or different yardsticks for judges depending on their connections to those who wield political power.

Where the spheres of independence and accountability become blurry is in the issue of judges' accountability for specific decisions they hand down. In some countries,[9] if a judge's ruling reveals patent ignorance of the law or gross negligence, it creates disciplinary and civil liability. One can also explain this by reference to the ethical-legal legitimization of the judge's power, since a judge must rule according to law: a person ignorant of the law cannot ascend to the bench. However, since we know that the law is not apodictic but lends itself to a variety of interpretations, calling judges into account in such circumstances is no easy task.

One plausible hypothesis for a comparative study is that the substantive regulation of judicial accountability varies little from one place to the next, though some countries may have more explicit, detailed regulations than others. In other words, we can assume that there exists a fairly widespread consensus as to the model of the good judge and the kind of deviations from the normative role that are sanctionable or, in society's view, should be sanctionable. A second hypothesis is that the avenues for demanding accountability, and the system's modus operandi, vary enormously from one country to the next. As a sociologist of law I would also posit that a country's *judicial culture* is more important than formal rules in the operation of justice.

An Independent and Accountable Judiciary

The foregoing clarification of notions of independence and accountability shows that these values can coexist as elements of good justice. They are, indeed, interlinked, but in practice the need for judicial independence can be used to excuse accountability, just as the need for accountability can be a tool for making judges answerable to politicians. With that in mind, I will end this paper with some practical recommendations on how countries can build a judiciary that is both independent and accountable.

---

9. For an analysis of the Italian case in different moments, see Ferrajoli (1978), Di Federico (1990), and Guarnieri (1992); for a comparative review with other countries, see Guarnieri and Pederzoli (1999).

The first recommendation would be to pay close attention to institutional mechanisms. If judges are independent it is not because their nation's constitution or laws so dictate: countries need an institutional apparatus or structure to guarantee the independence of the judiciary, watching over the appointment, evaluation, promotion, and accountability of judges. How such an apparatus operates will depend on a country's civic culture, and it would be a mistake to assume it to be readily transplantable. In a word, the institutional design of these mechanisms is all-important. The trend today is to have judges disciplined by their peers, with political control only of supreme court justices—but, even this can be moderated by the tradition of lifelong or lengthy appointments. Though this clearly is preferable to control by a justice minister, it is not enough. Every society needs mechanisms to continually review the performance of judges both individually and collectively.

A second recommendation is the strengthening of the judicial *ethos*. Judges should be imbued with the scope of their mission, understand the crucial role they play, and rise to society's expectations of them. This should be a core component of their training.

Aside from internalizing the importance of their role, judges must know that their performance will be routinely evaluated. The evaluations of greatest weight should come from the higher-ranking judiciary and from fellow judges. But this is only one avenue of assessment: another source of evaluation is statistics to implicitly or explicitly compare a judge's performance with that of his or her peers. Opinions of attorneys and others involved in the justice system are valuable inputs as well. Evaluations should center not on the caliber of judges' decisions (which falls into the realm of independence) but on their diligence, punctual and efficient discharge of their duties, intellectual qualifications, and creativity.

Judicial evaluation systems should give early warning of potential problems in a judge's conduct. In most cases, a timely word will be enough to keep a judge on the straight and narrow, so formal accountability mechanisms will not have to be activated. But there must be safeguards against any automatic solidarity among judges, which would thwart accountability systems.

I would like to conclude with a reminder of the importance of the collective responsibility of the judiciary and, perhaps, of those of us who have made the judicial system the focus of our work. Judicial systems should continually look inside themselves to gauge how they are performing in society: whether they are receiving the cases they should or are handling cases that could be better dealt with by other social agencies; if they are excluding or favoring certain sectors; and if the demand for justice is evolving or can be expected to change. These are issues of judicial policy that need to be fully understood, drawing on as extensive a body of information and analysis as possible. And the debate must spill over into the public arena.

It is not a question of having judges review their own performance or assigning that task to other judicial personnel. The key is to have independent investigators look at the system's workings, but make their findings available to the judiciary and other justice officials for debate. This will drive home to judges the importance of their work and its impact on different facets of societal activity. Only then will the debate on judicial policies be a rigorous and participatory exercise. I see this not only as a political responsibility of judges and judicial leaders, but also a responsibility of the scholarly or research community. Unless we continue in the footsteps of the giants who went before us, bringing imagination to the meticulous task of assembling and analyzing information, we will have failed to live up to that personal responsibility.

BIBLIOGRAPHY

Astuti, Guido. 1978. "Indipendenza e responsabilità del giudice: considerazioni introduttive." In A. Giuliani and N. Picardi, eds., *L'educazione giuridica III: La responsabilità del giudice*. Perugia: Libreria Editrice Universitaria.

Bancaud, Alain. 1993. *La haute magistrature judiciaire entre politique et sacerdoce*. Paris: Librairie Générale de Droit et Jurisprudence.

Becker, Theodore L. 1970. *Comparative Judicial Politics*. Chicago: Rand McNally.

Cappelletti, Mauro. 1989. *The Judicial Process in Comparative Perspective*. Oxford: Clarendon Press.

Correa Sutil, Jorge. 1993. "The Judiciary and the Political System in Chile: The Dilemmas of Judicial Independence during the Transition to Democracy." In I. P. Stotzky, *Transition to Democracy in Latin America: The Role of the Judiciary*. Boulder, Colo.: Westview.

Dahl, Robert. 1989. *Democracy and Its Critics*. New Haven, Conn.: Yale University Press.

Dawson, John P. 1968. *The Oracles of the Law*. Ann Arbor, Mich.: The University of Michigan Law School.

Di Federico, Giuseppe. 1990. "La crisis del sistema judicial y el referendum sobre la responsabilidad civil de los magistrados." *Revista de Estudios Políticos*. Madrid.

Ferrajoli, Luigi. 1978. "Posición institucional y función de la magistratura en el sistema político italiano." In P. Andrés Ibanez, *Política y justicia en el estado capitalista*. Barcelona: Fontanella.

Fix-Zamudio, Héctor, and H. Fix-Fierro. 1996. *El Consejo de la Judicatura*. México: Universidad Nacional Autónoma de México.

Forbath, William. 1991. "Courts, Constitutions and Labor Politics in England and America: A Study of the Constitutive Power of Law." *Law and Social Inquiry* 16.

Friedman, Lawrence. 1994. "Is There a Modern Legal Culture?" Ratio Juris 7.

———. 1985. *Total Justice*. New York: Russell Sage.

Frühling, Hugo. 1984. "Poder judicial y política en Chile." In J. de Belaúnde, ed., *La administración de justicia en América Latina*. Lima: Consejo Latinoamericano de Derecho y Desarrollo.

García Pelayo, Manuel. 1961. *Derecho constitucional comparado*. 6th ed. Madrid: Revista de Occidente.

Giuliani, Alessandro, and N. Picardi. 1978. "La responsabilità del giudice: problemi storici e metodologiche." In A. Giuliani and N. Picardi, eds., *L'educazione giuridica III: La responsabilità del giudice*. Perugia: Libreria Editrice Universitaria.

Griffith, J. A. G. 1991. *The Politics of the Judiciary*. 3rd ed. London: Fontana.

Guarnieri, Carlo. 1992. *Magistratura e politica in Italia*. Bologna: Il Mulino.

Guarnieri, Carlo, and P. Pederzoli. 1999. *Los jueces y la política. Poder judicial y democracia*. Madrid: Taurus.

Jacob, Herbert. 1972. *Justice in America. Courts, Lawyers and the Judicial Process*. 2nd ed. Boston: Little Brown.

Jowell, Jeffrey. 1999. "Of Vires and Vacuums: The Constitutional Context of Judicial Review." *Public Law*. Autumn.

Hammergren, Linn. Undated. "Diagnosing Judicial Performance: Towards a Tool to Help Guide Judicial Reform Programs." Draft prepared for Transparency International (unpublished).

Laubadère, André de, J-C. Venezia, and Y. Gaudemet. 1999. "Traité de Droit administratif." 15th ed. Paris: Librairie Générale de Droit et de Jurisprudence.

Linz, Juan. 1978. *The Breakdown of Democratic Regimes*. Baltimore: Johns Hopkins University Press.

Merryman, John Henry. 1999. *The Loneliness of the Comparative Lawyer*. The Hague: Kluwer.

———. 1985. *The Civil Law Tradition*. Stanford: Stanford University Press.

Muñoz Tebar, Jesús. 1891. *El personalismo y el legalismo*. New York.

Pásara, Luis. 1982. *Jueces, justicia y poder en el Perú*. Lima: Centro de Estudios de Derecho y Sociedad.

Pérez Perdomo, Rogelio. 2000. "Jueces y estado hoy," in G. Soriano (ed.), *Constitución y constitucionalismo hoy* (forthcoming publication).

——. 1995. "Políticas judiciales en Venezuela." Caracas. Ediciones IESA.

——. 1993. "En nombre de la República y por autoridad de la ley. Problemas de legitimidad del Poder Judicial en Venezuela." *Politeia* 16. Caracas.

——. 1990. "La organización del estado en el siglo XIX." *Politeia* 14. Caracas.

——. 1978. *El formalismo jurídico y sus funciones sociales en el siglo XIX venezolano.* Caracas: Monte Avila.

Rico, José María, and L. Salas. 1990. "Independencia judicial en América Latina: Replanteamiento de un tema tradicional." San José: Centro para la Administración de Justicia.

Santos, Boaventura de Sousa. 2000. "Law and Democracy: (Mis)trusting the Global Reform of Courts." To be published in J. Jenson and B. S. Santos, eds., *Globalizing Institutions: Case Studies in Social Regulation and Innovation.* Aldershot, New Hampshire: Ashgate.

Shapiro, Martin. 1993. "The Globalization of Law." *Global Legal Studies Journal* 1.

Tate, C. Neal. 1995. "Why the Expansion of Judicial Power?" In C. N. Tate and T. Vallinder, eds., *The Global Expansion of Judicial Power.* New York: New York University Press.

Toharia, José Juan. 1999. "La independencia judicial y la buena justicia." *Justicia y Sociedad,* No. 3 (UNDP).

Van Caenegem, R. C. 1987. *Judges, Legislators and Professors.* Cambridge: Cambridge University Press.

Zaffaroni, Eugenio Raúl. 1994. *Estructuras judiciales.* Buenos Aires: Ediar.

Independence and Accountability

An Asian Pacific Perspective

Hon. David K. Malcolm, AC

Chief Justice of Western Australia

Law reform on a global scale requires, and must necessarily have, at its core, the cooperation of law reformers of countries of differing political, social, and economic paradigms in order to have any chance of coming to grips with even the most basic legal reform concepts. Law reform covers a vast area of legal issues from the complex concerns of a treaty between foreign neighbors to the issues of judicial corruption.

I do not think it would be an overstatement to say that we live in exciting times in the context of international relations and rapid advances in technology. In recent times the advent of high-speed communications and the increasingly global nature of economics has meant the development of close bonds between the nations of the Asia Pacific region. Where the region was once the arena for combat of Western powers and then Western political ideologies, it has now become one of the most politically and economically important regions in world trade.

The rapid nature of information exchange and the increasingly porous nature of international boundaries through electronic communications and the movement of capital and labor have presented a range of new issues in the administration of justice. These have major implications for the courts and the role of the courts, particularly in newly liberalized economies. International trade has raised issues concerning both substantive law and procedure. Foreign investment in the region and the increasing affluence of particular socioeconomic groups in countries throughout Asia and the Pacific has seen increasing demands for the reform of the law and the methods of its enforcement in order to provide consistency and coherency in commercial relationships. These factors have been referred to by the Chief Justice of Singapore as Trade, Technology, and Tribe:

> Trade would refer to trends in international economics, the flow of goods and services and investments. Technology represents the broad implications of scientific advancement while Tribe describes how socio-economic forces can bind communities together or pull them further apart.[1]

It has been recognized for some time that an effective legal system administered by an independent judiciary is as essential to the infrastructure of a country as the transportation, communications, and the legislative, financial, and administrative systems in a country.

There have been some landmark developments in law reform in the Asia Pacific Region in recent years. Some of these have been the result of the efforts of the members of LAWASIA, the Law Association of Asia and the Pacific. The LAWASIA Region is coextensive with the region covered by the United Nations Economic and Social Committee for Asia and the Pacific (ESCAP), and following the collapse of the Soviet Union it now includes the Russian Federation: countries such as Kazakhstan, Uzbekistan, Kyrgyz Republic, as well as former countries that were members and still are from Afghanistan in the east swinging around to the Republic of Korea, down to New Zealand and Samoa in the Pacific Ocean, and across to Sri Lanka in the Indian Ocean.

For some years now I have been the Chair of the Judicial Section of LAWASIA and I have been responsible for the organization of the biennial Conference of Chief Justices of Asia and the Pacific since 1989. In recent years the Conferences have been attended by the Chief Justices of some 25–30 countries in the Region.

The Conference of Chief Justices is convened on behalf of the LAWASIA Judicial Section and, as is now the practice, held contemporaneously with the general LAWASIA Conference. The first conference took place in Penang, Malaysia in 1985 and subsequent conferences have been held in Islamabad, Pakistan (1987); Manila, Philippines (1989 and 1997); Perth, Australia (1991); Colombo, Sri Lanka (1993); Beijing, China (1995); and Seoul, Korea (1999). The Chief Justices Conference was first held in conjunction with the LAWASIA Conference in Perth in 1991.

---

1. The Hon. Yong Pung How. 1998. Keynote Address to the Asia Pacific Courts Conference, Manila. *Courts Systems Journal* 1: 138–147.

At the Sixth Conference of Chief Justices of Asia and the Pacific held in August 1995 in Beijing, the *Beijing Statement of Principles of the Independence of the Judiciary* was adopted as a statement of minimum standards to be observed in order to maintain the independence and effective functioning of the judiciary in the Region.[2] This is really quite a remarkable development, and it was foreshadowed by the United Nations when they adopted their *Basic Principles on the Independence of the Judiciary* and recommended that in various regions of the world the judiciary get together and adopt statements that were applicable to their particular regions. The Asia Pacific Region is the first region in the world where such a set of principles has been adopted.

It is almost universally acknowledged that one of the most fundamental aspects of the protection of human rights and the rule of law is the maintenance of an independent judiciary. A number of definitions of judicial independence have been advanced. Most academic definitions center on the absence of external influence in the administration of justice. For example, judicial independence has been defined as follows:

> The degree to which judges actually decide cases in accordance with their own determinations of the evidence, the law and justice free from coercion, blandishments, interference, or threats from governmental authorities or private citizens.[3]

Another definition has been offered in the context of a parliamentary democracy:

> The capacity of the Courts to perform their constitutional function free from actual or apparent interference by, and to the extent that it is constitutionally possible, free from actual or apparent dependence upon, any persons or institutions, including, in particular, the executive arm of government, over which they do not exercise direct control.[4]

It has been suggested that there is an additional aspect to judicial independence that many of these definitions omit, that is, the extent to which the

2. Nicholson, R. D. *Fifth Conference of Chief Justices of Asia and the Pacific: Evaluation Report*, p. 24.

3. Rosenn, K. 1987. "The Protection of Judicial Independence in Latin America." *University of Miami Inter-American Law Review* 19: 1.

4. Green, Guy, Sir. 1985. "The Rationale and Some Aspects of Judicial Independence." *Australian Law Journal* 59: 135.

judiciary holds the public confidence that it is the appropriate body to determine what is right or wrong.[5]

The maintenance of public confidence in the impartiality of judges is essential to public acceptance of the law and the legal system. A loss of that confidence can lead to instability and threaten the existence of society. The link between the independence of the judiciary and judicial impartiality is not well understood, however. One of the means whereby the links between independence and impartiality can be articulated is in the setting of minimum universal standards to protect judicial independence and thereby preserve judicial impartiality. Since the early 1980s, development of the concept of judicial independence at the international level, in particular by the enumeration of its key features, has proceeded apace through instruments such as the International Bar Association's *Minimum Standards of Judicial Independence* (1982) (*"New Delhi Standards"*), the United Nations' *Draft Principles on the Independence of the Judiciary* (1981) (*"Siracusa Principles"*), the UN *Basic Principles on the Independence of the Judiciary* (1985) (*"Basic Principles"*), and the *Draft Universal Declaration on the Independence of Justice* (1989) (*"Singhvi Declaration"*).

The *Beijing Statement of Principles of the Independence of the Judiciary* is quite comprehensive and I do not propose to give any detailed exposition of it. Briefly stated, though, what it does is provide a common definition of the judicial function that is accepted by judges in some 30 countries in the Asia Pacific region. Article 10 of the *Beijing Principles*[6] provides that the objectives and functions of the Judiciary include:

1. To ensure that all persons are able to live securely under the Rule of Law;[7]
2. To promote, within the proper limits of the judicial function, the observance and the attainment of human rights within its own society;[8] and
3. To administer the law impartially between citizen and citizen and between citizen and State.[9]

---

5. Larkins, C. 1996. "Judicial Independence and Democratization: A Theoretical and Conceptual Analysis" *American Journal of Comparative Law* 44: 605–610.
6. See also *Singvhi Declaration* Art. 1.
7. *Beijing Principles* Art. 11 (a).
8. *Beijing Principles* Art. 11 (b).
9. *Beijing Principles* Art. 11 (c).

These functions complement and overlap each other. For example, it is to the judiciary that the power of, and responsibility for, resolving disputes according to law is given.[10] The natural consequence of this allocation of responsibility is that the judicial power must be exercised by a consistent and unwavering application of the rule of law. It follows that the judiciary must apply the rule of law impartially to matters brought before it. As one judge has put it:

> The exercise of... judicial power... requires that judicial decisions be made 'according to law.' If the power is exercised on some other basis, and particularly as the consequence of influences whether of power, policy, private thoughts or money, it follows that an essential requirement of the judicial power is negated.[11]

In turn, a consistent, impartial, and unwavering application of the rule of law tends to protect persons from the infringement of human rights, to the extent that they are recognized by the rule of law that applies in a particular country. There is room, within the historical and cultural context of a country, for a legitimate debate about the appropriate scope of human rights within that country. However, insofar as those rights are recognized, the judiciary can play an important part in upholding them, whenever there is a powerful attempt to abridge them in an ad hoc or arbitrary manner. As Mr. L. V. Singhvi observed in his Final Report to the United Nations Commission on Human Rights in 1985:

> The strength of legal institutions is a form of insurance for the rule of law and for the observance of human rights and fundamental freedoms and for preventing the denial and miscarriage of justice.[12]

One area in which there is a potential threat to the independence of the judiciary is the financing of the work of the courts. In this respect it must be accepted that the courts will remain dependent, to an extent, on government for the provision of funding to operate the courts in the same way as any other arm of government. The provision of court infrastructure—things as

---

10. See generally Nicholson, R. D. *Judicial Independence and Accountability: Can They Co-Exist?* (pp. 410–11).

11. Nicholson, R. D. *Judicial Independence and Accountability: Can They Co-Exist?* (p. 405).

12. Singhvi, L. M. 1985. *Final Report.* See n44.

basic as office space, filing cabinets, and typewriters—is an important part of the efficient and effective administration of justice. A lack of funding of court structures, resulting in the understaffing of judicial positions and the lack of court facilities is often the root cause of delay and congestion in courts[13] and a loss of confidence in the legal system as a whole.

The direct control of the resources available to the judiciary by the legislature or the executive, coupled with the application of external measures or expectations of performance of the justice system, may leave members of the judiciary open to criticism from politicians for delays that may be beyond the scope of judicial control. This situation poses a direct threat to judicial independence.

At the Seventh Conference of Chief Justices of Asia and the Pacific in Manila in 1997, there was a short discussion on the models of administration utilized in the various courts and their impact on the independence of the judiciary. In particular, there was significant interest in the manner in which budgets were fixed and funds were provided to the courts. By way of a survey distributed in October 1998, I asked the chief justices present to provide me with information on the procedures applicable to the appointment of staff, the management and allocation of matters before the court and the setting of budgets. The objective was to obtain an overview of the administrative and financial structures of courts in the region. A draft survey was prepared and sent to the chief justices who attended the Seventh Conference of Chief Justices. Additional surveys were also sent to the chief justices of each of the Australian Supreme Courts.

There was considerable interest in the survey from the chief justices. By the end of July 1999, 35 responses had been received covering 37 courts. This figure represents a response rate of more than 65 percent. The comments that follow are an overview of the responses received from the chief justices. The references to "courts" in the following paragraphs are to those courts from which responses were received.

At the outset, two fundamentally critical points should be borne in mind. First, the review is necessarily brief. The task of reviewing the diverse administrative and judicial management structures of courts throughout

13. Shihata, I. 1995 "Judicial Reform in Developing Countries." In *The World Bank in a Changing World*. The Hague: Kluwer Law International See p. 152n.

the Region is enormous. In order to present the results to the Conference in a meaningful way, they necessarily must be presented in summary form.

Second, the review was not intended to identify and recommend to the chief justices the most appropriate form of management structure. To make such a recommendation, going beyond the general statements contained in Articles 36 and 37 of the *Beijing Principles*, would need to take into account differences in the cultural and legal or constitutional histories of each country, in addition to the resources available to each court. The review was designed to provide an opportunity for the chief justices to understand the differences between the jurisdictions represented at this Conference and to provide material to aid future discussion of the methods of ensuring the administrative independence of the judiciary.

The section on appointment and employment of administrative personnel dealt with the services involved in the reception, filing, and organization of the documents and legal processes relating to any legal proceedings; the management and listing for hearing of the cases to be heard; and the recording, processing, and implementation of the orders and judgments issued by the courts, together with the processing of appeals.

In all but three courts, administrative staff were employed as members of the relevant public service agencies. In the majority of courts, the administrative staff are appointed by a senior administrative officer or relevant public service agency in accordance with a legislative or other formal regime established by the legislature. While on its face this tends to suggest that the courts have little independence from the legislature or executive, it should be noted that in most cases, the appointment of administrative staff involved a senior administrative officer within the court or an appointment board or commission (or a combination). In a large number of courts, the chief justice is responsible for the discipline and supervision of administrative staff. For example, the administrative staff of the Subordinate Courts of Singapore are selected and appointed by the Public Service Commission, which delegates its authority to a Judiciary Personnel Board. The Board consists of members of the judiciary of the Supreme and Subordinate Courts in addition to a member of the Public Service Division. Following appointment, the administrative staff remains under the supervision of the registrar, subject to the control of the senior district judge. In the case of the Supreme Court of Nepal, administrative staff is appointed in a similar manner, in conjunction with a Judicial Service Commission, and remain under the supervision of the judges of the court to which they are appointed.

Of interest were the Supreme Courts of Pakistan, Japan, and the High Court of Australia. In the case of Pakistan, the administrative staff of the superior courts is appointed, remunerated, and supervised by their respective courts directly, in the exercise of a constitutional guarantee of independence. The process of appointment is governed by the rules of court. Once appointed, the junior administrative staff remains under the supervision of the registrar as administrative manager of each court, who is also appointed by the court.

Each court within the Japanese hierarchy manages the appointment and supervision of its staff directly by virtue of a similar constitutional guarantee of independence. In the Supreme Court of Japan, this guarantee is carried into effect, by virtue of Articles 12 and 13 of the Court Organisation Law[14]. Article 12 provides the following:

> In its conduct of judicial administrative affairs, the Supreme Court shall act through the deliberations of the Judicial Assembly and under the general supervision of the Chief Justice of the Supreme Court.

Article 13 provides the following:

> The Supreme Court shall have a general Secretariat which shall administer the miscellaneous affairs of the Supreme Court.

By comparison, the High Court of Australia manages its administrative staff by virtue of the establishment of an independent management structure by legislation. While the Commonwealth Constitution establishes a judiciary as an independent arm of government, the Constitution is silent in terms of the Court's administrative independence. Members of the administrative staff are appointed by the chief executive and principal registrar pursuant to the High Court of Australia Act of 1979, enacted some 79 years after the Commonwealth Constitution.[15]

While the ability of the judiciary to appoint administrative staff independent of interference by the legislature—or, more likely, a minister or other

14. Court Organisation Law, Law No. 59, 1947.
15. High Court of Australia Act 1979 (Cth).

member of the executive—is a desirable guarantee of independence, it remains an ideal. I note that in the majority of courts, the wages and salaries of administrative staff are paid either from consolidated revenue, or the budget of a government department, following its appropriation from a national budget. While the government continues to meet the financial demands of the court, it is only reasonable to expect that, in the majority of cases, they will seek to retain some control over the management of administrative staff. I will return to this point in the context of the review of budgetary structures.

In those jurisdictions where the judiciary has been established as an independent organization, administrative staff are paid by the Court itself. I have already outlined the structure of the Supreme Court of Japan. In the High Court of Australia, the payment of the wages and salaries of administrative staff is governed by the High Court of Australia Act. Section 37, for example, provides the following:

> Moneys paid to the High Court shall be applied only... in payment of any remuneration and allowances payable under this Act to any person other than a Justice.

Judges in the majority of the courts have personal staff. The nature of such staff varies widely from the inclusion of what could be termed "domestic staff," such as gardeners or housekeepers, through to the appointment of legally trained research assistants. In only 50 percent of those courts in which personal staff are appointed does the judge appoint the staff member himself or herself. In most other cases it is the registrar or manager of the court, or the government department charged with responsibility for the court, that appoints the judges' personal staff. In terms of independence, this may present a number of difficulties. For example, an inefficient or unsuitable staff member may have a direct impact on the efficiency of the judge, particularly in cases in which the judge relies on that staff member for services that he or she cannot perform himself or herself.

Although not included in the surveys, it may be appropriate to identify how the independence of personal staff members is guaranteed. For example, where the appointment and conditions of a staff member are subject to the control of an individual or agency separate from the judiciary, difficulties may arise if there is a dispute between the staff member and that department. A dispute about the level of remuneration is an example. Such a dispute would have a direct impact on the judge to whom the staff member is appointed. I note that in all cases, the wages or salaries of the judges' personal staff are ultimately paid from consolidated revenue.

In a little over one-third of the courts surveyed, the judges do not have personal staff. They are, however, often assigned additional administrative staff to support and assist them in their duties. In the majority of cases, similar issues to those that I have identified in relation to administrative staff would also arise.

In some jurisdictions these issues are dealt with by the establishment of a distinct administrative structure. In Japan for example, judges' personal staff are appointed in a similar manner to the balance of the administrative staff. In Hong Kong, the manager of judicial administrative affairs, called the Judiciary Administrator, appoints the staff. In both cases, a "pool" of available staff is created from which a Judge is assigned staff.

It should be noted that in the majority of those courts in which personal staff are appointed by a body that is external to the judiciary, the Judges to whom staff are assigned retain supervisory and disciplinary control over their day-to-day tasks.

The procedures adopted for case management and listings in each of the courts can be dealt with shortly. Scheduling the sittings of the court, the management of the lists, and the assignment of judges to particular matters are tasks that are generally undertaken under the supervision of, or with the direct involvement of, the chief judicial officer in each jurisdiction, a council or committee of judges, or the judge assigned to a particular matter. In all jurisdictions, therefore, this aspect of the administrative management of the courts is under the direct control of the judiciary. For example, in the Court of Appeal and High Court of New Zealand, the sittings of the Court are managed by the chief justice, pursuant to the legislation that establishes each Court. Section 60 of the *Judicature Act 1908* (NZ) provides the following:

(1)   The Court of Appeal may from time to time appoint ordinary or special sittings of the Court, and may from time to time make rules... in respect of the places and times for holding sittings of the court...

Section 52(1), subsections (a) and (b) of the Judicature Act, dealing with the High Court, provides the following:

(1) Any three or more judges, of whom the Chief Justice shall be one, may from time to time—

(a) Appoint sittings of the court for the dispatch of civil and criminal business; and

(b) Make for each place where an office of the High Court is established, rules respecting the places and times for holding sittings of the court, sittings in chambers, the order disposing of business... and such other matters.

In the superior courts of Japan, all matters are dealt with by the judicial conference of each court. I have already outlined the legislative provisions that give form to the conferences in relation to administrative staff. In the Supreme Court of Brunei Darussalam, the sittings of the Court and the listing of matters for trial are dealt with by the registrar in conjunction with the judges and the chief justice.

In those jurisdictions in which the court will go "on circuit" or sit in regional areas, the chief judicial officer also deals with the listing of matters and the designation of a particular judge to deal with the circuit, either alone or in conjunction with the registrar.

It is worth noting also that in all but one of the courts,[16] rules of court are made either by the council judges or by the chief judicial officer. In some jurisdictions, the rules are subject to disallowance by the executive or the legislature. Although not addressed in the survey, it may be interesting to identify the circumstances in which the executive or legislature can and will disallow rules made by the judiciary.

In the vast majority of courts, the regimes that apply to the internal administration of listings and procedure are largely free from interference by the executive or the legislature. This conclusion is significant. The removal or exclusion of external interference in the assignment of particular judges to particular matters, and the exclusion of interference in settling rules of procedure, also serve to remove or exclude bias, or an appearance of bias, from the judicial process. External interference in the judicial process, as distinct from the judicial function, will create an apprehension in the mind of the community that the judiciary is merely an administrative organ of the legislature or the executive. This leads into a discussion of the next section of the survey, which deals with the administrative structure of the courts in the context of the broader public administration.

16. The Supreme Court of the Maldives indicated that the president set rules of court in that jurisdiction.

The purpose of the section of the survey on the position of the court within the justice system was to identify the extent of judicial independence in practice. There were divergent answers given by the courts on this topic.

In Australia, a comprehensive study of forms of court governance was published in 1991. Entitled *Governing Australia's Courts*,[17] it provided a summary of the forms by which Australian courts were managed, incorporating methods of selecting staff and settling budgets. In that report, three models of court governance were utilized to compare and categorize the courts studied:

- The *traditional model* was used to describe those systems of administration in which the management of the court fell directly under the supervision of an administrative officer responsible to a member of the executive government, usually the attorney general. Until the late 1980s, most courts in Australia were administered in this manner.

- The *separate department model* was used to denote those systems of governance in which the provision of administrative services to the judiciary was administered by a separate department of state that falls within the portfolio of a member of the executive. Management responsibilities were shared between the chief judicial officer and a senior administrative officer responsible to the department. By reference to administrative services, I mean those services that fall into the first category that I outlined earlier.

- The final model was the *autonomous model* in which the chief judicial officer bears the responsibility for the management of both the administrative and judicial arms of the court. In some cases, the chief administrative officer is appointed by the chief judicial officer or by the government on the nomination of the chief judicial officer.[18]

In analyzing and comparing the various courts' structures throughout the Region, I have utilized these three models. I acknowledge that the three

17. Church, Thomas W. and Peter A. Sallman, 1991. *Governing Australia's Courts*. Melbourne, Australia: Australian Institute of Judicial Administration.

18. This style is also known as a "centralized" form in the United States; Graham C. 1993. "Reshaping the Courts: Traditions, Management Theories and Political Realities." In S. Hays and C. Graham, *Handbook of Court Administration and Management*, New York: Marcel Dekker, Inc. See p. 3 and subsequent pages.

categories are imperfect, as not every model of court administration utilized will fit precisely in one or the other of the three categories.

Only two of the courts surveyed fell within the traditional model in terms of their administrative structure. In the Supreme Court of the Maldives, the administration and management of the judiciary remains under the control of the president's office. Interestingly, the administration of the Supreme Court of Victoria remains under the control of the attorney general.

Six of the courts fell within the "separate department" model. All of the State Supreme Courts of Australia, except for Victoria, fall within this model. The administration in those courts is managed by departments that are structured in a similar manner. The management of administrative services for the Supreme Court of Brunei Darussalam is conducted by the civil service department.

The balance of the courts surveyed representing the great majority conform to the autonomous model. What is common to many of the courts that have applied this model is that the judiciary has been constituted as a distinct department of government as a means of guaranteeing judicial independence. In that case, a constitutional guarantee of "adjudicatory independence" has been carried through to create structures for "administrative independence."

Much from the previous sections of the survey carried over into the final section on court funding and expenditure. As I indicated earlier, complete administrative independence for the courts is the ideal. However, all courts remain dependent on government and, in particular, the legislature for the funds to maintain their operations and for the provision of administrative services. In all cases, funds are allocated to the courts from consolidated revenue or from an annual budget settled by the legislature. In almost all cases, Japan being the notable exception, the funds are allocated to the courts by the legislature, as an item in a national or provincial budget, or by a member of the executive from funds allocated to his or her portfolio.

It is notable that in all courts participating in the survey the budget estimate is settled either by, or in conjunction with, the chief judicial officer of each jurisdiction. In many cases, it is the principal or chief registrar of each court that has primary responsibility for settling the budget estimates and bears primary responsibility for the administration of the court's budget. This is because the registrar has day-to-day responsibility for the administrative management of the court's services. In a number of courts in which registrars perform judicial functions these responsibilities rest with an executive officer or equivalent.

I have outlined earlier the constitutional position of the Supreme Court of Japan. It is worth revisiting this in the context of budgetary arrangements for this court as it provides an example of the most secure method of ensuring independence while being dependent on the legislature and executive for the provision of funds. Article 83 of the Court Organisation Law provides that the amount to be allocated to the courts, as distinct from any broader justice portfolio, is to be independently appropriated by the national budget. The budget estimate for the Japanese courts is prepared by the Supreme Court Secretariat and receives the approval of the Judicial Conference. Once the budget estimate is received by the executive, the opinion of the Supreme Court on the estimate is sought.[19]

In terms of the final question in this section, an alarming number of courts reported that financial constraints had had an impact on the management of the courts and the judicial function. For example, the Supreme Court of Cambodia has acknowledged that lack of funds has meant that there has been some difficulty in arranging travel for witnesses in criminal trials. There is also a lack of judges with specialist training and there is little prospect for ongoing professional training. The Supreme Court of Mongolia has abandoned circuit work owing to a lack of funds to allow judicial officers to travel.

In April of 1997 the then-Chief Justice of Australia, Brennan CJ, announced in the course of opening the Twelfth South Pacific Conference in Sydney that the eight chief justices of Australia's states and Territories had that day released a *Declaration of Principles of Judicial Independence* relating to judicial appointments. It contains a set of principles adopted by the chief justices applicable to Australian circumstances.

Coinciding with this public announcement the chief justices published a statement to the same effect. In the statement the chief justices referred to the *Beijing Principles* indicating that the *Declaration* specifically took them into account and said:

19. Court Organisation Law, Article 18 (2).

In any state or country, the key to public confidence in the judiciary is its manifest impartiality.

There is a crucial link between judicial impartiality and the principles of judicial independence, understood as a set of protective safeguards. This *Declaration of Principles*, like the *Beijing Principles*, has as its aim the articulation and promotion of the principles of judicial independence.

The *Beijing Principles*, by articulating the benchmark principles of judicial impartiality and the rule of law, have the potential to make a substantial contribution to both the social and economic development of the Asia Pacific Region. As the Secretary General of the International Commission of Jurists has said:

> Far from being a luxury for a poor state, a legal structure which is quantitatively and qualitatively sufficient to carry out the services expected of it must be considered one of the necessary components of a society and a precondition for its progress.[20]

The adoption of the *Beijing Principles* represented the achievement of a remarkable consensus between the chief justices of a range of countries—from the two countries with the world's largest populations to some of the smallest. It was also necessary to accommodate the differences between those countries within the common law tradition and those within the continental or civil law systems. The common law tradition is reflected in a high degree of judicial independence and the absence of a career judicial service, with appointments made largely from the ranks of the private profession. The civil law system reflects both a collegiate system and a career judicial service undertaken as an alternative to private practice. There are also significant differences in the approach to procedure, as between the common law adversarial system and the inquisitorial system. The authoritarian traditions of some countries mark them off from those with more democratic traditions. There are numerous variations across a wide spectrum, many of which reflect the divergent cultures of the different countries in the Region. The achievement of a consensus on the principles of the independence of the judiciary in the Asia Pacific Region was a tribute to the determination of the chief justices to

---

20. Dieng, A. 1992. *The Rule of Law and the Independence of the Judiciary: An Overview of Principles.* See p. 35.

reach agreement on the minimum standards necessary to secure judicial independence in their respective countries.

The *Beijing Principles* were only one of the recent landmark developments in the Asia Pacific Region. The business world operates in a global village. While this has its economic rewards, disputes between parties to commercial transactions who reside in different countries create a range of problems regarding service of process, taking evidence abroad, the enforcement of judgments, and the like. There are very few countries in the region that are parties to individual agreements or treaties in the area. Recognizing the need for appropriate arrangements to deal with these problems, the Chief Justices of the 1999 Seoul Conference adopted the *Seoul Statement on Mutual Judicial Assistance in the Asia Pacific Region*. The Statement said:

> The prompt and fair resolution of civil and commercial disputes between residents of different countries in the Asia Pacific region requires the establishment of procedures for the efficient and effective service of process, taking of evidence and enforcement of judgments by a resident of one state in the territory of another.[21]

It was recommended to the government of countries in the region that "the formation of a strong network of arrangements on the service of process, taking of evidence and enforcement of judgments between countries" was necessary in order to achieve this objective. Annexed to the Statement was a proposed *Treaty on Judicial Assistance in Civil and Commercial Matters between Australia and the Republic of Korea*. That treaty was signed shortly after the Seoul Conference. It is hoped that this treaty will be used as a model and will encourage other countries in the Region to adopt similar treaties. For example, notwithstanding the interchange of trade and people between Korea and Japan, Korea and China, and other areas, no treaties exist between those countries. In fact, there are only one or two agreements that are currently in effect. I suppose the most important of those from Australia's point of view is the agreement between Australia and New Zealand, which has, in practical terms, the effect that while separate jurisdictions are maintained, jurisdiction can be exercised by judges of New Zealand in Australia and Australian judges in New Zealand.

---

21. *Seoul Statement on Mutual Judicial Assistance in the Asia Pacific Region.*

At the Seventh Conference in Manila in 1997 there was a session focusing on accessing worldwide information networks through the Internet, presented by Dr. Greenleaf, who is the architect of the AUSTLl program in Australia, which enables the judgments of participating courts in the scheme to be available on the Internet shortly after publication. We have a system in place in Western Australia that can put our judgments on AUSTLl on the Internet within 24 hours of publication. I think we currently hold the record, which is 45 minutes after the publication in court.

Since 1996 there has been a strategic relationship between Western Australian courts and the Singapore courts—in particular at the subordinate and district court levels. The relationship was originally proposed by the Chief Justice of Singapore. The courts in both Singapore and Western Australia had a common interest in the use and development of court technology in case management.

The most recent development from this relationship is the development by the Singapore Courts of the eJustice Judges' Corridor. This is a multi-jurisdictional judicial cluster established and organized by the subordinate courts. Its purpose is "to brainstorm court governance and jurisprudential issues and provide an opportunity for the diffusion of ideas."[22]

The eJustice Corridor is an e-mail network of a multi-jurisdictional character, organized by the Singapore Courts to brainstorm court governance and jurisprudential issues and provide an opportunity for the diffusion of ideas. The next topic listed for discussion on the e-Justice corridor, which has been subscribed to by judges in the region, is judicial reform.

In 1978 the International Commission of Jurists established the Centre for the Independence of Judges and Lawyers (CIJL) in 1978 "with the global mission of promoting and protecting judicial and legal independence."

The protection of judges and lawyers from persecution is a difficult task and one that requires constant vigilance and intervention by way of going on fact-finding missions or observing trials of the persecuted jurists. It was as a result of that kind of hard work that the position of the United Nations Rapporteur was established. The center recently held a seminar in February 2000 on *Combating Judicial Corruption*. The Conference adopted a policy framework

---

22. Keynote Address of the Hon. Chief Justice Yung Pung How, Republic of Singapore, Eighth Workplan Seminar 1999/2000.

for preventing and eliminating corruption and ensuring the impartiality of the judicial system. The framework has six aims that focus on the prevention, exposure, and elimination of judicial corruption for the purpose of creating an increasing public confidence in the judicial system.

The Chief Justice of Singapore, whom I referred to earlier, has said that the emerging economy (and society) is one that is premised upon, and shaped by, knowledge and knowledge workers. Knowledge, as embodied in human beings as "human capital" and in technology, has always been central to economic development. The advent of high speed communications and electronic commerce has the potential to change the face of business dramatically. The law concerning one of the most fundamental aspects of real estate law, indeed all business—namely, the communication of offer and acceptance in contracts—faces significant change. Electronic signatures and the instantaneous communication of both offer and acceptance means that many of the traditional methods of business may need to be reconsidered. On a more personal level, the courteous exchange of carefully worded correspondence has been replaced by the curt, shorthand nature of e-mail communications.

There can be little doubt that electronic mail and electronic commerce have achieved a staggering level of popularity in a short space of time. Although in development by the United States Department of Defense since the 1960s, the Internet was only opened to commercial traffic in 1991. The World Wide Web is an even more recent development having been publicly launched in 1993.[23] It was estimated that there would be at least 200 million users of the Internet in 1999.[24]

One of the potential uses of the Internet, which is quickly being realized by the private sector, is to attract customers. With the potential number of users being in the millions, the World Wide Web represents an inexpensive method of advertising a product and identifying buyers from all over the world. The United States Department of Commerce has estimated that by 2002 the Internet will be used for business at a volume that is worth more

---

23. Adams, M., R. Kuras, and J. Law. 1997. *Putting Australia on the New Silk Road: The Role of Trade Policy in Advancing Electronic Commerce.* Commonwealth of Australia. See p. 12.

24. Brown, Jack. 1997. "Obscenity, Anonymity and Database Protection: Emerging Internet Issues." *The Computer Lawyer* 14: 1.

than US$300 billion annually.[25] In his address to the Australian Information Industry Association in December last year, the Commonwealth Attorney General, the Hon Darryl Williams QC MP said:

> The Government believes that electronic commerce is a key factor in ensuring Australia's future prosperity... [T]he current growth in the Australian Internet consumer market has been unprecedented. The latest figures from the Bureau of Statistics show that Internet usage has increased 30% in the last six months, and is up almost 50% from the levels recorded in February this year.[26]

The use of electronic communications will have a significant impact on the law and, in particular, the law of contract. At an international level, work is currently underway on reaching uniform standards on electronic commerce in a number of fora including the United Nations Commission on International Trade Law, the World Intellectual Property Organisation, the Organisation for Economic Co-operation and Development (OECD), the World Trade Organization, and Asia–Pacific Economic Cooperation Group (APEC). It is important that common standards be adopted to determine such matters as when and where a contract has been concluded.

The use of e-mail also raises a number of issues in terms of the freedom of personal expression. Its international nature in particular raises some difficult international legal and political questions. Material that might be regarded morally objectionable or indecent material could foment difficulties. The issue that immediately comes to mind is the exchange of child pornography by Internet users. That is clearly objectionable and there would be little debate over the general nature of the material. What, however, of messages, images, or literary works that we do not consider subversive or objectionable or that are simply banned in the country in which they are being viewed, having been transmitted from some other country?

The difficulty of regulating Internet use has resulted in some Draconian methods of control in other jurisdictions. In China, Internet users are required to register with their local police stations. In Vietnam, Internet access

25. United States Department of Commerce. 1998. *The Emerging Digital Economy.* See p. 43.

26. The Darryl Williams QC MP, Speech to the Australian Information Industry Association, 14 December 1998; Available at <http://law.gov.au/ministers/attorney-general/Articles/AusInfInd.html>.

is restricted to universities and government agencies. In Saudi Arabia, access is limited to companies, hospitals, and universities.[27] The total prohibition of electronic communication is unrealistic, however, and I suspect impossible to enforce.

Even the partial prohibition of certain terms or subjects creates difficulties. For example, the filtering and restriction of messages by a carrier or service provider that contain the word "sex" would also exclude access to material on safe sex or even the English county of Sussex.[28]

It has been reported that in late 1995, the German government attempted to exert pressure on service providers rather than users to restrict access by Bavarian users to material that was deemed "explicit." As a result of the international nature of the communications, the effect was that 4 million users around the world were prevented from accessing the same sites. Sites as varied as Vatican pronouncements on sex and an academic commentary on pornography in China[29] dropped out of the Internet as a result of what Germany did. As this example illustrates, regulation by a single state could have far-reaching and potentially unforeseen effects on users all over the world. What might once have been seen as draconian internal battles over the restriction of access to subversive political literature could mean the proliferation of extradition applications, or alternatively, the imposition of the same internal restrictions on international users of the Internet.

The private commercial interests that are involved in the Internet network also constitute an obstacle to regulation by the state. The point is made by a number of commentators that internet users often consider that the internet is a "law-free" zone and a great deal of effort is put into steps to circumvent or subvert state regulatory practices.[30] Private Internet service providers are reluctant to enter into authoritative statements on content regulation as they infringe on the ability of users to use what is essentially a commercial service.

While it may be suggested that multilateral treaties on the use and access of Internet resources is a possible approach, one is immediately presented

27. Grabosky, P., and R. Smith. 1989. *Crime in the Digital Age*. Sydney: Federation Press. See p.125.

28. Grabosky and Smith (1989: 130) See note 28 for full reference.

29. Grabosky and Smith (1989: 133) See note 28 for full reference.

30. Grabosky and Smith (1989: 123) See note 28 for full reference.

with the same difficulties that I have outlined above in regard to internationally applicable standards of "objectionable," "indecent," or "subversive." For example, the United States Supreme Court has maintained a strong commitment to the First Amendment and the protection given to freedom of expression. Two recent examples provide an indication of the scope of electronic communications permitted and the reluctance of the Supreme Court to place any restrictions on the nature of those communications.

In 1996, the United States Government enacted the Communications Decency Act as part of the Telecommunications Reform Act. The Act prohibited the "patently offensive display of indecent material to minors." Neither "indecent" nor "patently offensive" were defined. In its decision in Reno v. American Civil Liberties Union[32], the Supreme Court found that the Communications Decency Act, while protecting minors from offensive material, interfered with the freedom of speech guaranteed by the First Amendment. The Court was concerned with the vague nature of the terms employed by the Act and the criminal sanctions that had been attached to a breach of its provisions. The Court noted that its role was not to "limit the level of discourse reaching a mailbox to that which would be suitable for a sandbox" and affirmed the right of adults to exchange and view material such as that struck at by the Act.[33] In its judgment, the Court said:

> The growth of the internet has been and continues to be phenomenal. We presume that governmental regulation of the content of speech is more likely to interfere with the free exchange of ideas than to encourage it. The interest in encouraging freedom of expression in a democratic society outweighs any theoretical but unproven benefit of censorship.[34]

In a matter that came before the United States Supreme Court earlier the same year, an injunction was issued preventing the enforcement of Georgia legislation that prohibited the use of an Internet user name which "falsely identified the person." The application for the injunction was brought by a number of civil liberties organizations, arguing that the use of false names allowed individuals to participate in discussions on sensitive topics or to

---

32. Unrep.; 26 June 1997; United States Supreme Court; 96–511.
33. Kirkland, E. 1997. "US Supreme Court Sends the White House Home to Think Again." *Computers and Law* 8: 19.
34. Kirkland (1997: 39). See note 33 for full reference.

express disapproval of government without fear of retribution. In granting the injunction, Judge Shoob said:

> On its face, the act prohibits such protected speech as the use of false identification to avoid social ostracism, to prevent discrimination and harassment and to protect privacy.[34]

Such an approach would of course have considerable benefits for authors wishing to publish works that may criticize or satirize government action or may be objectionable to others. The double-edged nature of the protection, as I mentioned earlier, creates a number of concerns. A laissez-faire approach to the content of communications also raises the specter of constitutionally sanctioned "hate speech."

As I have said, electronic communications and commerce offer opportunities for both personal and commercial growth. All of these important developments may not have been possible without the assistance of technology. Law reform on a global scale takes a concentrated effort over a long period of time. I think it was Michael Kirby who said, "law reform is for long distance runners." Years can pass while decisions and agreements are reached. Human rights continue to be violated, but this does not dull our spirits domestically or internationally. Each step we take is a step closer to achieving our goals of justice and fairness through the cooperation of countries, particularly in the Asia Pacific Region.

There are many challenges being faced by the countries of this Region. I have been inspired and encouraged by the willingness of the chief justices to join together in mapping out pathways to achieve judicial and other reforms to improve the administration of justice in the Asia Pacific Region. They have commenced a journey in the last part of the twentieth century that I hope will continue in the twenty-first century.

---

34. *American Civil Liberties Union and Ors v Miller* reported in Brown 1997, 4:14. See note 24 for full reference.

The Judicial System of Pakistan

Measures for Maintaining Independence and
Enforcing Accountability

Hon. Irshad Hasan Khan

Chief Justice of Pakistan

The Independence of the Judiciary

The concept of judicial independence has, along with changing international
relations, acquired a new impetus of placing a greater premium on the role of
the judiciary and the protection of human rights in the past half century. The
1948 Universal Declaration of Human Rights recognizes the right of individual to "a fair and public hearing by an independent and impartial tribunal, in
the determination of his rights and obligations and of any criminal charge
against him."[1]

Similarly, the 1966 International Covenant on Civil and Political Rights
states:[2]

> In the determination of any criminal charge against him, or of his rights and
> obligations... at law, everyone shall be entitled to a fair and public hearing
> by a competent, independent and impartial tribunal established by law.

And the United Nations Basic Principles on the Independence of the Judiciary stipulate the following:[3]

> Persons selected for judicial office shall be individuals of integrity and
> ability with appropriate training or qualifications in law. Any method of
> judicial selection shall safeguard against judicial appointments for im-
> proper motives. In the selection of judges, there shall be no discrimination
> against a person on the grounds of race, colour, sex, religion, political or
> other opinion, national or social origin, property, birth or status, except

1. Article 10.
2. Article 14.
3. Article 10.

241

that a requirement, that a candidate for judicial office must be a national of the country concerned, shall not be considered discriminatory.

The Sixth Conference of Chief Justices of Asia and the Pacific held in Beijing on August 19, 1995 adopted the Beijing Statement of Principles of the Independence of the Judiciary in the Law Association of Asia and the Pacific (LAWASIA) Region as follows (excerpts):

1. The Judiciary is an institution of the highest value in every society.

2. The Universal Declaration of Human Rights (Art. 10) and the International Covenant on Civil and Political Rights (Art. 14 (1)) proclaim that everyone should be entitled to a fair and public hearing by a competent, independent, and impartial tribunal established by law. An independent Judiciary is indispensable to the implementation of this right.

3. Independence of the Judiciary requires that:
   a. the Judiciary shall decide matters before it in accordance with its impartial assessment of the facts and its understanding of the law without improper influences, direct or indirect, from any source; and
   b. the Judiciary has jurisdiction, directly or by way of review, over all issues of a justiciable nature.

4. The maintenance of the independence of the Judiciary is essential to the attainment of its objectives and the proper performance of its functions in a free society observing the Rule of Law. It is essential that such independence be guaranteed by the State and enshrined in the Constitution or the law.

5. It is the duty of the Judiciary to respect and observe the proper objectives and functions of the other institutions of government. It is the duty of those institutions to respect and observe the proper objectives and functions of the Judiciary.

6. In the decision-making process, any hierarchical organization of the Judiciary and any difference in grade or rank shall in no way interfere

with the duty of the judge exercising jurisdiction individually or judges acting collectively to pronounce judgment in accordance with Article 3(a). The Judiciary, on its part, individually and collectively, shall exercise its functions in accordance with the Constitution and the law.

7. Judges shall uphold the integrity and independence of the Judiciary by avoiding impropriety and the appearance of impropriety in all their activities.

8. To the extent consistent with their duties as members of the Judiciary, judges, like other citizens, are entitled to freedom of expression, belief, association, and assembly.

9. Judges shall be free subject to any applicable law to form and join an association of judges to represent their interests and promote their professional training and to take such other action to protect their independence as may be appropriate.

Jurisdiction

33. The judiciary must have jurisdiction over all issues of a justiciable nature and exclusive authority to decide whether an issue submitted for its decision is within its competence as defined by law; and

34. The jurisdiction of the highest court in a society should not be limited or restricted without the consent of the members of the court.

Judicial administration and judicial independence are interlinked and intertwined. The independence of the judiciary cannot be maintained in letter and spirit until the basic factors and requirements relating to judicial administration are adhered to. In my view, factors that are relevant and have a bearing on judicial independence are the absence of coordination among the various tiers of judicial hierarchy, nonexistent court management and case processing mechanisms, lack of access to information technology, absence of competent and trained human resources, lack of infrastructure facilities, lack of automation, poor salaries to judicial officers and court staff, inadequate performance standards, inadequate data and statistics on performance, inefficient budgetary allocations, and so forth.

Numerous other international and regional human rights instruments also provide for judicial independence and the dispensation of quick but fair and impartial justice. The rationale for judicial independence and the impartiality of judges may be ascertained in an address given in 1997 by the Chief Justice of Australia (then Chief Justice of the State of New South Wales). He said, and I quote:

> Judges regard the judiciary as the third arm of government, separate from and independent of the two political arms, the legislature and the executive. Their duty is to maintain the rule of law, to uphold the constitution, and to administer civil and criminal justice, impartially, according to law.... The independence of the judicial arm of government is not a benefit won by judges on some ancient industrial battlefield, and now jealously guarded as a perquisite of office. It is a constitutional principle with a sound practical rationale. Justice must be, and be seen to be, administered with impartiality. Executive governments are themselves major litigants. Almost all criminal cases are fought as contests between the government and a citizen. Governments are frequently involved in civil litigation, either directly or through corporations in which they have a stake. Courts are sometimes called upon to determine disputes between different governments, or between the legislative and the executive branches of government. Judicial independence is an element of the constitutional system of checks and balances, and is the primary source of assurance of judicial impartiality.

The independence of the judiciary is a basic principle of our constitutional system of governance. The Constitution of Pakistan contains specific and categorical provisions for the independence of the judiciary. The Preamble and Article 2–A state that "the independence of the judiciary shall be fully secured"; and with a view to achieve this objective, Article 175 provides that "the judiciary shall be separated progressively from the executive." The rulings of the Supreme Court in the cases of Government of Sindh v. Sharaf Fafridi,[4] Al-Jehad Trust v. Federation of Pakistan,[5] and Malik Asad Ali v. Federation of Pakistan,[6] indeed, clarified the constitutional provisions and thereby further strengthened the principle of the independence of the judiciary, by

4. PLD 1994 SC 105.
5. PLD 1996 SC 324.
6. PLD 1998 SC 161.

providing for its separation from the executive branch, clarifying the qualifications for appointing High Court judges, prescribing the procedure and time frame for appointing judges and chief justices, and the transfer of a judge from a high court to the Federal Shariat Court. Furthermore, the supreme court judgments in the cases of Mehram Ali v. Federation of Pakistan[7] and Liaquat Hussain v. Federation of Pakistan[8] are also in line with the above rulings: they elaborate and reiterate the principle of judicial independence and the separation of the judiciary from the executive.

The Supreme Court in its recent unanimous verdict, authored by the Chief Justice of Pakistan, on the military takeover of October 12, 1999, observed:

> Notwithstanding anything contained in the Proclamation of Emergency of the Fourteenth day of October, 1999, the Provisional Constitution Order No. 1 of 1999, as amended and the Oath of Office (Judges) Order No. 1 of 2000, all of which purportedly restrained this Court from calling in question or permitting to call in question the validity of any of the provisions thereof, this Court, in the exercise of its inherent powers of judicial review has the right to examine the validity of the aforesaid instruments.

> In the exercise of its right to interpret the law, this Court has to decide the precise nature of the ouster clause in the above instruments and the extent to which the jurisdiction of the Courts has been ousted, in conformity with the well-established principles that the provisions seeking to oust the jurisdiction of the Superior Courts are to be construed strictly with a pronounced leaning against ouster.

On the subject of independence of judiciary the Court held:

> Stability in the system, success of the Government, democracy, good governance, economic stability, prosperity of the people, tranquillity, peace, and maintenance of law and order depend to a considerable degree on the interpretation of the Constitution and legislative instruments by the Superior Courts. It is, therefore, of utmost importance that the judiciary is independent and no restraints are placed on its performance and operation. It claims and has always claimed that it has the right to interpret the Constitution or any legislative instrument and to say as to what a particular provision of the Constitution or a legislative instrument means or does not mean, even if that particular provision is a provision seeking to oust the jurisdiction of this Court. Under the mandate of the Constitution, the

7. PLD 1998 SC 1445.
8. PLD 1999 SC 504.

Courts exercise their jurisdiction as conferred upon them by the Constitution or the law. Therefore, so long as the Superior Courts exist, they shall continue to exercise powers and functions within the domain of their jurisdiction, and shall also continue to exercise power of judicial review in respect of any law or provision of law, which comes for examination before the Superior Courts—to ensure that all persons are able to live securely under the rule of law; to promote, within the proper limits of judicial functions, the observance and the attainment of human and Fundamental Rights; and to administer justice impartially among persons and between the persons and the State, which is a sine qua non for the maintenance of independence of judiciary and encouragement of public confidence in the judicial system.

In a system of constitutional governance—one that guarantees fundamental rights and is based on the principle of trichotomy of powers—such as ours, the judiciary plays a crucial role of interpreting and applying the law and adjudicating disputes arising among governments or between state and citizens or citizens inter se. The judiciary is entrusted with the responsibility of enforcing fundamental rights. This calls for an independent and vigilant system of judicial administration so that all acts and actions leading to the infringement of fundamental rights are nullified and the rule of law is upheld in society.

The judiciary is required to oversee the performance of all state organs, including itself, to ensure that each organ remains within its allotted sphere and does not intervene in the affairs of the other(s). In a celebrated ruling, the Supreme Court of Pakistan in the case of the State v. Zia-ur-Rehman,[9] issued an authoritative interpretation of the relevant provisions of the Constitution. The Court's observation relates to the federal scheme of "distribution of subjects" and the system of "separation of powers"—and the role of the Supreme Court in implementing the same. The Court ruled:

> The functions of the State are distributed among the various State functionaries and their respective powers defined by the Constitution. The normal system under such a system, with which we are familiar, is to have a trichotomy of powers between the executive, the legislature and the judiciary. But each of these organs may itself be fashioned in a variety of different shapes and forms. Thus the legislature may be unicameral or bicameral; the legislative subjects may be divided between the federating units and

9. PLD 1973 SC 49.

the federation in a federal system or even the legislative power may be divided between the executive and the legislature as in our present system. The executive may take the Presidential or the Parliamentary form. The judiciary also may consist of various types and grades of Courts with the highest at the apex either as an ultimate Court of Appeal or a Court of Cassation. There may also be other administrative tribunals outside the judicial pyramid.

In all such cases, it will also be the function of the constitution to define the functions of each organ or each branch of an organ, as also specify the territories in which, the subjects in respect of which and sometimes even the circumstances in which these functions will be exercised by each of these organs or sub-organs. Limitation would, therefore, be inherent under such a system so that one organ or sub-organ may not encroach upon the legitimate field of the other. Thus, under a written Constitution, the legislature of a federal unit will not be able to legislate in respect of a subject which is within the field of the federal Legislature, nor will a federal Legislature be able to legislate upon a subject which is within the exclusive field of the Legislature of the federating units. It cannot, therefore, be said that a Legislature, under a written Constitution, possesses the same powers of "omnipotence" as the British Parliament. Its powers have necessarily to be derived from, and to be circumscribed within, the four corners of the written Constitution.

In a similar vein earlier, the Supreme Court in the case of Fazal-ul-Qadir Chaudhry v. Shah Nawaz,[10] had taken the view that in view of the constitutional scheme for the distribution of power among various state organs and authorities, the superior judiciary is allotted a crucial and delicate responsibility of containing organs and authorities within their allotted spheres of operation. Since the judicial review function of the Supreme Court is assigned to it by the constitution, it is the bounden duty of the Court to examine and pass necessary orders and directions to institutions and authorities to ensure strict adherence to the letter and spirit of the constitution. Thus, it may check the arbitrary tendency of state authorities and functionaries. The Court clarified that in performing this function, it does not arrogate to itself a supra-constitutional role, as the constitution obligates it to do so, so as to avoid encroachment of an organ or authority that is on the preserve or domain of another. The Court observed:

10. PLD 1966 SC 105.

So far, therefore, as this Court is concerned it has never claimed to be above the Constitution nor to have the right to strike down any provision of the Constitution. It has accepted the position that it is a creature of the Constitution; that it derives its powers and jurisdictions from the Constitution; and that it will even confine itself within the limits set by the Constitution which it has taken oath to protect and preserve but it does claim and has always claimed that it has the right to interpret the Constitution and to say as to what a particular provision of the Constitution means or does not mean, even if that particular provision is a provision seeking to oust the jurisdiction of this Court.

It is indeed for the purpose of realizing the above-mentioned objectives, that the constitution mandates the independence of the judiciary and its separation from the executive branch. With a view to attain such independence, the constitution prescribes a whole set of safeguards or guarantees so that not only the judiciary in its institutional capacity, but also judges in their individual capacity may remain shielded against any possible outside pressure or control or influence. Such independence is necessary, for otherwise the courts would not be able to administer justice freely, impartially, and without fear or favor to all manner of people, as is dictated by the constitution and the law. To ensure such independence, the constitution prescribes the qualifications for and mode of appointment of judges, security of tenure, service conditions, salary, and other privileges, together with grounds and mode of removal of judges and the courts' power to recruit their own ministerial staff and regulate the staff's employment terms and conditions. The constitution further provides for the immunity of courts from unwarranted criticism by the public or the legislature. It grants the courts the power to punish for its contempt. All the executive and judicial authorities are bound to aid the superior courts in the enforcement of their judgments and orders. In short, the constitution grants administrative and decisional independence to the judiciary.

The constitution makes it the exclusive power, responsibility (indeed, a legal obligation) of the judiciary to ensure the sustenance of the separation of powers system, based on checks and balances. The judiciary is called upon to enforce the constitution and safeguard the fundamental rights and freedom of individuals. To do so, it has to be properly organized and effective and efficient enough to quickly address and resolve public claims and grievances; and also has to be strong and independent enough to dispense justice fairly and impartially. It is such an efficient and independent judiciary that can foster an appropriate legal and judicial environment where there is peace and security in society, safety of life, and protection of property and guarantee of essential human rights and fundamental freedoms for all individuals and groups, irrespective of any distinction or discrimination on the basis of cast, creed, color, culture, gender or place of origin, and so on. Indeed such a legal and judicial environment also is conducive to economic growth and social development.

The Code of Conduct to be observed by the judges of the Supreme Court and all the High Courts in Pakistan inter alia enjoins:

> The prime duty of a Judge as an individual is to present before the public an image of the justice of the nation. As a member of his Court, that duty is brought within the disciplines appropriate to a corporate body.

> The Constitution, by declaring that all authority exerciseable by the people is a sacred trust from Almighty Allah, makes it plain that the justice of this nation is of Divine origin. It connotes full implementation of the high principles which are woven into the Constitution, as well as the universal requirements of natural justice. The oath of a Judge implies complete submission to the Constitution, and under the Constitution to the law. Subject to these governing obligations, his function of interpretation and application of the Constitution and the law is to be discharged for the maintenance of the Rule of Law over the whole range of human activities within the nation.

> To be a living embodiment of these powers, functions and obligations calls for possession of the highest qualities of intellect and character. Equally, it imposes patterns of behaviour which are the hallmark of distinction of a Judge among his fellow-men.

A congenial functioning environment for the judiciary is increasingly being emphasized locally and internationally. The present World Bank conference indeed aims at creating and strengthening such an environment. The President of the World Bank, Mr. James D. Wolfensohn, considers such an environment a key pillar of the Bank's strategy for spurring economic development and growth. In the Comprehensive Development Framework Plan, presented before the Bank last year, he emphasized the maintenance of the role of legal and judicial systems in improving governance:

Without the protection of human and property rights and a comprehensive framework of laws, no equitable development is possible. A government must ensure that it has effective systems of property, contract, labour, bankruptcy, commercial codes, personal rights laws, and other elements of a comprehensive legal system that is effectively, impartially, and cleanly administered by a well-functioning, impartial, and honest judicial and legal system.

To achieve the desired goals and objectives, the legal system and the system of administration of justice ought to be constantly reformed and improved. The system has to be cognizant of current issues and problems and geared toward meeting future challenges. It has to have an appropriate strategy for achieving the stipulated goals and objectives. There has to be a constant endeavor to improve the pace of delivery and quality of justice through timely changes and improvements in laws and procedures, introduction of newer methods and techniques of expediting trial, use of alternative methods of disputes resolution, upgrading of the human and physical facilities of courts, use of modern information technology, and improvement in the quality of legal education and judicial training programs.

This paper explains the system of administration of justice in Pakistan and the manner in which it functions. It highlights the issues and problems the judicial system is confronted with and the goals and objectives it seeks to achieve. It analyzes the constitutional and legal basis for the exercise of jurisdiction and powers by courts at various levels of judicial hierarchy. Finally, it studies the prescribed mechanism for ensuring judicial propriety, enforcing accountability, and the state of administrative, functional, and financial independence—as prescribed by the Constitution and the laws that are interpreted and clarified by the Supreme Court of Pakistan.

Judicial Organization

The judicial system of Pakistan may be broadly divided into the following hierarchical classes of courts:

1. Superior judiciary comprising the Supreme Court, Federal Shariat Court and high courts;
2. Subordinate judiciary comprising the district and session courts and civil/criminal courts; and
3. Special courts and administrative tribunals.

Superior Judiciary

The Constitution of Pakistan describes the organizational structure, as well as jurisdiction of the superior courts and terms and conditions of service of judges in such courts, in a fairly elaborate manner. Part VII of the constitution relates to the adjudicature. Article 175 provides for the establishment of the Supreme Court, a high court for each province and other subordinate courts. This Article also mandates the separation of judiciary from the executive. Articles 176–191 provide for the composition and jurisdiction of the Supreme Court, Articles 192–203 explain the establishment and jurisdiction of high courts, and Articles 203A–203J provide for the establishment and jurisdiction of Federal Shariat Court. Articles 204–212 contain general provisions relating to adjudicature—for example, provision for contempt, forum for and grounds for removal of judges of the superior courts, and the subjects in respect of which administrative courts and tribunals may be created.

Elsewhere the constitution provides for the independence of the judiciary.[11] It also entrusts the superior judiciary with an obligation to preserve, protect, and defend the constitution.[12] The remuneration of judges and other administrative expenditures of the Supreme Court and High Courts are charged on the federal and provincial consolidated funds.[13] Following the ruling of the Supreme Court in the case of Government of Sindh v. Sharaf Faridi,[14] the superior courts were given a degree of financial autonomy inasmuch as the chief justice of the Supreme Court and each high court were authorized to make reappropriation of funds within their budgetary allocations.

Supreme Court

The Supreme Court of Pakistan is the apex court of the land and is conferred original, appellate, and advisory jurisdiction.[15] It consists of a chief justice and 16 judges.[16] The chief justice of Pakistan is appointed by the president

---

11. Article 2A and Objective Resolution.
12. Article 178 and 194 read with 3rd Schedule.
13. Articles 81 and 121.
14. PLD 1994 SC 105.
15. Articles 184, 185, and 186.
16. Supreme Court (Number of Judges) Act 1997.

and other judges by the president after consultation with the chief justice of Pakistan. The qualifications prescribed for judges are as follows:

1. To be a citizen of Pakistan; and
2. To have been a judge of a high court for a period of five years; or
3. To have been an advocate of a high court for a period of not less than 15 years.

The Court is given original jurisdiction in intergovernmental disputes,[17] in other words, disputes between the federal government and any provincial government or provincial governments inter se. The Court has also been conferred upon the exercise of advisory jurisdiction.[18] Thus, the president may refer to the Supreme Court any question of law, of public importance, for opinion and advice. The Court is authorized to appoint its own staff[19] and can frame its own rules of procedure.[20]

Federal Shariat Court

The Federal Shariat Court consists of eight judges.[21] The judges are appointed by the president from among the serving or retired judges of the Supreme Court or a high court or from among persons who possess requisite qualifications for appointment as high court judges. Among the eight judges, three are required to be well-versed in Islamic law. The appointment is made for a period of three years, which the president may further extend.[22] Its jurisdiction is of two kinds:

- Examining and determining whether or not a certain provision of law is in conformity with the injunctions of Islam; and
- Exercising revisional jurisdiction over criminal courts in Hudood cases, which involve limits fixed by the Holy Quran for specific offenses. The Court can appoint its own staff[23] and can frame its own rules of procedure.[24]

17. Article 184(1).
18. Article 186.
19. Article 208.
20. Article 191.
21. Article 203–C.
22. Article 203–C.
23. Article 208.
24. Article 203–J.

High Courts

A high court is the principal court of a province. The number of judges assigned to each High Court is fixed, as follows:

1. Lahore High Court   50
2. High Court of Sindh   28
3. Peshawar High Court   15
4. High Court of Baluchistan   6

The chief justice of each high court is appointed by the president after consultation with the chief justice of Pakistan and governor of the concerned province. Other judges are appointed by the president after consultation with the chief justice of pakistan, governor of the concerned province, and the chief justice of the concerned high court.[25] The qualifications prescribed for the judges of a high court are as follows:

1. To be a citizen of Pakistan;
2. To be less than 40 years of age; and
3. To have been for a period of ten years an advocate of a high court; or
4. To be, and to have been for a period of not less than ten years, a member of civil service, and to have served, for a period of not less than three years, as (or exercised the functions of) a district judge; or
5. To have, for a period of not less than ten years, held, a judicial office in Pakistan.

The high courts exercise original jurisdiction with regard to the enforcement of fundamental rights, and appellate jurisdiction in respect of judgments and orders from the subordinate courts. Each high court has the power to supervise and control the subordinate courts in the province.[26] The court appoints its own staff[27] and can frame rules of procedure for itself as well as the subordinate courts.[28]

25. Article 193.
26. Article 203.
27. Article 208.
28. Article 202.

Subordinate Judiciary

The subordinate judiciary, again, may be broadly categorized into the following classes:

1. Civil courts;
2. Criminal courts;
3. Special courts and tribunals; and
4. Revenue courts.

Civil Courts

The civil courts consist of a district judge, an additional district judge, and civil judges first, second, and third class. Their jurisdiction is fixed by law. In keeping with the value of a lawsuit, appeals against these judges' orders or judgments lie before a district judge or the high court, as the case may be. These courts function under the administrative control of the respective high courts.

Criminal Courts

These courts comprise a sessions judge, an additional sessions judge, and judicial magistrates first, second, and third class. In keeping with the severity of the penalty imposed, appeals against their order or judgment go to the session judge or the high court. These courts also function under the administrative control of the high court.

Special Courts and Tribunals

The Constitution empowers the Federal Legislature to establish administrative courts and tribunals for federal subjects. Consequently, several special courts and tribunals have been created and are currently functional. Such courts and tribunals include the special banking court, special court custom, taxation and anti-corruption, income tax (appellate) tribunal, insurance appellate tribunal, and so on. Similarly, the Constitution also provides for the establishment of administrative courts and tribunals in matters relating to terms and conditions governing the employment of civil servants, and tortuous acts of government. Accordingly, service tribunals for the federal government employees as well as provincial government employees and judicial officers have been established.[29] Appeals against their decisions are addressed to the Supreme Court.

Revenue Courts

There also exist revenue courts, classified as board of revenue, commissioner, collector, and assistant collector. These courts were established and exercise their powers and functions under the Land Revenue Act 1967.

Issues and Challenges

The civil and criminal justice system of Pakistan is currently facing major issues, problems, and challenges. First and foremost is the perennial problem of case delays and accumulated piles of pending cases. This is a problem not unique to Pakistan, since other countries in our region as well as outside are also confronted with the same problem. The problem is an old and chronic one and is not restricted to developing societies alone. It is also a constant cause of concern for advanced nations such as the United States and the United Kingdom. Louis Lauer, then director of the Columbia University Project for Effective Justice in his address in 1964 to the New York Senate Judicial Committee remarked thus:[30]

> Remember that delay in the courts has the history that reaches past Shakespeare to Hammuarabi and, no doubt, past him to his ancient ancestors.

Similarly, Charles Dickens, in his famous novel, *Bleak House* depicted the classic case of Jarndyce v Jarndyce, not as a parody but as a fact and warned future litigants to avoid entering the portals of courts in the following words:[31]

> Suffer any wrong that can be done you rather than come here.

The problem seems to be intractable. Notwithstanding efforts to reduce delays, the problem has consistently defied solutions. This is so because haste may cause miscarriage of justice. An important principle of the criminal justice system is to punish the offender, after due process, and following the establishment of guilt, beyond any shadow of doubt. Similarly, the civil

29. Article 212.
30. Quoted by Jack Jacob in his book, *The Reform of Civil Procedure Laws*. London: Sweet & Maxwell Ltd. (1982 edition, p. 91).
31. Jacob (1982: 92). See previous note for full reference.

justice system also demands strict adherence to procedural law and the principles of equity, justice and fair-play. Such universally recognized and time-tested principles necessarily entail reasonable time and opportunities to parties and their counsel to present and defend their cases. Important though the issue of clearing the backlog and expediting the trial may be, it does not mean rushing to settling claims and deciding matters. The courts have to follow legal and procedural formalities and ensure due process. In the case of Mehram Ali v. Federation of Pakistan,[32] I had an occasion to deal with this issue, and made the following observation:

> The solution of the problem of Court-delay does not necessarily lie in a large scale addition of new Judges or creation of Special Courts but delay in the disposal of cases can be reduced only by Judges who are willing to insist that the lawyers/prosecutors/parties meet reasonable dead-lines for the conclusion of the trial. This effort will require concern and commitment on the part of the Judges. Judges will probably receive considerable "heat" from lawyers/prosecutors understandably upset by changes in their scheduling prerogatives. Be that as it may, delay in disposition of cases can be eliminated to a large extent through good Court management and not necessarily by creation of new Courts and increase in the strength of Judges. I would emphasise that it is for the Presiding Officer of the Court to evolve strategies within the parameters of the law/procedure for accelerating the pace of disposition of civil and criminal cases, resulting in reduction of delay and clearance of backlog. However, I would add a note of caution that sacrifice of justice to obtain speedy disposition of cases could hardly be termed as justice. A balance ought to be maintained between the two commonly known maxims, "justice delayed is justice denied" and "justice rushed is justice crushed." I do not suggest that speed and efficiency ought not to be ultimate measure of a Court but it should not be at the expense of justice.

Causes of Backlog and Delays

The causes of delays may be attributed to a variety of reasons and factors. In our own context, I have no hesitation in saying that the judicial system has not kept pace with increase in population and the bulk of consequent litigation. Increase in litigation is also attributable to increase in the literacy rate, general awareness of the people of their rights and interests, which is indeed indicative of civilized behaviour and respect for the rule of law. It is also true

32. PLD 1988 SC 1445.

that a number of complaints emanate from the arbitrary actions and abuse of discriminatory powers by state functionaries, impinging upon the rights, interests, liberties and freedoms of people who then resort to the court of law for redress. The problem of case delays and backlog may also be partly attributed to the inaction or too little action on the part of successive governments towards strengthening the administration of justice in the country. The courts—particularly the subordinate courts—do not have adequate resources for their effective performance and functioning. Indeed some of the courts have to operate in dismal conditions. There is a chronic shortage of judicial officers and administrative staff. In some areas the strength has to be doubled even trebled, so as to keep pace with the pending cases. There is a problem of lack of adequate courtrooms and residential accommodation for judges and court staff. They lack adequate equipment and have no access to modern technology. They do not possess even the essential law books in their libraries. I also take the view that the problem of slack supervision over the functioning of the subordinate judiciary is one of the causes for delay. I have, therefore, always emphasized upon internal assessment and evaluation of performance of the judges of subordinate courts by the respective high courts who are entrusted with the responsibility of control and supervision over such courts.

Lack of proper court management, deficient case processing, shortcomings in the system of legal education and judicial training, non-utilization of alternative dispute resolution mechanisms, archaic laws, and inflexible procedures further aggravate the situation. The march toward globalization, tendency toward urbanization, policy of privatization and its consequences in the shape of retrenchment of labor, and others further create waves in the social fabric and lead to a rise in crime. This state of affairs contributes to deterioration in law and order and dampens the prospects of economic growth. It also results in restricting, if not denying, access to justice, and disenchantment with the system of judicial administration.

Meeting the Challenge

Whereas the problems and issues confronting the judicial system are enormous and appear to be formidable, in my view, they also give us the greatest opportunity to address them. In my capacity as head of the administration of justice, I have tried, through a systematic strategy and after due discussions and deliberations in the relevant forums such as the Chief Justices' Committee, the Supreme Judicial Council, and the Pakistan Law Commission, to devise workable time-specific measures for redress. I would like to summarize these along the following lines:

Measures for Reform

1. Initiating the process of filling existing vacancies at all levels of judicial hierarchy, in the prescribed manner;
2. Constituting special benches in high courts for special subjects to ensure quick disposal;
3. Extending working hours to meet the specified target of case disposal;
4. Designing strategies for clearing the backlog of cases concerning deprived and underprivileged sections of society including widows, minor children, claims for maintenance by wives, child custody cases, and so forth;
5. Maintaining weekly and monthly reports on the progress in backlog clearance and fresh institution of cases in the high courts and the subordinate courts;
6. Measures for disciplining judicial officers and support staff through strict action for inefficient performance, impropriety or corruption, and the like;
7. Issuing guidelines and instructions to subordinate courts for the expeditious disposal of cases;
8. Giving orientation to and imparting pre-service training to newly recruited judges and judicial magistrates and in-service training to others; and
9. Giving appreciation and commendation certificates to judicial officers for exemplary performance.

After launching this program, the initial results for the past three months were very encouraging. I should like to explain the results through charts, showing the backlog disposal rate at various levels of the judicial hierarchy. The performance of all courts including the Supreme Court, high courts, and subordinate courts has improved. This is clearly shown in the following charts, which provide the figures of pending cases, fresh institution, disposal, remaining balance, and reduction in pending cases. The charts also present relevant data on judicial hierarchy, financial expenditure on judiciary, strength of judges in Supreme Court, Federal Shariat Court, high courts and subordinate courts, strength of court staff, number of law colleges, number of law officers, number of practicing lawyers, number of police personnel, and so on.

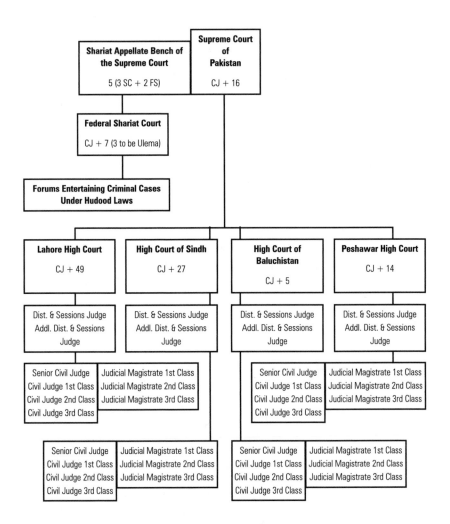

HIERARCHY OF COURTS AND STRENGTH OF JUDGES

**Number of Judges in the Supreme Court, Hight Courts, Districts and Session Judges/
Senior Civil Judges &Civil Judges, and Administrative Staff of the Subordinate Courts**

	Supreme Court of Pakistan	Lahore High Court	High Court of Sindh	Peshawar High Court	High Court of Baluchistan
Chief Justice and Judges	17	50	28	15	6
Administrative Staff of Supreme Court and High Court	507	1,199	865	344	249
Districts & Session Judges/ Senior Civil Judges & Civil Judges, under each High Court	n.a.	649	390	177	123
Administrative Staff of the District Courts under Administrative Control of High Courts	n.a.	6,376	3,940	1,725	663

n.a. Not applicable.

List of Advocates

	Supreme Court of Pakistan	Lahore High Court	High Court of Sindh	Peshawar High Court	High Court of Baluchistan
a) Advocates	2,406	13,000	4,500	2,026	350
b) Advocates of Districts Courts under each High Court	n.a.	14,500	5,270	4,342	384
c) Advocates-on-Record	190	n.a.	n.a.	n.a.	n.a.

n.a. Not applicable.

Pendency, Institution and Disposal of Cases in the Supreme Court of Pakistan, High Courts and Subordinate Courts, April 1–30, 2000

Name of the Court	Pendency on Apr. 1, 2000	Institution Apr. 1–30, 2000	Disposal Apr. 1–30, 2000	Balance on Apr. 30, 2000
Supreme Court of Pakistan				
Petitions	6,363	540	972	5,931
Appeals	5,474	130	199	5,405
Lahore High Court	70,633	8,369	10,769	70,004
High Court of Sindh	71,949	3,785	3,822	71,912
Peshawar High Court	1,221	106	179	1,148
High Court of Baluchistan	892	231	213	832
Punjab	516,784	75,701	70,820	521,665
Sindh	7,555	1,088	3,887	4,756
NWFP	5,801	1,849	3,651	3,999
Baluchistan	145	91	70	166

Pendency, Institution, Disposal, and Balance of Special Category Cases April 1–30, 2000, in the Province of the Punjab

S. No.	Special category	Pendency on Apr. 1, 2000	Institution Apr. 1–30, 2000	Disposal Apr. 1–30, 2000	Balance on Apr. 30, 2000
1	Family cases	29,330	9,312	16,453	22,189
2	Custody of minors	4,137	1,228	1,939	3,426
3	Maintenance	8,565	2,538	4,390	6,713
4	Dower.	4,084	834	1,464	3,454
5	Admn. of Estate of Deceased	270	57	180	147
6	Eject. from houses	2,372	409	807	1,974
7	Cases of widows	1,581	492	978	1,095
8	Cases of orphan children	852	236	378	710
9	Crl. Cases carrying penalty up to two years imprisonment	37,706	9,301	5,265	41,742
10	Small disputes	2,043	34	130	1,947
	Total	90,940	24,441	31,984	83,397

Pendency, Institution, Disposal, and Balance of Special Category Cases April 1–30, 2000, in the Province of the Sindh

S. No.	Special category	Balance as of Apr. 1, 2000	Disposal on merit	Dismissed in default	Total disposal	Balance as of Apr. 29, 2000
1	Matters relating to widows (specify law & section)	248	115	26	141	107
2	Matters relating to orphans (specify law & section)	4		2	2	2
3	Suit for administration of the estate of the deceased persons	81	31	1	32	49
4	Suits for maintenance	420	129	41	170	250
5	Suit for dower	208	57	21	78	130
6	Cases for custody of minors	484	160	65	225	259
7	Other family suits	2,566	906	272	1,178	1,388
8	Cases relating to ejection from houses only	1,508	571	95	666	842
9	Criminal cases (punishable by not more than 2 years)	1,622	900	61	961	661
	Total	7,141	2,869	584	3453	3688

Pendency, Institution, Disposal and Balance of Special Category Cases Apr. 1–30, 2000, in the Province of the Baluchistan

	Family cases (divorce, dowry, maintenance)	Custody of minors	Cases of widows	Cases of orphan children	Suit for administration of the estate of deceased persons	Rent cases	Taxation cases	Criminal cases	Civil suit
Previous Pendency	145	35	23	0	26	137	0	269	909
Institution	91	8	2	0	13	34	0	125	269
Total	236	43	25	0	39	171	0	394	1,178
Disposal	70	10	12	0	13	41	0	156	256
Balance	166	33	13	0	26	130	0	238	922

Statement Showing Pendency, Institution, Disposal and Balance of Special Category Cases Apr. 1–30, 2000, in the Province of the NWFP

S. No.	Category of cases	Pending as of Apr. 1, 2000	Institution Apr. 1–30, 2000	Total for disposal	Disposal Apr. 1–30, 2000	Balance
1	Family cases	3,387	943	4,330	1,876	2,454
2	Custody of minors	397	118	515	270	245
3	Cases of widows & orphans	409	144	553	240	313
4	Rent cases	764	563	1,327	529	798
5	Minor cases	802	64	866	696	170
6	Admin. of estate of deceased	42	17	59	40	19
	Total	5,801	1,849	7,650	3,651	3,999

Budgetary Allocation for the Judiciary During the Financial Year 1999–2000

S.No		(Rupees. in Million/Thousands
1	Total Budget of Federal Government	RS. 525, 904.4 (Million)
2	Budget of Supreme Court	RS. 79.408 (Million)
3	Percentage of Federal Budget	0.0150
1	Total Budget of Federal Shariat Court.	RS. 23.254 (Million)
2	Percentage of Federal Shariat Court	0.004
1	Total Budget of the Punjab Province	RS. 90, 940.834 (Million)
2	Budget of the Lahore High Court	RS. 715.751 (Million)
3	Percentage of Punjab Budget	0.786
4	Administration of Justice in the Punjab	RS. 715, 751.000 (Thousands)
1	Budget of Sindh Province	RS. 50,249.392 (Million)
2	Total Budget of High Court of Sindh	RS. 307.323 (Million)
3	Percentage of Sindh Budget	0.610
4	Administration of Justice in Sindh	RS. 307,323.200 (Thousands)
1	Total Budget of the NWFP	RS. 35,492.973 (Million)
2	Budget of the Peshawar High Court	RS. 165.704 (Million)
3	Percentage of NWFP Budget	0.464
4	Administration of Justice in NWFP	RS. 165,704.000 (Thousands)
1	Total Budget of Baluchistan Province.	RS. 17,151.689 (Million)
2	Budget of High Court of Baluchistan	RS. 85.395 (Million)
3	Percentage of Baluchistan Budget	0.495
4	Administration of Justice in Baluchistan	RS. 85,395.240 (Thousands)
	Federal and 4 Provinces Budget	RS. 719738.288 (Million)
	Budgetary Allocation to Supreme Court, Federal Shariat Court, 4 High Courts and Subordinate Courts in 4 Provinces	RS. 1274.173 (Million)
	Percentage Expenditure on Administration of Justice	0.177

Gender Balance: A Look at the Numbers of Women in Bar Associations

Year	Bar Associations	Total	Women	Percentage
1997	Supreme Court	456	7	1.53
1995	NWFP	6,750	112	1.65
1994	Baluchistan Bar Council	350	6	1.71
1995	Punjab Bar Council	27,000	271	1.00
1995	Sukkur Division	663	11	1.65
1995	Larkana Division	477	4	0.83
1995	Hyderabad Division	1,111	59	5.31
1995	Mirpur Khas Division	265	1	0.37
1995	Karachi Bar Association	2,080	262	12.59

The Numbers of Law Officers in the Supreme Court and Provinces

	Supreme Court	Punjab	Sindh	NWFP	Baluchistan
Law officers	25	205	97	48	34

The Numbers of Law Colleges by Area

Federal Territory, Islamabad	Punjab	Sindh	NWFP	Baluchistan
1	24	10	8	1

The Police Force in Numbers: The Provinces, Islamabad/Railways/AJK, and Northern Areas

	Punjab	Sindh	NWFP	Baluchistan	Islamabad	Railways	AJK	Northern Areas
Police Force	97911	93555	31481	15954	7036	7715	6274	2857

Reform Strategy

Our reform strategy is structured around the following steps:

1. The various forums for improvement in the administration of justice have been activated through regular meetings and monitoring performances. In case of defects or shortcomings, remedial action is to be promptly suggested and implemented.

2. The judiciary recommends law reforms to the government, through the Pakistan Law Commission, to modernize laws and bring them in consonance with changing times and realities.

3. Implementation cells, headed by the respective registrars, have been established at the level of the Supreme Court and each high court. Similarly, cells have also been created at the level of courts of district and session judges.

4. Liaison officers have also been appointed at the levels of the Supreme Court, each high court, and the courts of district and session judges to monitor progress in backlog clearance and expeditious disposal of cases, particularly in special categories of cases—namely, family cases, cases of child custody, cases of widows and orphan children, cases of ejection from residential houses, suits related to estate administration disputes following deaths, and minor criminal cases.

5. Regular evaluation of the work and performance of judges of high courts by the Supreme Judicial Council will be carried out.

6. The respective chief justices of high courts have nominated their judges to monitor the working and functioning of the subordinate courts for securing compliance with the decision of the Chief Justices' Committee and so as to enhance efficiency and to check irregularities.

7. Close liaison is maintained with the members of the bar. They are being recruited as partners and consulted. As chief justice of Pakistan, I invited the elected representatives of the bar throughout the

country to a meeting to inform them of the decisions of the Chief Justices' Committee and to secure the cooperation of the members of the bar for implementing the same. The response of the members of the bar was indeed very encouraging and to the satisfaction of all concerned.

8. The media (print and electronic) have been successfully associated with the process of judicial reform and with ensuring speedy disposal of cases. Thus, lists of backlog clearance and case disposal performance are being shared with the media through a transparent strategy. To help the relevant court in identifying the cases of litigants in special categories, the respective high courts notify the general public through the media—television, radio, and newspapers—to file applications with the court for expeditious redress of their grievances.

9. Steps are underway to increase the number of judicial officers and administrative staff, build courtrooms, provide equipment, and consider enhancing the emoluments of judicial officers and court staff.

10. In addition to the above measures, at the appropriate time the scope of the consultative process will be widened to all users of the administration of justice by arranging workshops, seminars, and conferences involving various segments of society, including lawyers, the executive branch, business communities, workers, women, jurists, professionals, Islamic scholars, and others.

These are only a few measures, some already applied and operational and others envisaged and planned for the future. But much more is required. New goals have to be set and new benchmarks need to be prescribed. Judges and court staff engaged in the process have to be motivated, trained, and given the necessary tools and equipment to enable them to rise to the occasion and seek to accomplish the prescribed goals.

Such activities would require financial resources, however, which is a major constraint faced by the system of justice administration in Pakistan. The country is resource deficient, and there are several demands on the scarce state resources. There is an overall economic slowdown as the gross domestic product (GDP) growth during the past few years has barely kept pace with the growth of population. And a considerable portion of the meager resources goes to debt servicing; the debt burden equals the entire national income. Therefore, budgetary constraints impede not just the delivery of justice to its users but also social sector development. This is obviously a serious issue that has to be tackled and resolved; if we fail in this regard, the ideal of opening up access to and quick dispensation of justice for all segments of the population (and in particular for the deprived and underprivileged classes) cannot be realized.

Judicial Accountability

Independence is defined as a state or condition of being free from the control, dependence, subjection, or subordination of an outside agency or authority. Such independence is given to the judiciary to ensure that it is able to administer justice freely, impartially, and without any fear or favors involved—and the judiciary may be taken to task and held accountable if it fails to administer justice in accordance with the law and established procedure. The judicial process should also be expeditious and economical.

Under Pakistan's Constitution, a full-fledged mechanism for the accountability of Superior Court judges has been prescribed. Article 209 details the grounds as well as the forum and procedure for the removal of these judges. A code of conduct has been prescribed for the judges of the Supreme Court and high courts as well. The code is fairly elaborate, covering public and private conduct, strict observance of elements of judicial propriety, and efficient performance.

Such accountability is carried out through the Supreme Judicial Council. The Council consists of the Chief Justice of Pakistan as Chairman and the two next most senior judges of the Supreme Court and two most senior chief justices of high courts as members. On a reference received from the president, the Council inquires into the allegations of misconduct or physical or mental incapacity and may recommend the removal of a judge. The president then, acting upon these recommendations, may remove the judge from office. A judge of the Supreme Court or a high court may not be removed except on the stipulated grounds by the Council, following due process. Thus, the Constitution ensures the freedom, independence, and impartiality of the judges of the superior courts.

Following a constitutional dictum for the separation of the judiciary from the executive branch and the ruling of the Supreme Court in the case of Government of Sindh v. Sharaf Faridi,[33] the Court observed:

> The concept of judicial independence warrants the elimination of financial control of the executive branch over the budgetary allocation of the judiciary and therefore the respective Chief Justice should be authorized to make necessary re-appropriation funds within approved budgetary allocation of the court.

Such authorization has since been given. In my view, financial independence is an essential ingredient of judicial independence. Having said so, however, I should also emphasize that to be able to derive full benefits of financial autonomy and independence, we need to put in place appropriate mechanisms for control through good management, and establish priorities through proper planning, monitoring, and reporting systems.

This brings me to the concluding part of my paper, in which I tried to explain the accountability law and procedure as designed and being practiced in the subordinate courts of Pakistan. The subordinate courts, both civil and criminal, are supervised and controlled by the concerned high courts, which are the principal courts of the province. The administration of justice is a provincial subject, and the organization of subordinate courts and the terms and conditions of service for judicial officers are determined under provincial statutes and rules. The Public Service Commission recruits the judicial officers generally through competitive examination. The high courts are also associated in the selection process as judges sit on interview panels. As regards posting, transfer, promotion, and disciplinary proceedings, the respective high courts are empowered to take appropriate action in all such matters. The judges of the subordinate courts function under their respective provincial codes of conduct. In my view, such codes are inadequate to cover all aspects of judicial performance, and therefore the Pakistan Law Commission is currently examining a new code of conduct for subordinate court judges. The codes are enforced by the respective high courts through efficiency and discipline rules and due process is followed. After the initial inquiry and investigation, a report is submitted to the respective chief justices who can impose the appropriate penalty. The justices' orders may be

33. PLD 1994 SC 105.

appealed to the provincial judicial service tribunals, which comprise the judges of high courts.

The high courts exercise supervisory functions by inspecting and calling of records of the courts. They exercise judicial control through their power of revising and overturning upon appeal orders and decisions of the subordinate courts.

The judicial system of every country is unique, unique because it is based on the country's peculiar historical, cultural, and politico-legal evolution. But there are some attributes and features that are common in all systems, and judicial independence and accountability are among those. These are realized and sustained through different and diverse institutional mechanisms and legal safeguards, however. I have tried to list and explain the salient features of our judicial administration. Conferences, such as the present one, help in making comparisons and learning from each other's experiences, to further strengthen the system of administration of justice.

Judges, particularly superior court judges who have to interpret the law and the constitution, perform a crucial role of not just settling claims and disputes but also seeking to converge the latent and patent thought and philosophy and expound the same through rational and logical propositions. In doing so, they become trendsetters.

This is indeed an onerous responsibility and cannot be adequately performed but by impartial, independent, competent, and courageous judges. This is how the courts tend to determine the stand of contemporary society on fundamental issues. The various components of judicial independence are meant to bolster the role of courts in doing so; only then may the judiciary contribute to the growth and development of the society. George Washington was right when he stated, "The true administration of justice is the firmest pillar of good Government." And Alexander Hamilton, writing in the Federalist Papers,[34] maintained, "The ordinary administration of criminal and civil justice... contributes, more than any other circumstance, to impressing upon the mind of the people affection, esteem, and reverence towards the Government." It is an independent and capable as well as accountable judiciary that can contribute toward establishing good and beneficent administration of justice for the welfare of the people and growth and development of the nation.

34. Federalist Paper 17.

How Does Legal Training Improve Participation in the Reform Process?

The Many Facets of Training

Hon. Sandra E. Oxner

President, Commonwealth Judicial Education Institute

Halifax, Nova Scotia, Canada

Reform Is Change

Judicial and legal reform to a great extent involves changing the habits and behavior of humans—often contrary to their personal and vested interests. This is not as easy as building roads and bridges—most people by nature tend both to resist change and to revert to former ways when a short-term pressure for change goes away. Experience shows us that successfully achieving long-term behavioral change requires a combination of incentives to change, participatory identification and articulation of changes required by those to be most affected by the reforms, and sanctions for failure to change. To achieve this we need to create an environment that is open to change—an important part of which is to inculcate in the judges, support staff, and bar an ethos of service and openness to reform.

In legal and judicial reform there is the added challenge owing to the necessity of doing it in a way that protects the independence of the bar and the judiciary while creating or strengthening the accountability and transparency of their processes and procedures. In addition, the legal profession, including the judiciary, is often a conservative element strongly resistant to change.

Reform Requires Training

Few now dispute that the foundation for behavioral change required for reform is one of training and consensus building. Education is, therefore, a common component in legal and judicial reform projects. However, other reform project components that may not seem to do so on the surface, require training. In one country I found that machines for recording evidence in courtrooms were still sitting in their unopened boxes three years after delivery, stacked in a storeroom. No one knew how to install or operate them. Evidently no training had been provided.

In many countries I have seen computers provided to judges for research or case flow management lie on their desks under thick layers of dust—or in use by clerical staff. One-on-one computer training for judges, preferably linked to Web searches of professional and personal interest, will go a long way toward ensuring the success of a judicial computerization component. Even in the renovation or building of courthouses, a comparative study of various floor plans that promote efficiency and security and a review of the significant body of literature on courthouse planning now available can prevent the expenditure of funds on new additions to the current line-up of obsolete and dysfunctional structures.

Judicial education is the foundation of judicial reform. The desired end-product of judicial education is improved service to the community, delivered by an impartial, competent, efficient, and effective judiciary whose performance attracts the confidence and respect of the people it serves.

Objectives of Judicial Reform and Training

What are the objectives of judicial reform?[1] In my view, they are identical to those of judicial education. I like to use the acronym "ICEE," pronounced icy, to identify them. I am told this is not inappropriate for a Canadian.

"I" stands for both the reality and the perception of impartiality. This includes the following concepts:

1. An impartial and independent judiciary;
2. Transparency—from the appointment process to the rendering of judgments comprehensible to the public;
3. A transparent and accessible judicial complaint process; and
4. An articulated and publicized code of judicial ethics and conduct so that the community is aware of the standards they have the right to require of a judiciary.

"Impartiality" and "independence" are often used interchangeably. I choose "impartiality" to describe the personal and intellectual integrity of

---

1. This section is based on a paper on judicial education and judicial reform written by the author and published by JUTA in 1997.

the judge. In the analysis of judicial independence, shown in chart 1 in the annex, you will see that I choose to use "judicial independence" to mean far more than judicial independence from the executive and legislature or control over budget and administration. This analysis includes mechanisms that have been found to be supportive of the environment that is most likely to ensure an impartial judicial mind. It includes the following:

1. Substantive independence—which means that in the discharge of his or her functions a judge is subject to nothing but the law and the commands of his or her conscience;
2. Internal judicial independence—which requires that the judge be independent from directives or pressures from his or her fellow judges regarding his or her adjudicative functions; and
3. Collective independence—which extends to the independence of the judiciary as a whole, as a corporate body and is measured by its administrative independence.

This concept of judicial impartiality-independence identifies roles and responsibilities for the judiciary, the executive, the media, the legal profession, and the public.

The creation and support of an impartial mind has a different focus depending on which country you are in. For example, in the post-Soviet states the focus is on developing an impartial independent dispute resolution mechanism that is free from state interference. In such countries as Canada, the United Kingdom, and Australia, judicial education places emphasis on "social context" training to eliminate hidden bias from the judicial mind in fact finding, particularly in relation to gender and ethnic issues. A major impartiality issue facing many jurisdictions is the reality or perception of corruption among judges and judicial support staff. While anti-corruption campaigns must be multi-pronged, important aspects include wide judicial consultation to articulate required standards of behavior on and off the bench; the preparation by the judges of an annotated code of ethics and conduct linked to an accessible and transparent judicial discipline and complaint process; and intensive education programming to ensure that judges are familiar with the code of conduct standards and sanctions.

"C" stands for competency. This, of course, refers to an adequate level of legal knowledge—both substantive and procedural. In many developing countries there is insufficient information and material provided to the judges to maintain an adequate level of competency.

"E" stands for efficiency, which includes efficient judicial court room management, case flow and process efficiency, reform of rules and procedures to narrow the issues early on and encourage timely settlements, court-annexed and free-standing mediation and other alternative dispute resolution (ADR) practices. Efficiency also relates to appropriate physical structures, adequate equipment, and timely access to such judicial tools as laws, precedent cases, legal texts, and other scholarly writing.

Jurisdictional restructuring is a basic reform method that is successfully used in many countries to achieve greater efficiency. Examples of how this may be done include the following:

1. Downloading cases to subordinate courts by increasing their jurisdiction. (As a byproduct, this makes them a better training ground for the elevation of their members to higher judicial office. This in itself may be a supportive reform method, as recruitment to superior courts from the private legal profession is a problem in many countries owing to the great disparity in income between judges and lawyers in private practice. A career judicial path is an incentive to attract well-qualified candidates to subordinate courts.)

2. Making room in subordinate court lists by using out-of-court settlement techniques for quasi-penal and regulatory matters. These may be enforced by a refusal to issue government licenses (namely, motor vehicle licenses) to those with outstanding fines or court appearances.

3. Free-standing small claims courts, perhaps sitting in the evening to meet public convenience. These may be presided over by nonjudicial members of the legal profession and may or may not allow representation by counsel and appeals.

4. Elimination of preliminary hearings or proper use of paper committals in jurisdictions that retain preliminary hearings.

5. Decriminalization and diversion processes for appropriate cases.

The second "E" stands for effectiveness and describes several aspects of judicial effectiveness. One is bridging the gap between law and justice by judicial techniques such as domestic application of international human rights norms, judicial activism in interpretation of constitutions or through the exercise of discretion. All these judicial techniques are currently in use to achieve justice in particular cases.

Judicial predictability is a second aspect of judicial effectiveness. A third aspect is the collective judicial responsibility of listening to the community's complaints about the justice system and using the judiciary's influence to shape the justice system to respond to responsible complaints. For example, judges often do not consider a low rate of judgment recovery their responsibility. In many countries, however, difficulties in enforcing judgements make successful litigation a hollow victory and bring the judiciary into disrepute. There are legal and administrative ways of improving judgement recovery. Should the judiciary not be interested in supporting these?

As discussed under "I" above, another aspect is the reality and perception of impartiality to attract the confidence of the community that the judiciary serves.

Training for Judges

Definition

What is judicial education? A definition of judicial education includes collegial meetings (international, national, regional, and local); all professional information received by the judge, be it print, audio, video, computer disk, satellite television, online; mentoring; and feedback.

The targets of judicial reform training are as follows:

1. Aspirant judges;
2. Newly appointed judges;
3. Sitting judges;
4. Judicial support staff;
5. The legislature;
6. The executive;

7. The media;

8. School children; and

9. The community at large including nongovernmental organizations (NGOs) and civic society organizations (CSOs).

Levels of Judicial Training

There are several levels of judicial training:

1. The provision of basic legal information—such as updated statues and case reports—that is necessary for the judge to effectively do his or her job (and that is not always easily provided in the developing world).

2. Making sure that judges understand new laws that define a shift in philosophy—for instance, the laws of a new regime creating a democracy, or legal framework reform to support a market economy.

3. Teaching a judge a new intellectual approach such as the judicial exercise of discretion, domestic application of human rights norms, or developing schools of jurisprudential thinking, such as "law and economics."

4. Inspiring behavioral change required to create an impartial and accountable bench that can rise to social expectations. As discussed above, in some countries the change required may relate to gender or racial bias. In others, the behavioral change required involves encouraging the judicial ethos of service in the community and the fact and perception of judicial independence, integrity, and impartiality. In many countries the serious backlogs and delays require changed behavioral patterns to make the process more efficient.

Attitudinal and behavioral change is the most difficult area of education in any field. It is the essence of reform. It requires motivated and inspired teachers who are properly trained and who are respected and trusted by the judges. For this reason judges or former judges who have acquired a high level of teaching skills are likely to be effective judicial educators.

Curricula Development

How does a judiciary determine what to study? In many common law countries, judicial education began with judges electing to spend their study time considering the law of evidence and procedure. However, community criticism of the justice system rarely seems to find fault with judicial application of the law of evidence and procedure. Criticisms dwell on other weaknesses that are perceived.

You may recollect the story of the chief justice of England during medieval times who wished to petition the King to seek improvements in the benefits of judicial office. Thinking it tactful to take a soft approach the Chief Justice wished to begin the document with the following preamble "mindful as we are of our inadequacies..." The judges, however, were not prepared to agree that they had inadequacies. The following compromise was arrived at "mindful as we are of each other's inadequacies."

Therefore, mindful as we are of each other's inadequacies, what should judges study? The content of judicial education programming must respond to community perceptions of judicial weaknesses. The community (in this context) includes not only the judiciary, the bar, and court users, but also the business sector and society at large. Judicial education is expensive—one must take into account the judges' days off the bench, the cost of maintaining courthouses, and paying court staff during judicial absences, as well as travel and accommodation expenses for participants, and program delivery costs. To justify these expenditures, programming must go beyond the old standbys of "evidence" and "procedure" and visibly respond to areas of perceived weakness. A curriculum committee may employ several tools to identify areas requiring improvement:

1. A broad-based needs assessment survey of the community;
2. A review of complaints against judges;
3. A review of media complaints on justice issues;
4. An assessment of areas of the law that call for frequent appellate review;
5. An analysis of the role and function of a judge;[2] or
6. A combination of all of the above.

2. Ibid.

A sample needs assessment is contained in chart 2 (see annex). It is interesting to note that an additional benefit of such a needs assessment is that it often produces a prioritized list of needed judicial reforms. It also tends to enhance public confidence in the judiciary as soliciting court users' opinions assures the public of judicial sensitivity to the community it serves.

Any finding of guilt or innocence or rights between parties determined by the facts is based on subjective beliefs of the trier of fact. In many jurisdictions a single judge sitting alone without a jury is the finder of fact. The greatest power of a common law judge lies in the function of being a finder of fact, as for all practical purposes a judge cannot be reversed on appeal in this area.

A judge should also be aware, as most of any experience are, of the fallibility of the human powers of observation and memory. The experiments of psychologist Elizabeth Loftus[3] have shown us how sympathy can make honest people see things inaccurately. Many experienced judges think that their function in making findings of credibility is not in danger of being usurped by a lie-detecting machine, as in their experience most people have convinced themselves that their evidence is true by the time they get to the courtroom.

The science of fact finding in judicial decision-making is an important but neglected issue. While legal writers have given some attention to this issue[4] their analysis is different from the process of belief and proof that is considered by Seniuk.[5] His work points out that because of the power of the finder

3. Loftus, Elizabeth. 1979. *Eyewitness Testimony.* Cambridge, Mass.: Harvard University Press. Loftus, Elizabeth. 1980. *Memory, Surprising New Insights into How We Remember and Why We Forget.* Reading, PA: Addison–Wesley Publishing Co..

4. Abella, R. S. 1987. "The Dynamic Nature of Equality." In S. Martin and K. Mahoney, eds., *Equality and Judicial Neutrality.* Toronto: Hardwell (pp. 3–8). Shientag, B. L. 1975. "The Virtue of Impartiality." In G. R. Winters, ed., *Handbook for Judges.* Chicago: The American Judicature Society. Wilson, Bertha. 1990. "Will Women Judges Really Make a Difference?" *Osgoode Hall Law Journal* 28: 507. For example, Wigmore, J. H. 1937. *The Science of Judicial Proof,* 3d ed. Boston: Little, Brown; Twining, W. L. 1985. *Theories of Evidence: Bentham & Wigmore.* London: Weidenfeld & Nocolson; Gold, N., C. Mackie, and W. L. Twining. 1989. Learning Lawyers' Skills. London: Butterworths; Twining, W. L. 1990. *Rethinking Evidence: Exploratory Essays.* Oxford: Basil Blackwell. For a number of articles considering a new academic movement called the "new evidence scholarship," which considers the implications of decision theory, probability and statistics for the study of evidence, see "Decision and Inference in Litigation" (1991) in *Cardozo Law Review* 13 (Special Issue): 253. I am indebted to the Honorable Judge Gerald T. G. Seniuk for this reference.

5. Seniuk, Gerald T. G. 1994. "Judicial Fact-Finding and a Theory of Credit." Paper given at the Nova Scotia Judicial Education Seminar, Halifax, Canada. February 16.

of fact, the outcome of a case is often determined by which judge is drawn. This, in essence, leaves the outcome as much to chance as would the flip of a coin.[6] His conclusion is supported by mock findings of guilt or innocence made by judges in judicial education programs. Having viewed a video that depicts a trial in which a young female from a troubled past alleges a retired war-disabled veteran sexually assaulted her, the judges are polled for their verdicts. When used throughout the Commonwealth, the result has almost always been an approximate 40/60 split on the part of the experienced judicial decision-makers.[7] Programs assisting judges to analyze, detect, and improve biases in their fact-finding process are important to the success of the judicial reform process.

Faculty Development

The identification and training of judicial education leaders is key to effective judicial education and reform. Few judges have teacher training. However, most are accomplished learners and with professional educator support can design programs that motivate and inspire judicial reform. Skills that judicial educators need to acquire include adult pedagogy, resource networking, the methodology of curriculum development, the development of teaching plans and tools, distance learning techniques, and fundraising.

Evaluation

The first measure of successful program content is how well the program responds to the community's concerns about its judiciary. Achieving this goal, however, is only the first step. Program topics must respond not just to program objectives; individual sessions within a program should articulate sub-objectives that can also be evaluated. These precisely defined session objectives should be linked to participation evaluation forms to measure the learning achieved. For example, a program on detecting bias in fact finding

6. Rabelais' Judge Bridlegoose did decide cases by tossing a coin—see *Gargantua and Pantagruel* (1955), transl. J. M. Cohen, Vol. 3, Chs. 39–43, Penguin. Another unusual story of a coin-tossing judge is that of the Manhattan judge who used this method to decide the length of a jail sentence. He also asked courtroom spectators to vote on which of two conflicting witnesses to believe. He was removed from office in 1983 by the New York State Commission on Judicial Conduct. *The Times,* February, 3, 1982.

7. Experience gleaned from the use of the video at Commonwealth Judicial Education Institute programs.

may have the following session objective: *"The participant will learn three biases of which he or she was previously unaware."* In assessing the session, the participant evaluation form would ask: *"Did you learn of any biases you hold of which you were previously unaware? If so, how many?"* This would allow quantifiable evaluation of whether programming objectives were achieved or, unhappily, not achieved.

The measurement of learning achieved, however, is relatively simple when compared with the challenge of evaluating how the learning process produces attitudinal and behavioral change. Professionals in the field spend many long hours developing effective performance indicators. While they are still fine-tuning these tools, a combination of the following is often used:

1. Pre-, post-, and year-end focus groups and surveys of internationally accepted standards;
2. Participant satisfaction and self-evaluation interviews;
3. Assessment of court data and records;
4. Personal interviews with designated officials; and
5. Independent expert appraisal.

The behavioral change that is the basis for sustainable judicial reform is likely, however, to take one or even two decades to have an impact. While obviously mileposts along the way are necessary, donor agencies need to understand that in judicial reform projects the full impact cannot be measured in a three- or five-year project term. A project is not unsuccessful if the seeds for change have been planted and nurtured. Donors need to establish evaluation techniques for judicial reform projects that do not put pressure on program managers to choose project components that have little sustainable behavioral change impact.[8]

A further aspect of judicial education that needs to be evaluated is the effectiveness of presentation. In the old days, any incumbent of a distinguished office was considered an adequate speaker to fill up judicial education hours. Failing this, a quickly established panel of those present would be talked into convening an ad hoc discussion. Long lectures—highly conducive to judicial

---

8. See general discussion on this point in Toope, Stephen J. 1997. "Programming in Legal and Judicial Reform: An Analytical Framework for CIDA Engagement." September. p. 17.

nap-taking!—were a matter of course. Today, adult education studies have shown that an average adult (hopefully, a judge is better than average) retains only 7 percent of what he or she hears. Visual aids, teaching plans, provision of background material, and interactive teaching methods are now de rigueur in order to achieve an acceptable score in programming evaluation.

Legal Education

I leave this specialized area of academic and professional qualification training and continuing professional legal education to my more knowledgeable colleagues on the panel. However, I wish to note that it is an important foundation area for judicial reform.

In most jurisdictions judges come from law schools if not through the bar. The ethical and public service values instilled or failed to be instilled in them in their law schools and professional training will shape the bench. Their legal analytical and research skills will determine the quality of their profession. Their jurisprudential understanding of the theory and philosophy of law is particularly important in those jurisdictions with constitutionally entrenched charters of rights and in countries developing modern market economies. A failure to achieve acceptable standards of basic legal education inculcating a jurisprudential understanding of the function of law as the underpinning of the economic and social well-being of the community reduces law schools to trade schools and provides a poor foundation for reform.

A recent publication[9] analyzed civil process reform in 13 countries; the study concluded that the one constant in efforts to reform justice systems in both common and civil law countries, developed or developing, was the opposition of the organized bar. This comes as no surprise to those of us who have undergone judicial reform or who have worked on the judicial reform projects of others. The bar has a great deal of political clout in most countries and there are many examples of how bars have successfully impeded reforms that they perceive as threats to their vested interests.

While an ethos of public service will alone not serve to overcome the resistance of the bar to change, where it exists, it is a powerful support for reform. Linked with high professional standards imposed and enforced by

9. Zuckerman, Adrian A.S. 1999. *Civil Justice in Crisis.* Oxford: Oxford University Press.

an effective self-disciplinary bar, it can go far to promote pressures to overcome resistance to change. Continuing professional legal education can only provide a supportive environment for a justice system that effectively serves the community.

Unfortunately bar associations in some developed and many developing countries have not assumed or do not exercise the necessary control over admission standards, continuing education, or the professional conduct of their members. Judicial reform projects would do well to encourage the assumption by the bar of these responsibilities. This requires support for the regular reform process of widespread dissemination of information on comparative best practices, wide spread consultation to achieve articulation of desired reform appropriate to the national culture, identification and training of emerging reform leaders, and formulation and stakeholder adoption of a step-by-step reform process and implementation of the reforms. Training is involved at every stage.

Training for the Media

Many countries have a career judicial pattern with a highly professionalized judiciary that makes little use of lay judges or juries. In such situations and where there is a strong media, this plays an important role in creating the image of justice. Few people attend court hearings. Relatively few people are involved in the administration of justice as litigants, witnesses, or jurors. This means the public information about the impression of judges and the justice system is shaped by the members of the media. Their understanding—or lack of it—of the justice system will color their reporting and the public perception of the justice available to them. For this reason, it is important that programs are established to teach the media the principles underlying a well-functioning judiciary. Members of the media need to understand the principles and processes of an independent judiciary and they need to know the standards the community has the right to demand of its judiciary so that they can scrutinize, monitor, and report accurately on the degree of attainment of these standards

Unnecessary and inappropriate undermining of the judiciary because of a lack of knowledge and understanding of how it should function is as dangerous to high standards of judicial service as is a failure of the media to scrutinize and analyze where it fails. In addition to collegial short training programs on such topics as access to justice or basic constitutional judicial issues for members of the media, longer-term legal studies—such as Bachelor of Laws programs made available to meritorious journalists interested in specializing in legal reporting—contribute to higher standards of judicial service.

It is also important that lines of communication are kept open between the media and the judiciary. This can ensure an understanding on the part of one essential element of democracy about the objectives, principles, and difficulties of the other. This opening of communication lines has been accomplished in some jurisdictions by the creation of bench and media committees.

Community Training

The need for community training is threefold. The first need is to ensure that there is popular understanding and support for the need for judicial independence to allow the courts to protect civil and human rights from executive excesses and to ensure that the legislature acts within constitutional limits. To ensure the right of the individual to equality before the law and the protection of the law, the judiciary must be able to exercise its function without pressure from the state, the rich, and the powerful. The independence of the judiciary is a cornerstone of a society that cherishes the rule of law.

The courts are impotent without the support of the executive branch. They have no capability of carrying out their orders against the state without executive compliance. This is being dramatically illustrated now in the news reports emanating from Zimbabwe concerning court orders that are not being followed by the police. In a democracy the executive is ultimately controlled by the people. And only if the people understand the importance of an independent judiciary can they exert their will that the executive and legislative branches discipline themselves to support judicial independence— through positive actions and by obeying court orders against the state. Chart 2 in the annex lists a number of mechanisms that have been found to be supportive of the environment that is most likely to ensure an impartial judicial mind. It is an entertaining yet effective educational tool—one that can assist both those who are legally trained and others who are not—to measure the support their country gives to an independent judiciary.

Second, the community must be informed of the standards that it has the right to demand from its justice system. This not only means the right to an impartial hearing and the right to have easy access to a transparent, efficient, and effective judicial complaint process. Appropriate court access also means that access to justice is not denied for economic, geographical, physical, or other reasons, such as illiteracy or lack of understanding of the official court language. In some countries the official court language differs from the vernacular; in multilanguage countries interpretation services are often inadequate.

Targets of Community Education

The targets of community education necessary to foster the judicial reform process are broad. They include educating the legislative branch, the executive branch, school children, disadvantaged groups, and the community at large—including NGOs and CSOs. In a constitutional democracy it is imperative that the legislators are provided with sufficient information and training to make them sensitive to their responsibilities in relation to maintaining an independent judiciary. In addition, and this is particularly the case in countries that have recently undergone significant legal changes and are engaged in legal framework reform, it is important that the bills presented to the executive cabinet and legislature be accompanied by information and training programs explaining the reasons requiring the new legal framework and the economic and social impact of the proposed bills. The information to allow meaningful reaction to complex legal framework reforms so often funded by donors cannot be presumed to be in the minds or hands of the legislators.

As indicated in chart 1 (see the annex), the executive branch in a well-functioning state must actively support the judiciary—in other words, prosecuting those who would corrupt the judicial process, and obeying court orders directed against the state—and at the same time restrain themselves from interfering in the decision-making process or undermining public confidence in the judiciary.

To ensure a public that is educated in the importance of a well-functioning justice system, school curricula should include programs on principles of judicial independence, access to justice, and the standards that the community has the right to demand from its justice system. Disadvantaged groups such as women and minorities need to have special efforts made to acquaint them with their legal rights and assist them to reach out to the law for protection. Sensitivity training for judges, judicial support staff, and lawyers is more effective if the disadvantaged groups are trained to understand their legal right to equality before the law and the procedure to claim the protection of the law.

Programs on access to justice delivered locally not only teach legal rights and the legal path to obtain them, but often include training in mediation and conciliation skills to establish or strengthen local ADR processes and institutions. This training has not only the direct benefit of supporting extra-judicial dispute resolution—thereby lightening the court workload—but also the indirect benefit of bringing mediation and conciliation skills to families and the community.

Finally, experience has shown that judicial reform makes the best progress if pressures that are external to the formal justice system instigate and support initiatives for judicial reform. The training of trainers in NGOs and CSOs to provide information and discussion at the local or village level for the purpose of garnering public support to create these pressures is an essential impetus for effective judicial reform.

Training for Those Involved with Judicial Reform

We have discussed above the need for training to develop national judicial reform leadership—both inside and outside the formal justice system. There is, however, another area that merits examination. The upsurge of interest in judicial reform has created a need for judicial reform specialists to act as consultants on judicial reform projects. To do this requires learning in many areas. Some of the most important are these:

1. We need to understand that theories and principles may transplant but that institutions and processes often do not.

   A good example comes from my home jurisdiction of Nova Scotia which was, in 1749, the first settled English colony in what is now Canada. The early settlers were dominantly of English stock and one would have thought admirably suited to receive English legal institutions and processes. The first governor instituted courts of sessions presided over by volunteer lay justices of the peace on the English model. The early records indicate the poor attendance of the lay judges and the reluctance of the settlers to sit on juries. With hindsight the reason is clear. There were no members of the landed gentry in the province derisively called "Nova Scarcity" who could afford to donate their time for civic duty.

Inevitably reality overcame the theory and the need to get on with the judicial process resulted in the abandonment of volunteer judges and the development of the highly professionalized judiciary of modern Canada. The lesson well known to Nova Scotian law students is that English institutions and process which admirably suited England were not transplantable even to English settlers in "New Scotland." The formal abandonment of the aboriginal dispute resolution created both social and legal injustice for aboriginal Canadians.

A study of legal history of other English colonies shows that often no effort was made to transplant an independent judicial process in the subordinate courts, but rather control of the subordinate judiciary was kept in the hands of the colonial administrators to ensure them control over public order and judicial officers sympathetic to the colonial administration. While to my knowledge the executive branch controls the subordinate courts now in only two Commonwealth countries—Zimbabwe and Bangladesh—this emancipation of junior but powerful judicial officers is relatively recent in many countries and goes a long way toward explaining the slow development of judicial independence in the subordinate courts in these countries.

To understand the present problems judicial reformers need to understand the past. Sustainable change cannot be planned without taking into account the legal history and the culture it created.

Judicial reformers need excellent listening skills as well as a broad-based knowledge of a variety of legal cultures to understand the context of a justice sector weakness and to be able to recommend solutions that are custom designed to suit not only the problem but the context in which it is found. Western solutions imposed on non-western cultures may not work or may only work during the life of a project to be followed by a creeping return to pre-reform ways. A good example is the Philippine situation where western-style time limitations imposed on judges without treating the underlying causes of delay have resulted in some judges filing fraudulent work returns and others preferring not to file at all and to suffer the penalty of nonpayment of their salaries. A similar example may be found in a story from Asia of a judge, also desperate to meet his monthly quota of cases, who resorted to the practice of hearing two cases at the same time—one in the courtroom, presided over by his clerk and another in his chamber, over which he presided. His monthly quota of cases was met, but it must have appeared to the judgeless litigants in the courtroom that the priority product to be delivered by the justice system was efficiency and not the reality or perception of a fair trial.

2. The judicial system works within a national culture. There is no universal prescription that will necessarily work for common problems. Let us look at a few examples.

Enforcement of Judgements

One component of delay is often inefficient and ineffective enforcement of judgements. The causes of this can differ. For example in Yemen, the official executing court orders may be met with armed resistance; in many jurisdictions the problem is corruption of the court officers (or delegated private firms) enforcing court civil judgements; in some West African countries the culture will not permit the attachment of land traditionally used by the community; in still other countries delay in enforcement may be caused only by lack of appropriate legal framework, inefficient processes, and inefficient personnel.

Bankruptcy Law

Another example of a national culture resisting international best practices may be found in Uganda where there is almost no use made of a perfectly functional bankruptcy law. This is because of the strong social pressure against both those undergoing the bankruptcy process and those who seek to use it.

Corruption

It is unreasonable to expect that judges will naturally have ethics superior to those of the culture from which the judges come. Without question, a certain number of people in all walks of life in every country have high standards of integrity which they follow regardless of temptations and cultural norms. We know from such varied countries as

Bangladesh and Uganda that the members of the superior courts are able to rise above national ethical standards and enjoy the confidence of at least the legal community. (As discussed below the community at large generally takes its image of justice from the subordinate courts.)

Anti-corruption campaigns are founded on large-scale community education programming and are many-pronged. They include a widely disseminated code of judicial conduct on and off the bench that allows the community to know what standards it has the right to demand. It requires a transparent and easily accessible judicial complaint and discipline process which is efficient and fair to judges and provides for visible imposition of remedial and punitive sanctions to judges who have transgressed the code. As the code requires of the judges a standard of conduct that prevents not only the reality but the perception of corruption, they require an annotated code with hypothetical and precedential fact situations to clearly articulate to the judges the conduct required of them. To develop the requisite ownership of the code necessary for effective implementation (to attract even the grudging support of the judiciary) requires its development through the involvement of the whole judiciary. Further consultations and continuing education sessions are required to ensure widespread understanding of expected standards of conduct throughout both the judiciary and the community.

3. Judicial reformers need to understand the delicate balance between ministries of justice and judiciaries.

Some tension between the executive and the judiciary is healthy, as the function of the judiciary is to protect the citizen from executive misuse of power. "It is an accepted fact that in all countries with working democratic systems, strains develop between the judiciary and the Legislature or the Executive."[10]

However, when the tension grows to interrupt necessary communication between the two branches of government to the extent that it paralyzes all or part of the judicial function, it becomes destructive.

---

10. Georges, P. Telford. 2000. "Report on the Independence of the Judiciary in Trinidad and Tobago." February 16. p. 14; <http://www.ttlawcourts.org/reports/georges>.

The most current example of this is the refusal of the executive branch in Zimbabwe to carry out court orders. It serves to remind us that a judiciary is impotent without executive support. Judicial reformers need to be very careful not to exacerbate the tensions between the two branches of government, since tensions tend to escalate during reform projects.

4. We need to collect information and share ideas. Only by building up a body of literature, only by collecting and analyzing empirical data, by exchanging information on our successes and failures and creating files on lessons learned can we become more effective. The World Bank has given leadership and impetus to this quest for judicial reform learning in several ways, one being this "Global Conference" bringing together so many leaders and workers in the field. Other ways in which it has made significant contributions are through the establishment of a World Bank Web page linking together people and information in the field and the publication of important judicial and legal reform publications.[11] Only through the rigorous evaluation of training programs and their relevance to priority needs can legal and judicial education to support judicial reform be improved. Only through application of appropriate evaluative techniques to the work we do can we discharge our duty to be accountable to the public and ourselves for the time and money spent on judicial reform.

5. Judicial reformers, including judges, from developed countries need to appreciate the difficult position of the judge in a developing country. The position of the subordinate court judge is particularly onerous.

   The subordinate court presents the image of justice to the people. It is the court that has the greatest public contact. The opinion held of the subordinate court colors the reputation of all courts. If the subordinate court has fallen into disrepute, if it does not provide an efficient

---

11. Dakolias, Maria, and Said, Javier, World Bank Legal and Judicial Reform Unit, "Judicial Reform a Process of Change through Pilot Courts"; Buscaglia, Edgardo, and Dakolias, Maria, World Bank Legal and Judicial Reform Unit, "An Analysis of the Causes of Corruption in the Judiciary"; Messick, Richard E., "Judicial Reform and Economic Development: A Survey of the Issues." All in the February 1999 *World Bank Research Observer* 14(1): 117–36; <http://www1.worldbank.org/legal/ljrconference.html>.

dispute resolution service, if it is reputed to harbor corruption, the public's faith in the state and the judiciary is eroded. Furthermore, the perception and reality of the unpredictability, costs, and inefficiencies of the court system block national, social, and economic development by driving away local and foreign investment.

Subordinate court judges are poorly paid, usually not housed, made by necessity to travel to and from court on public transport with the witnesses and litigants who appear before them, and are intensely scrutinized and criticized. In some jurisdictions, their decision making process is interfered with by some of their many superiors. They often must watch the people who come before them wait in dirty and run-down courthouses, without information services, unable to provide even copies of documents, and they know that the poor record-keeping and lack of case flow management are invitations for corruption for which they will be criticized.

There is usually no adequate in-service professional growth program to assist them to improve their competency and confidence, few tools to spark intellectual interest in the philosophy of law and justice, and little contact with external judiciaries to discuss solutions found elsewhere to common problems.

Training is needed to point out to the senior judiciary, the legal community, the Ministry of Justice, and the community that more tribute needs to be paid to the subordinate court. Its defects are perceived and public dislike of the defects—which are often beyond the court's ability to remedy them—earns it disrespect.

The judiciary is a hierarchical institution. The subordinate judiciary is at the bottom of the judicial tier. Despite its important and essential function as the workhorse of the judiciary and despite its wide jurisdiction (some have unlimited civil jurisdiction and have the power to impose the death penalty), its achievements are not much heralded. The leadership of the judiciary, the government, the bar, and the community need to be agents for change in publicly recognizing the importance of the court, encouraging its judges to set and attain high personal goals of integrity and professional competence, and demonstrating respect for the office of the subordinate judge.

Judges in nearly all developing countries are inadequately paid. In many jurisdictions they work without basic tools and equipment and live in modest government housing that often lacks potable water. In some instances they are so overburdened with judicial reform consultants and projects that there is little time left to hear cases. They have electronic technology pressed upon them by donors; some, having conquered the computer and e-mail, find their phone and power cut off as a result of their electronic legal researching costs having exhausted the judicial budget allocation. Intellectually and emotionally they are torn by being asked to solve in their courts issues that are social and economic and usually beyond their state's capacity to fund.

Conclusion

The question put to us is, "How does legal training improve participation in the reform process?" My response is that it creates an environment for reform through knowledge. Judicial training improves participation in the reform process in the following ways:

1. It identifies the community perception of judicial weaknesses;
2. It designs and delivers effective remedial programming to respond to the identified weaknesses;
3. It develops leaders in judicial education and reform and equips them with the skills to inspire others;
4. It lays the foundation and provides continuing support for the sustainable behavioral change that is the essence of judicial reform;
5. It strengthens the fact and perception of the impartiality, competence, efficiency, and effectiveness of the judiciary;
6. It builds public confidence in the judiciary; and
7. It creates pressures within and outside of the judiciary for reform.

Judicial education is not only a separate component of judicial reform projects; it is a supporting thread running through all.

Annex

Chart 1 Needs Assessment

The_____ Judicial Education Curriculum Committee would like to solicit your opinion on topics for judicial education, the study of which would strengthen the Judiciary. Would you kindly prioritize the following topics ranked in order of preference from ONE to TEN, number ONE being the most important? More than one topic may share the same numerical rank. Please write in any additional topics you might like to suggest, assigning them a numerical rank.

You will note the topics are divided into four general categories:

1. Impartiality   _____
2. Competency
3. Efficiency
4. Effectiveness

Please rank the above-noted categories in order of their priority to you. More than one category may be assigned the same rank.

A. Impartiality, Independence, and Accountability (Please enter a number between ONE and TEN for each item. Two or more items may share the same rating.)

1. The Principle and Practice of the Independence of the Judiciary   _____
2. Accountability to the Public Judges Protect and Serve   _____
3. Judicial Ethics and Conduct, On and Off the Bench   _____
4. The Science of Fact Finding—Recognition of Judicial Bias   _____
5. Sensitivity Training in Contemporary Social Issues   _____
6. Gender, Ethnic, and Other Disadvantaged Groups Sensitivity Training   _____
Other: _____   _____
_____   _____

B. Competency—Professional Skills Updating—Continuing Education in Substantive and Procedural Law (Please enter a number between ONE and TEN for each item. Two or more items may share the same rating.)

7. Criminal Law   _____
8. Sentencing   _____
9. Evidence   _____
10. Constitutional Law   _____
11. Family Law   _____
12. Civil Procedure   _____
13. Criminal Procedure   _____
14. Legislative Interpretation   _____
15. Torts   _____
16. Contract Law   _____

17. Administrative Law _____
18. Assessment of Damages _____
19. Property Law _____
20. New Developments in the Law _____
Other: _____ _____
_____ _____
_____ _____

Economic Laws (Please enter a number between ONE and TEN for each item. Two or more items may share the same rating.)

21. Intellectual Property Law _____
22. Bankruptcy Law _____
23. Banking Law _____
24. Modern Corporate Law _____
25. Principles of International Trade and the Roles of Financial Institutions and Banks _____
26. Evidence Laws for Administrative Tribunals _____
27. Foreign Exchange Laws _____
28. International Trade Procedures _____
29. International and Domestic Arbitration Laws _____
30. Competition Law _____
31. Communications Law _____
32. Labor Law _____
33. Income Tax Law _____
34. Environmental Law _____
Other: _____ _____
_____ _____
_____ _____

C. Efficiency (Please enter a number between ONE and TEN for each item. Two or more items may share the same rating.)

35. Computer Training _____
36. Case Flow Management _____
37. Time Management _____
38. Mediation Skills _____
39. Alternative Dispute Resolution _____
40. Stress Management _____
41. Court and Docket Management Skills _____
42. Management Skills _____
Other: _____ _____
_____ _____
_____ _____

D. Effectiveness (Please enter a number between ONE and TEN for each item. Two or more items may share the same rating.)

43. Judicial Techniques to Bridge the Gap between Law and Justice _____
44. Interpreting Constitutional Charters of Rights _____
45. Domestic Application of International Human Rights Norms _____
46. Exercise of Judicial Discretion _____
47. Media-Bench Relations _____
48. Judgement Writing and Delivery _____
49. Judicial Skills—Chairpersonship of the Proceedings—Maintenance of a Dignified, Orderly, Efficient Pace of Proceedings _____
50. Sensitivity to Needs and Rights of the Witnesses, Litigants, and Public _____
51. Communication Skills—in the Courtroom, with Stakeholders and the Community at Large _____
52. Adapting to Change _____
53. Social Impact of Judicial Decisions _____
54. Economic Impact of Judicial Decisions _____
55. Legal and Judicial Reform _____

Other: _____ _____

_____ _____

_____ _____

Comments: _____ _____

_____ _____

_____ _____

Chart 2–Index of Judicial Independence

Impartial appointment process	Impartial discipline process	Adequate salary	Constitutionally protected salary	Security of tenure	An independent bar	Physical security	Civil immunity for judicial functions
Executive support to enforce judgments even against itself	Executive restraint from interference in judicial decision-making process	Executive support to prosecute and punish attempted or actual judicial corruption	A government that is sensitive to public opinion	An educated public that demands an impartial judiciary	Articulated judicial ethical standards	Freedom from interference in decision-making from superior judicial officers outside of the appellate process	Integration of Subordinate Court as full members of the Judiciary
Emancipation of the Subordinate Court from the Executive	A lack of retrospective legislation	Judicial control of its own budget	Judicial control of its own administration	Constitutionally entrenched courts	Freedom from geographic transfer without consent (unless it is term of employment)	Free and informed press	Judicial control of the curriculum and faculty of judicial education

Improving the Reform Process through Legal Training

Akua Kuenyehia

Dean, Faculty of Law

University of Ghana

Introduction

In recent years many developing countries have embarked on various structural reforms of institutions supported by donor agencies. One of the main objectives of these structural reforms has been to create an environment that will attract investment and enhance private sector growth and development, and also improve access to and the delivery of services to the citizenry.

It has become apparent that a country's legal environment plays a highly significant role in fostering investor-friendly conditions as well as promoting private sector growth. It also plays a large role in improving the conditions of living for the ordinary citizen. It is crucial that institutional reform and restructuring, capacity building, technology enhancement, and the strengthening of the various institutions of law in general be undertaken if the right conditions are to be created that will foster investment, encourage an active private sector as well as encourage full participation of all beneficiary groups in the development process.

Legal education and training are important components of legal reform. The training of lawyers by academic institutions and continuous education for lawyers in private practice and in various institutions and for judges, as well as training for support and administrative staff are critical in this process. Additionally sensitization and awareness creation of the processes of the law—especially the operations of the judiciary and other institutions—for the general public are important to ensure a constant evaluation of the role of the legal sector in the development process.

Legal Training Institutions

Faculties of law and law schools, where lawyers are trained, have an important role to play. The training they provide for lawyers has an influence on the kind of legal environment that exists in any country. This is especially the case in developing countries where these institutions may operate under severe economic restraints.

Curricula in these institutions ought to be constantly reviewed so that subjects that are taught are relevant to the needs of the country while at the same time keeping pace with developments in the rest of the world.

It is important that these training institutions pay special attention to emerging areas of law that have a direct impact on the development process. They need to provide adequate instructions in these emerging areas of law so that the lawyers who are trained will be able to function effectively, rendering appropriate service to society.

In view of the above there is a need therefore to ensure that the training institutions are adequately financed so that they will be able to have the needed resources to provide the required training for lawyers.

The teachers in these institutions also need to constantly update their knowledge through participation in conferences, seminars, workshops, and other activities both at the national and the international level. This way, they would be able to monitor and evaluate the training that they are providing for lawyers in the country. Links with other institutions are an important part of the training provided by the training institutions. Links that allow the exchange of students and staff can provide an excellent opportunity to learn from the experiences of others as well as keep abreast with the developments of the law in various areas. It also provides exposure to new ways of looking at old problems and new strategies for dealing with problems.

Continuous Legal Education for Lawyers

This can be broken down into education and training for lawyers in private practice and those employed in various institutions, both in government and in the private sector.

This is crucial for progress in any country. Since law is dynamic, it is necessary to put in place an effective system of continuous legal education for lawyers that would help them update their knowledge. This should be a requirement for every lawyer wherever that lawyer works.

The world is moving so fast that developing countries are lagging behind in a great number of areas. Especially in information technology there is the need to tailor the training to meet the identified training requirements of the various institutions. The important thing is that training and education need to be an integral part of the program of institutional activities and actions.

The rapid pace of development in information technology means that there has been a dramatic change in many areas of the law. The only way in which lawyers can keep up their knowledge is to have consistent periodic programs of going back to the classroom to deliberate and learn about new developments in the law. There are many ways of exposing lawyers to new learning and all the possibilities ought to be exploited and fully utilized in the effort to keep lawyers abreast of new developments.

One cannot overemphasize the need for continuous learning for lawyers in all sectors. This is especially true in the context of reforms. Lawyers cannot be effective participants in the process of reform unless they receive training in new areas as well exposure to new thinking on old areas of the law. Lawyers themselves must be willing to take the initiative and strive to equip themselves with resources that will enable them to keep abreast with new developments in the law.

As has been observed continuous education could take many forms depending on the type of practitioner under consideration. For lawyers in private practice, the Bar Association needs to organize a program for updating their knowledge. This must be a requirement for all lawyers in practice and must be a prerequisite for obtaining a license to practice.

For those employed in the Ministry of Justice and other institutions both within government and the private sector, there is the need for a variety of training programs targeting different areas of operations. Since reforms include both revisions of laws as well as the introduction of new laws, lawyers in these institutions need training in new areas of law as well as in drafting skills.

The training could take the form of formal periodic courses at local as well as foreign institutions, participation in seminars, workshops and conferences both at home and abroad, as well as in-house training provided by experienced lawyers imparting their knowledge and skills to newly employed ones.

In situations in which resources are scarce, every avenue for training ought to be explored and utilized for the benefit of the institutions. This actually forms part of the reform in that it fosters an economic utilization of scarce resources.

Enhanced library facilities to facilitate research in these institutions should be part of the process. Access to the Internet and of course training in the use of it for research purposes all help to improve lawyers' knowledge and thus equip them to be a vibrant part of the reform process.

This way, lawyers are able to play an effective role in the process of reform by bringing their skills and knowledge to bear upon the revision of laws as well as the introduction of new laws.

The Judiciary

In most countries, especially in developing ones, very little attention is paid to the training needs of the judiciary. As a result the judiciary tends to be the weakest link in the legal chain. It is therefore important to pay special attention to the training of judges and other personnel involved in the administration of justice. These include the administrative staff, some of whom may be judges, and court personnel as well as other support staff.

Judges

Judges do not receive specialist training for the bench. They are normally appointed to the bench based on their experience at the bar or in academia.

Even though upon appointment they are given short orientation courses, they mostly rely on their aforementioned experience. It is important that a system be put in place to give the judges some training in judicial reasoning and discretion. This will go a long way in helping them dispense justice satisfactorily. These are skills that are acquired; they do not necessarily come naturally to the individual.

Judges also need to be exposed to the Internet and be granted access to comprehensive libraries so that they can carry out research that would add to their knowledge and aid them in the discharge of their duties.

Some of the problems that the judiciary in developing countries face arise because it is assumed that judges, once appointed, know how to be judges. They need training in judging cases, especially in using new ideas as part of their everyday working experience.

Judges play such a crucial role in the reform process that their training needs cannot be overlooked. In view of this role, they also need to be trained in areas of economic and commercial laws—such as laws and regulations governing banking transactions, capital markets and securities, insurance, intellectual property, consumer protection, electronic commerce, economic crimes, and associated fields.

Development is such that judges ought to be abreast with the emerging areas of the law if they are to assist in ensuring that the legal system is responsive to both the private sector and the citizenry during this development process. Lack of knowledge of new areas of the law can be a serious drawback to judicial dispute resolution, which in turn can have very serious repercussions for the development process.

The training of judges, just as that for lawyers, should be a continuous one. It is therefore necessary to establish an institution that is well equipped to provide the necessary training in all areas and, especially, in the emerging areas of law.

This way, judges would be able to handle competently all types of cases that come before them thereby helping to provide the needed environment for investment as well as enhancing access to justice for the population.

There is also a need to provide management-training skills for those judges who have administrative responsibilities. This enables them to discharge their administrative responsibilities efficiently. It must never be assumed that a judge has the necessary administrative skills to manage, as well as to be a judge.

Most often, this training is not given, and judges are therefore not able to discharge the added obligations of their position efficiently.

Court Personnel and Support Staff of the Judiciary

For any judiciary to function efficiently, it is necessary for the judges to be well versed in the law and its operations. It is also necessary for the staff who work in the various sections of the judiciary to be trained so that they have the required skills that will enable them to discharge their responsibilities effectively. This is important, since one of the major objectives of any reform process is to have a judicial system that is transparent and efficient.

Most often, in developing countries, court personnel such as court clerks, bailiffs, ushers, and interpreters are not provided with any training, whether in-house or externally. They thus become stale and in some cases unfamiliar with court processes. In order to increase their efficiency in the discharge of their responsibilities, it is necessary to provide them with short-term training on a regular basis that would reinforce their knowledge of court processes and also enhance their skills in discharging their obligations. This will help them in realizing that they play an important role in the administration of justice. More important, it helps reinforce their pride in the work they do and encourages them to give their best to the persons they serve.

Most often, because such staff are unfamiliar with the court process, they tend to abuse the very process that they are charged to administer. This in turn leads to corruption or perceptions of corruption within the system.

A system that allows the staff to be trained and have their knowledge refreshed and updated regularly leads to better efficiency. It also allows them to participate in the reform process from an informed perspective. It helps them appreciate their role in the whole reform process.

Additionally, training in the use of new technologies, especially information technologies, is important for support staff in order to enhance the role of the judiciary in the reform process. In cultures in which computers are the exception rather than the norm, it is important to ensure that support staff have access to training programs that would introduce them to the use of computers, e-mail, and the Internet. Without these skills the reform process will not make much of an impact. The administration of justice does not depend on judges alone, but more importantly on the staff who support the judges and deliver the associated services. Regular management training courses that are organized or made available to judicial staff will help them keep abreast with modern trends in management and thus enhance their efficiency.

In countries where there are lay adjudicators, training of such personnel in the basics of law and the legal system is crucial to their successful participation in the adjudication process. It is important for these persons to be conversant with legal concepts involved in the dispensation of justice.

Public Awareness

The public—the user of the services provided by the legal sector—has an important role to play in the reform process. When the general public is conversant with the processes connected with the administration of justice, they are able to demand performance, and corruption is minimized, if not totally eradicated.

The situation that prevails in most developing countries, however, is that processes are obscure and cumbersome—the public lacks knowledge about court processes, land registration, and associated processes, and this makes them susceptible to exploitation by junior and senior workers alike within the institutions charged with rendering the necessary services.

It is possible for awareness to be created among members of the public so that they would play an active role in the reform process. Through various campaigns and fora, awareness of court and associated processes can be created to enable the public to demand accountability and performance from the service providers. This has the added advantage of encouraging the service providers to do what is right at all times, since ignorance on the part of the public will no longer provide them with protection for wrongdoing.

It must be noted that this process needs to be ongoing, and it ought to be an integral part of any reform process. Without creating public awareness—enabling the public to use the process without hassle, and also to call attention to abuses—there will be no effective way of monitoring and evaluating the effectiveness of the reform.

Conclusion

Training is an indispensable and crucial part of legal reform. Without training, reform is seen only in the context of revision of laws and the introduction of new laws. Reform, to have a lasting and effective impact, must aim at revising old laws as well as introducing new ones. But more important than that, it is necessary to pay attention to the institutional framework within which reform takes place as well as the human resources that make the institutions function.

Any reform program that does not have a clearly defined training component for the different groups within the legal system involved in the administration of justice is bound to fail. Training is important to make reform last for the benefit of society. Not only will training for lawyers and others who run the legal system improve the reform process, it will also enrich and accelerate the process. The individuals involved will be in a position to fully appreciate the benefits of an efficient and transparent system and therefore work harder to achieve the bigger picture.

Legal Training in a Transitional Democracy

The Georgian Experience

Dr. Lado Chanturia

Chief Justice

Republic of Georgia

The collapse of the Soviet Union and the creation of new, independent states across Eastern Europe, the Caucasus, and Central Asia have presented an opportunity for legal reform unlike any other time in modern history. My homeland, Georgia, has proudly joined the family of democratic nations and has taken great steps toward establishing a market economy and a society based on the rule of law.

As I begin my remarks, I must first stop to express the deep thanks of my nation and its government—particularly its judiciary—for the assistance provided by international organizations such as the World Bank in helping us draft and implement the changes necessary to reform our legal system. Historically, Georgia has many links to the continental law system and we have benefited from a close collaboration with European legal experts. We have also relied on the American legal community for help in those areas in which we have chosen to model our system more closely on the adversary system in the United States.

While building our new legal system in Georgia, we learned many lessons. We realize that we must have strong institutions that are able to implement the numerous changes from the old Soviet system. But we also have learned that our institutions are only as strong as the people who serve in them. We recognize that successful legal reform cannot occur without lawyers and judges who understand the advantages of a system based on the rule of law. We also realize that to have lawyers and judges with such understanding, we must reform our system of legal education.

The importance of reform in our method of educating those who will practice and judge the law is clear to us in Georgia. We also know that it is not only the future lawyers and judges, but also all public servants, who must understand our new legal system.

But I must leave the topic of reform of our legal education system for another time. Today I want to focus my remarks on the critical areas of judicial reform and training for those who currently sit in judgment of the legal disputes that come before the courts of Georgia.

In 1998, Georgia took a historic step to ensure that its judges knew and understood the many new laws in our nation. We began judicial qualification examinations for all those who were judges under the old Soviet system and for new judicial candidates.

This was a crucial reform in our system. It gave the people confidence in the judiciary of our newly independent country and ensured that judges would be appointed based on their legal knowledge.

An indication of the level of change this reform brought to our judicial system is the fact that since 1998 we have had six judicial qualification examinations. Over 1,500 candidates have taken the examinations but only 287 have passed and only 70 of those were former judges.

There are 388 judicial positions in Georgia and we have filled 206 of these positions with men and women who have passed the judicial qualification examination. As a result over half our judiciary consists of these newly qualified judges. This is a reform that we are truly proud of and from which we will never turn back.

Passing the qualification examination is just the beginning of the reform process. Good judges must not only know the law, they must know how to apply the law and to fulfill their duties as judges. That is why we have now placed judicial training among our highest priorities.

Let me provide details of some of the ways we are giving our new judges the tools necessary to do their job in the most professional way.

We have created the Judicial Training Center to determine the areas in which judges themselves feel the greatest need for instruction and then provide training and seminars in those fields. The Center coordinates the assistance provided by international organizations such as the European Union, Council of Europe, World Bank, United States Agency for International Development (USAID), and the German Agency for Technical Cooperation (GTZ) in arranging seminars and workshops for the judges. In many of these, Georgian judges serve as speakers and help organize the training sessions.

Seminars are arranged in various locations around the country to make sure that training is provided to judges in all the regions.

We have made maximum use of foreign legal experts to share their experiences with our new judges. These experts provide practical examples to show judges how cases can be heard and decided. During the Soviet regime, the judiciary was never exposed to outside experiences and we know the damage that such isolation caused. Judges have a crucial role to play in a democratic society with a market economy. Our judges need to closely cooperate with, and learn from, European and American judges and legal experts during our transition period.

We have begun a program of training Georgian judges in the methods of teaching their fellow judges. We have created a group of judges from our Supreme Court and our appellate courts who are specially trained to conduct seminars and provide workshops for their associates.

Important changes have also been made in our court organization in Georgia. Court reform laws created an appellate court level in our system and restructured the function of the Supreme Court, which has now become a court of cassation. As a result of this reform, judges have required training in hearing and deciding cases on appeal from lower instance courts. It has become important for appeal judges to learn the process of discussing and analyzing the decisions of lower courts and identifying possible errors in those decisions. Seminars on these topics have become a tradition in our Supreme Court and appellate courts and we recognize this as an important area of judicial training.

The publication of court decisions has also had a great impact on the level of legal education of our judges. The decisions of the Supreme Court are now published and distributed to every judge in the nation. This is part of our effort to develop a body of law that can be applied consistently throughout our court levels.

An important part of our training system has been our ability to send Georgian judges on training tours of European and American courts. These tours allow judges to observe practices in other courts and to apply these experiences when they return to Georgia. The World Bank has been very helpful in this field and our Supreme Court has cooperated with the Supreme Court of Germany (BGH) and GTZ in providing six-week training courses in Germany for our judges. We have been also been able to send judges for training in the United States and France in addition to programs in Germany. The sharing of experiences with judges of different nations is of great importance to our developing court system.

In Georgia we are in the unique position of being able to draw upon two legal systems in creating our training programs. We have strong historical links to the family of European continental law but we are also learning from experts in common law courts. Our legal education is strongly linked to continental law so our training programs for judges are designed to emphasize this connection. Judicial education programs based on continental law help the judges in applying the relevant law to the facts of a case and reach a decision that complies with the requisites of the law and court procedures.

Our friends in countries using the common law system, particularly judges in the United States, have been of great assistance in sharing their experiences about court administration and case management. Also, American judges have conducted many seminars on judicial discipline and judicial ethics. Their contributions to our knowledge in these fields have been of crucial importance as we begin our effort to establish a disciplinary system for the judges of Georgia.

These training programs have all been organized to accomplish our goal of improved judicial knowledge and professionalism. Our training system takes three forms:

1. Joint discussions between Georgian judges and foreign experts about the facts of a case and the possible methods of resolving the dispute in accordance with applicable law.
2. Identification of problems in court practice and administration and use of foreign experiences to solve these problems.
3. Translation of decisions of Georgian judges into foreign languages and assessment of those decisions by foreign judges who discuss their conclusions with our judges.

We have found all three methods extremely useful and apply the appropriate training method to the particular problem facing our system.

I should mention one practical problem that we face in conducting all of these training programs. Judges must first of all be judges—they must spend time in their courtrooms hearing cases and in their offices giving consideration to their opinions. As a result, we have tried to schedule as many seminars and training sessions as possible for weekends and we have arranged for regional training sessions so that judges can gather in one place and meet for workshops and seminars together with foreign experts.

Finally, I must mention our great need for legal textbooks and commentaries. Our judicial reform turned all our old law books based on the Soviet system into paper for our fireplaces. The judges need new textbooks and commentaries to help them gain insight into the application of all the new legislation that our Parliament has enacted to implement these reforms.

Again, international organizations have played a crucial role in helping us prepare and publish such commentaries. The Netherlands Ministry of Foreign Affairs–Center for International Legal Cooperation, USAID, and GTZ have all been closely involved in this effort in connection with our Civil Code. The American Bar Association has sponsored publication of commentaries by one of our Supreme Court judges on the new Criminal Code, which will be distributed to every Georgian judge at the upcoming Conference of Judges.

Our law library has benefited from purchases of literature by USAID, GTZ, the American Bar Association (ABA), and Open Society Georgia Foundation (OSGF). Without their assistance, we would have very limited research materials. The American Bar Association is assisting the Supreme Court in designing and equipping our Supreme Court Law Library, which will be open not only to judges but also to law faculty, students, and the public.

Let me end these remarks with a very special word about our relationship with the World Bank. The Bank plays a key role in our judicial training effort and without their financial and technical assistance many of the projects I have discussed today could not exist. The Judicial Training Center is a prime beneficiary of the Bank's support and our credit agreement makes judicial reform a reality in Georgia. The training of our judges, the reform of our court structures, and the modernization of our equipment is possible because of the World Bank's support.

With the help of our friends in the World Bank, the United States, and throughout Europe, each new day brings Georgia closer to its goal of a modern, professional court system that is the foundation of a society based on the rule of law. This is the dream of every judge in Georgia and of each of our citizens.

Bringing Sub-Saharan African Lawyers into the Legal Reform Process

Experiences and Lessons of the International Law Institute— Uganda Legal Centre for Excellence

Swithin J. Munyantwali

Executive Director

ILI–Uganda Legal Centre of Excellence

Introduction

It is common knowledge that most Sub-Saharan African lawyers do not participate in law reform activities in the transition economies of the Region. Reform initiatives, such as privatization, infrastructure-finance transactions, and commercial law reform, are largely the domain of Western consulting firms and highly priced consultants with no real understanding of local conditions. But law reform programs in Sub-Saharan Africa can succeed only if indigenous lawyers are fully involved.

This paper argues that a lack of continuing professional legal education (CLE) is a major cause of the marginalization of indigenous lawyers from legal reform processes. It demonstrates that the establishment of the International Law Institute Legal Centre of Excellence in Uganda (ILI–Uganda) is a positive response to the need for post-professional legal training and has, in its two years of existence, provided vital programs for public and private sector lawyers in Sub-Saharan Africa.

The central argument of this paper is that CLE is an essential factor in enabling these lawyers to participate in legal reform processes, and that increased efforts by the Sub-Saharan African public and private sectors to augment their knowledge through periodic training will result in more meaningful participation in the process and, therefore, more successful results for reform programs.

The paper begins by demonstrating that legal education in the Region has not responded to the need for CLE and how ILI–Uganda, established in 1998, has begun to address the CLE needs of Sub-Saharan African lawyers and related professionals. It then describes related capacity-building initiatives in which ILI–Uganda is involved, such as technical assistance related to training and research.

Background and Problem Analysis

If lawyers are to work effectively in a world of accelerating legal, financial, and commercial change, regular participation in CLE is essential. Even in societies that provide excellent law school education, a practicing lawyer soon finds a continuous need to be current with changing conditions. This need is particularly severe in Sub-Saharan Africa, where basic law school education is often inadequate.

In Uganda, and typically throughout Sub-Saharan Africa, law schools have traditionally provided a narrow focus on antiquated views of traditional subjects. The universities have neither the resources nor the infrastructure to provide an updated and comprehensive legal education. This leaves the law school graduate with a general understanding of the law, but without the tools necessary to function effectively as a lawyer. Additionally, because a sophisticated employment marketplace does not exist, there is no environment that provides opportunities or motivation to sharpen skills or provide effective, ongoing CLE training. The result is a cadre of young lawyers who never fully become experts in their fields and older lawyers who, notwithstanding longer service, also do not possess the necessary expertise in their fields.

Sub-Saharan Africa has not had regional entities capable of providing CLE on the latest issues affecting both domestic and international law. In addition, a lack of sufficient facilities, limited libraries, outdated materials, and research documents that do not address regional conditions, prevent legal and business professionals from performing their functions in both the private and public sectors. Consequently, indigenous professionals in Sub-Saharan Africa are at a disadvantage in developing the essential skills and perspectives needed to function effectively and productively at home or on the international scene.

All too often, because the skills of indigenous lawyers are not updated regularly to meet the changing needs in their respective countries or in the world at large, the result is an inferior level of professional service. A lawyer from a more developed country, who frequently updates his or her skills by attending mandatory CLE seminars in their country, can then more effectively represent clients in matters involving new and complicated legal matters, such as those in a complex joint venture transaction, privatization, debt management, international arbitration, commercial negotiations, international finance, or an intellectual property and technology transfer agreement. In addition, government officials or related professionals who receive CLE training are then able to perform their duties more efficiently and productively.

The lack of capacity within the legal sector affects practically every aspect of a country's operation. It is well understood that business and law operate together. A legitimate business transaction can occur only within a dependable and reliable legal environment. Domestically, governance is not rendered as completely or as efficiently as it should be. Essential services and programs do not reach their intended beneficiaries, are not run efficiently, or are not completed because of the lack of the essential legal structure to fully develop the programs and to strictly enforce their application. In addition, the inadequacies of the legal sector create an insecure environment that is hostile to foreign and domestic investment.

Internationally, the lack of capacity within the legal sector is even more damaging. The globalization of the world economy has become so increasingly complex that it now heavily influences the development of a country's economy. Highly trained legal and business professionals have become essential to the majority of the complicated transactions required for successful operation within the global economy. When faced with new issues in an international transaction, or involving negotiations with a lawyer from a more developed country, the majority of Sub-Saharan African lawyers are frequently at an extreme disadvantage in representing their clients.

This results in severe discrepancies harming economic growth. First, local governments usually receive an inferior bargain or insufficient terms in contract negotiations with foreign companies and governments. Second, domestic companies are not able to benefit fully from global economies of scale because they lack the capacity to operate efficiently and negotiate internationally, which results in stagnant domestic growth and employment. Third, foreign companies and organizations operating in the region do not use local representation, resulting in less effective operations because of a lack of local knowledge. And finally, since governments and large companies are forced to use foreign legal representation, this hampers current local employment and prevents the influx of resources into the legal sector needed to facilitate the development necessary to provide these services in the future. The use of foreign consultants is not cost-effective for the government or the corporations and cannot be continued into the indefinite future.

This is a vicious cycle that will continue without the intervention of effective CLE training. Current resources are insufficient to train Sub-Saharan Africa's legal and related professionals adequately so that they can contribute to the creation of economic wealth. Without the creation of economic wealth the current resource base cannot be improved, and the cycle becomes one of inadequate input resulting in inadequate output. The lack of adequate advanced legal services deprives a country of the tools needed for economic growth and acts as a dead weight against all efforts toward that end.

The problem is deeply aggravated because Sub-Saharan Africa lacks institutions offering effective CLE programs. Efforts in the past have concentrated exclusively on the building of training institutions for economic policy. To be sure, sound economic policy is essential to a country's development and growth, yet it cannot be implemented in practice and expected to produce efficient results without a concurrent growth in legal resources. Successful economic and human development requires structurally sound rules of law.

In the past, local CLE training programs have been sporadic donor-financed projects, run by existing institutions whose focus is in other areas. Thus, CLE programs were irregular, inconsistent, and lacking in long-term planning. In the case of Uganda, the Law Development Centre (LDC) was supposed to provide CLE training but has almost completely failed to do so (further discussion below).

Discussions with various bar associations in East Africa have shown that they do not possess the resources to provide CLE training to their members. This is also true of most bar associations in other parts of Sub-Saharan Africa. A few fortunate lawyers (mostly from government institutions and the relatively few successful private sector companies) manage to attend courses offered abroad, but this occurs at great expense and as a result is done infrequently.

Not only are the resources not currently available for CLE training, there is also a void in research materials and services necessary to keep abreast of legal developments. The libraries of the current institutions are antiquated and un-derfunded, and since they are cut off from the international network they cannot acquire the vast materials that are needed to provide useful facilities. Furthermore, with the growing importance of online legal research, there is a need in Sub-Saharan Africa for computer facilities and online research train-ing. Most law schools in more developed jurisdictions now devote consider-able time to training their students in online research methods, and the gap in training will become a further impediment to the African lawyer.

An effective CLE program with modern research programs and facilities will intervene in the vicious cycle in African legal education and post-profes-sional training and will improve the region's legal capacity, which will in turn provide the resources and create the demand for a higher level of legal ser-vices. The effect will be that the beneficiaries of CLE training will be able to design, analyze, and implement successful programs that will improve their country's productive capacity. They will manage their organizations more ef-fectively, have the skills to implement advanced policies, provide legal ser-vices without the need or expense of foreign consultants, and negotiate on equal footing with foreign investors, financiers, governments, multilateral or-ganizations, contractors, consultants, exporters, suppliers, and licensors.

The Need for a Professional Legal Education Center of Excellence

In Sub-Saharan Africa, there has been a failure of the respective national legal institutions to provide CLE for private and public sector lawyers once they graduate from law school. The problem with these institutions is that they are supply-driven, poorly funded, inefficiently run, with poor quality person-nel, and they lack critical resources (for example, libraries). The case of the Ugandan LDC described below is symptomatic of the crisis in continuing professional legal education that plagues Sub-Saharan Africa.

The need for a permanent professional legal education center of excel-lence to provide CLE training in Uganda was stated in the Report of the Committee on Legal Education Training and Accreditation in Uganda (Odoki Report, July 1995). This report, which was funded by the World Bank and requested by all the relevant stakeholders was subsequently adopted as Government of Uganda policy, and it provided the rationale for the creation of ILI–Uganda. There is no other institution in Uganda that offers CLE on a systematic basis, and there are no significant CLE programs in other countries in the region.[1]

The Odoki Report noted that the curriculum at Makerere Law School "is rather narrow, and unduly occupied with traditional subjects which were fashionable twenty-five years ago in English law schools...";[2] and further that "continuing legal education is increasingly recognised as essential in view of the unavoidably limited coverage of university and Law Development Centre (LDC) programmes, the emerging specialist areas, and new developments and trends in the law."[3]

As a result of these educational deficiencies, Ugandan lawyers are frequently deficient in "emerging areas of specialised commercial practice such as international trade, international investment, joint ventures, intellectual property law... and international commercial arbitration."[4] These are all areas in which the Centre offers training.

The situation with the LDC in Uganda is representative of the problems facing institutions in Sub-Saharan Africa. Although the LDC has the statutory responsibility to provide continuing professional legal education programs in Uganda, it is widely recognized that this is not possible given its current resource constraints, and may even be undesirable. This view is strongly supported by key officials in government, including the Attorney and Solicitor General. The Ministry of Justice, which is responsible for the overall policy on continuing professional legal education, strongly supports the approach of this function by an independent organization such as ILI–Uganda. The Odoki Report noted that while it may have been desirable in 1971 to centralize many legal functions in the LDC (the LDC statute lists no less than 15 separate responsibilities), "constraints on resources and capacity have made it impossible to operate such a multi-functional establishment. LDC is no longer in a position to carry out such a complicated

1. The Law Development Centre (LDC), which is managed by the Ministry of Justice, is charged with providing CLE in addition to a host of other duties, but has never had the resources to mount a significant program. It is generally accepted that the LDC's resources are inadequate even for its basic mission of postgraduate practical training for new lawyers. Neither Makerere nor universities in Nairobi or Dar es Salaam provide significant CLE programs. To our knowledge, most CLE projects in Sub-Saharan Africa are provided by donors on a sporadic basis in response to particularly acute needs.
2. Odoki Report, p. 8.
3. Odoki Report, p. 3.
4. Odoki Report, p. 6.

diversity of legal tasks."[5] For instance, the LDC is presently responsible for training graduates of Makerere Law School for the post-graduate bar course, but can only partially fulfill this function. LDC can presently train only half of the Makerere Law School graduates who apply for the post-graduate bar course, and even then the quality of training these students receive has been questioned and has resulted in the recommendation that this function be privatized to include other training providers.

Given the inability of the LDC and other similar institutions in Sub-Saharan Africa to respond to the need for CLE programs for state attorneys and private practitioners, it is reasonable that such programs should be privatized. The Ugandan plan was to originally use donor support, with the facilities of the International Law Institute–Washington (ILI–Washington) and other international providers to form a model so that "it should be possible to plan a longer programme which is however locally based."[6]

The Response—The Establishment of ILI—Uganda Legal Centre of Excellence

With funds from the World Bank-funded Uganda Institutional Capacity Building Project (UICBP), ILI–Washington established operations in Uganda in 1997 to provide CLE training for the benefit of public and private sector lawyers in Uganda. The program, which was eventually opened to the Sub-Saharan African Region, attracted participants from many states in the Region. In April 1998, the institution was registered as a local indigenous NGO and the regional Centre was established. This is the first regional center of excellence in Sub-Saharan Africa. I like to think of the World Bank project as the pregnancy that nurtured and carried ILI–Uganda to term. I would like to further point out that the only two other institutions in the world that offer CLE on a continuous full-time basis are the ILI in Washington, and the International Development Law Institute (IDLI) in Rome. After the formation of ILI–Uganda, ILI–Washington began to withdraw control of the African operations, and now serves as a partner to provide a declining level of technical support. The Washington, D.C. operations, as a separate entity, are extremely valuable to the operation of ILI–Uganda for the knowledge,

5. Odoki Report, p. 71.
6. Odoki Report, p. 67.

expertise, credibility, and contacts created in over 40 years of successful operation in international law.

In August of 1998, we received a significant grant from the Austrian government for the building and implementation of the facilities and programs that form our current institution. With this grant and the revenue generated by program fees, consulting contracts related to training, and a modest in-kind contribution from the Ugandan government, we moved into a new facility, hired new staff, created the beginnings of a library, launched a successful internship program (discussed later), and managed, over the last two years, to serve a Sub-Saharan African constituency of over 1,000 government officials, legal and business professionals, and scholars from our base in Kampala. Participants to the Centre have come from Kenya, Tanzania, Zanzibar, and Rwanda in East Africa; Zambia, Zimbabwe, Botswana, Angola, Namibia, Swaziland, South Africa, Malawi, Lesotho, Mauritius, and Seychelles in the Southern African region; and Ghana, Nigeria, Cameroon, and Mali in West Africa. We recently received applicants from Greece who will be attending the fall programs. The grant has recently been renewed for a similar financial contribution and is part of the ongoing funding plans. In addition, the Norwegian government has recently indicated their interest in cofinancing the program and have already pledged $250,000.00 as their contribution for the remainder of this year.

We are now a fully operational African center of legal excellence, which is staffed, run, and controlled by African lawyers and professionals. The seminars are taught using a combination of foreign and local experts so that international theory can be applied to local conditions. The courses offered by the International Law Institute in Washington and the Centre do not require any particular legal background. All of the courses offered at the Centre or ILI–Washington, are attended by individuals from nations with vastly different legal backgrounds. For example, over the years, ILI–Washington, and to a lesser extent ILI–Uganda, have had participants from the civil and common law traditions. The interest by these individuals in courses such as debt management, arbitration, privatization or even foreign investment, derives from the fact that the issues or problems raised in each of these subject areas is the same regardless of the underlying legal structure existing in a participant's country. Consequently the legal background of the faculty member does not in any way affect the quality of the seminar.

The experts we have used tend to be from the United States with strong international and local insight into the subject matter. With close collaboration with ILI–Washington we have sourced these experts from public international institutions such as the World Bank and International Finance Corporation (IFC). From the private sector, numerous individuals at the world's leading law firms in London, Paris, New York, and Geneva who deal with these issues on a day-to-day basis are frequent lecturers at ILI–Uganda. We also source many leading academics from leading U.S. educational institutions such as Harvard Law School, Georgetown University Law Center, and University of California at Los Angeles. We are constantly increasing our base of European and regional experts to provide a worldview in each of our programs, and will continue do so under the new programs offered by ILI–Uganda.

Since our main emphasis is on the development of African capacity, the importance of using indigenous and local experts of world-class standing cannot be underscored enough. Many regional experts, in a wide variety of fields, have attended training seminars in Washington or Kampala and now return to lecture and teach in our seminars. We are increasingly using highly skilled regional professionals for our seminars. These have included the CEO of the Nairobi Stock Exchange, the legal director and company secretary of Kenya Airways who led the privatization and initial public offering of the airline, and many of the region's justices and magistrates, to name a few, including a significant number of experts from South Africa. Under our agreement with the ADB mentioned below, the ADB will provide some of its staff as lecturers for selected courses.

Our recent publishing success with *Capital Markets in Uganda,* by Stuart Cohn and Fred Zake, a foreign and a regional expert in their respective fields, demonstrates the commitment and success of the North–South capacity-building aspect of our program. Stuart Cohn, from the University of Florida Law School, was a lecturer in the capital markets course under the World Bank program, and Fred Zake, an investment lawyer in Uganda, was a student in the course. We encouraged their cooperation in writing the book, which was finally edited and published by ILI–Washington. The book is a clear and concise explanation of Uganda's capital market and is intended to assist in its development by providing guidance and information to private and public sector organizations, firms, and individuals in positions to facilitate market growth and development. Another publication on comparative experiences of privatization in the subregion is forthcoming and should be released in the fall. The principal authors are Gerald Tanyi, formerly an attorney with the respected Wall Street firm of Sullivan and Cromwell, and presently with the World Bank Group, and several former regional participants—experts in privatization who attended a course on legal issues in privatization in the fall of 1998. We are now building a library to house our publications and materials gathered during our operations, and with appropriate funding, it should be the basis for an expanded research center open to professionals from the subregion. With the success of our seminar offerings and increased demand from across the region, we are increasing our seminar offerings from 20 this year to 27 in 2001. Courses covered include a wide selection of essential areas, such as: government integrity/corruption, debt management, foreign investment negotiation, legislative drafting, international commercial arbitration, WTO participation, international human rights, the nature of international organizations, and intellectual property.

Playing a Role in Law Reform and Economic Development

In order to achieve full and successful participation in the global economy, a nation requires a market infrastructure, a stable legal environment and updated legal framework, functioning capital markets, and trained executives and professionals in the private and public sectors. Overall law reform is an indispensable aspect of this process. ILI–Uganda promotes an orderly path to effective participation in a world economy through its programs of training lawyers and related professionals in business, finance, law, and governance for governments and institutions throughout Sub-Saharan Africa.

As part of a multi-pronged response to Africa's capacity deficiencies, we focus on developing a stable and effective legal environment, which is a fundamental aspect of a successful economic development program. It produces the reliability and integrity within a country that is conducive to attracting the domestic and international investment necessary for growth. While we are committed to providing the CLE training that is necessary for the growth of Sub-Saharan Africa's legal structure, its benefits for economic development go well beyond legal training.

It is important to emphasize that even though we sponsor research projects and can provide extensive programs of technical assistance, we are not a "think tank." We have pragmatic goals. We work to build functional capacity by training professionals in business, finance, law, and governance. We are dedicated to the encouragement of open markets and successful participation in the international economy. Because of the high quality, importance, applicability, and variety offered in our training seminars, many of the Centre's seminar participants are not trained lawyers. They are professionals from the public and private sectors in business, government, finance, economics, and law. In fact, managers and policymakers from other capacity-building and development agencies from throughout the Region often attend our seminars. Our training infrastructure allows the Centre to conduct seminars on other economic issues as easily as legal topics, and many of our seminars are on hybrid subject areas. In the past we have covered such areas with seminars that have included legal issues in privatization, debt management, international business transactions, project procurement, WTO participation, securities and capital markets, international loan negotiation and renegotiations, foreign investment, and development and regulation of securities and capital markets. Furthermore, our previously discussed publication, *Capital Markets in Uganda*, is reflective of the hybrid subject matter being dealt with by ILI–Uganda.

Our courses are constantly being revised to meet the changing nature of private sector development and public concerns in the Region and are therefore demand-driven. We have already drawn up our agenda of courses for 2001, which will include seminars on banking regulation (following the recent banking crisis in the Region), utility reform and privatization, telecommunication policy and regulation, and improving foreign investment flows to Sub-Saharan Africa. Through the Centre's high quality seminars, the capacity needed to design, analyze, and implement successful economic programs is being built.

Our effectiveness in capacity-building extends also to providing assistance to the economic institutes and universities in the Region. The possibilities for cooperation in capacity-building programs between ILI–Uganda and the Region's economic policy analysis and training institutes are among the most promising opportunities currently being explored. Our access to a wide range of prominent international faculty and the flexibility to quickly meet specific demands make us the perfect complement to the programs of the established economic institutes. In addition, the resources and facilities we offer make us an ideal training facility for faculty from other institutions, either to attend topic specific seminars, instructor-training seminars, or to use the resources for research and publishing.

In informal discussions with the Masters Programme in Economic Policy Management—a project funded by the African Capacity Building Foundation (ACBF)—at Makerere University, Kampala, the practicality and benefit of co-operation with ILI–Uganda was immediately obvious. The possibilities for areas of collaboration, from our upcoming list of seminars alone, included having our faculty provide supplemental instruction in the areas of international negotiation, privatization, foreign investment, public enterprise, WTO participation, and capital markets and securities development. In addition, there is recognition of the benefit and interest in the possibility of members of their faculty attending or instructing at future seminars. This situation is likely to be found in most of the economic institutes across Sub-Saharan Africa. The quality and diversity of our training and expertise make us a powerful tool in economic capacity-building in Sub-Saharan Africa, on our own or in collaboration with existing institutions and universities.

We aim to develop further our regional activities. We are currently the only institution in Sub-Saharan Africa that is able to provide a systematic program of continuing legal education to the Region's public and private sector lawyers and related professionals. We would like to expand so as to centralize CLE activity for the Sub-Saharan Region and also serve as the hub for a developing network of legal experts, practitioners, and researchers. Regional, rather than national, training institutions generally will serve human and institutional capacity-building needs more cost-effectively. From our training seminars over the last two years, we have developed an in-depth understanding of the developing-country issues that affect important matters such as foreign investment, privatization, joint ventures, debt management, procurement, capital markets, and other significant policy issues. Our access to the foremost experts—who are sensitive to the developing country perspective—in each of the courses offered under our present and proposed curriculum allow these experts to pass on the benefit of their experience to lawyers and related professionals in the Region who are actors in this dynamic marketplace and who, with the benefit of the Centre's seminars, can make more informed policy decisions affecting their respective countries and the Region at large.

We have submitted requests for funding to various donor programs. These funds would allow us to expand our operations. The expansion of the Centre would allow us to better meet the demand for our seminars, but also it would allow for the improvement of training facilities to world-class levels. CLE does not produce fully effective results with only one-time training seminars. CLE is an ongoing process of instruction and education. Seminar graduates need facilities and updated courses so that they can keep abreast of changes and developments within their fields. Furthermore, successful graduates will often advance workplace production to a level requiring more advanced or related training that was not applicable with their old skills. We will serve to develop the human and institutional capacity-building needs of Sub-Saharan African professionals through our training programs, research facilities, and publications.

The Link to Improved Regional Law Reform Efforts

There has been an outpouring of positive feedback from the region's public and private sector stakeholders since the inception of ILI–Uganda. Based on independent surveys that we have carried out and unsolicited feedback from heads of department in ministries and other public and private sector institutions across the region, there is a consensus that our training programs have made a positive impact on the contribution of public and private sector lawyers in overall law reform and other efforts. Following are samples of these responses.

Recent participants representing 11 countries from Sub-Saharan Africa attended a course on legislative drafting, which is a course we have introduced since expertise in this area is indispensable to most regional law reform efforts. Three anonymous participants had the following comments.

"This seminar was refreshing in that after having practical experience in the field of legislative drafting I have been able to remove doubts I have about situations I have actually faced in real life, and it has buttressed my knowledge of this field."

A second respondent stated that "I am going back home a more polished draftsman than I was before coming to the course..."

Finally a third respondent stated that "I can now draft a bill based on the knowledge acquired from the seminar."

The manager of the Kaduna State Water Board (KSWB) in Nigeria commented late last year that his staff's participation in our courses had greatly increased their effectiveness at work, and that their recent commendation by the World Bank as the best performing water authority in Nigeria was in large part attributable to their participation in ILI–Uganda training programs. The KSWB continues to send its staff to our courses.

Several attorneys general and training managers at ministries of justice across the region have expressed appreciation for our courses as they relate to overall law reform. The following was an excerpt from a letter written by Uganda's Attorney General, Hon. Bart Katurebe to us: "The Ministry of Justice does appreciate the contribution made by ILI in the training of our lawyers, and we shall continue to support the work of the Institute in this country."

A senior partner of a small but growing commercial practice in Uganda commented that he substantially relied on our two-week seminar and course materials in joint ventures and franchising, which helped him put together a joint venture agreement between a South African telecommunications firm he was representing in a joint venture with a Ugandan concern.

These are just a few of the responses we have received from across the region. Our impact in improving the changing face of law reform in the Region will continue to grow as more and more regional public and private sector lawyers and related professionals get to know our work.

Finally, the espirit de corps created by the attendance at our courses of a diverse group of regional professionals has resulted in useful networking of participants toward improving legal services. For example, a reputable growing mid-size Tanzanian commercial firm is already in merger talks with a similar Ugandan firm following the senior partner's attendance of the Managing a Legal Practice seminar held earlier this year. Furthermore, the existence of many of our alumni in high level positions around the Region has provided for a fertile ground when setting up local training or technical assistance projects in their respective countries.

These are some of the tangible benefits, which over time will positively contribute to the regional law reform process.

Future Activities of the Legal Centre of Excellence

Our primary function will continue to be the provision of CLE seminars. In addition, the Centre will continue training judges from around the Region, engaging in research and publishing on issues of public and private international law and international economic relations, and hosting conferences and symposia on these subjects, in addition to other relevant activities. The beneficiaries of our work will continue to be all Sub-Saharan African public and private sector professionals in business, finance, and law. The objective is to establish ILI–Uganda into a self-sustaining institution, which will provide these services into the indefinite future, without direct donor support.

We are registered as a Ugandan nongovernmental organization (NGO), established to provide broad legal services that cover the aforementioned mandate. At present, we are registered as the International Law Institute–Uganda Legal Centre of Excellence, but are strongly considering changing the name to the ILI Regional Centre of Excellence to give us a more regional character and appeal. ILI–Washington (through subcontracts with ILI–Uganda) will continue to provide important albeit diminishing level of technical assistance to us in the coming years. The next steps in our growth include the following:

1. Providing a broader range of demand-driven seminars in continuing professional legal education for the benefit of public and private professionals in business, finance, management and law in Sub-Saharan Africa;
2. Engaging in research and publishing in the areas of public and private international law and related economic development issues;
3. Increasing the use of and opportunities for Sub-Saharan African academics and experienced regional public and private sector experts to lecture in our seminars;
4. Establishing an attachment program through which key individuals from public sector institutions in the Region are attached (following attendance in a particular course) to well-established and relevant institutions in the Region or the United States and Western Europe to enhance their skills in relevant areas of their work;
5. Providing support to visiting senior researchers, and academics from Sub-Saharan Africa, and the rest of world conducting research focused

on vital areas of law, finance, and related economic issues in Sub-Saharan Africa; and

6. Formalizing and substantially expanding our marketing program to obtain tuition-paying participants with a view to attaining 100 percent self-sufficiency.

Since legal training is the main source of revenue for the Centre in reaching self-sufficiency, it will, therefore, be our principal business activity.

We will continue to engage in research on various issues broadly related to private sector development and public and private international law. As mentioned earlier we have already developed a modest library from the seminars we have been offering since our inception and will be using this opportunity to add to its collection. In time, we will have developed a library where officials from ministries of justice, other important public and private sector institutions, and representatives from academia in Sub-Saharan Africa are able to research and collect the latest information and trends on various issues on public and private international law and related economic issues. To enhance this process, we are already in discussions with reputable international online research companies such as Lexis/Nexis and Westlaw. This will allow Africa's researchers to access a wealth of constantly updated materials available online.

In continuing with our objective of enhancing the skills of law students from universities in Sub-Saharan Africa and the rest of the world, the future will see an expansion of our present internship program. The program, which began two years ago is very competitive and attracts leading students from around the world, with diverse backgrounds, to work on important projects, provide research input to ongoing assignments, and help in preparation for planned conferences and seminars. The program has also provided an opportunity for these students to attend selected meetings and therefore interact with local professionals, officials, and lawyers, including the opportunity for some field activities. The program further presents an opportunity for law students to learn about current issues in law, finance, governance, and other related issues affecting Sub-Saharan Africa while providing hands-on experience working on a wide range of projects. To date, the program has attracted interns from as far away as the United States (Cornell Law School), Germany

(District Court of Stuttgart), and England (University of London), working with others from Uganda (Makerere University Law School) and from around the Region. This month students from Georgetown University Law Center, Cornell Law School, and Makerere Law School begin an eight-week internship program. It is a unique and productive opportunity.

As mentioned earlier, ILI–Washington will continue to provide a diminishing degree of oversight and technical assistance to the Centre. It will assist with cash management, financial systems, controls and reports, administrative and personnel systems, foreign faculty logistics, obtaining research publications and documents, and in marketing efforts. However, at every stage of our development we will work very closely with ILI–Washington, as there will always be a benefit to its wealth of experience spanning over 40 years.

Our specific goal in marketing will be to steadily increase the number of participants attending the courses on a tuition-paying basis, so that the program can become self-sufficient and operate without the need of additional direct donor support. Our numbers to date indicate an impressive performance since the World Bank project in 1997. The comparison between participant revenues under the World Bank project, and the first year of operation as an independent institution resulted in a 76.5 percent gross increase in the latter period. When comparing the first quarter of 1999 with this year, we registered a 176.86 percent gross increase. The projections for the rest of the year are even more impressive. As of October 1999, the closing date for our first year of operation, we were 36.8 percent self-sufficient based on revenue generated in that period. As of today, six months after the last reporting period, present income and commitments far exceed the revenue we generated in the previous 12 months. This year will be a much more successful one than the last. This is testament to the fact that as we enter the new millennium it is increasingly clear that from Accra to South Africa, Sub-Sahara's public and private sector institutions are growing to rely on ILI–Uganda as an important resource to improve the skills of their staff and to provide training-related technical assistance in areas broadly related to finance, management, law, and governance.

Our impressive performance is also an indicator that improved marketing will largely increase the possibility of our achieving 100 percent self-sustainability in the long term. Currently, the resources directly available have limited the marketing of our seminars. We would like to expand our marketing budget to enable us to improve our Web page, to create additional awareness within the public and private sector of the entire Region, to improve our visibility with increased advertising in all the major publications of the Region, and to allow our staff to take more trips within the region to develop contacts and create interest in our seminars.

Our affiliation with ILI–Washington will continue to bring an added cachet to the marketing efforts. ILI–Washington already has an impressive worldwide reputation for its programs of professional training, technical assistance, and publishing. Through an expanded and intensive marketing effort (which will be helped by the expanding reputation and networking of ILI–Uganda) and the offering of demand-driven seminars, we will attract a larger number of paying participants from around the region. Already the participant demand for our seminars is growing rapidly with modest marketing efforts throughout the Region. The public donor community has supported a majority of these participants in the past, and new scholarship agreements are being developed with agencies such as the African Development Bank (ADB), and the United Nations Institute for Training and Research (UNITAR), which has provided a reliable revenue source facilitating cofinancing and allowing our continual investment in marketing and expansion as discussed further below. As mentioned earlier, the Norwegian government has also recently joined our growing list of donors to invest in the program. As African legal communities develop, however, it is expected that increasing amounts of support will be available from the private sector, and that CLE in Africa will eventually resemble the privately supported systems found in developed countries today.

Examples of Technical Assistance and Other Activities of ILI–Uganda Related to Law Reform

The activities of the Legal Centre of Excellence discussed above are only one aspect of the capacity-building functions of ILI–Uganda. While seminars are—and will continue to be our primary function, the knowledge and expertise developed through their administration allows us to fulfill other roles related to broad commercial law reform in the subregion. A few of these are highlighted below:

Uganda Commercial Court Project

At the request of the Uganda Commercial Court (UCC) and funded by the Danish International Development Agency (DANIDA), we were retained to examine and make recommendations related to case management and alternate dispute resolution, the lack of which result in the poor adjudication of disputes before the UCC. ILI–Uganda in collaboration with ILI–Washington put together an impressive team of experts, which included a former judge of the English Commercial Court (ECC), a member of the Judicial Committee of the House of Lords, a former Registrar of the ECC, and other prominent members of the English bar and bench.

At the conclusion of the project, ILI–Uganda issued recommendations, which included jurisdiction of the UCC; composition of the UCC; case management; procedures; court facilities; alternative dispute resolution; and training.

Currently DANIDA is examining our recommendations before proceeding with a more extensive follow-up project.

Rwanda Procurement Reform Project

In 1998 ILI–Washington was retained by the Government of Rwanda through the National Tender Board (NTB), to begin developing a regulatory framework for the conduct of public procurement in Rwanda. The project involved the drafting of a code to establish the NTB, and a decree regulating public procurement in Rwanda. The code is currently before Cabinet, and will thereafter be debated by Parliament. The project was funded by the World Bank.

The project resulted in a memorandum of understanding (MOU) between the Government of Rwanda (GOR), through the NTB, and ILI–Uganda, which calls for conducting training seminars and technical assistance in the areas of policy and operations management, capacity-building and career development, public procurement management, and procurement information management.

In early 2000, ILI–Uganda won a contract to continue capacity-building and technical assistance activities for the benefit of the NTB, and related stakeholders in Rwanda. The project, which is also funded by the World Bank, involves the following:

- Review and finalization of the draft law establishing the NTB and regulatory decree. Activity involves discussion with all key public and private sector stakeholders involved in public procurement in Rwanda;
- Preparation of implementing procurement regulations;
- Preparation of Standard Bidding Documents;
- Identification of other aspects of procurement-related legal framework for possible review and modernization. This will involve a survey of legal and regulatory areas ancillary to procurement law and regulations themselves. We will identify key areas of the law that need to be reviewed for modernization.

2001–2003 Agreement with UNITAR

Following successful implementation of a two-year scholarship agreement between ILI–Uganda and UNITAR a new agreement has been entered into for a three-year period, beginning in 2001. In addition to scholarship assistance, it will cover two of the following areas. Under the first, we will be contracted to perform national profile assessments (NPAs) of the present legal infrastructure for debt and financial management in Uganda, Tanzania, and Rwanda. Recommendations from the NPAs will seek to strengthen the legal infrastructure for debt and financial management in the three countries. Finally, ILI–Uganda and UNITAR will develop a joint Web site, which will provide important information on debt and financial management, such as sample loan agreements, key introductory terms for all the ILI–Uganda/UNITAR courses on debt and financial management, a list of regional and international experts on debt and financial management, and cross references to related Web sites of the United Nations and other sources.

The agreement is an important vehicle in allowing us to meet our operating costs and to promote capacity-building in the Region.

African Development Bank Agreement

We recently entered into an agreement with the African Development Fund (ADF) under which the ADB like UNITAR will fund participants from Regional Member Countries (RMCs) to attend courses at ILI–Uganda. The MOU provides for scholarships to benefit mid- to high level government officials from RMCs to attend training seminars in the following fields: WTO accession, compliance and disputes, and regional integration efforts; privatization;

public-private sector partnership; development and regulation of securities and capital markets; procurement as it relates to governance issues; intellectual property and transfer of technology; best procurement practices; debt management and related negotiation issues; legislative drafting; arbitration and related alternate dispute resolution matters; and financial sector restructuring. The agreement also contemplates technical assistance and training by ILI–Uganda as the ADB develops its new governance program.

The MOU is another vehicle, which will lead to increasing self-sustainability for ILI–Uganda.

Common Market for East Central and Southern Africa (COMESA) Agreement

We also recently signed an MOU with COMESA under which we will provide technical assistance and training primarily in the areas of trade and competition policy. The agreement also provides for training in areas of interest to COMESA such as procurement reform.

The increasing demand for our services by governments and regional bodies in Sub-Saharan Africa is reflective of the primacy of a solid legal framework toward the analyzing, designing, and implementation of any significant reform and development programs and management schemes.

We hope to increase our human and material resources to meet the increasing demand for our training-related consulting, research, and design analysis services.

The Centre and Research

It is fundamental to our role in building human and institutional capacity in Sub-Saharan Africa that we are able to serve as a central coordinating mechanism to the professional community for publishing, research, information provision, advice, and analysis. To serve this need, we will continue to build our library, make available training manuals, provide access to our collection of legal materials and texts, and work to publish more works on law and economics in Sub-Saharan Africa.

Since the inception of the current CLE program, we have accumulated a library on various commercial subjects broadly related to private sector development. This library is drawn mainly from the subject matter in the seminars and some related texts contributed by ILI–Washington. The American Bar

Association will also soon be providing some texts on the subject of bankruptcy. As part of the capacity-building effort we have provided the libraries of LDC, Law Reform Commission, Makerere University Law School, and the Ministry of Justice in Uganda with literature covering subjects such as international business transactions, foreign investment negotiations, international trade agreements, international loan negotiation and renegotiation, legal issues in privatization, capital markets development and regulation, international project procurement and contract negotiation, computer law and contracts, joint ventures and franchising, intellectual property and transfer of technology, international commercial arbitration, and debt management. In addition, other private and public sector individuals from Uganda and participants from Sub-Saharan Africa buy these materials at cost. In fact, the Ugandan Inspectorate of Government Office, which is charged with fighting corruption recently purchased copies of our entire catalog of seminar binders. This is highly valuable material that is not available elsewhere in the region.

We will continue to expand this base of information to include other important and increasingly relevant subject matter offered in our seminars, and drawn from our conferences and symposia.

Past participants have frequently contacted us with questions on how to handle a particular negotiation question, procurements, sale of public enterprise, and various other matters related to their public or private sector responsibilities. We have responded to these requests by providing the individual or institution with relevant literature on the subject or put them in touch with our experts to handle the question—or both.

We plan for an expanded research center, which will allow for the addition of invaluable research texts, treatises, hornbooks, scholarly journals, legal publications, and many other essential materials. Additional funding will allow us to incorporate computers and online capabilities into the research facilities. Access to the wealth of constantly updated materials available online through legal research providers, such as Lexis–Nexis or Westlaw will open up invaluable research tools to us. Further, any professional in Africa, whether a lawyer, policy analyst, educator, or manager, can benefit from the speed and availability of information online to complement their research. A fully functional library, providing access to a variety of powerful research tools, open to professionals from across the Region, in conjunction with first-rate seminars and access to world-class experts will form a complete and effective CLE training institution prepared to tackle the overwhelming need for human and institutional capacity-building in Sub-Saharan Africa.

Institutional Objectives

Long-Term Objectives

Our long-term objectives are as follows:

- To improve the capacity in Sub-Saharan Africa of the overall delivery of professional services in business, finance, and law in the public and private sector by creating a strong human resource nucleus of African lawyers, professional policy analysts, and managers who are trained in and kept abreast of the most recent developments and techniques in their fields;
- To facilitate the development of skills that will allow indigenous African lawyers to deal on an even level with the best foreign-trained lawyers, creating more effective, cost-efficient, and beneficial economic dealings with foreign governments, corporations, banks, NGOs, and investors;
- To create a permanent institution in Sub-Saharan Africa that will ensure that the Region has the capacity to train enough local legal and economic policy professionals to decrease the region's dependence on foreign technical assistance and overcome the shortages created by the brain drain of talented Africans to industrial countries; and
- To serve as a central legal coordinating mechanism for Sub-Saharan Africa, capable of providing modern continuing legal education training, research facilities, technical support, and publishing services in subjects that are fundamental to legal development, policy analysis, and economic development.

Short- to Medium-Term Objectives

In the short to medium term we hope to achieve the following targets:

- Expand our marketing program to reach a wider target audience across the whole Sub-Saharan African Region and to provide better information access through our publications, Web site, staff visits, and advertising;

- Increase our physical capacity to meet the growing demands for our training seminars and for technical support to the region's governments and organizations through the expertise of ILI–Uganda; and
- To build a comprehensive library that will symbiotically support our seminars in continuing legal education by providing access, research materials, and facilities to professionals from throughout the Region allowing them to keep updated in current legal developments.

We cannot achieve our long- and short-term objectives without the strong support of key multilateral institutions such as the World Bank and other European donors such as the Austrian and Norwegian governments. Strategic worldwide alliances discussed below are one possible avenue of achieving our goal of legal capacity-building through training and effective law reform.

Strategic Worldwide Alliances

Increased multilateral alliances with institutions such as the World Bank, which initiated this process of our development and other donors, such as the Austrian and Norwegian governments, which have ensured our continued existence, will be more important in the future.

Our long- and medium-term plans will require much more funding in the immediate future if we are to achieve our objectives. We cannot get to the "next level" without financial assistance from major donors to purchase our own premises, hire more competent staff, advertise in each major publication of the Region to attract the most qualified participants and therefore reach the required levels of self-sustainability within our three-year projections, make the required structural changes to our facilities to offer classroom space and related facilities of a world-class standard, or provide library and research facilities with the most up-to-date technological innovations to enable regional researchers to have access to the latest global trends on a cross section of issues in public and private international law and related economic issues.

This kind of assistance is crucially important and immediately necessary for us to be able to achieve our objectives. We have proven through verifiable data that we have the capacity and potential to create a regional institution that is capable of making a profound contribution to overall law reform efforts through training in the Sub-Saharan African Region.

Examples of some of these strategic alliances could include the following:

- Provision of scholarship assistance to regional participants who cannot afford to attend our courses. We have found that there are a substantial number of mid- to high-level lawyers and other professionals in the public and private sector who cannot afford our course fees. As already stated we have successfully exercised such an arrangement with UNITAR over the last two years. We hope to finalize a similar arrangement with the ADB soon;
- Provision of grants to provide needed capital expenditures;
- The World Bank Institute (WBI) and ILI–Uganda could partner in developing distance learning programs for Sub-Saharan African professionals and institutions. Such an arrangement could finance the establishment of technological infrastructure at ILI–Uganda to allow online seminars for longer courses such as legislative drafting, and corporate finance. This would allow extremely busy senior lawyers and other professionals who do not have the time to attend Kampala seminars to attend courses online and improve their proficiency while receiving the certification that is necessary to improve their skills and opportunities for career advancement at the same time. This so-called e-learning is already taking off in the United States and has resulted in the creation of such companies as Unext.com, University Access, and Pensare. Already New York University, Columbia University, and others have set up for-profit Web ventures for post-career training. The target groups are mid- to high-level public and private sector professionals—the same target audience for the ILI.

Conclusion

We at ILI–Uganda have also seen tremendous growth in the demand for our training programs in the Region. We foresee an increase in technical assistance and advisory assignments in the future and will seize the opportunity to make a difference in legal and judicial development. Through our training programs, which have greatly benefited numerous institutions throughout the Region, we have created a reputation for effective and world-class training. This has increased the demand for our training services. All of these activities will result in increased revenue generation for a stronger, self-sustainable institution providing these services into the long term. We will consequently be well positioned to tackle the overwhelming need for human and institutional legal capacity-building in the Sub-Saharan African Region.

Only through the creation of a functional enabling environment for high quality domestic legal outputs can a country's efforts toward sustainable economic growth and development be realized. We will continue to promote an orderly path into the world economy through our programs of professional training and technical assistance for public and private sector professionals in business, finance, law, and governance. However, without the important strategic alliances with important donors around the world, we will not be able to achieve our laudable objectives.

If we meet these challenges, together we will be able to successfully expand our efforts toward overcoming the lack of human and institutional legal capacity in Sub-Saharan Africa.

How Does Global Knowledge Sharing Foster Civil Society Participation?

Pending Challenges of Judicial Reform

The Role of Civil Society Cooperation

Alfredo Fuentes Hernández

Executive Director

Corporation for Excellence in Justice

Colombia

Background

The recent history of judicial reforms in Latin America and the Caribbean cannot be conceived in isolation from the reformulation of development strategies and the restructuring of the role of the state in society and the economy. Since the late 1980s, the regional development agenda has underlined the role of the market, international competition, and private initiative as growth engines. Nevertheless, it has also approached the debate on the revitalization of certain public areas in order to respond to pending social challenges—among them, the lack of basic services, infrastructure and qualified human resources, as well as regulatory and institutional flaws that hinder the rule of law.

There is growing concern about the need to improve the judiciary's role in social and economic development, by enhancing its responsibilities of guaranteeing law enforcement, facilitating transactions, and avoiding arbitrary actions and corruption.[1]

The debate on the scope of state restructuring has been enriched with economic analysis emphasizing the relationship between explicit or implicit rules of society and economic performance. Leading research on institutional change and economic development emphasizes how formal and informal

---

1. The World Bank's 1997 *World Development Report,* devoted to the issue of the role of the state, explains how economic welfare is unreachable without institutions that (a) allow for the resolution of disputes among corporations, citizens, and governments, (b) clarify the ambiguities of the law, and (c) endeavor to enforce obligations and contracts.

legal rules of conduct are the fundamental drivers of economic growth, since they define an incentive structure. Legal and judicial systems are key to the performance of the economy, as they ensure the enforcement of contracts and property rights, and allow different branches of the state to make decisions within a framework of legal security. This reduces the cost of transactions as well as the costs and risks of economic activity.[2]

Judicial reform is deemed to be an essential component for strengthening democracy to the extent that it is an effort to redefine interactions between a state and its citizens, aimed at increasing efficiency, equity, and predictability in the resolution and prevention of conflicts. Moreover, the reforms to the justice system, while trying to establish reliable and enforceable legal rules, nonarbitrary procedures, and judicial organizations capable of acting with transparency and effectiveness, also uphold the use of law as a tool for peaceful and equitable coexistence.

Today it is widely recognized in governmental as well as nongovernmental circles, that supremacy of law in a democratic society cannot be firmly established and safeguarded without an effective and well-functioning judiciary. Notwithstanding such recognition, judicial reforms still lag behind and the agenda for the future calls for a wide range of critical work in many areas.

Reform efforts in the Region have been aimed at overcoming various obstacles to the provision of a good service, including: (a) the judiciary's limited independence, b) insufficient and inefficient allocation of resources to operate the system, (c) cumbersome procedures and requirements, (d) lack of an entrepreneurial approach in the management of courthouses and legal cases, (e) inadequate selection and training of personnel, (f) powerless sanctions to anti-ethical conduct, and (g) limited scope of alternative dispute resolution (ADR) mechanisms.

In spite of the wave of justice reforms, there are still serious delays in legal processes, a great accumulation of cases in the courts, limited access to services (especially by the poor), corrupt practices, scarce predictability of judicial decisions, and a high level of mistrust among citizens regarding their judicial powers.[3]

2. North, Douglass, 1990. *Institutions, Institutional Change and Economic Performance.* Cambridge, United Kingdom: Cambridge University Press.
3. Buscaglia, E., M. Dakolias, and W. Ratliff. 1995. "Judicial Reform in Latin America: A Framework for National Development." Stanford, Calif: Hoover Institution on War, Revolution and Peace, Stanford University.

Given the current dissatisfaction with justice services in the Region, a "third generation of reforms" has been recommended by experts in their evaluations of achievements and pending challenges.[4] This would consist of a more pragmatic fine-tuning stage, based on the understanding of that which does not work, learning from experiences of other countries in order to introduce better practices, and paying greater attention to cultural issues that hinder the transition process. The new approach to institutional change would require the adoption of a political and economic conception of the reforms—one that acknowledges the interests of supporting or opposing groups, and regards the incentives and merit systems equally relevant to improving the poor performance of the administration of justice.

Such an approach would imply a change of the rules of the game between the political actors, in order to keep old vices from prevailing or appearing with greater momentum in the reformed institutions. In this new phase of reforms nongovernmental organizations (NGOs) are playing an active role. Indeed, during the past decade there has been a welcome emergence of NGOs concerned with legal and judicial reforms. These organizations are undertaking impartial activities to foster the reform process.

Nongovernmental organizations have often filled the gap left by governments, providing legal aid, promoting public awareness of the legal system, research, legislative support, and court reforms. NGOs' increased involvement has provided monitoring mechanisms of judicial performance, increased public consciousness of the adverse effects of inefficiency, and enhanced understanding of the importance of independence and integrity of the judicial system. As a result, the NGOs in Latin America working on judicial reform have become an integral part of the process to strengthen the rule of law in the Region.

Innovative Approaches to Judicial Reform

The most relevant elements of these new approaches to judicial reform are summarized below. In the first place, regarding reform leadership, experts

---

4. Hammergren, Linn. 1999. "Fifteen Years of Judicial Reform in Latin America: Where We Are and Why We Have Not Made More Progress?" In Corporation for Excellence in Justice, *Judicial Reform in Latin America*. Bogotá, Colombia.

acknowledge the need to counteract the low political capital of Latin American judiciaries. In most cases they have a poor level of public acceptance and institutional limitations to generate sound reform proposals and innovative amendments to motivate the participation of social groups. Hence, it is of critical importance to promote alliances among the executive branch, the spokespersons from the legislative branch, and civil society organizations and international agencies to overcome problems in the reform process stemming from weak leadership and lack of continuity.[5]

Above all, there is a need for better coordination among those who promote the reforms, and for building coalitions for the sake of public interest, in order to compensate for the opposition of groups who will necessarily lose power and privileges once the institutional rules of the game are modified.[6] These alliances are also important for promoting a suitable environment for investment and economic development; to consolidate a rule of law capable of protecting human rights and vulnerable groups; and to strengthen regional cooperation mechanisms aimed at defending democracy from the threats of transnational crime.[7]

In the second place, the success of future reforms will depend on the removal of cultural impediments that pose obstacles to well-designed and timely reforms. Aside from formal rules, there are further informal restrictions that are deeply entrenched in traditions, culture, and corporate behavioral patterns; these generate perverse incentives and deter individuals from undertaking change. Discussions on this subject point out how the defensive culture toward innovation in the judiciary may be historically explained. In fact, in one example, once country independence was attained, no significant changes were introduced to the formal and authoritarian institutional model of law and justice prevailing in the Spanish colony, and no adequate room

5. Carrillo, Fernando. 1999. "Challenges of Justice Reform in Latin America." In *Judicial Reform in Latin America* (see previous note for full reference).

6. In countries such as Spain, the judicial power summoned the parliament, the government and Spanish society to enter into a suprapartisan agreement for justice, whereby the majority government parties and the opposition accorded the priority necessary to the reforms set forth in the Libro Blanco de la Justicia (White Book of Justice) so that they could prevail as a long-term plan or objective. See General Council of the Judicial Power. 1997. *Libro Blanco de la Justicia*. Madrid.

7. García, Jorge. 1999. Keynote presentation of the Seminar on Judicial Reform in Latin America, held in Bogota, Colombia, July 1998. In *Judicial Reform in Latin America* (see note 5 for full reference).

was left for local dispute resolution methods or for the development of customary law traditions.[8]

Within this context, any reform process should give priority to the modification of a set of informal and formal rules that determine the extremely conservative nature of judicial power. Sound policies have to be designed to fight the scarce creativity of judges regarding the cases they handle, subordination to the initiative of the parties, and adhesion to hierarchy and corporate culture, rituals, and written forms. The policies also should confront reluctance to delegate, insufficient dissemination of judges' decisions, and deductive judicial reasoning centered on preexisting rules, which often neglect the economic and social context of cases under trial.

In the third place, new approaches to reform should grant increasing attention to the search for efficiency and effectiveness in the system, based on a better allocation of physical, human, technical, and financial resources. From the public finance perspective, there is consensus that the "expansion phase" of judicial reforms in the Region is coming to an end. This highlights the challenge to achieve a strong recomposition of public spending in order to fund activities aimed at substantially raising service quality. In this respect, the reallocation of resources should give priority to initiatives such as broadening alternative dispute resolution mechanisms; training and undertaking the continuing education of judges, prosecutors, and lawyers; and providing technological equipment for case management in courts. This investment-productivity approach may be facilitated by "de-judicialization" and outsourcing policies of certain procedures and complaints.[9]

The discussion about improving the distribution of resources gives rise to the question of how to increase effectiveness through incentives that encourage policy measures for private resolution of socially relevant disputes, keeping litigation from reaching excessive levels. Within a context of scarce

---

8. Saez, Felipe. 1999. "The Nature of Judicial Reforms in Latin America: Some Strategic Considerations." In *Judicial Reform in Latin America* (see note 5 for full reference).

9. To achieve such a reallocation of resources it is crucial to count on expedited judicial budgeting and auditing capacities. Besides, the body representing the judicial branch must have technical abilities and legitimacy to participate in budget debates and negotiations, linking the demand for financial resources with the adoption of measures that ensure high productivity in the performance operators. Fuentes, Alfredo. 1999. "Justice for the New Century: Proposal for the Colombian Goverment 1998–2002." In *Judicial Reform in Latin America* (see note 5 for full reference).

resources, no justice system can pretend to deal with every interpersonal conflict, and therefore it is necessary to apply "corrective policies" to modify the gaps between private incentives and the social costs of using the system.

These policies should promote the configuration of a more rational, plural, and diversified system to solve and prevent disputes, which transfers litigation costs to the parties involved (direct settlement, conciliation, arbitration, risk insurance, among others). Likewise, corrective policies should also comprise, in some cases, the use of the price system (court expenses, rates or fees), which reflects the fact that although justice bears elements related to the public good, it may also allow regressive appropriation of benefits by private individuals or organizations.[10] For an adequate design of such systems, it is key to count on better empirical knowledge of the characteristics of society's demand for justice and of possible alternative mechanisms that would facilitate a better service within the context of scarce resource allocation.

In the fourth place, justice administration reforms in Latin America are faced with the challenge of insisting on incorporating as a priority objective the improvement of access for disadvantaged sectors of society, such as the poor, indigenous peoples, and women. While discussing policies, there is insistence on the fact that justice spending tends to be regressive to the extent that those who have access to justice are basically those who can afford its services. This bias would continue to justify the adoption of corrective policies aimed at subsidizing programs such as legal aid and public defenders for the poor, in order to correct undesirable and inequitable "sub-litigation" situations and maximize the social profitability of resources. In order to overcome access barriers, the current debate strongly recommends focusing efforts on the promotion of better knowledge of citizens' rights and obligations and learning how the system functions to enforce them.[11]

---

10. Such private appropriation of the benefits of numerous judicial processes is the result of the gratuitous nature of justice which subsidizes litigation costs, especially for high-income litigators. The use of the price system to rationalize the use of the service, or mechanisms for the parties to assume the cost of the resolution of their conflicts would contribute to a more rational supply of justice. Except in cases of legal assistance for the poor, there doesn't seem to be any justification for certain litigation procedures to continue being cheap or gratuitous in situations of high judicial workload. For a complete discussion on the subject, see Shavel, S. 1996. "The Fundamental Divergence between the Private and the Social Motive to Use the legal System." Center for Law, Economics, and Business. Harvard Law School, Discussion Paper No. 206. November.

11. Cox, Sebastián. 1999. "Legal Aid for the Poor: The Experience of Forja." In *Judicial Reform in Latin America* (see note 5 for full reference).

In the fifth place, a new generation of reforms should avoid past short-comings due to lack of definition of a precise agenda of transition, objectives and strategies, and it should determine which would be critical interventions and what the expected results would be. Public justice policies or the failure to adopt them, often represent private and social costs and benefits that must be measured to justify and facilitate the transition toward better practices.[12] It is also key for specific transition agendas to define the responsibilities of the various actors of the justice system and the tools they require to fulfill their duties to their fullest extent.[13] Finally, the agenda needs to comprise the task of disseminating the reforms, so that citizens, as direct beneficiaries of the justice service, are able to have access to it, submit proposals for its improvement, and responsibly exercise their rights and duties.

Participation of NGOs in Judicial Reform

Given the aforementioned shortcomings that have prevented the judiciary from becoming more fair and efficient, one may ask about the role that nongovernmental organizations have in supporting the reform process. Though NGOs are not civil society itself, their political importance and coverage empower them to pass judgment on the legitimacy of institutional and cultural change. By promoting the participation of and alliances with sectors such as mass media, trade associations, universities, and the private sector in general, NGOs become a powerful instrument in judicial reform processes as they monitor and follow up on the reforms. At the same time, NGOs end up promoting trust and support for state institutions when they disseminate successful results of reform initiatives.

Nongovernmental organizations may also significantly contribute to the diffusion and evaluation of comprehensive, reliable, and timely statistics on

---

12. Regarding the benefits and costs that such reforms would yield for economic activity, there is a wide range of methodologies based on empirical research or business surveys, which unveil the hidden costs assumed by taxpayers, citizens, and the economy as a whole, as a result of the poor performance of the judicial system. See Castelar, Armando. 1999. "Hidden Costs of Judicial Inefficiency in Brazil." In *Judicial Reform in Latin America* (see note 5 for full reference).

13. For example, the quest to overcome dilatory habits should embrace systemic policies determining responsibilities and qualifications for lawyers, citizens, and those in charge of administering justice and managing administrative tasks. See Lopez, Luis. 1999. "The Spanish Experience of Judicial Reform." In *Judicial Reform in Latin America* (see note 5 for full reference).

the justice sector, which bears several advantages for a sector characterized by secretive handling of information and resistance to accountability. A great deal of NGOs are directly involved in the rendering of legal and educational services to the community, as well as in private conflict resolution activities. Given the incomplete commitment or lack of leadership of judicial and government officers, many organizations in the Region are also promoting multidisciplinary justice reform efforts supported by the legal community and international organizations.

Among specific judicial reform activities being pursued by NGOs in the Region, the following may be of interest:[14]

- Support the judiciary in designing merit-based judicial appointment and evaluation systems, taking into account positive incentives and negative sanctions.
- Review of disciplinary and sanction enforcement mechanisms for judges to improve ethical behavior, as well as motivating public vigilance of disciplinary complaints.
- Compilation of statistics and evaluations of judicial performance and making them available to the public.
- Building alliances with the judiciary to establish pilot projects in order to apply innovative case management methods and to carry out training programs needed to fight court delays.
- Working with judicial schools to design high quality continuing education programs for judges and prosecutors.
- Organization of legal awareness educational programs to promote better knowledge of rights and duties, and comprehension of judicial mechanisms and procedures.
- Provision of ADR services, legal aid, and public defender programs to low-income citizens and communities.

However, both within individual countries and regionally, the impact of the work of NGOs has been diminished by insufficient communication

---

14. Cárdenas, Marcela. 1999. "Civil Society and Justice: Some Experiences." In *Judicial Reform in Latin America* (see note 5 for full reference).

among them and a consequent inability to profit from and build on each other's advances. Insufficient cooperation also has a negative impact on donors' work in that they are frequently unaware of potential partners and useful pilot projects that they might incorporate into their programs. A regional conference held in Bogotá in July 1998, under the auspices of a local NGO—the Corporation for Excellence in Justice—was a worthy example both of the way to learn about innovative programs being undertaken by a variety of private and public sector actors throughout the Region, and of the potential benefits to be derived by encouraging this kind of interchange.

The achievements attained by NGOs that shared experiences in this conference, as well as the institutional changes they have been promoting through their novel approaches, are worth mentioning. Among these entities are those that are private in nature and financed locally; others that receive various degrees of international funding; an organization composed of officials of the judicial branch; and an entity directly supported by the Supreme Court of Justice. In general, they are independent NGOs, and therefore not subject to the interference of political parties. Grass roots organizations include some devoted to defending the rights of women, children, indigenous peoples, and other vulnerable groups. It is interesting to note the determined commitment of the entrepreneurial sector to judicial reform processes, and the strategic role played by mass media in supporting reform. Although most of the organizations carry out training activities, they have no formal relationship with the education sector.

The Inter-American Network for Judicial Reform

Good governance requires information, transparency, and participation. The initiative to create a regional network grew out of the April 1998 Summit of the Americas in Santiago, Chile. Three months later, NGOs from eight Latin American and Caribbean countries joined forces in the aforementioned regional conference in Bogotá, in order to establish the Inter-American Network for Judicial Reform, RIRJU, which is currently housed in Bogotá's private Corporation for Excellence in Justice. The project seeks to formulate a network for organizations that are participating in judicial reform in Latin American countries. Since these organizations have the common aim of strengthening justice systems in their respective countries, they know that they can gain insight and support from peers with better knowledge.[15]

By working together in cyberspace NGOs can have instantaneous access to information—specifically, insights and feedback about successes and failures of the participatory process and activities implemented by other NGOs, courts, and other entities working in the field. It is of common interest to use these lessons in ongoing and planned operations. Research and evaluations on judicial performance and monitoring of how the public is affected by changes in the judiciary will also allow donors and international agencies to better assess the social impact of the projects they finance. In addition to the benefits mentioned above, this network will further assist in strengthening the role of justice systems by keeping doors open to participation, thereby helping to enhance judicial credibility and adherence to the rule of law.

To sum up, the main objectives to be achieved by RIRJU are as follows:

1. To use the network to increase communication and information exchange among NGOs, public sector entities, and individuals working on judicial reform.
2. To use the network—and the entity charged with organizing it—to identify and facilitate discussion of common problems facing reform programs and the various means adopted to resolve them.
3. To encourage interorganizational cooperation in the development and implementation of research and action projects at national and regional levels. Such cooperation might itself be virtual (that is, conducted via an electronic network), or it may entail the physical pooling of human and financial resources.
4. To help donors and international organizations learn more about the activities of the members and to identify organizations that could possibly collaborate in their operations.

Following those objectives, the network promotes specific activities such as the following:

15. Dakolias, Maria. 1999. "La Red Latinoamericana de Reformas Judiciales." In *Judicial Reform in Latin America* (see note 5 for full reference).

- Exchange of publications, magazines, research findings, and all other materials.
- Dissemination of activities to be undertaken by each of its members.
- Cooperation to channel resources from international agencies.
- Organization of periodic meetings on experiences of modernization and access to justice in the hemisphere.
- Coordination with other networks pursuing similar objectives, with the purpose of avoiding duplication of effort.
- Discussion and meetings through electronic media.
- Dissemination of the network's activities through mass media.
- Support initiatives aimed at strengthening the justice system in every country, upon members' request.
- Exchange of experiences through visits to countries with pilot projects on modernizing justice and access to justice.

The Network has been modeled after the information mall program currently being used for the Global Cultural Heritage Network at the World Bank. The mall is managed by a technical group responsible for updating the sites on a regular basis, with the valuable support of the Bank. Information on the mall includes descriptions of each participating organization, their activities, publications, contact people and links to their own Web pages, discussion groups on various topics, kiosks with project announcements, issues and events, ongoing cases, and so forth.

NGOs (there are already 24) and other institutions, such as the World Bank, Inter-American Development Bank (IDB), U.S. Agency for International Development (USAID), and United Nations Office for Project Services (UNOPS) are members of the Network and have the ability to contribute on an ongoing basis by updating their own kiosks with information on their projects, events, and research. Donors and loan institutions can use the Network to keep abreast of reforms in various countries and have a better understanding of what kind of activities are having an impact on the reform process.

In addition, as a result of the 1998 Summit of the Americas in Santiago, Chile, the participating governments agreed to establish the Justice Studies Center for the Americas as an intergovernmental, self-governed entity that will promote the exchange of information and cooperation to facilitate support for the modernization of justice systems in the Region. Based on consultations with the directors of the Center, it is now envisaged that the Inter-American Network for Judicial Reform may support the Center's endeavor to serve as a clearinghouse for the collection and distribution of information on national experiences pertaining to reforms and for the dissemination of indicators and data related to justice in the western hemisphere.

According to the Network's policies and bylaws, which relate to membership and governance, the members of the Network shall annually designate an executive committee composed of three of their members. This committee approves new members and leads the Network toward achieving the proposed objectives. It is presently formed by the following organizations: Corporación Latinoamericana de Desarrollo (CLD), Ecuador; Asociación Civil Primero Justicia, Venezuela; and the Corporation for Excellence in Justice (CEJ), Colombia, which is coordinating the technical updating, maintenance, and translation of the information mall, with the support of the World Bank.

There are three possible ways to participate in the Network: as an active member; as a provisional member; or as a user. The first is a person or an entity, who after actively participating in the Network during a provisional period, has been accepted as an active member and has assumed the corresponding commitments to share knowledge on a permanent basis. The final admission of a provisional member shall depend on his or her active participation during a time period not exceeding one year. The user shall be a person who, in spite of using some of the services offered by the Network, is not interested in participating on an active and ongoing basis.

The sustainability of the Network will depend mostly on NGOs using the system rather than on monetary fees. The monthly cost to maintain the site is being financed by a World Bank grant. This amount covers Internet service provider fees and management costs. It has been agreed that the Bank will service the Network on the technical operational aspects while the Network members will handle, through their coordinators, the substantive issues. This Network could later be expanded to other regions. The intention is to link up with previously established non-hemispheric networks on judicial reform.

Final Remarks

This paper examines the issue of dealing with pending challenges of judicial reform in Latin America and defining the role of NGOs, as well as promoting their regional cooperation in order to foster the needed process of change. As far as the objectives of the reform are concerned, preeminence is given to the following tasks: (a) adopting an economic conception of how to promote institutional change aimed at increasing the effectiveness of the judicial system; and (b) improving access for low-income segments of the population to justice services by identifying policies to overcome access barriers.

Increasing effectiveness is considered to be closely related to the improvement of resource allocation in the sectoral budget. The functioning of the judiciary is usually intensive in human resources, salaries, and physical infrastructure, so that other items closely related with the increase of efficiency and effectiveness of the judicial system are generally underinvested. Having reached the goal of removing disincentives caused by poor remuneration in the judiciary, the recommended next step involves efforts to adopt an investment-productivity approach to encourage expenditure in training and continuing education of judges, prosecutors, and lawyers. In the same vein, modernization policies related to the adoption of new technologies and management techniques in courts should be implemented. Achieving a strong recomposition of public spending to fund activities aimed at raising service quality should be mixed with the de-judicialization of and outsourcing policies for certain procedures and complaints.

Concerning the task of improving access, priority should be given to broadening the scope of alternative dispute resolution mechanisms and contending with cultural barriers that deter citizens, corporations, and public entities from bringing their cases before conciliators, mediators, arbitrators, justices of the peace, or administrative officers. Efforts need to be made to promote a better knowledge of such mechanisms and of the type of complaints, rights, and obligations related to the reconciliation process. Also, given the regressive bias of justice expenditures, the adoption of corrective policies is recommended to subsidize public defenders and legal aid programs.

The goals of a judicial reform program could miscarry if no attention is paid to cultural barriers that hinder the transition process. A "fine tuning" approach is needed to identify components that do not work, and to define critical interventions and expected results within a precise agenda of transition. This approach might facilitate a better perception of the interests of those groups that support and oppose the reform.

Nongovernmental organizations have developed capabilities to undertake impartial activities that foster and support judicial reform processes. They have become an integral part of activities that strengthen the rule of law in the Region. In different countries, NGOs have helped to counteract the low political capital of Latin American judiciaries, bringing leadership and continuity to reforms. Through the promotion of alliances within civil society, they have become able to fight against a culture that is reflexively defensive toward innovation, and to oppose the conservative nature of judicial power.

It is extremely important for future reforms to take advantage of the aforementioned learning process developed by NGOs. A first step is to thwart insufficient communication among such organizations by encouraging a process of building on each other's advances. The recent creation of the Inter-American Network for Judicial Reform constitutes a positive example of a way to learn about innovative programs for institutional and cultural change in the Region. Such international alliances are powerful instruments to monitor reforms better and to diffuse and evaluate their outcomes.

Legal Reform, Global Knowledge, and Civil Society

The Kenyan Experience

Hon. S. Amos Wako

Attorney General of Kenya

I am delighted to be a participant at this important World Bank conference on "Comprehensive Legal and Judicial Development: Toward an Agenda for a Just and Equitable Society in the 21st Century." That the World Bank has organized this conference is to me an important watershed, a landmark in the transformation in the thinking of the World Bank on its functions and role in economic and social development. Gone are the days when the World Bank and our development partners focused exclusively on financing economic and social projects such as roads, schools, health centers, water projects, and other easily quantifiable efforts. In a world in which careers depended on visible and quantifiable achievements, something as abstract as justice was bound to find no suitors in the halls of the donor community among those responsible for setting the agenda for development.

I am glad there is now recognition that a solid foundation for economic and social progress requires consolidation of democracy as well as respect for the rule of law and human rights: that the enabling environment for economic and social development lies in good governance, respect for the rule of law, the dictates of universal human rights, and the effective pursuit of democratic ideals.

Parallel to this development, which recognizes the centrality of the legal and judicial sectors in development, there has also been further thinking on the elements or factors that enhance democracy at the national and international levels. No longer is democracy viewed simply in terms of universal and equal suffrage. People exercising their right to vote and to be elected at genuine periodic elections is just the beginning; democracy also means people have a say and can advance views and opinions and influence decisions that affect them on an ongoing basis. Whereas governments formerly operated on the basis that the making of decisions and policies was their exclusive preserve and jealously guarded the information on which such decisions and policies were based—under such legislation as the Official Secrets Act—now it is increasingly recognized that the people's role is not just to vote at elections, but also to be consulted and to contribute from time to time during the decision-making process. This they do either directly or through non-governmental organizations (NGOs) or civil society. Hence the rise of the right to access to information.

Whereas in the past civil society, which attempted to influence government decision-making, was seen as an opposition force and not entitled to any relevant information in possession of the government, today it is increasingly recognized as a partner of government, sharing its aims and objectives, particularly in the area of legal and judicial development. It is apparent that the sharing of information between civil society and government will contribute to the best solution in any circumstance and thereby contribute toward the goal of an equitable society underpinned by an efficient, transparent, and just legal and judicial system.

It is well established that the actors in civil society can be an independent third force alongside industry and government in actively helping to combat social, political, and economic problems, as well as ecological degradation and in helping create an impartial system of administration of justice. Instead of playing complementary roles, traditionally, NGOs and government have been divided by mutual suspicion, lack of understanding, and even hostility. To avoid the destructive force inherent in this conflict, there is a need to build linkages and understanding between civil society and government. Both must work to harmonize and reinforce their objectives. This synthesis can only be obtained within the context of knowledge-sharing.

There is no doubt that global knowledge-sharing has helped dispense with unjustified fears such as the initial presumption that trade and environment would be fundamentally incompatible. The two major social movements that may be the biggest legacies of the twentieth century—human rights and environmentalism—were largely a product of the struggle of civil society. In the case of the latter, the United Nations Conference on Environmental Development (UNCED), which adopted Agenda 21 in Rio de Janeiro in 1992 marked a major milestone as the first significant global interaction between civil society and governments. Two years ago in Rome, during the Diplomatic Conference on the International Criminal Court, there was a sharing of knowledge between governments and civil society. The door having been opened and no monsters having been found on the other side, trust started to emerge between the international community as represented by governments and international civil society.

The confrontational approaches between government and civil society must give way to consultative engagement, which can yield positive results if the knowledge is shared. The way forward is through constructive dialogue. However, in this transitional period there will be those on either side who will engage in the tactics of yesteryear when confrontation was the name of the game, without realizing that a new order of collaboration between government and civil society has emerged.

That may be one of the reasons why in July 1997, the Secretary General of the United Nations stated in his blueprint for reform (DOC A/51 /950) in the chapter entitled "Reaching Out to Civil Society":

> Civil Society constitutes a major and increasingly important force in international life.... Yet despite those growing manifestations of an evermore robust civil society, the United Nations is as at present inadequately equipped to engage civil society and make it a true partner in its work.

The Secretary General went on to appeal to all the United Nations entities to be open to and work closely with civil society organizations that are active in their respective sectors, and to facilitate increased consultations and cooperation between the United Nations and such organizations.

These consultations and cooperation among governments, their intergovernmental organizations, and NGOs can only be successful and effective for the good and in the best interest of society if they share values, objectives, and information. Sharing knowledge has the effect of diffusing controversies and building essential confidence and trust. That is one of the reasons why at the international level, institutions such as the World Bank—which is an intergovernmental institution whose operations are such that it is a repository of a wealth of information from governments—have to evolve ways and means of sharing their information with and receiving information from civil society.

At this juncture, permit me to put in a word of caution. There is a proliferation of nongovernmental organizations in the world and particularly in Africa. There are certain limitations that have to be taken into account as governments and intergovernmental organizations engage civil society in constructive dialogue. I will mention only three.

First, many of the organizations have been formed primarily as a means or source of income for the officials and members and lack genuine commitment to the ideals and noble objectives they espouse, and grass-roots support.

Second, because these organizations are formed with a specific objective in mind, they can pursue this objective at the expense or to the detriment of other equally important objectives, which may not have the support of an organization with resources. Governments therefore have a duty of balancing the various objectives in the national and public interest.

Third, the question must be asked: to whom are the nongovernmental organizations accountable? In a democratic system there are many ways to hold government and its officials accountable. The ultimate weapon is to vote out a governmental administration at an election. Nongovernmental organizations must be held to even stricter rules of transparency and accountability.

The fact that global sharing fosters civil society participation is not in doubt. I would like to go over my own experiences in Kenya and Africa before I conclude this paper.

When I assumed office following my appointment as attorney general in May 1991, I informed the country that constitutional and legal reform were going to be my priority areas of concern. As was the case with virtually all countries in Africa at that time, Kenya was in the midst of great and exciting political changes, which eventually saw the country move from a single- to a multiparty state in December 1991. Furthermore, I knew that the bulk of Kenya's procedural and substantive law was a colonial heritage totally unsuitable for a modern democratic state whose economic philosophy was government facilitation of private sector as an engine of economic growth.

I knew that speed was of the essence in undertaking the law reforms. I further knew that the institutional mechanism for law reform was undercapacitated and thus incapable of speedily midwifing the reforms I thought were necessary. I therefore decided that constituting task forces to review the laws was the best way forward. I sold the idea to my colleagues in government, and it was agreed that the instrumentality of Kenya's law reform would be the task forces. In all, 15 task forces were established, covering important areas such as penal laws and procedures; security legislation; company law; laws relating to children, women, persons with disabilities; legal education; landlord and tenancy laws; press laws; agricultural laws; land laws; public health laws; labor laws; and so on. Eleven out of 15 have submitted their reports so far.

In setting up the task forces, we followed a deliberate policy to ensure that the composition of each task force was representative of the various social and professional interests, with a proven record and expertise in the particular area of reform. I reached out to civil society and recruited a fair mixture of academics, legal practitioners, judicial officers, members of the business community, women, members of the clergy, persons with disabilities, and so forth. The task forces were under instructions not only to consult widely but to crisscross the country and meet the people who had views to express on the area covered by their mandate.

Why did I decide to involve civil society in the law reform process? I decided to do so because first, I wanted to tap into the knowledge that I knew civil society had in the area of the law to be reformed. When it comes to law reform, governments all over the world have tended to be more conservative and to move more slowly than the situation warrants. This may not be necessarily bad. Governments have to ensure that peace, stability, and cohesion in society are not compromised as reforms are undertaken. This leads governments to be, at times, more cautious than is necessary. Civil societies, by contrast, want reforms; they want to change society. This tension, if properly handled, is good for society as a whole. In Africa, whereas governments look inward, civil societies look not only inward, but also outward and establish linkages regionally and internationally. They therefore have access to outside information and know more than the government about what trends and developments are going on in any area of law worldwide. Furthermore, governments of most African countries have yet to computerize or have access to the Internet whereas reputable NGOs have already cleared that hurdle. By appointing members of civil society to these task forces, I ensured that the information they had was available to the task forces.

Second, because of the experience they have in working in that area of the law to be reformed, civil society members have a wealth of experience on its shortcomings. Third, by involving civil society, I involved that part of our society most affected by the law or interested in the operation of that law, and therefore they felt a sense of ownership when the law was enacted. My task of steering the legislative outcome of these processes would be made easier if the government could be seen as having not acted on its presumed wisdom, but as having engaged interest groups and the public in the process of law-making.

The government came to realize that it was of no use reforming the laws unless the public perceived that the machinery of justice was an integral and indispensable component of an efficient national infrastructure. The following were some of the issues that had to be dealt with: complaints of inefficiency and delay in delivery of legal services whether by the judiciary, or by legal practitioners whether private or public; inordinate delays in the disposal of cases, whether criminal or civil; the condition of legal registries; and the general decline in professional conduct and discipline. It was during the process of reforming the legal machinery that an enabling environment would be created for the reformed laws to serve the purposes for which they were enacted.

The coordinating committee on legal sector reform was therefore constituted with the mandate to review the legal sector comprehensively and to recommend appropriate measures to enhance its operational efficiency. It was to strive for a holistic and integrated approach to legal sector reforms and be guided by the best practices in the world.

I will focus on reform methodologies since that is what is relevant for the purposes of this conference. In terms of composition, in addition to ensuring that those institutions or offices involved in the legal sector—such as the judiciary, the Attorney General's Office, the Law Society of Kenya, faculties of law, and so on—were represented at a high level, we made sure that consumers of justice, represented by civil society, such as the business community, women's organizations, and the like, were also on the committee.

The committee's approaches on any issue are participatory and, in conjunction with stakeholders, it has developed a lobbying strategy for successful legislative and administrative reforms. In this regard, two national stakeholders workshops were held: the first one was held in June 1999 and formulated an agenda for reform; the second one was held in December 1999 and used the results of the first national stakeholders conference to formulate an action plan for reform within the sector. Over 150 stakeholders attended the workshops. The workshops increased understanding of the varied perceptions of the sector's problems, formulated interventions that had been arrived at through consensus and that heightened the sense of ownership of the sector among the stakeholders.

Interestingly, these workshops also provided rare fora in Kenya for representatives of the three branches of the legal profession—namely, the judiciary, the bar, and the public sector—to discuss the state of their sector and to move forward as one on this matter. Prior to this, the various institutions in the administration of justice area tended to talk at each other rather than *with* each other by shifting blame for who was responsible for shortcomings in the sector. By sharing knowledge we have found that we can create an enabling environment to find solutions to problems in the administration of justice.

I have stated briefly what is going on in Kenya in the way of knowledge-sharing and civil society participation. Now I would like to widen the scope of this discussion and talk a little bit about the regional scene and the African scene. As I have earlier stated, in general, civil society in Africa has been better organized than governments when it comes to issues of law reform. They have not only had access to information, but have for many years now formed regional and international linkages. The African Bar Association, for example, which is composed of the national bar associations of the commonwealth countries in Africa, has been in existence since the early 1970s. Most national bar associations in Africa either belong to the International Bar Association or its counterpart in francophone countries. The International Commission of Jurists has many chapters in African countries. Civil society in Africa has therefore been on the forefront in demanding and undertaking studies and research on issues touching on the independence and accountability of the judiciary, the independence of the bar, the standards required in legal education, and so on. In fact, African civil societies have made attempts to address each of the specific topics covered in this conference.

By contrast, governments in Africa have not been as organized. I believe one of the first attempts to get them to address the issue of administration of justice was when I convened in Nairobi, in October 1992, a meeting of the ministers of justice and attorneys general from Eastern and Southern African states to discuss this topic. I called the meeting because I was anxious to hear my colleagues' experiences in dealing with the administration of justice in their respective countries. It transpired from the discussions we held that each one of us in our capacity as legal advisor to our respective governments shared many concerns on the state of the administration of justice in our countries. We recognized the indispensability of the rule of law and the administration of justice to the development process. We discovered that throughout the region there was neglect by governments in terms of budgetary allocations, and we appealed to our governments to rectify the situation and allocate more resources to the sector. We also squarely put the administration of justice on the agenda of development. We also recognized donors as development partners in furtherance of the ends of an efficient, just, and equitable legal and judicial system. I was mandated to put forth this viewpoint at the Vienna Conference on Human Rights whose Declaration states in part:

> This Declaration provides those concerned with administration of justice and with its importance in development, with a juridical basis for seeking support both at the national and international levels.

In the statement, we identified constraints in the legal and judicial sectors—and indeed in the administration of justice as a whole—that militate against full realization of human rights and hence the creation of a just and equitable society. We identified the problems in law enforcement agencies, the judiciary, the penal systems, and the Attorney General's Offices. We also touched on the importance of legal aid services. We stated the urgent need to establish workable and sustainable legal aid schemes.

I am mentioning this meeting because it showed clearly the value of shared knowledge and experience. Until this conference each one of us had thought that the seemingly insurmountable problems he was facing were unique. After the conference, at least there was added determination to tackle the problems and face the challenges, which we now know are common to all of us and on which together we can more effectively lobby our respective governments.

Following this meeting the potential and value of exchange of knowledge within the African continent has shown itself in many ways. For example:

1. When I wanted to draft and enact the Community Service Order Act, I set up a task force on this, consisting, as I said before, of representa-

tives from government and civil society. We realized that we should not be reinventing the wheel. Therefore some members of the task force visited Zimbabwe, Swaziland, and South Africa where such schemes are operational. We also involved some regional and international nongovernmental organizations such as Penal Reform International and the African Coalition Against Child Abuse Network. The result has been good legislation, which will not only assist in the reformation and rehabilitation of convicts, but also reduce the prison population.

2. It is the intention of the Government of Kenya to constitute by legislation the Kenya National Commission on Human Rights. Experts from similar organizations in Uganda and South Africa have been consulted and have participated, in addition to the local and international nongovernmental and governmental organizations, in the workshops finalizing the draft legislation.

3. It is the intention of the Government of Kenya to put in place a legal aid scheme that is affordable. I have set up a committee consisting of representatives of government and those nongovernmental organizations currently offering some legal services to the public without payment of fees. Again, we involved experts from the United States of America, the United Kingdom, South Africa, and Zambia where such schemes are already in place.

The foregoing highlights the importance of establishing some networking on the African continent where knowledge in the legal and judicial sector and the reform of laws generally can be shared between governments and civil society as a matter of course.

At the government level, opportunities have arisen for us to meet and consult at various fora provided by meetings at the regional and African levels. However what is now lacking is the linkage between African governments and their civil societies, particularly in the area of legal and judicial reform. Within the East African region, the East African Law Society has been formed, and we are in the process of institutionalizing cross-border practice, and members of the branches of the legal sector are given opportunities to meet and consult on various aspects of the legal sector.

My experience in Africa is that even though we may have different legal traditions, the problems we face are the same and the sharing of knowledge, experiences, modalities, and solutions to the problems will be extremely useful because in some cases implementation of programs that have proved useful in one country could be replicated with some modification in other countries. Sometimes I become aware, just by having a casual discussion with my counterpart or with a nongovernmental organization, that in a particular country they have enacted legislation that closely follows what I was contemplating drafting, and this has made my task easier because of the available precedent and that country's experience in implementing that legislation. There is no doubt Africa stands to benefit from knowledge-sharing between governments and civil society.

In conclusion let me summarize my points.

1. There are certain limitations on the part of civil society that should be taken into account by governments and intergovernmental organizations as they engage civil society in a constructive dialogue. Some NGOs were formed primarily as a source of income for its officials or members and only secondarily to espouse certain ideals. They often lack transparency and accountability, and pursuing one track—as nearly all nongovernmental organizations do—can be detrimental to other equally important tracks. Governments and intergovernmental organizations have a duty to see the overall picture and make decisions in the interest of society as a whole.

2. The involvement of civil society in decision-making makes better public policy and enhances transparency and public accountability. The comprehensive legal and judicial reforms aimed at creating a just and equitable society in the new century are more amenable to this involvement because members of the legal fraternity, whether they be in the judiciary or in the public and private sectors, whether they are human rights activists or lawyers, share common values and objectives when it comes to the issues of the rule of law, protection of human rights, and an independent, efficient, and accountable judiciary and bar. Each of the groups brings to the table its own perspective on how

these objectives can be achieved, and through shared knowledge and information, our training is such that a solution or the way forward is found.

3. Global knowledge-sharing is necessary because in putting all sides on an equal footing as far as the information they have is concerned, it promotes the understanding of each other's role and competence and helps build the capacity of each to meaningfully contribute to enlightened decisions.

4. In Africa today, there is an urgent need to have linkages and improve communication and information-sharing if we are to improve, in a cost-effective manner, the administration of and access to justice and undertake comprehensive legal reforms toward this goal.

5. There are cost implications to legal reform, to putting in place an independent, transparent, and efficient administration of justice system and to providing the necessary linkages with the institutions and civil societies with interest in the rule of law, and other legal and judicial matters. I hope the World Bank can attach priority to this neglected area because on it depends economic and social development.

How Can Effective Strategies Be Developed for Law and Justice Programs? Are There Models for Legal Reform Programs?

Legal Reform in Developing and Transition Countries

Making Haste Slowly

Julio Faundez

Professor of Law

University of Warwick

United Kingdom

Introduction

The organizers of this conference have asked me to address two questions:

- Why is legal reform slow and difficult to achieve? and
- Are there are models for legal reform?

I am delighted that these questions are on the agenda of this important conference. I am delighted because these questions confirm that law has finally established itself as an essential component of the development agenda. This is good news, for until recently those involved in the practice and study of development ignored or avoided law altogether.

I am also delighted because the questions suggest an awareness that law is a complex and often contradictory instrument. This is a welcome development because some publications on legal technical assistance depict law as simple and unproblematic.[1] The message that these publications seem to convey is that there is a single model for legal reform and that all one needs to achieve success is to take into account the five attributes of market-friendly legal systems; namely, rules known in advance; rules actually in force; availability of mechanisms for the application of the rules; independent

---

1. See, for example, Cooter, Robert D. 1996. "The Rule of State Law and the Rule-of-Law State: Economic Analysis of the Legal Foundations of Development." In *Annual World Bank Conference on Development Economics 1996,* pp. 191–237. Washington, D.C.

bodies to resolve conflicts over the interpretation of rules; and procedures for amending the rules.[2] The questions I have been asked to address suggest that perhaps there are doubts as to whether in fact there is a single model applicable to all developing and transition countries.

Finally, I am delighted because by linking the process of judicial and legal reform with the objective of achieving a just and equitable society, the organizers of this conference acknowledge that a just and equitable social order is not a byproduct of economic processes, but a goal that has to be consciously and deliberately pursued. If we take this goal seriously we cannot afford to ignore law and legal institutions.

The questions posed above, though they delight me, are also daunting. In order to carry out my task I will do the following: I will first offer a brief and schematic response to each of these questions. I will then explore selected issues that arise from this initial response.

Why Is Legal Reform So Slow and Difficult to Achieve?

Because it is a process and, as such, it requires careful preparation, meticulous planning, effective execution, elaborate coordination of public officials and disparate institutions, as well as the agreement or at least acquiescence of those directly affected by it. Success in carrying out legal reform requires considerable commitment, patience, and a certain amount of good luck. But success is elusive as the process of legal reform often has unintended consequences and sometimes is blocked by unexpected events. There are, of course, many examples of successful reforms. Yet, their success is difficult to measure and evaluate. Regardless of how success is measured, the number of new laws drafted and enacted is not the sole criterion. Indeed, although the enactment of new rules is generally part of the process, new rules often restrain rather than facilitate the objectives of the reform process.

Are There Models of Legal Reform?

Yes and no. Yes, if by model we understand a simplified description of what the reform process should achieve and it is used to assist those in charge of designing and implementing the reform process. Indeed, how could any

2. World Bank. 1992. *Governance and Development.* Washington, D.C. See p. 30.

process of reform proceed were there no model or vision of what the reformers seek to achieve? If, however, by model we mean blueprint—that is, a detailed plan of the form and content of the reform process—then the answer is no. Yet, the question that should be addressed is whether a model, derived from an ideal type of market and legal system, can be made to work in every country, regardless of local circumstances.

I am aware that my answers are far too general and raise more problems than they solve. This paper addresses some of these problems. The first section below examines whether and if so why legal reform is slow and why foreign legal experts tend to regard legal reform as mainly an exercise in legal drafting. Two examples, one from the United States and the other from Peru, are used to show that legislative change is not always the only or the best alternative available to legal reformers. The second section explores some issues that arise from externally funded projects. It examines the argument as to whether importing laws is better than allowing home-grown products to develop, and includes brief remarks on the role of foreign legal experts. It also discusses the political impact of externally funded projects in recipient countries. Under the rubric "local ownership," the third section explores some issues related to the long-term sustainability of legal reform projects. Two aspects of local ownership are examined: technical ownership through legal drafting and legal ownership through training and legal education. The concluding remarks highlight some of the main points.

What follows is based largely on my experience in the area of legal technical assistance in Latin America and Africa. I have also drawn on the work of many colleagues who have similar experience in other parts of the world. I do not, however, purport to offer a comprehensive review of the literature in the field of legal technical assistance. The purpose of this paper is to raise questions and draw attention to aspects of the process often neglected both by academics and practitioners. To facilitate the reading of this paper I have avoided expressions of hesitancy. This is merely a stylistic device as the paper only purports to put forward provisional answers to the issues it raises. I will have fulfilled my purpose, however, if one or two of my comments provide the basis for a debate that helps us find solutions to the many problems encountered by legal reformers.

The Reform Process

Is Legal Reform Really Slow?

The evidence of the past two decades seems to indicate that legal reform is neither slow nor difficult to achieve. After all, during this period there has been an unprecedented amount of legal reform. It started with the current wave of democratization, which prompted many countries to adopt new constitutions or to amend old texts. The comprehensive restructuring of the political rules of the game was followed by an equally comprehensive redefinition of the rules governing economic policy as virtually every country in the world incorporated the "Washington consensus" into its legislative framework. This new legislation provided the platform to launch major programs of liberalization, deregulation, and privatization. A well-known example of the speed and impact of the current reform process is the regulation of foreign investment. While in the 1970s foreign investment codes were largely hostile to foreign investment and imposed various hurdles, today they are entirely different. Instead of rejecting foreign investment they welcome it, and instead of hurdles they contain various mechanisms to attract it.[3] This shift in the content and style of foreign investment regulation is replicated at the international level by the proliferation of bilateral and plurilateral investment treaties. The evidence of the last two decades thus suggests that legal reform is not only relatively easy to achieve, but that it can also be achieved in a relatively short period of time, both at the national and international levels.

It is undeniable that over the past two decades, developing and transition countries have enacted a large number of new laws. This process, however, has been both narrow in scope and partial. Narrow because it has focused on a relatively small area of legal regulation and partial because it has consisted mainly in the enactment of new legislation.

Legal reform has, so far, focused primarily on the linkages between national economies and world markets. In the case of transition economies, the focus has also been on the establishment of comprehensive frameworks to

---

3. For an analysis of the impact of a foreign investment code, see Nichols, Philip M. 1997. "The Viability of Transplanted Law: Kazakhstani Reception of a Transplanted Foreign Investment Code." *University of Pennsylvania Journal of International Economics* 18: 1235.

regulate private transactions.[4] Yet, these reforms, though narrow in focus, have nonetheless radically altered the basis upon which the state and legal systems operate. The interventionist state of yesterday is in the process of being replaced by a new, leaner, and less obtrusive state—a state that is friendly to the market. The dramatic transformation of the state has generated its own momentum making national governments and international organizations aware of the need to extend the process of reform to other areas of legal regulation. Thus today, the reform agenda has expanded to include areas such as judicial reform, decentralization, labor standards, equal opportunities, gender equality, land tenure systems, criminal law, and the protection of the environment.[5]

Although the reforms carried out so far have already had a major impact, they have, nonetheless, been partial as they have concentrated mainly on the relatively easy task of drafting and enacting new legislation. The task that most national governments face today is ensuring that the laws they have so effortlessly enacted are rigorously applied, fairly interpreted and, if necessary, promptly amended. This is a complex process that requires time, patience, and considerable political and legal skills. Not surprisingly, national governments and international organizations have already begun to shift their attention toward the task of strengthening and developing the capacity of the newly established or recently reformed state institutions. Accordingly, the emphasis today is on training and on changing the culture of public bureaucracies to ensure that the reforms already in place are not undermined by practices that in the past plagued the political and legal systems.

The process of legal reform has thus entered a new stage. The reform agenda is now broader. Perhaps some would say that it is too broad. Moreover, the efforts to ensure that new legislation is successfully implemented require legal reformers to look beyond the limited confines of legal doctrine and consider the compatibility of the new rules and institutions with the rest of their legal and political systems. This new stage of the process of legal reform will be more difficult than the first and will undoubtedly be slower.

4. See Gray, Cheryl W. et. al. 1993. *Evolving Legal Framework for Private Sector Development in Central and Eastern Europe.* Washington, D.C.: World Bank.

5. On the expansion of the reform agenda, see Shihata, Ibrahim F. I. 1997. "The Role of Law in Business Development." *Fordham International Law Journal* 20: 1577, 1586.

Legal Drafting—A Fatal Attraction

I am certain that few would dispute the proposition that legal reform is a process and that it is not simply about drafting and enacting new rules. Yet, when foreign legal experts assess the legal needs of developing countries they almost always seem to assume that the problems they have identified can be resolved by the enactment of new legal rules. While in some occasions this diagnosis is correct, quite often it is not. Why is it that the prescription offered by these experts almost always tends to be the same?

There are several possible answers to this question. First, simply because legal drafting is something that most lawyers do well and enjoy doing. Second, because by training lawyers are attached to closed systems of rules that are capable of resolving current problems and anticipating problems in the future. And third, because foreign legal experts often do not have the time or the resources to inquire how the legal systems of recipient countries work before deciding whether prevailing rules and practices are effective or whether new rules are necessary.

The attraction that foreign legal experts have for new legal rules is curious. Indeed, most lawyers and policymakers know that social problems are not always resolved by enacting new rules. In fact, it is often the case that new legal rules are not the best solution either because there is no agreement in society as to the content of the rules or because the rules simply do not reach the groups that the rules are meant to reach. The case of affirmative action in the United States and of the administration of justice in a remote community in the Andes illustrate this point.

A Foreign Lawyer Looks at Affirmative Action in the United States

Suppose that a lawyer from a developing or a transition country who has learned about the five attributes of market-friendly legal systems—rules known in advance; rules actually in force; availability of mechanisms for the application of the rules; independent bodies to resolve conflicts over the interpretation of rules; and procedures for amending the rules—is invited to visit the United States to examine how affirmative action works in this country. What would she notice? What would surprise her? I suppose that for a lawyer who believes in the generality and certainty of the rule of law one of the most baffling features of affirmative action in the United States is how difficult it is to know with any degree of certainty which types of affirmative action measures are legal and which are not.[6] This uncertainty is not caused by the absence of rules as there is an abundance of federal or state regulations on this topic. She would also be surprised to learn that despite several attempts, the Supreme Court has not clarified this point. Indeed, and judging by the large number of law review articles published after each decision, our friend could well conclude that Supreme Court decisions add layers of complexity to an already complicated issue. Our friend would also be bewildered by the inconsistency between the policies of the federal government and that of some states.[7] She would probably ask: why doesn't the federal Congress intervene—setting out, once and for all, clear rules of the game? After all, uncertainty over affirmative action is bound to undermine the way firms operate and such confusion is not market-friendly. Aware that Congress is reluctant to legislate on this matter, our friend would probably turn to the Court and ask the same questions again and again.

If our friend turned her attention to the political arena she would soon realize that, even though everybody agrees that affirmative action is an issue of fundamental political and social importance, there is no consensus as to how best to deal with it. Upon reflection she would realize that despite the absence of clear rules, law does play an important role in channeling the debate and in the practice of affirmative action.[8] It does not, however, work as a mechanical device. It is part of a complex and often contradictory social process.

Conflict Resolution in the Andes

The assumption that legal reform requires new rules is especially absurd in cases in which the formal legal system does not reach the whole territory of the state. This is indeed the case in many developing countries where the state either does not have the resources or the legitimacy to rule effectively over its entire territory. In most of these cases local communities are governed partly by their own customary practices and partly by the rules of the formal legal system. It is not self-evident that the existence of a plurality of

---

6. For a recent and very stimulating discussion of affirmative action, see Rubenfeld, Jed. 1997. "Affirmative Action." *Yale Law Journal.* 107: 427.

7. On California's policy on affirmative action see Spann, Girardeau A. 1997. "Proposition 209." *Duke Law Journal* 47: 187.

8. On this point see Sunstein, Cass R. 1996. "Public Deliberation, Affirmative Action, and the Supreme Court." *California Law Review.* 84: 1179.

legal systems is a problem. Indeed, allowing diversity and customary practices to flourish is probably the best way to improve the quality of governance and to democratize both the form and content of legal regulation.
In any event, managing legal diversity is not an easy task. The integration
of local communities within the state is certainly a matter of legitimate
concern for state authorities. It is not the case, however, that this matter
can be resolved by enacting laws or issuing executive decrees. This type of
official intervention is likely, more often than not, to create rather than
resolve problems.

The experience of an indigenous rural community in a remote area of the
Andes, about 90 miles from Ayacucho, in Peru, is a case in point. With the financial support of the British Council I recently had the opportunity to visit
this community and observe how the local people run their affairs. This is a
community of some 200 families of Quechua-speaking peasants who live
high up in the Andes in a place of extraordinary physical beauty, but where
life and farming conditions are extremely difficult. In recent years, this community has had to cope with untold atrocities. First they were victims of the
activities of the Shining Path, a terrorist group which sought its support
through intimidation, torture, and murder. Later on, when the government's
military campaign against the terrorists reached their area, several members
of the community were accused by the military of belonging to Shining Path,
and there followed another round of intimidation, torture, and summary
executions. Caught between the crossfire this small community was nearly
destroyed.

At the time of my visit, violence had subsided and the members of the
community, with admirable courage and resilience, were attempting to re-
constitute their social life. With the support of a local nongovernmental organization (NGO) they had elected a committee of seven to lead this process.
The committee performed several functions, one of which was to resolve disputes between members of the community. This was an important function
because as a consequence of the recent upheavals, there was considerable
confusion as to who had a right to cultivate the various plots of land owned
by members of the community.

I attended one of the hearings of the committee. It involved a dispute between two women over a plot that each claimed had been cultivated
by their respective partners. Both partners had been victims of the recent

violence: one had been murdered by the terrorists and the other had been killed when the army had come in search of terrorists. After a brief hearing during which the women made eloquent speeches in support of their case and answered questions from members of the committee, a solution emerged. The solution proposed by the committee split the difference between the two claims. In his closing speech, the president of the committee stressed the importance of resolving disputes peacefully, highlighting the fact that despite occasional differences they should remember that both parties were equally poor and dependent on the land for their livelihood. He finally urged the two women to accept the committee's recommendation. The parties accepted it.

The risks involved in this type of informal justice are well known.[9] There is always a danger that this type of procedure may degenerate into pure political justice. It is also likely that strict rules of due process will not be observed. What then is the solution? Self-help? Require the parties to travel a day on foot to seek justice from the nearest state court where proceedings are in writing and in Spanish? Or should the parties instead wait for the government to deliver its commitment to carrying out a comprehensive program of judicial reform? A few days after visiting this community I attended a seminar in Lima where one of the participants proposed that the solution was to pass legislation ensuring that community organs, such as the local committee near Ayacucho, would carry out their activities within the terms of the constitution. As a lawyer, I must confess, I find this proposal attractive since it addresses my concerns about the constitutionality of the committee's activities and about the possibility of conflicts of jurisdiction. Yet, on the basis of my limited knowledge of the area and of politics in contemporary Peru, I would not endorse it as I would be concerned that any form of legislative intervention would derail the process of reconstruction that is taking place in this community.[10] Perhaps in the future some form of state intervention might be helpful. Not now.

9. On this topic, see, for example, Cranston, Ross. 1997. "Access to Justice In South and South-East Asia." In J. Faundez, ed., *Good Government and Law*, pp. 233–55. London: Macmillan.

10. For an overview of the plight of indigenous people in Latin America, see Dandler, Jorge. 1999. "Indigenous People and the Rule of Law in Latin America." In Juán E. Méndez et al., *The (Un)Rule of Law and the Underpriviledged in Latin America*, pp. 116–51. Notre Dame, Ind.: University of Notre Dame Press.

Taking the Context Seriously

The importance of understanding the local context is widely acknowledged in the literature on legal technical assistance.[11] The examples discussed in the preceding two subsections underscore the importance of understanding local conditions before deciding whether legal reform is necessary, and if so, how to implement it. Yet, despite the widespread agreement on this point, it seems that, in practice, a thorough analysis of the local context is rarely carried out either because of time constraints, shortage of resources, or simply because there is no agreement on how it should be done.

I suspect, however, that one reason why legal experts from Europe and the United States who advise government in developing and transition countries often appear to disregard the local context is because in their own jurisdictions they can afford to take that context for granted. Where institutions are stable and have the capacity to adapt to change legal, reform slips into the process of social and political change in a relatively unproblematic way. To be sure, legal reform in industrialized countries is not easy, but it generally does not have the traumatic impact on the political system or society that it often has in developing environments. Thus, it is not surprising that when lawyers reared in a stable milieu visit other countries as advisers they take local conditions for granted and assume that legal reform process is as easy as it is at home. Hence, not surprisingly, they become easily frustrated at the slow pace of the reform process and often assume that the reason for it is that local officials are either lazy, corrupt, uninterested, or inefficient.

I am not concerned here with the important methodological question as to how best to carry out a proper analysis of the local context.[12] I would like,

11. See World Bank. 1995. *The World Bank and Legal Technical Assistance*, p. 11. Washington, D.C.: World Bank, Legal Department.

12. There are good accounts by scholars and consultants who have taken the wider context of the reform process into account. Perhaps the most elaborate theoretical and practical statement on this topic is the Seidmans' account of their experience as legal advisers of a United Nations Development Programme (UNDP) project in China. [See Seidman, Ann, and Robert B. Seidman. 1996. "Drafting Legislation for Development: Lessons from a Chinese Project." *American Journal of Comparative Law*. 44: 101. See also Seidman, Robert B. 1987. "Drafting for the Rule of Law: Maintaining Legality in Developing Countries." *Yale Law Journal* 12: 84.]

Bernard Black and Reinier Kraakman's account of the new company law in Russian provides a good illustration of how modern general principles in a particular area of the law can be adapted to an environment where the private sector is at a relatively early stage of development [Black, Bernard, and Reinier Kraakman. 1996. "A Self-Enforcing

however, to highlight one feature of developing countries that international legal consultants often tend to forget; namely, that most of them have weak institutional frameworks. Those familiar with the literature on political development and with World Bank publications on governance know that this is an important issue.[13] As a recent World Bank publication reminds us, it is also a problem that cannot be resolved overnight.[14] Yet, some international legal consultants seem to ignore the bearing that weak institutional frameworks have on the outcome of the reform process.

A state that has a strong institutional framework is one that can get things done in accordance with pre-established procedures and with the minimum use of coercion.[15] A strong state is not necessarily authoritarian or ruthless. It is also not necessarily a large state—indeed size is often the reason for a state's weakness. Strong states can implement policies and laws, while weak states are generally unable to "get things done," to formulate and implement policy or to secure compliance with the law by its citizens. State strength is, of course, a relative matter. In Latin America for example, few countries have all the attributes that one associates with strong institutional frameworks. Some have strong party systems; others have competent judiciaries; some have strong and lively civil societies; others have efficient bureaucracies; some have good systems of legal education and others have good parliamentary procedures. Yet, there is probably no single country in the region where the state has all these attributes. Some transition countries, as evidenced by the

---

Model of Corporate Law." *Harvard Law Review* 109: 1911; for a critique of this approach see Nikulin, Yevgeniy V. 1997. "The New Self-Enforcing Model of Corporate Law: Myth or Reality." *Journal of International Law and Practice* 6: 347].

For a case study of an African country, see William L. Andreen's (2000) article on Tanzania ["Environmental Law and International Assistance: The Challenge of Strengthening Environmental Law in the Developing World." *Columbia Journal of Environmental Law.* 25: 17]. It describes his experience drafting environmental laws in Tanzania and offers interesting insights on the bearing that the institutional framework has on the process of legal reform.

13. See Frischtak, Leila. "Political Mandate, Institutional Change and Economic Reform." In J. Faundez, ed., *Good Government and Law,* pp. 95–119 (see note 9 for full reference). See also the excellent collection of articles on this topic edited by Grindle, Merilee S. 1997. *Getting Good Government.* Cambridge, Mass.: Harvard University Press.

14. World Bank. 1997. *World Development Report 1997: The State in a Changing World,* p. 151. Oxford: Oxford University Press.

15. On weak and strong states, see Migdal, Joel S. 1988. *Strong Societies and Weak States.* Princeton: Princeton University Press.

case of the contemporary Russian Federation, are also affected by the problem of weak institutional frameworks.[16]

In countries where the institutional and political systems are weak, legal reform, indeed any major reform, is difficult and at times almost impossible to achieve. In such countries it is difficult to distinguish the process of lawmaking from the process of institution building. Some publications on this topic point out that in order to strengthen the institutional framework the rule of law must be observed.[17] In many respects, this statement begs the question as it presents us with the classic chicken and egg dilemma. How can the rule of law be secured in countries where the institutional framework is weak; and how can the institutional framework be strengthened, if the legality and the rule of law are constantly flouted? This dilemma, though frustrating in practice, should not lead us into despair. It should, however, serve as a reminder that in countries where the institutional framework is weak, lawmaking and institution building are processes that cannot always be easily distinguished. Hence the importance of ensuring that managers of legal reform projects do not take the institutional framework for granted.

Undermining the Local Context

A paradox of the current stage of the reform process is that while one of its stated aims is to strengthen the institutional framework of recipient countries, in practice, the process itself may undermine it. As the agenda of legal reform expands, there is a serious danger that the institutional framework of many states may deteriorate as a result of the large number of reforms that have to be processed over a relatively short period of time. An overcrowded reform agenda makes it difficult for officials in charge of the reform process to spare the time to understand its wider implications. An overcrowded agenda also reduces the time for consultation and deliberation. Hence, apart from weakening the institutional system, an overcrowded reform agenda may unintentionally also undermine the democratic process.

16. See Hendley, Kathryn. 1996. "Law and Development in Russia: A Misguided Enterprise?" *American Society of International Law: Proceedings* 90: 237.17. See World Bank, *World Development Report 1997*, p. 80. (See note 14 for full reference.)

It must be noted that the relative success of the reforms introduced so far may also act as a brake on the pace of the current reform process. Indeed, as explained above, the reforms already introduced have largely achieved the objective of radically restructuring the state in developing and transition countries. Most of the agencies of these recently restructured states are new and their personnel, though technically well-qualified, are often inexperienced. Hence, burdening them with a large number of new projects may have the effect of stunting their development. Thus, paradoxically, the success of the first generation of legal reforms may undermine the reform process during this second stage.

External Factors

The Inevitability of Politics

In general terms, all externally funded and externally managed technical assistance projects constitute a form of intervention in a domestic environment. Whether or not this intervention is consistent with international legal standards does not concern me here. My concern is to highlight the fact that whether the project has had its origins in a direct request by the government, or a set of conditions for soft loans, or a foreign aid package, externally funded or externally managed projects always have the potential of becoming the focus of political controversy in recipient countries. This potential for controversy is especially acute in the case of projects of legal reform as the power to legislate free from external constraints is an important attribute of sovereignty.

A certain amount of controversy and public debate over the reform is perhaps unavoidable. Indeed, in some circumstances, it may be a sign that there is local interest in the project. There are cases, however, in which the agencies entrusted with the delivery of legal reform projects, unaware of local political sensitivities, create unnecessary political resentment or exacerbate existing tensions. In some cases, decisions by managers of the project may, unintentionally, deepen divisions within the bureaucracy or create rifts between NGOs. It could well be that the project attracts controversy because of the relatively large budgets controlled by those associated with the project. While many of these problems are unavoidable, there are some that can and should be avoided.

It is important to remember that recipient governments are not passive spectators in this process. Indeed, it is often the case that governments make use of externally funded projects to further their own party political agendas showing little regard for the objectives of the project. In these situations multilateral agencies are caught in a difficult dilemma: either withdrawing on the ground that the government is not seriously committed to the project; or continuing on the expectation that despite the government's behavior the project will, in the long run, benefit the country as a whole. The dilemma that multilateral agencies face is difficult and not often fully appreciated by their critics.[18] Multilateral agencies should, however, confront this problem honestly and openly to ensure that political misunderstandings arising from their projects do not undermine the objectives of the project.

The (Real) Fear of Legal Imperialism

In addition to the immediate political impact that any technical assistance project is bound to have, legal reform projects also generate resentment as they are often depicted as tools designed to impose alien legal regulatory schemes that undermine the indigenous legal culture.[19] This criticism comes from all sides of the political spectrum. Some focus on the economic components of the current process of legal reform, while others focus on its political components. Thus, while some depict the measures that have led to the liberalization and deregulation of national economies as evidence of a new form of international domination, others see the current stress on human rights as confirmation that imperialism is alive and well.

Academics from industrialized countries often dismiss these views as a symptom of naive nationalism. Whether or not this assessment is correct, what is relevant for our purposes is to bear in mind that honest and competent officials as well as responsible citizens in recipient countries genuinely believe that externally funded projects are either part of an alien political

18. The failed negotiations of a loan for judicial reform between the World Bank and Peru is a good example of the difficult dilemmas that multilateral agencies face when governments are less than forthcoming regarding their commitment to the objectives of the reform process. For a critique of the World Bank's role in this process see Lawyers Committee of Human Rights. 2000. "El Banco Mundial y la Reforma Judicial en el Peru." *IDEELE (Revista del Instituto de Defensa Legal)* (Lima) No. 126, March, pp. 73–76.

19. For an interesting proposal on how comparative lawyers can avoid undermining local legal cultures, see Demleitner, Nora V. 1999. "Combating Legal Ethnocentrism: Comparative Law Sets Boundaries." *Arizona State Law Journal* 31: 737.

agenda or pose a serious threat to their legal culture and national identity. The interminable debate in the United Kingdom between the Euro-skeptics and pro-Europeans—a debate that cuts across political class and generations—is a helpful reminder that concern about foreign imposition and control is not only an infantile disorder affecting so-called "young nations." As far as I understand it, however, the Euro-skeptics oppose deepening the process of European integration because they do not want to surrender control of key political decisions—mainly, monetary policy—to a federal type of organization or to unelected officials of the European Union. I am not concerned with the merits of the British debate over Europe. I simply want to underscore the impact that the perception of alien political domination has on political debates. If citizens and responsible politicians of an old and stable country such as the United Kingdom are genuinely worried about the political consequences of deepening a process of integration that began nearly half a century ago, it should not be surprising that their counterparts in developing countries should have the same reaction toward projects that seek to integrate local institutions to the global economy.

The fact that legal reform projects are externally funded or externally managed is, of course, not always a source of controversy in recipient countries. Indeed, more often than not, governments of developing and transition countries actively seek the support of international agencies and bilateral donor agencies. In some areas, such as human rights, for example, the establishment of alliances between local and international groups often provide the impetus to prompt reluctant governments into action. Moreover, many of the legal reforms currently implemented in developing and transition countries enjoy widespread legitimacy as they merely seek to incorporate into the legal systems of recipient countries standards and principles adopted by international organizations.[20] This is the case, for example, of international labor standards, of measures dealing with the protection of the environment, and of the many new areas of regulation that have recently become part of the agenda of the World Trade Organization.

In any event, officials from international agencies in charge of managing projects of legal reform should not forget that, whether justified or not, these projects raise sensitive issues that should not be ignored or lightly dismissed.

20. Some may of course argue that decision-making processes in some international organizations should be improved in order to enhance the legitimacy of their decisions.

Imports Versus Home-Grown Products

The debate as to whether imports or home-grown products are preferable is, in some respects, a restatement, at the technical level, of the political debate about legal imperialism. Though academically interesting, this debate, has, in my view, received far more attention than it merits. Perhaps its prominence is because legal technical assistance projects have hitherto placed excessive emphasis on the drafting process.

The terms of the debate are fairly simple. Those against the importing of legal texts generally point out that it is a form of colonial imposition and, as such, contrary to the principles of democratic governance.[21] Importing is also seen as objectionable because it undermines indigenous legal cultures. On the other side, there are those who argue that waiting for the home-grown product to emerge through social practices is inefficient and unrealistic—inefficient because it takes a long time for social practices to develop and unrealistic because it is unlikely that social practice will be as clear or as coherent as rules contained in codes based on the experience of more advanced jurisdictions.[22] It has also been pointed out that copying and borrowing saves time, contributes to the process of harmonization, and generally avoids having to reinvent the wheel each time policymakers confront a new problem.[23]

We have all heard about lawyers who fly the world "drafting" laws based almost word for word on the laws of their own countries.[24] Most observers are in agreement that this approach to legal technical assistance is in the end counterproductive as it is unlikely that such laws will ever be fully implemented, let alone understood by the recipients. Moreover, this approach is rejected because it breeds cynicism toward the legal system, not to mention discrediting the enterprise of legal technical assistance. As ever, there are

21. For a lucid summary explanation of this argument see Walde, T. W., and J. L. Gunderson. 1999. "Legislative Reform in Transition Economies: A Short-Cut to Social Market Economy Status." In Ann Seidman, Robert B. Seidman, and Thomas W. Walde, eds., *Making Development Work*, pp. 84–89. Cambridge, Mass: Kluwer Law International.

On this topic see also Gopal, Mohan Gopalan. 1996. "Law and Development: Toward a Pluralistic Vision." *American Society of International Law—Proceedings* 90: 231.

22. David, René. 1963. " A Civil Code for Ethiopia: Considerations on the Codification of the Civil Law in African Countries." *Tulane Law Review* 37: 189.

23. Watson, Alan. 1974. *Legal Transplants*. Edinburgh: Scottish Academic Press.

24. See, for example, the anecdotes recounted by deLisle, Jacques. 1999. "Lex Americana?: United States Legal Assistance, American Legal Models and Legal Change in the Post-Communist World and Beyond." *University of Pennsylvania International Econic nics Law* 20: 179. [verify journal title]

always examples that appear to show that sometimes this approach to legal technical assistance does indeed work.[25]

While reckless copying of foreign legal texts should not be encouraged, policymakers and legislators, however, should have a sound understanding of the experience of other countries—preferably countries that have similar features—in order to assist them both in the choice of policy and in the drafting process. Such understanding should enable them to identify good practice in specific policy areas. Given that public officials and their advisers do not generally have the time or the resources directly to carry out research on best practices, model laws prepared by international organizations or private associations are helpful tools, provided that they are prudently and wisely used.

In any event, as Alan Watson reminds us, modeling institutions on the experience of another country or on a general model is a long-standing practice.[26] As such, sometimes it fails and sometimes it succeeds. Some, for example, regard presidentialism in Latin America as an example of a failed transplant. Inspired by the United States Constitution, most Latin American constitutions adopted a presidential regime. Yet, while in the United States the presidential regime has evolved within a dynamic and open system of government, in Latin America presidentialism is, according to its critics, the main factor that has led many countries into authoritarianism.[27] Regardless of of whether or not these critics are right, there is no doubt that the Latin American version of presidentialism is quite different from the model on which it was based.

A contemporary example of a successful transplant is the case of the Office of the Ombudsman in Peru, the *Defensoría del Pueblo*. As we know, the ombudsman originated in Sweden and from there it spread to several industrialized countries and then to the rest of the world. Many constitutions enacted by developing countries in recent years make provision for such an office.

---

25. See, for example, Paul Drake's (1989) study of legal and economic technical assistance by a Princeton Professor in Latin America during the 1920s: *The Money Doctor in the Andes*. Durham, North Carolina: Duke University Press.

26. Watson, Alan. 1996. "Aspects of Reception of Law" *American Journal of Comparative Law* 44: 335.

27. See Linz, Juan J., and Arturo Valenzuela, eds. 1994. *The Failure of Presidential Democracy: Volume 2—The Case of Latin America*. Baltimore: Johns Hopkins University Press. For a critique of this view see Mainwaring, Scott, and Matthew Soberg Shugart. 1997. *Presidentialism and Democracy in Latin America*. Cambridge, United Kingdom: Cambridge University Press.

The objective of the Office of the Ombudsman is to protect members of the public against abuses committed by public officials. It does not have enforcement powers. It merely investigates and makes representation to public authorities on behalf of members of the public. In Peru, the *Defensoría del Pueblo,* based on the Spanish model, was established in 1979 and has recently become a major force in the promotion and defense of civil, political, and social rights.[28] Remarkably for Latin America, and particularly for Peru, the *Defensoría* has managed to maintain its independence from the government.

The *Defensoría's* leading role in the protection of human rights has been widely acknowledged. To a large extent the prominent role of the *Defensoría* stems partly from the weakness of the judiciary caused mainly by the notorious tendency of the government to interfere with the courts. Given these circumstances, the *Defensoría* has stepped in to fulfill the demands for justice and fair treatment, particularly from the weakest and poorest sections of the population. So far, the success of the *Defensoría* is largely attributable to the courage, intelligence and diplomatic skills of the incumbent and of his talented team of lawyers. Whether the *Defensoría's* excellent record in the defense of human rights will continue beyond the term of office of the present incumbent is an open question. I hope it does, although countries in Latin America have a poor record at institutionalizing good practice. In any event, the experience of Peru's *Defensoría del Pueblo* is a good example of how imported institutions can flourish and develop in unexpected ways even in relatively hostile political environments.

The foregoing shows that the discrete and careful use of model laws and model legislation does not necessarily undermine legal culture. On the contrary, it often enriches and adds diversity to local legal cultures.

Foreign Legal Experts

The participation of lawyers in technical assistance projects is sometimes viewed with suspicion by members of the local bar. It is of course not surprising that lawyers from different countries and often different cultures should view each other with a degree of reticence as lawyers are, by training, parochial. They are experts in the operation of a single legal system and tend

---

28. See de Noriega, Jorge Santistevan. 1997. "La Defensoría del Pueblo." in Ana Teresa Revilla Vergara, ed., *Acceso a la Justicia,* pp. 63–68. Lima: Oficina Técnica de Proyectos de Cooperación Internacional del Poder Judicial.

to view rules and institutions with which they are not familiar as exotic, silly, or incomprehensible. These parochial attitudes—which could be described as epistemological self-righteousness—occur at all levels. It is well known that many lawyers trained in civil law have great difficulties accepting that common law is a "scientific" legal system. Likewise, many common law lawyers believe that lawyers of the civil law tradition are good at memorizing rules, but not at applying them. Even lawyers who belong to the same legal tradition display considerable intolerance toward colleagues from other jurisdictions. Indeed, despite the apparent respect and close links that exist between Wall Street lawyers and city of London solicitors, I wonder whether they really regard each other as equally competent.

Given the parochialism prevalent among lawyers it is not surprising that when they are called upon to advise foreign governments they almost invariably offer their own laws as solutions to every problem they encounter. Moreover, their parochialism leads them often to behave arrogantly, dismissing as irrelevant or silly what they cannot understand. It should be noted, however, that international legal consultants often irritate local colleagues simply because of their ignorance of local practices. If in order to compete in global markets multinational companies train their employees in local customs, why shouldn't multilateral banks require their legal consultants to take similar courses?

Despite these problems, the contribution that international legal experts can make is invaluable. An area in which they do make an important contribution is in the diagnosis and assessment of the legal and political systems of recipient countries. In my experience, I find that the most interesting studies of my own country—Chile—are those written by scholars from other countries who, apart from being experts in their respective fields, take the time and trouble to understand local conditions.[29]

In the drafting of new legislation, international legal consultants also make a valuable contribution.[30] Yet, in order fully to take advantage of their skills they should form teams with local lawyers who should always have the ultimate responsibility for the drafting process. Foreign lawyers should not

29. See, for example, Ieetswart, H. 1981. "Labour Relations Litigation: Chile, 1970–1972." *Law and Society Review* 16: 625.
30. See generally, Seidman, Ann, Robert B. Seidman, and Thomas W. Walde, eds. 1999. *Making Development Work.* Cambridge, Mass.: Kluwer Law International.

attempt to lead the team. If they feel that their local counterparts are inefficient, slow, or uninterested they should pause and consider whether their feelings have any factual basis or whether they stem from their impatience and parochialism. It is true, of course, that often international teams such as the one I am proposing do not work effectively because recipient governments regard the drafting process as a purely technical task.[31]

Ownership

The concept of property has slipped, perhaps inadvertently, into the analysis of the reform processes in developing and transition countries. Experts on these processes now speak about local ownership of reform projects.[32] By local ownership they mean that all those directly affected by the project should be informed and consulted, and, one hopes, they should participate in its design and implementation. Local ownership is regarded as essential for the long-term sustainability of the project. These are splendid objectives—which I am sure many endorse, provided, of course, that the methods through which ownership is "acquired"are genuine. That is, provided that the efforts to secure local ownership of projects are not mere gestures by irresponsible politicians or unscrupulous local or international bureaucrats determined to demonstrate at any cost that local communities want, understand, and share the objectives of a particular project.

Although strategies to develop local ownership focus mainly on securing the support of the wider community—in other words, the stakeholders— there are two aspects of local ownership that are especially important in projects of legal reform. One concerns the understanding and technical expertise of local officials; and the other concerns the extent to which, in the long run, the local legal profession is capable and willing to sustain the reform process.

Technical Ownership

It is generally agreed that local input in the conception, design, and drafting stages of a project of legal reform is essential. The literature on legal technical assistance contains helpful tips on how to secure this objective. Policymakers should have a clear idea of what they are seeking to achieve; they should

31. See the section on "Technical Ownership" below.
32. World Bank. 2000. *World Development Report 1999/2000—Entering the 21st Century*, pp. 18–21. Oxford: Oxford University Press.

thoroughly understand the objectives and implications of the project; there should be widespread consultation of stakeholders, local lawyers should be involved in the drafting process, and there should be suitable mechanisms to evaluate the project's outcome.[33] Applying this advice in practice is, as ever, quite difficult. My participation, as an external legal adviser on two International Labour Organisation (ILO)-sponsored projects, one in Namibia and the other in South Africa, illustrates this point. The projects involved advising the departments of labour on the design, drafting, and implementation of policies to eliminate discrimination in employment and to improve employment opportunities for the victims of apartheid.

Both Namibia and South Africa have democratically elected governments which enjoy overwhelming popular support. These democratically elected officials also control the majority of seats in their respective legislatures. In both countries affirmative action (as it is called in Namibia) or employment equity (as it is called in South Africa) was seen as part of the wider process of dismantling apartheid. The aims of the legislation were twofold: to secure both equitable representation in employment for individuals belonging to groups excluded from the job market by the apartheid regime; and to achieve a culture of nondiscrimination in the workplace in line with constitutional principles and international labor standards. In both countries the potential beneficiaries of the new legislation are the majority of the population. The differences in the process of implementation of the two projects are quite interesting. While in Namibia the process was slow and plagued by intrabureaucratic problems, in South Africa the process was fast, efficient, and lively.

Affirmative Action in Namibia

In Namibia the project was launched in 1990, shortly after independence. The members of the ILO team immediately concentrated all their efforts in ensuring that government officials as well as all relevant stakeholders—employers' associations, trade unions, women's groups, representatives of the disabled—were informed and consulted about the new initiative. This stage of the project was not subject to rigid deadlines as the ILO team was

33. See, for example, Knieper, Rolf, and Mark Boguslavski. 1999. "The Concept of Legal Counselling in Transformation States." In Ann Seidman, Robert B. Seidman, and Thomas W. Walde, eds., *Making Development Work*, pp. 115–44. Cambridge, Mass: Kluwer Law International.

conscious that it was essential to ensure that all relevant groups were properly consulted. The outcome of this stage was, however, disappointing. Meetings between the ILO team and Department of Labour officials were difficult to arrange, had spotty attendance records, and were often unexpectedly cancelled. Other government departments showed little interest in the project. The Prime Minister's Office, which has overall responsibility for public sector appointments and, at the time, was busy making new appointments, was reluctant to participate in consultations. Indeed, at times, officials from the Prime Minister's Office seemed positively hostile toward the project. Equally disappointing was the lack of interest shown by grassroots organizations that represented those who stood to benefit most from the project. The response of employers' associations was, however, quite different. They attended every seminar and offered written comments and proposals to the Department of Labour. Though they regarded the project as unnecessary and potentially dangerous, they made many helpful suggestions, many of which were incorporated into the draft bill.

The project had envisaged that the bill on affirmative action would be drafted by a team of three: two local officials—one from the Department of Labour and the other from the Prime Minister's Office—and a foreign legal consultant. The team, however, never quite worked as such since the local officials assigned to the team had neither the time nor the interest to participate in the project. One was quite senior in his department and was understandably busy with other matters. The other, with neither seniority nor relevant experience, was dissatisfied in her current job and was actively seeking a transfer to another department. In any event the drafting team was doomed from the start as neither the Minister of Labour nor his Permanent Secretary understood the importance of having such a team. They simply expected the ILO to provide them with a draft bill in the shortest possible time—a week was considered long enough. Their sole objective was to get the bill approved by parliament as soon as possible.

In the event, ILO submitted a draft bill less than a year after the project was launched. The expectations of the Department of Labour of getting the bill approved by parliament were, however, not fulfilled because the process was blocked by the cabinet. Four years later, after the appointment of a new minister of labour, the project was revived. In 1998, after another round of consultations that were more successful than the first, the bill was finally approved by parliament, some eight years after the initiative was launched.

Employment Equity in South Africa

The development of employment equity legislation in South Africa was quite different. In 1996, with the support of local and international consultants, the government launched the process with the publication of a consultative document.[34] This document set out in general terms the objectives of the proposed legislation and requested feedback on specific topics. After receiving responses to the consultation document, the government appointed a drafting team made up of three South African lawyers all of whom worked in private practice. I joined the drafting team as external consultant.

The consultation document issued by the government, though comprehensive, was vague on the crucial and difficult question concerning the meaning of the phrase, "employment equity." Did employment equity require preferential treatment of those who had been discriminated against by the apartheid regime; or, was employment equity merely designed to secure equal opportunities without seeking to remedy the present consequences of past discriminatory practices? As this was a key matter of policy, the drafting team sought clarification from the Department of Labour. After further consultations with employers' associations, trade unions, and other stakeholders, the Department decided that employment equity should include preferential treatment for individuals who belonged to groups discriminated under apartheid. After the policy was clarified, the drafting team completed its task and submitted the first draft of the bill to the government. The draft submitted by the drafting team was discussed within the Department of Labour and in December 1997 was published in the Official Gazette. The publication of the draft opened up an intense period of consultations during which unions, employers' organizations, and other stakeholders expressed their views on the text and made concrete proposals for changes. After completing this stage of the process the government, with the assistance of the drafting team,

34. Republic of South Africa. 1996. "Employment and Equity Proposals." *Government Gazette*, Vol. 373, No. 17303.

prepared a new version of the bill. The bill was approved by parliament in October 1998, two years after the government published the first consultation document.[35]

Comparing the Two Experiences

The relative ease with which the South African Government developed its employment equity legislation contrasts sharply with the difficulties that the process encountered in Namibia. There are, of course, many factors that account for the differences between the two processes. In Namibia the process was launched at the wrong time, only days after independence, when the new political leaders who had virtually no administrative experience were busy dealing with more urgent issues. Moreover, the new political leaders could not count on the loyal or efficient support of the civil service personnel appointed by the preceding administration. The government in South Africa, by contrast, had a diverse and politically experienced leadership, many of whom had been active during the long years of struggle against apartheid. Moreover, the transition to democracy in South Africa had been preceded by a lively political debate—which involved all sections of society and yielded a complex, but interesting document. The most important factor that accounts for the differences between the two processes, though, is that while in South Africa affirmative action was a live political issue, in Namibia it had little, if any, resonance in civil society. In South Africa, the government was confronted with the need to establish a legal framework for affirmative action not only because the constitution allowed it, but because affirmative action had become a social fact that required urgent regulation. Indeed, soon after the advent of democracy, the private sector, in an attempt to distance itself from the previous regime and anticipating what it regarded as inevitable, had begun to implement policies of preferential treatment. The fact that affirmative action was already a social and political fact prompted the government to respond quickly by introducing rules to regulate the process. Thus, while in South Africa the government was catching up with social change, in Namibia the Department of Labour wanted to bring about change that, at the time,

---

35. Mandala, T. H. 1999. "Affirmative Action—A South African Perspective." *SMU Law Review* 52: 1539.

neither officials from the government nor stakeholders understood or regarded as urgent.

The irony of this story is that many of the reports, background papers, and drafts of the bill prepared during the slow process in Namibia provided invaluable assistance to policymakers and legal drafters in South Africa. Indeed, some key clauses in the South African act are based on drafts prepared during the years when the reform process in Namibia was at a standstill.

Legal Ownership

The role of lawyers in the process of development was a matter of great concern for the group of American law professors who in the 1960s launched the well-known, but short-lived law and development movement.[36] In their view, legal education in developing countries was inadequate as it placed excessive emphasis on rote learning of legal rules and doctrine, a method that, in addition to being dull, did not enable the students to understand social and economic reality properly. As a consequence, lawyers in developing countries were unable to make full use of the law either to protect the rights of citizens or to further the objectives of economic development.[37] As these law professors believed that lawyers had a major role to play in the development process they set out to help a select number of developing countries reform legal education. As we know, the enterprise was cut short because funds dried up and the professors became aware that it was futile to attempt to export legal liberalism.[38]

The diagnosis of legal education by the law and development movement is still valid today, as the quality of legal education in developing countries has not significantly improved since the mid-1970s. Although it is self-evident that a well-trained legal profession is essential for ensuring the long-term sustainability of legal reforms, the issue of legal education is notoriously

---

36. For an authoritative history of the law and development movement, see Trubek, David M., and Marc Galanter. 1977. "Scholars in Self-Estrangement." *American Journal of Comparative Law* 25: 492.

37. For a critical analysis of the educational objectives of the law and development movement, see Gardner, James. 1980. *Legal Imperialism: American Lawyers and Foreign Aid in Latin America*. Madison, Wis.: University of Wisconsin Press.

38. See generally, Merryman, John Henry. 1977. "Comparative Law and Social Change: On the Origins, Style, Decline and Revival of the Law and Development Movement." *American Journal of Comparative Law* 25: 457.

absent from current debates on legal reform. I am, of course, aware that the World Bank and other multilateral agencies support the establishment of judicial academies and sponsor training programs for judges and lawyers in various countries. These activities are undoubtedly useful, but do very little to improve the overall quality of legal education in recipient countries. Although I feel strongly that the reform of legal education in developing and transition countries is urgent, I do not believe that multilateral banks should add legal education to their already heavy agendas. The primary responsibility for this task lies with governments, universities, and local professional associations. International agencies can do much to support activities that contribute to improving the quality of legal education; they should not, however, attempt to lead the process.

Bilateral donors also have a part to play in this process. One important activity that bilateral donor agencies have supported, but which in recent years seems to be losing popularity among donors, is sponsoring transnational links between law schools. These links provide a lively and relatively inexpensive mechanism with immediate practical benefits—such as updating and facilitating curriculum development—as well as long-term intellectual benefits as they enable legal academics to organize conferences and launch joint research projects on topics of mutual interest. It must be noted that, contrary to what happens in legal technical assistance projects, these exchanges benefit both sides. This is the case of my own institution which, with a relatively small budget, currently has formal and informal links with law schools in more than 20 countries. I would like to think that our partners have benefited from these links as much as we have. For my colleagues and me at Warwick University these links are essential as they allow us fully to develop our teaching and research potential.

Concluding Remarks

Legal reform is slow, because it is a process. I restate this platitude because, in practice, it is often forgotten. Recipient governments tend to forget it because most politicians operate within restricted time frames and naturally want to take credit for the introduction of major legal reforms. Multilateral agencies also often behave as if they are unaware that legal reform is a complex and slow enterprise. Their impatience is probably attributable to budget restrictions and a heavy agenda. I am afraid, however, that their impatience may also stem from a misplaced devotion to theory. Indeed, while it may be true that, theoretically, market-friendly legal systems have some attributes in common; in practice, the interplay among law, the state, and markets is complex and far from predictable. Hence my skepticism about excessive legal drafting and my insistence on taking local contexts seriously.

I am concerned that those who are impatient with the slow pace of reform may end up endorsing authoritarian regimes on grounds of efficiency and speed. Indeed, it was not long ago that some multilateral agencies applauded Third World tyrants because of their ability to get things done. Today things have changed. Democratization is now the prevailing trend. Yet, many of these new democracies are fragile. It would be a disaster if impatience led to the re-emergence of authoritarian regimes—which, as before, would cynically proclaim their adherence and loyalty to the reform process in order to achieve international legitimacy.

Amartya Sen has recently reminded us about the importance of democracy in the process of development.[39] I am certain that most of those who are impatient with the slow pace of legal reforms share his views and are keen to safeguard and further enhance the current wave of democratization. The successful implementation of the current package of legal reforms should contribute toward cementing the link between development and democracy. It should also provide the foundation for ensuring that the benefits of globalization are equitably and fairly shared. The reform process should be carried out with vigor and commitment—both its objectives and pace should, however, be realistic.

39. Sen, Amartya. *Development as Freedom*, pp. 146–59. Oxford: Oxford University Press.

Making People the Focus

A Risk Worth Taking

Hon. Luis Paulino Mora*

Chief Justice of Costa Rica

Introduction

It is well known that democracy is a prerequisite for equitable, balanced, and sustainable social development. Latin America has recently succeeded in paving the way for democracy, notwithstanding various difficulties that have yet to be overcome and that continue to undermine efforts to promote democratic consolidation. As Enrique Iglesias[1] pointed out during a recent visit to Costa Rica, the level of social violence in our region is three times higher than in the United States and Europe, the concentration of wealth has created a huge income gap, and economic growth continues to lag despite efforts to accelerate it.

Against this background, our Region must also deal with the impact of economic globalization, a phenomenon that simultaneously offers many opportunities and poses pressing challenges to the survival of our economies.

Generally speaking, the people are afraid, and there seems to be no clear perception of how to deal with the changing circumstances we are experiencing. As a result, passions run high in discussions of such issues as the size of the state, the role of the market, participation by civil society, political corruption, and disillusionment with democratic institutions. At the same time, it has not been possible to bridge the gap between the benefits expected of democratic regimes and reality as it actually unfolds.

In this setting it is absolutely *crucial* that ways be found promptly to strengthen the rule of law and, in so doing, the judiciary as well.

---

* Translated into English from the original text in Spanish and edited in English.

1. Presentation on May 19, 2000 at the National Theater, San José. Enrique Iglesias is president of the Inter-American Development Bank.

However, the loss of trust in the judiciary—as high as 85–90 percent[2] in some countries—reported by some surveys, along with the aforementioned developments, has created a dangerous vacuum, which populists and supporters of the military are exploiting.

For example, during the 1990s a number of presidents in Latin America asserted at various times and to varying degrees that by virtue of their popular support, their right to govern was above the law and they were not beholden to their parties. There is no reason to think that these are atypical or fleeting symptoms.

As the gap between the promise of democratic regimes and what they actually deliver continues to widen, the landscape of Latin America is unfortunately beginning to closely resemble that of its past.

Our Region urgently needs to reform its trading practices and restore credibility in its democratic institutions—particularly those responsible for ensuring that the rule of law prevails—so that it can consolidate democracy and take advantage of the benefits of the new world economic order. I firmly believe that justice and economic development go hand in hand, for if economic development and market forces are to thrive, they both require a modern, reliable, efficient, and strong system of justice that not only guarantees its citizens access to and the protection of the system, but also ensures a climate that is hospitable to investment and development.

A weak legal system—as evidenced by a high crime rate, excessive bureaucracy, and restricted access to justice—adversely affects investment and national development. Indeed, the impact of "noneconomic" forces on investment is becoming increasingly apparent. In Colombia, for example, an increase of 10 homicides per 100,000 inhabitants translates into a 4 percent decline in investments. If the figure rises to 20–80 homicides per 100,000 inhabitants, gross domestic product decreases by as much as 2 percent annually.[3]

Moreover, the legal bureaucracy—whether within or outside the judicial system—increases transaction costs, thereby affecting the national and inter-

2. In Venezuela, for example. See Prillaman, William. 1999. *Judicial Reform and Democratic Consolidation in Latin America.* Charlottesville, Va.: University of Virginia.

3. Rubio, M. 1995. *Crimen y crecimiento en Colombia–Coyuntura económica.* Cited by Martínez, M. 1998. *Rule of Law and Economic Efficiency.* Washington, D.C.: Inter-American Development Bank.

national competitiveness of a country's products and forcing businessmen to waste time and money figuring out how to evade the laws instead of investing in producing goods or devising ways to improve their products.

If we add to this the fact that cases can drag on for years as they make their way through the judicial system, the cost to businesses of protecting their commercial or related rights becomes extremely high.

It is absolutely essential to strengthen the rule of law in Latin America, in the interests of both democratic consolidation and economic growth. Accordingly, what should our strategic focus be? Why have our efforts at legal reform been inadequate? What does the judiciary require to be efficient and trustworthy?

For the past 15 years we have discussed the prerequisites for an efficient and reliable judiciary, including economic and functional independence, accessibility, updated and less bureaucratic codes of procedure, a career path and training for judges, an efficient disciplinary system, establishment of parameters for measuring how judges perform, and separation of administrative functions to enable judges to devote all their time to the administration of justice. Finally, although most of our countries have to varying degrees adopted measures that have had very positive results, these measures have neither increased our credibility significantly among the population nor enabled us to make up for lost time.

I shall now focus primarily on the Costa Rican experience in order to shed light on these questions, for I am confident that there are common denominators applicable to judicial reform in general.

Factors That Have Had an Impact on Judicial Reform

One key lesson which the judicial reform process has taught us in recent years is that we have been underestimating its complexity and scope. While focusing on implementing measures proposed by domestic and external bodies and advisers to the letter (independence, access, and so forth), we have failed to take the following factors into account:

Increase in Crime and Social Conflict

As the population has grown and the gap between the rich and the poor has widened, a heavy demand has been placed on the judicial system. Crime and social violence have increased far more than ever expected. In addition,

Costa Rica has an extremely litigious populace which, for historical reasons, has tended to resolve disputes through the courts instead of turning to alternative dispute resolution arrangements or (fortunately) taking justice into its own hands. In the past year alone, 710,000 new cases were brought before the country's courts—this for a population of approximately three million inhabitants. This figure also reflects the fact that Costa Ricans are well-informed about their rights and can exercise them because they enjoy easy access to the courts at no cost to themselves, as in the case of the Constitutional Court.[4] Thus, improved access and a citizenry better informed about its rights result in more lawsuits, and this in turn escalates social conflict and places a substantial burden on the judicial system. This burden is a positive one, in that it is a sign that the people have faith in the legal system as a peaceful mechanism for dispute resolution.

Reforms Based on a Purely Technical Perspective,
Without Reference to the Political Context

Since the second half of the twentieth century, Costa Rica's judiciary has taken the lead regarding all legislative initiatives in the area of judicial reform, with the exception of the 1989 reforms of the Constitutional Court. Although this situation, which is unique to my country, has been very positive from a technical and legal standpoint, judges and magistrates have been trained in such a way that the political ramifications of judicial reform have simply been overlooked. We have approached the reform process as a technical exercise, whereas in reality it has both political and technical elements. "Political" here does not, of course, refer to partisan matters, but rather, to far-reaching changes in the rules of social interaction, which boils down to the question of who obtains what, how, and when. Moreover, we have done little to convince others of the importance of judicial reform for national development, and have treated it as something separate from our day-to-day lives and the government reform process. We have forgotten to persuade others that strengthening justice is a strategic necessity, not only in order to

---

4. Writs of habeas corpus or actions for enforcement of *amparo*—which pertain to the defense of fundamental rights-are informal and may be submitted by any means: written (including via fax or telegram) or verbal. The court receives complaints 24 hours a day and is even accessible to minors, who need not be represented by a lawyer. In its 10 years of existence, the Constitutional Court has received nearly 65,000 cases.

guarantee the stability of democracy, but also to drive economic development. We have limited ourselves to preparing bills and sending them to the legislature, without undertaking the lobbying required to ensure that our proposals receive priority attention.[5] When the bills are finally adopted, they will have taken so long to make their way through the legislative process that reforms are introduced four or five years after they were needed.

The Lack of Strategic Planning to Make Room for Integral,
Ongoing Judicial Reform

Judicial reform has been approached as a mechanistic undertaking directed at solving specific problems. There has been no systematic focus or planning.

Only in April 2000 did the Costa Rican judiciary adopt a strategic plan with clear objectives covering a five-year period. Junior personnel in all areas, judges throughout the country, and magistrates participated in this effort to develop a mission and vision for the judiciary with strategic objectives and clear targets to be achieved by 2005. This is the first time that the leadership of the judiciary will work on the basis of a plan devised through a participatory process bringing together a representative group of officials and judges from all regions to ascertain our strengths and weaknesses and define our short- and medium-term goals.

In other words, until recently efforts at reform have been piecemeal and limited in scope, reflecting a restricted vision dependent on the personal initiatives of magistrates or presiding judges. If efforts focused on penal reform, the problems experienced by the civil courts probably were not discussed, and vice versa. Or, if efforts were made to improve the codes of procedure, then administrative reforms or technological innovations did not receive the same close attention. As a result, the budget lacked a broad focus as far as investments were concerned and essentially reflected the subjective preferences of the magistrates sitting on the Budget Committee. For example, if they were criminal judges, their specialty area very likely would receive funding,

5. The conservative approach displayed by the leadership of the judiciary to its political responsibilities has been a major factor here. The leadership is wary of getting involved with deputies or politicians, since it clearly draws no distinction between the judicial functions of judges and their political functions, which also include diplomatic functions. In Costa Rica, the Political Constitution assigns management and administrative responsibilities relating to the judiciary to judges, with the result that judges perform both judicial and political functions simultaneously.

meaning that investments depended for the most part on the enthusiasm, vision, and individual preferences of each committee member. Inasmuch as the full Court had no concrete action plan either, budget bills usually were adopted as proposed by the Budget Committee, whose membership has tended to vary from one year to the next. The prevalence of this mechanistic approach narrowly targeting specific problems undoubtedly had a negative impact on progress with respect to the independence of the judiciary, access to justice, the protection of fundamental rights, and other areas.

Strategic planning is therefore essential to a professional, nonimprovisational, approach to work, and to tackling priorities in an integral, planned manner, thereby preventing the diversion of resources to less important tasks.

Relying Too Much on Imitation and Too Little on Innovation

We imitated what we observed, without stopping to think. Judicial form was for a long time limited to solving specific problems (the mechanistic approach), primarily through procedural and legislative change, and we have followed that example, perhaps in the belief that because that is how things were done in developed countries, it was automatically the best solution for us as well.

Taking this approach, until recently we assumed it was sufficient to study procedural and substantive advances in more developed countries and import them with some adaptations in order to keep our own systems of justice up to date. The General Law on Public Administration, the Code of Civil Procedure, the Civil Code, and many other instruments responded in part to this tradition. Even the existing Penal Code was, at the time it was promulgated, identical—with the exception of two or three provisions of its own—to that of Córdoba, Argentina. Our judges and lawyers were trained overseas, mainly in Europe, and their experience has led us to reproduce the same approaches in our systems of justice without even considering whether those approaches were consistent with our national character and our own history.

Because we did not recognize that there was no magic formula for judicial reform, in many instances we reproduced problems from one country to the next by importing solutions foreign to our culture and history. This made us overconfident that we were doing the right thing and prevented us from seeking our own solutions.

Spain is an obvious case in point. For years we took every opportunity to follow its example. We adopted Spain's solutions with few modifications, even though the Costa Rican mentality is very different from that of Spain. The Spanish system—as the Spanish themselves acknowledge—is formal and bureaucratic, and not very accessible, which probably resulted from a different approach to justice. By contrast, our informality and level of freedom require a more accessible, fast-moving, simple, and nonbureaucratic system. Costa Ricans and Spaniards therefore have very different levels of tolerance in such matters.

The *Libro Blanco de la Justicia*[6] is one example of something we have tried to copy from a system that is very different from our own, from what we desire, and from our historical reality. In so doing, we behaved like a colony, and there are still many who believe that our neighbors have the answers, that we need not introduce any innovations or, as doing so would of course imply, risk seeking our own solutions.

Losing Sight of the True Target of Justice: Individuals, and the Need to Solve Their Problems

For many years the legal culture of Latin America has been a rigid product of the Napoleonic era. Most of our judges are still trained in this authoritarian tradition at university. The entire system was in general designed to apply the law in a mechanistic fashion, and has paid insufficient attention to the individual or the social conflict underlying court cases. Form became substance, leaving an endless stream of unresolved disputes mired in meaningless bureaucratic obstacles. Our codes of procedure—which, as I have noted, usually were imported—have played a major role in encouraging this rigorous and excessive formality.

Our citizens lack access to justice and find it difficult to invest resources and time in lawsuits. They are forced to deal with cold, distant judges who are out of touch with social reality, reluctant to change, and totally unaware of their true role in a democratic society.

Our Napoleonic heritage—vertical and authoritarian—has bequeathed to us judges who consider themselves "lords and masters" of their domain and

6. See "La Experiencia Espanola de Reforma Judicial: El Libro Blanco de la Justicia," L. López Guerra, OAS, sladlciw@oas.org.

are convinced that isolation and absence of controls are the natural consequences of judicial independence. This vision is still attractive to many
judges, since they can impose their will, enjoying uncontested sovereignty
not only with respect to the cases they choose to consider but also over the
office they manage. Also prevalent is the notion that judges deal with case
files instead of people. The exercise of judicial discretion has been discouraged, and judges have been cautioned to avoid the "contamination" that
might result from speaking with individuals and dealing with reality instead
of considering only the facts contained in case files. Another major constraint has been that our system has compelled the parties involved in a dispute and judges to express their views in writing. The ideology underlying
the system reinforces this behavior, for according to this ideology, judges do
not serve as guarantors of citizens' rights in a democracy; rather, they serve
the objectives of the system.

Failure to Invest Adequate Resources

Finally, one factor that has significantly affected the outcome of judicial reform efforts has been our failure to invest adequate resources.

I am referring not only to the lack of planned investments I mentioned
earlier, but also to the shortsightedness of national and international policy
in failing to recognize *soon enough* how important the strategic role of justice
is as an instrument of both democratic stability and economic development.

Until recently, the judiciary was viewed with the same passivity with
which it viewed itself, and the political, social, and economic consequences
of poor or mediocre performance by the judiciary in developing countries
were underestimated. Consequently, for years our countries kept the judiciary on only a "maintenance" budget, making a few mechanistic and therefore isolated efforts to improve the system, efforts that—for the reasons I
have indicated—have proved completely inadequate for the purpose of
building a modern, up-to-date, reliable judiciary. Excessive reliance was
placed on economic reform, which clearly could not—indeed, could never—
resolve the problems faced by Latin America, a developing region in constant turmoil. We have come to realize that reforming the state is, once
again, a prerequisite for sustainable development and good governance, and
only now do we acknowledge the strategic role that the judiciary must play
in this process.

The Costa Rican Strategy: Making People the Focus of the Justice System

After meeting virtually all the requirements experts deemed essential for an effective judiciary—in other words, after trying almost everything—we were surprised and dismayed to find that the public still lacked confidence in the judicial system and that the system had a heavier backlog of work than it had faced prior to the reforms. The factors mentioned earlier are some of the main reasons this happened. Our focus now is twofold: (a) we are pursuing efforts already underway to promote the economic and functional independence of the judiciary, judicial career paths, accessibility, judicial training, discipline, procedural reform, investment in technology, and other areas; and, even more important, (b) we are striving to encourage a philosophical shift in order to reorient the judiciary toward its true purpose, namely to serve the public, making the individual—not judges—the central focus of its attention.

Management planning on both these fronts is in progress, to which end a strategic planning process has been launched with broad participation at all levels (administrative and judicial) in order to guide all activities, decisions, and investments relating to the judiciary, as described above. The concept of a system of justice as a public service focusing on the individual clearly implies a profound change of course. The justice system can no longer be considered a power unto itself and must refocus its mission on the human person. Consequently, independence and all the other traditional features of the judiciary will play *instrumental* roles in creating a sound system of justice—which, besides being efficient and effective, must also be transparent to the public and earn its trust.

To achieve this goal the courts must first prove that they are accountable and, inevitably, must become independent in the true sense of the word. Second, civil society must be incorporated openly and transparently in the work of the judicial system (this undoubtedly means establishing a strategic alliance between the two). Third, a shift in mentality and organizational culture is required to enable the system to develop a customer service orientation.

Accountability

In a democracy, only the people hold sovereign power. All other powers are delegated and those who hold them are accountable for their actions.

Accordingly, not a single public official or other authority is exempt from control. No one has this privilege, not even Parliament. Moreover, the people do not merely hold sovereign power; they also finance our work through the taxes they pay, and they are entitled to honest answers regarding how their money is spent.

Therefore, in a democracy the independence of the judiciary must exist by virtue of, and as a guarantee for, the people, in order to preclude any doubt that the courts have acted fairly and transparently.

Unfortunately, we have focused intently on independence for years, treating it as virtually the only priority objective, and have used it as a shield enabling us to work behind civil society's back to prevent ourselves from being questioned or held accountable for our actions. On occasion, independence has been used as a weapon during strikes, in an effort to prevent anyone from interfering with our work, particularly if the dispute concerned the establishment of remuneration guidelines or proper disciplinary procedures.

Because the courts are considered a public service in a democracy, secrecy is out of the question, which means that the independence of the judiciary must always be viewed as a tool and not as an end in itself. The objective must be to provide the population with a reliable justice system.

Accordingly, independence neither is nor should be the major focus of the judicial reform agenda, and we should move on to tackle other priority matters of concern to our citizens. Studies show that the independence of the judiciary is not the public's major concern at present. The following issues are more important in their view: the degree of access to the justice system, the efficiency and speed with which cases are resolved, cost, and the professional caliber of judges.[7] *The public believes that independence alone does not guarantee adequate justice for all.* In fact, many people's concern is not that there is a lack of independence, but that there is too much, as the writer Fransico de Quevado has already warned, "Excess was always poisonous," or as Mckechie (1996) observes, "Independence without responsibility is an illusion, and independent powers should be given only to those who account for how they exercise them."[8]

7. A survey conducted by officials in the State of the Nation program indicates that the public's main concerns are equality of access and greater flexibility and speed.

8. Toharía, J. 1999. In "La independencia judicial y la buena justicia." *Justicia y Sociedad,* No. 3.

A Strategic Alliance with Civil Society

Neither the state nor the market has managed thus far to resolve the major issues on society's agenda. We firmly believe that it is essential to incorporate civil society in an open and transparent manner at all levels of government (in the broadest sense of the word), particularly in the judicial arena. This is necessary because, as I have already pointed out, the judiciary has been silent, has hidden itself from public scrutiny, and worked in secret, partly as a result of having dangerously distorted the concept of independence and, undoubtedly, failed to make the individual the focus of its attention.

We have learned that listening to the people, hearing their needs, their concerns, and their suggestions, and including them as our allies in our reform effort, is the appropriate way to restore confidence in the judiciary and clear up any distortions the public may harbor concerning the way we work.

We have taken a risk to accomplish this, by making our operations transparent to the community and the media, and also by looking inward. On this last point, as I have already noted, we have initiated a participatory dialogue at all levels within government and the judicial system to elicit the views of staff regarding existing problems and determine the strategic objectives that should be adopted to resolve them. This effort resulted in the preparation of the first strategic planning document on planned management for the judiciary.

However, our boldest step has been our unprecedented effort to open up our operations to the public. We began by being totally transparent in our dealings with the press, providing it with access and information. We are also engaged in an ongoing dialogue with reporters from all the media—print, television, and radio, rural as well as national—regarding our plans and projects, progress made, and obstacles encountered. Our hope is that this will increase understanding of the judiciary and thus ensure that the public is accurately informed. We also want to encourage the media to take an interest in the positive aspects of justice and its role in society, in order to counteract their practice of focusing on crime and accident reports as if this information about the system were all that mattered.

We have also launched a series of meetings with other key actors in society, including lawyers, politicians, and businessmen, to hear their views and inform them about our plans and objectives. For the same reason, the

Supreme Council of the Judiciary has visited all of the country's communities, with very positive results. We learned, for example, that both rural and urban inhabitants have a mistaken view of the role of the judiciary, in that they associate us with the increase in crime and with a lack of supervision and patrols—in other words, with problems that are the responsibility of other components of the judicial system.

We are using these opportunities to hear the people's concerns and teach them about the role of the judiciary, and are also developing an educational video concerning the judiciary (to be distributed to schools, communities, and the press) in an effort to correct misinformation regarding our role. One interesting fact in this connection gleaned from opinion polls is that the judiciary is less popular among persons who have not had any dealings with the courts than with those who have. This indicates that considerable misunderstanding exists about the role of the judiciary and that the public is unfamiliar with the judiciary's activities and programs.

We are also taking steps to improve our Web page[9] so that girls and boys throughout Costa Rica will have access to the history of the judiciary, its functions, programs, and projects, and will be able to communicate online with judges to express their opinions, offer suggestions, or criticize how the judiciary operates. By strengthening our Web presence, people anywhere in the world will be able to reach us and consult records of our proceedings and jurisprudence.

As another indication of our desire to reach out to the public, to ordinary citizens, we have been given a one-hour time slot each month[10] on the country's most popular radio program, during which callers can speak directly to judges on any matter of interest to them. We also use this time to inform listeners of progress made, as well as projects and programs.

A Shift in Mentality and Organizational Culture in order
to Develop a Customer Service Mentality

If we are to shift from a philosophy that the judiciary is all-powerful to one that holds that the judiciary must serve the population and that civil society

---

9. <www.poder-judicial.go.cr>.

10. This slot will be available only this year, since it is a collaborative effort with the company. Lack of funds will, unfortunately, prevent us from continuing to participate.

must be able to contribute fully, major reforms naturally are required. These should focus in particular on the service we provide, and we must therefore develop appropriate diagnostic and monitoring tools and disciplinary measures to improve how we assist and respond to the public.

A Judicial Services Inspection Unit is therefore needed to facilitate communications between users and the judiciary, detect problems, and find solutions to enhance service effectiveness, through both corrective and preventive measures.

The Unit will complement the Judicial Inspection Office, ensuring that matters not requiring disciplinary measures are dealt with the utmost dispatch.

In addition to contributing to the modernization process, the Unit will also strengthen the people's trust in the administration of justice, encourage the public to participate in supervising the provision of services, and foster the rational use of public resources. It will also help both to enable the people to exercise their right to petition the judiciary so that they can express their views on the quality of services received, and to ensure that their requests are dealt with and resolved.

The proposal calls for the establishment of a Central Inspection Unit as well as 11 subunits to be set up gradually throughout Costa Rica as part of a three-stage process ending in 2002.

The proposal is now under consideration, with budgetary issues posing the primary obstacle.

In introducing the measures described above, Costa Rica is relying on the community as its best ally in the effort to modernize its judicial system and strengthen the rule of law. We know now that the silence behind which we cloaked our operations for so many years generated distrust and ignorance of the role of the judiciary, seriously undermining its credibility and reliability. Although we do not expect this strategy to be a panacea, it is a major tool for developing a more democratic, open, and transparent judicial system. The fact that it calls for ongoing supervision should encourage us to make continuous improvements.

Before I conclude my statement, I would like to mention briefly a number of other efforts underway to improve traditional indicators relating to judicial reform:

- Procedural reforms to promote orality and simplification of cases.
  A General Code of Procedure has been prepared which increases the number of statements that may be presented orally and is designed to bring judges and parties together more easily and to accelerate case processing. A Code of Administrative Procedure has also been prepared to update the Law Regulating the Administrative Court System, assigning the public a greater role in monitoring administrative procedures.

- More judges.
  We have learned that a severe shortage of judges is one of the reasons the judicial system is faced with a backlog of work. We therefore decided to increase the budget to recruit at least 100 judges initially, a step that will lead to more appropriate workloads.

- Investment in technology.
  We are investing heavily in technology thanks to support from the *Corte–Bid* Project. Our projects include direct notification to users' servers; consolidation of electronic case processing, allowing remote access from anywhere in the country or the world; access to the legal information system, enabling judges and the public to consult the jurisprudence of the four chambers of the Supreme Court or the Court of Cassation (*Tribunal de Casación*), the opinions of the Office of the Attorney General, and current legislation from their computers; links between judicial circuits via telephone to consolidate Internet connections, and implementation of the final phase of work permitting automatic withdrawal of funds and remote access for major users.

- Elimination of atypical jurisdictional responsibilities.
  We are also considering eliminating atypical jurisdictional responsibilities, which increase the cost of administering justice by diverting resources from other priority areas and distorting the role of the judiciary.[11]

---

11. One example is the removal of uncontested traffic cases (accounting for over 200,000 cases annually) from the competence of the courts. Another example is the

Conclusion

1. There is a consensus in Latin America that the rule of law must be strengthened as the key to consolidating democracy and ensuring economic efficiency.

2. Costa Rica, motivated by a desire to ensure that its judicial system is transparent, efficient, egalitarian, and worthy of trust, and that it contributes to the country's economic and democratic development, has therefore launched a carefully planned—not improvised—effort adapted to its particular needs. This undertaking is comprehensive, covers all the factors that are essential for an efficient legal system, and focuses on the individual, in a strategic alliance with civil society.

---

relocation of the Office of Notaries, which handles disciplinary matters pertaining to notaries; although this is not a matter within the competence of the courts, the Office receives substantial budgetary resources, diverting funds that could be used for the administration of justice.

The Example of the Organization for the Harmonization of Business Law in Africa (OHADA)

Seydou Ba

Presiding Judge

Common Court of Justice and Arbitration

OHADA

In the interest of greater cooperation among African states, countries in West and Central Africa, together with the Islamic Federal Republic of the Comoros, decided to harmonize their legal systems in the area of business law. To this end, the Treaty establishing the Organization for the Harmonization of Business Law (OHADA) was signed on October 17, 1993 in Port Louis.

Accession to the Treaty is open to all member states of the Organization of African Unity (OAU) that were not original signatories of the Treaty, and to any other state invited to become a member of OHADA by common consent of all the signatory states. The Treaty entered into force on September 18, 1995.

OHADA, which at present has 16 members, seeks to provide a secure legal and judicial environment for businesses.

The initiators of the Treaty on the Harmonization of Business Law in Africa justified their effort by emphasizing the need to eliminate legal and judicial insecurity in the business sector.

The causes of judicial insecurity had been identified as stemming, in particular, from a lack of knowledge or understanding of applicable legal texts (because official gazettes were not published or were published irregularly and the legal decisions comprising jurisprudence went unpublished). This resulted in a climate of uncertainty, which was incompatible with the minimum level of predictability regarding legal issues that is necessary for economic activity.

There were many reasons for this judicial insecurity, including the following:

- Inadequate training of judges and judicial personnel;
- Instability of jurisprudence; and
- Dissatisfaction within the judicial profession, in terms of both technical support and the material circumstances of judges.

Such shortcomings contributed to a climate of uncertainty regarding the outcome of judicial proceedings. This uncertainty has been acknowledged as one of the major causes of the deterioration of the business environment, resulting in paralysis or the exodus of some businesses operating in key sectors. To address this problem, it was deemed necessary to introduce mechanisms to enable all the states concerned to adopt the simplest, most modern, and most appropriate legal procedures—those that were the most effective and most easily accessible to businesses wanting to invest or already operating in OHADA countries. Thus the goal was to ensure a secure and predictable legal environment for businesses through the adoption of uniform acts. Measures to improve the security of the legal environment of businesses are the subject of the first part of this paper.

While adopting uniform legal texts admittedly has many positive aspects, it was not sufficient to ensure complete security. Above all, the judicial environment had to be improved by developing a corps of judges and judicial personnel capable of appropriately applying the uniform laws; establishing a body responsible for ensuring uniform interpretation and enforcement of uniform legal texts; and, finally, developing simplified procedures for collecting debt and strengthening enforcement mechanisms. Measures to improve the security of the judicial environment of businesses are the subject of the second part of this paper.

Legal Security

Uniform law took concrete form with the adoption of texts called uniform acts. These acts were prepared by the Permanent Secretariat of OHADA in consultation with the governments of the states that were parties to the Treaty which established OHADA. The Council of Ministers, a body established under the Treaty, discussed and adopted the acts on the advice of the Common Court of Justice and Arbitration (CCJA). It is useful to keep in mind that national parliaments are excluded from the proceedings for adopting uniform acts. The Council of Ministers has sole competence in this area. This makes it possible to avoid the drawbacks of indirect procedures that could lead to the adoption of conflicting legal texts that would be difficult to implement.

The acts become effective immediately after they are published in the Official Gazette of OHADA, without the need for additional regulatory legislation from the treaty party states. They are directly applicable and binding in all OHADA countries, notwithstanding any contradictory provisions in existing or future national laws.

Uniform law is of considerable benefit to private investors. It ensures them better legal information and a completely revised body of business law. The adoption of identical rules for business law has many advantages, such as the following:

- The elimination of conflicts of laws, which frequently occur in international trade relations. Judges no longer need to determine which national law is applicable to the parties, since the applicable law is identical for all OHADA member countries.
- The ability of businesses to know which laws apply or will apply to their international activities. It is sufficient to know what law is applicable in a given country.

The revision of business law is evident in three critical areas: the status of businesses, stronger guarantees for creditors, and the relevance of the collective procedures for discharging liabilities to the problems businesses face.

Reforming the status of businesses calls for reforming structures and professional relations. The adoption of modern business laws governing commercial firms and economic interest groups is all the more commendable if one considers that except for Senegal, Mali, and Guinea, the remaining member states of OHADA had been operating under outdated provisions of the civil code and the laws of July 24, 1867 and March 7, 1925.

One particularly welcome development is that sales of goods and services between business professionals are now carefully regulated from the development of the sales contract to its execution or cancellation.

Finally, the adoption of a unified accounting system will considerably facilitate the evaluation and comparison of company asset and liability positions, not only within the same country, but also among countries.

Strengthening debt security for creditors is also a concern of OHADA. The limited scope of this paper prevents us from giving a detailed account of the Treaty's provisions in this area; however, it is possible to indicate a few of the innovations. The first demand guarantee, derived from international business practice, was introduced, definitively established, and regulated under substantive law. The ranking of creditors holding secured debt, somewhat complicated by unclear provisions in the civil code, was considerably simplified and clarified. Various warrants (for the hotel, oil, and agricultural sectors, for example) formerly governed by antiquated and widely scattered legal documents were brought together under common rules and given a new name—schedules of equipment and merchandise inventories used as collateral.

Finally, outdated nineteenth century bankruptcy legislation inherited from the commercial code was replaced with collective procedures for discharging liabilities. The new procedures are adapted to the range of constraints businesses face, without sacrificing the interests of creditors.

Thus, two mechanisms were introduced to prevent businesses that are unable to continue their operations from failing to fulfill their debt obligations: internal measures that alert executives of the enterprise, and preventive regulatory procedures that allow the company to devise a reorganization plan with the agreement of creditors.

Naturally, if cessation of payments does occur, provision is made for standard procedures to deal with the situation, namely court-supervised rehabilitation and liquidation of assets. However, court-supervised rehabilitation is based on the reorganization plan, which allows traditional delaying mechanisms (time extensions and forgiveness of debt) as well as other technical, financial, and legal measures that are favorable to the recovery of the business.

A final reason that private investors stand to benefit from the fact that a group of African countries (currently 16) have adopted uniform and binding business laws is the establishment of the Trade and Personal Property Register (RCCM) established under the Uniform Act on General Commercial Law, which entered into force on January 1, 1998.

Prior to the adoption of this Act, the majority of the states that were parties to the Treaty were governed by the French law of March 18, 1919, under which the trade register was merely a directory of information without legal force.

The Uniform Act adopted by OHADA indicates that the purpose of the RCCM is to record the registration of individuals engaged in commercial activities, commercial firms, other corporate bodies, and branches of foreign companies exercising a commercial activity within the territory of the signatory states.

In addition, the Uniform Act provides that the RCCM will also record registrations of securities on movables such as pledges of goodwill as collateral, goodwill vendor's liens, equipment pledges, and especially pledges of stocks and company shares, reservation of title clauses, and leasing contracts. This represents an innovation for all the states concerned except Senegal and Mali.

The overall objective of the RCCM initiative is to offer businesses the most extensive commercial information on the legal and financial status of their business partners, as well as the opportunity to put in place reliable legal guarantees to facilitate commercial transactions. To support this objective, the initiative sets up a national RCCM file in each state, and a regional file in the Office of the Clerk of CCJA.

Judicial Security

To achieve the goal of creating a secure judicial environment for businesses, OHADA established a Regional School for the Advanced Training of Judges and Judicial Personnel (*École Régionale Supérieure de Magistrature,* or ERSUMA). The school offers specialized training for judges and judicial personnel to enable them to properly apply the uniform legislation for the business sector.

A CCJA was established to ensure the uniform interpretation and application of the Treaty, its implementing regulations, and the uniform acts.

Finally, it was necessary to set forth simplified procedures for debt recovery, and to strengthen enforcement measures without challenging the existing organization of the judicial systems of the treaty party states.

This paper will briefly describe, in turn, the Regional School for the Advanced Training of Judges and Judicial Personnel and—the cornerstone of the reform effort—the Common Court of Justice and Arbitration (CCJA) of

OHADA. Finally, it will discuss the simplified debt recovery procedures and enforcement measures.

Regional School for the Advanced Training of Judges and Judicial Personnel

The school's mission is to train judges and judicial personnel from the states that are parties to the Treaty for the Harmonization of Business Law in Africa.

The establishment of this school represents an innovation for several reasons:

1. If judicial personnel receive the same professional and legal training, irrespective of country of origin, one can assume that this will guarantee satisfactory application of the harmonized business law by courts of first instance and courts of appeal. These jurisdictions typically play a decisive role in lawsuits since not all cases reach the court of cassation, the highest appeals court. Moreover, when an appeal on points of law is made, before the jurisdiction responsible for ruling on appeal intervenes, various measures may already have been undertaken by trial courts, and these measures will have a decisive bearing on the final outcome of the lawsuit.

2. The training offered by the school is designed both for judges and for all judicial personnel (including court clerks, receivers, judicial experts, attorneys, notaries, and process servers).

3. Finally, the school can train judicial personnel in other areas of uniform law that are not within the purview of OHADA, such as intellectual property (the OAPI[1] Treaty), banking law (the WAEMU[2] Treaty), and insurance law (the CIMA[3] Treaty). This extends the scope of judicial training offered by the school. Article 41 of the OHADA Treaty places no restriction on the subject areas in which the school may offer

---

1. African Intellectual Property Organization (*Organisation africaine pour la propriété intellectuelle*), (OAPI).
2. West African Economic and Monetary Union (WAEMU).
3. Inter-African Conference on Insurance Markets (CIMA).

training. The school is responsible for training and upgrading the knowledge and skills of judges and judicial personnel of the treaty party states and can therefore provide both preservice training and continuing education.

The Common Court of Justice and Arbitration (CCJA)

The adoption of common legal texts by the states that were parties to the Treaty establishing OHADA is not sufficient to guarantee effective harmonization of business law, a factor that will help ensure a secure environment for foreign investment (which was the goal of the initiators of the Treaty).

In addition, it is particularly important to ensure that the uniform legal texts are consistently applied and interpreted, which means that the same body of jurisprudence should serve as a reference throughout the OHADA area.

Introduction to the Common Court of Justice and Arbitration of OHADA. The Common Court of Justice and Arbitration is one of the four institutions envisaged in Article 3 of the Treaty. The other three institutions are the Council of Ministers, the Permanent Secretariat, and the Regional School for the Advanced Training of Judges and Judicial Personnel. Of the four institutions, the CCJA is the one that best symbolizes OHADA's ambitious goals, by virtue of the scope and specificity of its jurisdictional powers. Occupying a strategic position in the overall process of legal and judicial reform, the CCJA performs the following functions:

- Ensures that the Treaty, its implementing regulations, and the uniform acts are consistently interpreted and applied by all the states parties;
- Can be consulted by all signatory states, the Council of Ministers, or national courts regarding all the matters discussed above;
- Acts as a supra-national court of cassation for rulings handed down by appeals courts in the signatory states or for court rulings of which no appeal is likely in all matters related to the application of the uniform acts and regulations envisaged in the Treaty; and
- Through relatively strict monitoring of judicial proceedings and arbitral awards, ensures that arbitration is promoted and given credibility as an instrument for settling contractual disputes.

The powers and prerogatives of the CCJA are as extensive as they are varied and specialized. For this reason the CCJA often arouses curiosity and prompts questions. It is a unique entity in the legal-judicial structure of Africa, and for that matter, in the world. It is rare that the same court is simultaneously a supra-national court of cassation, a high court with tertiary jurisdiction (when an application is made for judicial review, the court may assume cognizance of a case and rule on its merits), a legal adviser to signatory states and community institutions, and an arbitration body.

At a somewhat comparable level, the Court of Justice of WAEMU in West Africa and the Court of Justice of the European Communities in Luxembourg do not have as many powers and prerogatives as the CCJA.

This brief discussion of the CCJA will conclude with a description of its composition, organization, and functions. Articles 31 to 39 of the OHADA Treaty and Articles 6 to 19 of the Rules of Procedure imply that the CCJA is similar to our national high courts of cassation—staffed with a presiding judge, judges distributed among its chambers, and a chief clerk of court, who also functions as general secretary for arbitration. The only difference is that the judges of the CCJA are elected by the Council of Ministers for a specified term.

Terms of reference and competencies of the CCJA. Article 14 of the Treaty stipulates that the CCJA has three functions:

- *Consultation.* The Court is consulted and advises on drafts of uniform acts before they are submitted and adopted by the Council of Ministers. It can be consulted by any member state or by the Council of Ministers on any matter related to the application or interpretation of uniform acts or their implementing regulations. It can also be consulted by national courts about lawsuits before those courts on matters relating to the uniform acts.
- *Litigation.* The Court serves as the appellate judge in a court of cassation in place of national courts of cassation in all matters relating to harmonized business law. When an application is made for judicial review, the court may assume cognizance of a case and rule on its merits.
- *Arbitration.* Pursuant to an arbitration clause or an arbitration agreement, any party to a contract—whether one of the parties is domiciled or has its habitual residence in a signatory state, or whether the con-

tract is executed or to be executed wholly or in part within the territory of one or several signatory states parties—may submit a contractual dispute to the CCJA under the arbitration procedures envisaged in the Treaty.

These three functions must be exercised in accordance with specified procedures. This paper will not elaborate on the procedures, but will simply note the following:

- *Consultation procedures.* Neither the Treaty nor its Rules of Procedure specifically say so, but it is reasonable to assume that the opinions of the CCJA cannot be imposed on signatory states, the Council of Ministers, or originating jurisdictions. These entities seek the CCJA's guidance mainly in order to appropriately apply or understand a uniform act or a related implementing regulation (for example, application over time and specific domestic measures to be taken).
- *Litigation procedures.* Bringing a case before the CCJA suspends all appeals proceedings undertaken in a national court against the contested decision (Article 16 of the Treaty, second paragraph). Bringing a case before the CCJA does not, however, suspend execution proceedings. In cases in which a dispute is brought before the CCJA and a national court of cassation has declared itself competent to render a verdict and has done so, the decision is considered null and void if the CCJA rules that the national court wrongly asserted its competence (Article 18 of the Treaty, third paragraph).
- *Arbitration procedures.* The CCJA is involved in the arbitration activities of OHADA even though it does not itself settle disputes (Article 21 of the Treaty, second paragraph). It appoints or confirms arbitrators. It is also informed of the progress of legal proceedings and examines draft awards before they are signed by the arbitrator. In the context of examining the award, the CCJA can only propose changes with respect to issues of form. It thus exercises, upstream, the role of "monitor" with the sole objective of making the arbitration activities of OHADA credible. Downstream, Article 25 of the Treaty confers a jurisdictional role on the Court with respect to the execution of arbitral awards, which must be the subject of an exequatur—which the CCJA alone is empowered to

issue—in order to be enforced. Similarly, as set forth in the arbitration rules, the CCJA has jurisdiction in cases in which the validity of an award is contested and it also hears appeals against writs of enforcement once an exequatur has been issued. However, responsibility for appending the enforcement order falls to the national authorities.

Effects of CCJA decisions. The effects will be defined on the basis of litigation decisions rendered by the CCJA.

According to Article 20 of the Treaty, the decisions of the CCJA have the authority of a final court ruling and the force of law. No ruling contrary to a decision of the CCJA may be enforced within the territory of a signatory state.

It is therefore useful to analyze the aforementioned article in terms of (a) the effects attributed to the authority of CCJA decisions, and (b) the effects resulting from the enforcement of such decisions.

- *Effects attributed to the authority of CCJA decisions.* Two important effects may be inferred from the assumption in Article 20. First, the decisions of CCJA are to be treated as equivalent to decisions rendered by courts in the signatory states, making it unnecessary for the states to monitor those decisions. Second, the authority of the CCJA extends to the territory of each signatory state. Thus, the authority of a final ruling by the CCJA would, for example, be an obstacle to reopening a case in Togo that had already been pursued in Mali—and vice versa.
- *Effects resulting from the enforcement of CCJA decisions.* The decisions of the CCJA are enforceable within the territory of each signatory state under the same conditions as decisions made by national courts. The enforcement order is almost direct, and the local judge does not have to issue an exequatur decision as is customary for rulings delivered by foreign jurisdictions.

Article 42 of the Rules of Procedure specifies *a fortiori* that the decision has the force of law from the day it is handed down. Article 46 of the Rules of Procedure adds that the enforcement order is appended without any formality other than verification of the authenticity of the decision by the national authority.

The CCJA is nevertheless the sole authority that can suspend an enforcement order (Article 46 of the Rules of Procedure) or entertain exceptional review procedures (such as third-party proceedings or reconsideration of decisions).

As the foregoing information indicates, the decisions of the CCJA are characterized by autonomy and detachment from the legal order of, and the everyday events experienced by, the national courts. At the very least, this contributes to the simplicity, speed, and efficiency of the judicial process, all factors that can be attractive to investors. This attractiveness was a major impetus for the Treaty.

Simplified Debt Recovery Procedures and Enforcement Mechanisms

One uniform act deals specifically with simplified procedures for recovering debt and measures for enforcing the procedures without challenging the organization of the judicial system in the states parties.

The act deals solely with procedures that are most commonly used by creditors.

Simplified debt recovery procedures. The procedure relating to an order to pay is applicable in all OHADA countries, although some countries are not aware of it.

The procedure involves obtaining a petition from a judge ordering the debtor to pay. If after the notification is served, the debtor does not execute the order or does not contest it within a specified period of time, the order becomes final and enforceable.

This simplified procedure is applicable to any liquid and payable debt that has a contractual basis, or is represented by a negotiable instrument or check.

The second simplified procedure relates to the obligation of the debtor to deliver an item in execution of the contract (such as a sale, an exchange, a contribution to a partnership's assets, a deposit, a loan for use) or to return the item if the contract is annulled or terminated. This procedure is called an injunction to deliver.

Finally, provision is made for clearance of mutual debts between public-law corporations and individuals under private law.

Enforcement mechanisms. A creditor may have recourse to provisional attachment only if recovery of a contested claim is in serious jeopardy and the creditor is not in possession of a writ of execution.

A judge must authorize the creditor to carry out such an attachment unless the claim concerns a negotiable instrument, an unpaid and contested check, or unpaid rent certified by a formal order to pay that has not been honored. Previously, national laws of the states concerned required the authorization of a judge for all debt claims.

Moreover, the creditor has a strict time limit of one month (or the attachment will lapse) during which to institute substantive proceedings and obtain a writ of execution. Once the writ has been obtained the attachment of goods occurs without intervention of a judge. The court's process server simply serves notice. Notification makes legal proceedings for validation optional. Validation would take place only if the debtor wished to contest the attachment by referring it to a judge.

Procedures for the attachment of movable property assume that a writ of execution has been issued and that the attached items are goods, financial claims, or earned income.

The attachment of goods is dependent on the prior issuance of an order to pay. The innovation in this Act is that the debtor is allowed to sell the confiscated goods through a private sale with the agreement of creditors. The inherent costs of a public sale are thus avoided and a better sale price for the property is obtained.

The attachment of claims other than earned income is limited to the sum due and the amount in question is awarded immediately to the creditor even if attachment claims are presented subsequently by other creditors. Limiting the attachment to the amount owed abolishes the former principle of the indivisibility of the attachment, which tied up a higher sum than was actually owed to the creditor.

Owing to the sensitive nature of the attachment of earned income, it was thought preferable to retain the standard procedure of preliminary intervention by a judge with attempts at reconciliation, which is the practice in the countries concerned. The payments are processed by the clerk of court. In the case of multiple attachments, creditors are ranked by the amount they are owed, subject to the priority of their claims (for example, maintenance claims).

A specific procedure was provided for the attachment of securities and partnership rights, which were previously treated in the same manner as either financial claims or goods. Attachment and replevin complete the simplified procedure for the injunction to deliver and return movable property.

Finally, under the procedure for distributing proceeds introduced by the Act, the most diligent creditor may initiate legal proceedings if an amicable agreement between the creditors has not been reached. The rules that govern this procedure are, for the most part, similar to those for the attachment of movable property and real estate.

Attachment of real estate. The attachment of real estate raises two fundamental issues that need to be resolved.

The first issue arises from gaps in the registration of real estate, since arrangements differ in the various countries concerned. The solution requiring the creditor to have the debtor register the property before a writ for payment is served if the property has not yet been registered (as is the practice in Senegal and Gabon) is preferable to the situation under Malian law, which only requires a statement certifying that the debtor has rights in rem to the property under litigation.

The second issue relates to fixing a reserve or upset price for the real estate. The solution, which prevails at present under French law, consists of letting the plaintiff freely set the price. This approach is generally criticized as inviting abuse, since it allows the creditor or plaintiff to assign a ridiculously low price to the property. Nevertheless, the practice under Senegalese law of having the judge establish the reserve price seemed too cumbersome a procedure, and it was considered preferable to let the plaintiff determine the reserve price by setting a floor price equal to one-fourth of the market value of the property, subject to possible review by the judge.

Finally it is useful to note that assets subject to attachment as real property include outlays on real estate improvements by the debtor on land that he or she does not own, but that was granted to him or her by the decision of an administrative authority.

EPILOGUE

Perceptions of the Rule of Law in Transitional Societies

Dr. Mamphela Ramphele

Managing Director

The World Bank

I am—like Amartya Sen—neither a lawyer nor a legal expert, but simply an international public servant and concerned citizen, so please indulge me while I say a few words for the next few minutes.

This presentation is concerned with civil society perceptions of the rule of law in post-conflict states. Later, specific reference will be made to my country South Africa. As you know South Africa was embroiled in conflict. However, my comments are equally applicable to societies in conflict and those emerging from it. Specifically, those with a history of being directly oppressed by the apparatus of the state and its rules—the recently toppled kleptocracy in Zaire being a prime example.

What about the youth of Nigeria, born to a society where corruption is the rule rather than the exception? Where, during the Abacha era, 125 million people were held hostage by an autocrat? Where the rule of law was determined and hence undermined by one individual?

How do you heal societies where the youth see greater value in being big chiefs rather than productive citizens? Bad governance and corruption are pandemic in the states and civil societies of Africa—and these factors, along with deadly conflict, are chiefly responsible for the ineffectiveness of the rule of law on the African continent.

That said, there are some "citable" though not seminal examples of post-war states that have managed to rebuild civil society *confidence* in the rule of law and simultaneously yet slowly reconstruct their own legal and judicial systems. As the ombudswoman has already stated, post-1991 Namibia is a good example. Others are post-1993 Ethiopia and Eritrea, and post-1994 Mozambique. Although Namibia is moving forward in this regard, Ethiopia and Eritrea have been engaged in a disheartening war that has stifled their development processes, and Mozambique is struggling to rebuild its basic infrastructure in the wake of the horrific floods that ravaged it earlier this year.

I am hard pressed to identify one African state that can be referenced as a *seminal* example.

How does Africa teach its children to respect authority and the rule of law and to be productive citizens *when the state does not respect them?* How does one teach young people to respect the rule of law when they have no experience of it working in their interests?

Even outside the scope of the postwar context, can you imagine rural African women in many countries today, bringing claims against their employers for sexual harassment—let alone influence the state to institute claims against men for rape, or bring civil suits themselves? If during peacetime, women cannot find a venue to adjudicate their grievances, what about the hundreds of thousands in Africa who have been victims of war crimes?

A society that respects its government and the rule of law will continue to do so amidst chaos or crises. For example, the people of Mozambique have dealt with the crises of flooding in spite of the chaos around them with great dignity. Likewise, the people of Sierra Leone were so troubled with the coup d'etat that toppled the democratically elected government of Tijan Kabbah in 1997 that they held mass protests and even militarily challenged the illegal junta.

The key issue is, how do we inculcate respect for and adherence to the rule of law, and for that matter liberal democracy, in societies that have a history of—or are emerging from—authoritarian, autocratic, clientelistic, dictatorial, and corrupt regimes, or mass civil war? How can post conflict civil societies respect the rule of law when the state has been the referent of their oppression?

Similarly, how can they embrace and respect popular notions of liberal democracy as espoused by the West/North, when the West/North applies a double standard to Africa? For example, in my country, it was clear that the system of apartheid was not only illegal under international law but customary international law, as defined by Nuremberg. Why did not the international community fulfill its international obligations and take *decisive* action against South Africa's racist apartheid regimes, as opposed to selling them weapons, for example? Or, why was the international community lethargic in responding to the crises in Rwanda and Sierra Leone, yet it acted expeditiously to the crisis in Kosovo? If the international rule of law were applied equally in both cases, perhaps, today, Sierra Leone would not be in a state of crisis.

If African leaders do not respect international law owing to such disparities, or for any other reason, how can we expect them to govern under its auspices? And how can we expect African civil society to know about, understand, and respect international law?

Do you see the pattern? If African leaders ignore international law and best practices, how do you think they view their domestic law or vice versa? How can societies pull themselves out of poverty without strong legal systems and frameworks? Amartya Sen's analysis of development as freedom makes the case for entrenching democracy and the rule of law.

These are important questions because, today, domestic and international law are deeply intertwined, and in small and weak states, international law and best practices, whether economic or human rights law, have a strong impact on the character of states and hence civil society. It is in recognition of this impact, that donor countries tie liberal democratic development—whether it is political, economic, or legal—to aid.

We know that in democratic countries the law is the glue of society. It holds everything firmly together in a systematic fashion. It serves as society's equalizer, especially when a respectable judiciary complements it. Yet, how can we expect post-conflict societies to embrace and respect the rule of law, when the law—whether traditional, national, or international—has not brought them justice?

Stated differently, how can the international community expect victims of unjust laws to be productive citizens and defend and uphold the rule of law? What are the roles of the judiciary, lawyers, legal academics and the like in this regard? It is always easy to discuss what others can and should do, but what are each of you going to do differently when you get back to your home bases and places of employment, to help advance these ideals?

Yes, it is true that I have many questions! But that is because throughout the years, I have heard so few answers! Answers that, today, are needed more than at any other time!

Allow me to discuss the case of South Africa for a moment.

During apartheid, black South Africans were deeply affected by a four-tiered legal system. We lived under (1) traditional law; (2) apartheid law, which at the time was the national law; (3) regional law and policy, as espoused by the Organization of African Unity (OAU) and other independent free African countries, which sought to end apartheid; and (4) (in my view a defunct) international legal regime. During this period and even today, black South Africans pondered the question, if apartheid is wrong, if it is illegal, then how did the "civilized" world allow it to continue?

All of these legal regimes greatly affected how the laws of apartheid were established and nurtured, some with contradictory effects. While white rulers in South Africa did not have to adhere to the rule of law, and in fact were above the law, black people were forced to coexist with their white fellow citizens under a barbarous system.

Today, the new democratic South Africa is forced to contend with the legacy and experiences of citizenship and subjugation. The implications of ongoing white privilege and the need for black empowerment in the context of societal imperatives for the development and entrenchment of a free and democratic civic culture are enormous. How does one get a people with a "protest culture," and legitimate historical disregard for the state apparatus to adhere to, and respect the rule of law under the new dispensation? How does one get them to see themselves as "citizens" with responsibilities beyond their own lifetimes? It is easy to have free and fair elections, and subsequently declare democracy, but what about all of the *obligations* and *privileges* that democratization demands? How does one create a civic culture? Not only for civil society, but also for the military and political leaders—who, by the way, should be a part of civil society?

For example, in 1995, during the anti-apartheid struggle, a prominent African National Congress (ANC) member and provincial leader from the Western Cape, was accused of embezzling large amounts of money donated for poverty reduction for the poorest of poor people. He was stripped of his ambassadorship to Geneva, and has been criminally prosecuted, found guilty and jailed. It is a tribute to South Africa's criminal justice system that it acted firmly against this disgraced leader in spite of protests from the ANC leadership.

Yes, crime occurs in every society, however, the rationale behind why crimes are committed may vary. There appears to be a nexus of circular causation between the general disdain for the rule of law in South Africa, which persists to date, and the black population's experiences during apartheid. The survival strategies essential for that period are dysfunctional to the culture appropriate for democracy. Other countries—such as Nigeria, Liberia, Guinea–Bissau, and the Democratic Republic of Congo—will and are having to deal with similar legacies.

The Way Forward

So what can be done to assist such countries to foster strong legal systems and build respect for the rule of law and hence a responsible citizenry?

On a structural level, more resources are needed for capacity building. In most African countries the judiciary is nonfunctional in rural areas. Justice must be available to poor people beyond the urban core. And even in the urban core, poor people suffer in this regard.

Information technology is crucial in this respect. The Red Terror Trials in Ethiopia provide a good point of departure here. The state is prosecuting over 6,000 persons from the Mengistu regime for genocide under the 1957 Ethiopian Penal Code, which by the way is one of the most comprehensive penal codes in the world. However, only one-sixth of the cases have gone to trial and several of the regional courts that have jurisdiction to adjudicate cases are not functional. At this pace, this process could take another 10 years before all of the cases are disposed. This is notwithstanding the fact that several donor governments have provided some technological assistance (computers, typewriters, recording equipment, and so on) and other resources to the Ethiopian judiciary. Greater international support for Ethiopia's judiciary would certainly make it more efficient.

The international community, including donor states and the multilateral institutions, must commit more resources for building and strengthening legal systems in the developing world. The World Bank has begun to engage in this capacity-building process. This conference is a visible sign of our commitment.

What needs to be done?

Courts must be built and properly equipped.

Lawyers and judges must be trained, not just in domestic law, but in international law as well. In this regard, such organizations as the National Judicial College, which trains American judges and foreign judges from across the globe, should be studied closely and supported, and their experiences used to assist the developing world, to develop appropriate institutions.

Civil society must be educated about the rule of law and have better access to the judiciary; it should not be a mystery to them. Poor people, especially women and children, must be exposed to information about where they can be advised about their rights and responsibilities. Advice offices in poor communities are a good investment in this regard.

And finally, Africa and other developing countries must harness and institutionalize the strengths of customary law and do away with exploitive chauvinistic practices.

There cannot be authentic democratization and hence development without adherence to, and respect for the rule of law. The law permeates every facet of society, it is the glue that holds the apparatus of the state together, and the latter accountable to the people. Without it, lawlessness and corruption become endemic and taint the cultural fabric of society. Only just and impartial institutions steeped in the rule of law can revive a civic culture and turn victims, non-believers, and pessimists into CITIZENS.

Biographies of Authors

Martín Abregú

Martín Abregú is the rights and citizenship program officer for the Andean and Southern Cone Regions at the Ford Foundation. Formerly, he was the executive director of the Center for Legal and Social Studies in Buenos Aires, as well as the representative in Argentina of the Center for Justice and International Law located in Washington, D.C. He has also been a foreign consultant at the School of Judicial Training of El Salvador and a dean's fellow at the American University Washington College of Law in Washington, D.C.

Mr. Abregú earned his law degree from the School of Law at the University of Buenos Aires, where he focused on international public law and criminal law, and later received a Master of Laws from the American University Washington College of Law, where he specialized in international protection of human rights.

Mr. Abregú has also authored many articles on human rights, criminal law and democracy and has lectured frequently both in Argentina and abroad.

Omar Azziman

Omar Azziman is the minister of justice of Morocco. He earned his law degree from the Mohamed V University of Rabat and a certificate in business law in Paris, and later received his doctorate degree in private law. Dr. Azziman subsequently served as a professor at the University of Rabat Faculty of Law.

Dr. Azziman is also the president of the Hassan II Foundation for the Moroccan Community Living Abroad and a member of the Arab-Portuguese Chamber of Commerce and Industry Arbitration Council and of the Euro-Arab Superior Council of Conciliation and Arbitration in Paris.

Dr. Azziman also represents Morocco at United Nations annual sessions on international trade and has served as a delegate minister to the prime minister in charge of human rights in government. Moreover, Dr. Azziman has authored several books, focusing on the juridical structure of banks in Morocco and the legal profession in Morocco.

Lado Chanturia

Lado Chanturia is the chairman of the Supreme Court of Georgia and has been a key player in drafting national legislation for Georgia. He was a member of the State Commission in Charge of Drafting the Constitution of Georgia and of the Editorial Group in Charge of Drafting the Civil Code of Georgia. In his position as a member of the Council of Justice and as the Minister of Justice of Georgia, he made numerous contributions to implementation of judicial reform in Georgia.

Dr. Chanturia graduated from the Faculty of Law at the Iv. Javakshvili State University in Georgia and pursued post-graduate work at the Moscow Legislation Institute. As a grant holder of DAAD, he studied at the Faculty of Law at the Goettingen University in Germany.

Dr. Chanturia is a professor of law at Tbilisi State University and has authored extensive publications, focusing primarily on Georgian law and legal reform.

Julio Faundez

Julio Faundez obtained his LLB degree from the Catholic University of Chile and his LLM and SJD degrees from Harvard University. He established the postgraduate program in International Economic Law at Warwick University, where he teaches courses on various aspects of international law. His recent books include *Governance, Development and Globalization* (co-editor) (Blackstone Press, 2000), *Good Government and Law* (editor) (Macmillan Press, 1997) and *Acciones Positivas en el Empleo y la Ocupación: Perspectivas Internacionales* (ILO/OIT, Lima, 2000).

Prof. Faundez has advised the Governments of South Africa and Namibia on affirmative action in employment. He acted as advocate and counsel for Namibia before the International Court of Justice in the Case Concerning Kasikili/Sedudu Island and is a legal consultant to Denton Wilde Sapte, a London-based law firm. He is currently conducting a major evaluation of legal and judicial reform projects for the Inter-American Development Bank.

Alfredo Fuentes Hernández

Alfredo Fuentes Hernández is the executive director of the Corporation for Judiciary Excellence in Colombia. Prior to this, he served as the technical coordinator of the National Trade Union Council, adviser to the High Council on Foreign Trade in Colombia, and chief executive officer of the Colombian-Venezuelan Chamber of Commerce and Integration.

Dr. Fuentes earned his undergraduate degree from the Gimnasio Moderno and his Doctor of Laws from the University of the Andes in Bogotá. He received his Master of Laws from Harvard University Law School and his Master of Arts in Economics from Boston University.

Dr. Fuentes has published extensive articles and books on economics in Colombia, integration, development, and the administration of justice in Latin America.

Denis Galligan

Denis Galligan is a professor of socio-legal studies at the Faculty of Law at the University of Oxford, as well as the director of the Centre for Socio-Legal Studies at Wolfson College at the University of Oxford and a fellow of Wolfson College. Prof. Galligan is also a frequent visiting professor at the Central European University.

Prof. Galligan earned his Bachelor of Laws from the University of Queensland and his Bachelor of Civil Law from the University of Oxford, where he graduated with first class honors and later went on to pursue both his Master of Arts and Doctorate of Civil Law degrees. Prof. Galligan has also been a Rhodes scholar.

Prof. Galligan has authored various publications, focusing primarily on administrative justice and law, particularly in Central and Eastern Europe.

Bryant G. Garth

Bryant G. Garth has served as the director of the American Bar Foundation since August 1990. Prior to this, Dr. Garth pursued a career in academia, as a professor of civil procedure, the legal profession, international and comparative law, and human rights at the Indiana University School of Law, Uppsala University in Sweden, the University of Michigan School of Law, and the European University Institute. He later became dean of the Indiana University School of Law.

Dr. Garth received his Bachelor of Arts in American Studies with highest honors from Yale University and his Juris Doctor from Stanford Law School, where he was also the editor-in-chief of the Stanford Journal of International Studies. He subsequently earned his Doctor in Laws from the European University Institute.

Dr. Garth has also authored and co-authored numerous publications, primarily focusing on international legal concerns and access to justice.

Bience Gawanas

Bience Gawanas is the ombudswoman of the Republic of Namibia and is actively involved in advocating and lobbying for the promotion of human rights and gender-sensitive policies, programs, and laws. Prior to this post, she lectured on gender in law at the Law Faculty of the University of Namibia. Ms. Gawanas also served as the secretary general of the Namibia National Women's Organization for several years.

Ms. Gawanas earned her Bachelor of Laws from the University of Warwick in the United Kingdom, where she graduated with honors, and qualified as a barrister from the Inns of Court, School of Law in the United Kingdom.

Ms. Gawanas does a great deal of national and international public speaking on issues focusing on women, law, gender, governance, and development. She has also authored works on these same issues and is active in radio and television.

Kathryn Hendley

Kathryn Hendley is an associate professor of law and political science at the University of Wisconsin in the United States, as well as the Director of the Center for Russia, East Europe and Central Asia at that same university. She has also served as a scholar-in-residence at the Law Library of the U.S. Library of Congress and as a visiting scholar at the Documentation Office for East European Law at the University of Leiden in the Netherlands.

Dr. Hendley received her Bachelor of Arts in history from Indiana University and her Juris Doctor from the UCLA School of Law. She subsequently earned a Master of Arts in Russian Area Studies and a PhD from the University of California at Berkley in political science. In addition, she has been awarded numerous fellowships and grants, the most recent being a research grant from the National Council for Eurasian and East European Research.

Dr. Hendley is the author of many publications and book reviews. She is currently studying contractual relations among Russian enterprises during the transition and working to develop a theory on the role of law in the context of transition.

Irshad Hasan Khan

Irshad Hasan Khan is the chief justice of Pakistan. In this capacity, he also serves as the ex-officio chairman of the Supreme Judicial Council, the Chief Justices' Committee, the Pakistan Law Commission (the federal statutory institution responsible for the systematic reform and modernization of the legal system and the administration of justice), and the Judicial Policy Body (entity responsible for strengthening institutional capacities for judicial and legal reform). Chief Justice Khan is also on the Panel of Arbitrators at the International Center for Settlement of Investment Disputes in Washington, D.C.

Chief Justice Khan received his law education from University Law College in Lahore and was a visiting professor at the Himayat-e-Islam Law College. At present, he is a member of the Board of Governors at the International Islamic University in Islamabad.

Chief Justice Khan has participated in various symposia, workshops, conferences, and seminars, including, for example, the World Peace Through Law Conference, the Seminar on the Role of Government in Industrial Relations, and the Islamic Conference.

Akua Kuenyehia

Akua Kuenyehia is the dean of the Faculty of Law at the University of Ghana in Legon. She has taught a variety of subjects at the Faculty, including criminal law, labor law, and international law. She currently teaches the subjects of gender and the law, and international human rights law. Dr. Kuenyehia received her education from the University of Ghana and Oxford University.

Her research focuses primarily on family law, where she explores legal issues of interest to women such as property rights of married couples, particularly following divorce. Dr. Kuenyehia currently directs a research project on women and law in West Africa, which encompasses Ghana, Gambia, Nigeria, and Sierra Leone.

Dr. Kuenyehia has also been involved in the legal sector reform process currently underway in Ghana. In this vein, she has coordinated and synthesized reports from various consultants regarding different aspects of the legal system, facilitated a stakeholders conference, and prepared a strategic plan to move forward with the reform process.

David K. Malcolm

David K. Malcolm is the chief justice and lieutenant governor of Western Australia, as well as a companion of the Order of Australia. He is also the chairman of the Judicial Section of the Law Association for Asia and the Pacific, chairman of the Advisory Board of the Crime Research Center at the University of Western Australia, president of the Western Australian Branch of the International Commission of Jurists, and a member of the Board of Directors of the Society for the Reform of Criminal Law.

Chief Justice Malcolm earned his Bachelor of Laws from the University of Western Australia where he graduated with first class honors. Chief Justice Malcolm was subsequently a Rhodes Scholar and received his BCL at Oxford with first class honors. He has practiced in many areas of law including commercial and corporate law, mining, media, shipping, and administrative law.

Shahdeen Malik

Shahdeen Malik works primarily with the Bangladesh Legal Aid and Services Trust, the largest legal aid organization in Bangladesh. He is also closely associated with Adarpur Legal Aid Association, which resolves the disputes of the poor and marginalized rural people through mediation.

Dr. Malik earned his Bachelor of Laws from City Law College in Dhaka, Bangladesh. He received a Master of Laws from both Patrice Lumumba University in Moscow and from the University of Pennsylvania Law School in Philadelphia, and his PhD from the School of Oriental and African Studies at London University. He currently works as an adjunct professor at the Independent University of Bangladesh in Dhaka.

Moreover, Dr. Malik has worked as a consultant for a number of national and international organizations and has published articles in law journals in Bangladesh, India, and Germany. He is the editor of the Bangladesh Journal of Law, published by the Bangladesh Institute of Law and International Affairs.

Grizelda Mayo-Anda

Grizelda Mayo-Anda is the assistant executive director of the Environmental Legal Assistance Center in the Philippines. In this capacity, Ms. Mayo-Anda has focused on environmental litigation, staff supervision and coordination, policy advocacy, environmental research and fact-finding, and building relationships among both Philippine and international governmental and nongovernmental groups.

Ms. Mayo-Anda has also been a representative of the Pala'wan NGO Network to the Pala'wan Council for Sustainable Development, a member of the Committee on Forestry Affairs at this same council, and a member of the Prosecution and Adjudication Committee of the Bantay Pala'wan Program, a provincial environmental program.

Ms. Mayo-Anda earned her Bachelor of Laws from the University of San Jose Recoletos in Cebu City, graduating cum laude. She received a Bachelor of Commerce from St. Theresa's College in Cebu City, where she also graduated cum laude.

Swithin J. Munyantwali

Swithin J. Munyantwali is the executive director of the International Law Institute at the Uganda Legal Center of Excellence, a regional center that trains lawyers and related professionals in sub-Saharan Africa and works in regional technical assistance in the field of commercial law reform. Mr. Munyantwali is responsible for the overall management of the Center, including acting as a liaison with regional and international organizations such as the African Development Bank, the Common Market for East and Central Africa, UNCTAD, and UNITAR.

Mr. Munyantwali received his law education in the United States, earning his Master of Laws in international and comparative law from the Georgetown University Law Center in Washington, D.C. and his Juris Doctor from the Case Western Reserve Law in Cleveland, Ohio.

Mr. Munyantwali has presented papers at numerous conferences on subjects such as trade and competition policy, privatization, governance and accountability, corporate governance and the importance of capacity building in the region.

Sandra E. Oxner

Sandra E. Oxner is a retired judge of the Nova Scotia Provincial Court in Canada, where she served for 25 years. Throughout her career she has been a leader in judicial education at the provincial, national, and international levels. Judge Oxner was the founding director of the Canadian Institute for Advanced Legal Studies and has organized or taught in judicial education programs in Canada, the United States, England, Australia, East, South, and West Africa, the Caribbean, Yemen, China, and Russia.

In addition to lecturing for nine years at the School of Journalism at the University of King's College and presenting papers at judicial education programs throughout the world, Judge Oxner has been a guest lecturer at many law schools.

Judge Oxner is also a judicial reform specialist and has worked on judicial reform projects in 24 countries, including the former Soviet Union, as well as countries in the Middle East, Africa, the Caribbean, and Asia.

Rogelio Pérez-Perdomo

Rogelio Pérez-Perdomo is the academic director of the program in International Legal Studies at Stanford University in California. He is also a professor at the Instituto de Estudios Superiores de Administración in Caracas. Dr. Pérez completed his post-graduate work in Paris and at Harvard and has also earned a doctorate from the Universidad de Venezuela.

As part of his scholarly pursuits in the issues of law and society, Dr. Pérez has been active in the Research Committee on the Sociology of Law of the International Sociological Association. Moreover, he is the former director of the International Institute for the Sociology of Law, located in Spain.

Dr. Pérez has written extensively on the legal profession, on litigation, and, most recently, on the comparative study of governmental corruption.

Mamphela Ramphele

Mamphela Ramphele, a South African national, became managing director of the World Bank in May 2000. Prior to joining the Bank, Dr. Ramphele served as vice chancellor of the University of Cape Town, the first black woman to hold this position at a South African university.

Dr. Ramphele has been honored widely for her contribution to the struggle against apartheid. She has also worked as a medical doctor, civil rights leader, community development worker, and academic researcher. Dr. Ramphele has received numerous prestigious national and international awards, including 10 honorary doctorates acknowledging her scholarship, her service to the community, and her leading role in raising development issues and spearheading projects for disadvantaged persons throughout South Africa.

Dr. Ramphele qualified as a medical doctor at the University of Natal. She also holds a PhD in social anthropology from the University of Cape Town, a Bcom degree in administration from the University of South Africa, and diplomas in tropical health and hygiene, and public health from the University of Witwatersrand. She has published various books and articles on education, health, and social development issues.

Geoffrey Robertson

Mr. Robertson is a Queen's Counsel (leading trial lawyer) who has argued many landmark cases involving human rights and media law in England and throughout Europe and the British Commonwealth. He has served as counsel to international commissions investigating political corruption and arms trafficking and, most recently, the administration of justice in Trinidad. He is credited with saving the lives of hundreds of Caribbean death row prisoners through cases he has brought on their behalf in the Privy Council, and in 2001 he led the successful legal challenge to the legitimacy of the military-backed government of Fiji. A long-standing Commonwealth counsel to Dow Jones Inc., he has defended its journalists against civil and criminal actions throughout the world.

Mr. Robertson is the author of *Crimes Against Humanity—The Struggle for Global Justice* (Penguin/New Press, 2000). He has also published *The Justice Game* (Random House, 1998) and the textbook *Media Law* (Sweet and Maxwell, 4th Edition, 2001). He is visiting professor in human rights at the University of London (Birkbeck) and serves as a recorder (part-time judge) in London.

Pierre Truche

Pierre Truche is the honorary first chairman of the Court of Cassation in France. He also chairs the National Consultative Commission on Human Rights, the Reflection Commission on an International Criminal Court for ex-Yugoslavia, and the Reflection Commission on Justice, and is a member of the Criminal Justice and Human Rights Commission. Previously, Judge Truche served as the public prosecutor at the Court of Cassation, as well as the public prosecutor at the Court of Appeals of Paris. He has also been a judge and assistant public prosecutor in Dijon, Lyon, and Marseilles.

Judge Truche holds a Bachelor of Laws degree and has reviewed various articles pertaining to different aspects of the legal field. His most noted work is *The Anarchist and his Judge.*

Maher Abdel Wahed

Maher Abdel Wahed is the attorney general of Egypt. He is also the member of various committees on legislative reform, private sector development, banking and credit laws, and administrative reform. Attorney General Wahed has headed numerous delegations, such as those in charge of negotiating a cooperation agreement on legal affairs with Tunisia, a treaty on legal and judicial cooperation with Bahrain, and a cooperation agreement on legal affairs with France.

Attorney General Wahed holds a Bachelor of Laws, as well as diplomas in administrative sciences and public law, and has lectured on civil and commercial procedure law at Wahran University in Algeria.

Attorney General Wahed has also published several works and reviews on a variety of topics, including civil law, maritime concerns, and rights.

S. Amos Wako

S. Amos Wako is the attorney general of Kenya. Prior to this post, he was a partner at Kaplan & Stratton and has also served as the chairman of the Law Society of Kenya and of the Association of Professional Societies in East Africa, and as secretary general of the African Bar Association.

Attorney General Wako earned his Bachelor of Science in Economics from the University of London, specializing in international affairs. He graduated from the University of East Africa with a Bachelor of Laws degree and from the University of London with a Master of Laws degree. He is also a fellow of both the International Academy of Trial Lawyers and the Chartered Institute of Arbitrators, as well as an advocate of the High Court of Kenya.

Attorney General Wako has been a member of various committees and commissions working in the field of human rights and has also participated in numerous legal and judicial panels and boards.

Editor's Note: Regrettably, it was not possible to obtain biographical information for all the authors at the time of publication.